NORTH AMERICAN FREE TRADE: ISSUES AND RECOMMENDATIONS

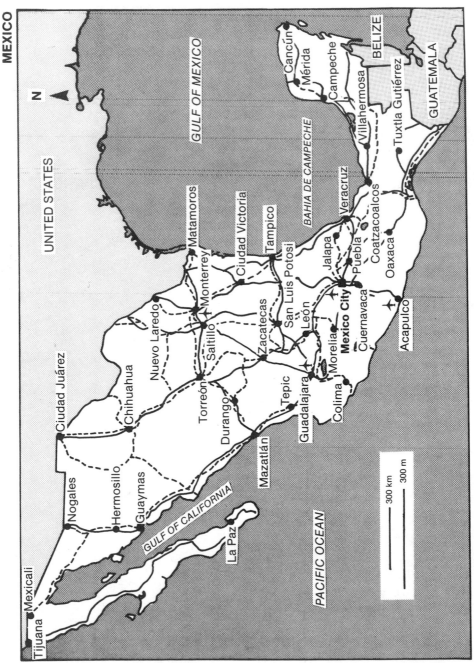

GARY CLYDE HUFBAUER AND JEFFREY J. SCHOTT

North American Free Trade: Issues and Recommendations

Assisted by Lee L. Remick, Diana E. Clark, Rosa M. Moreira, and Joanna M. van Rooij

INSTITUTE FOR INTERNATIONAL ECONOMICS
WASHINGTON, DC 1992

Gary Clyde Hufbauer is a Visiting Fellow at the Institute for International Economics and Marcus Wallenberg Professor of International Financial Diplomacy at Georgetown University. He was formerly Deputy Director of the International Law Institute at Georgetown University, Deputy Assistant Secretary of the Treasury for International Trade and Investment, and Director of the International Tax Staff at the Treasury. He is author or coauthor of numerous publications on international trade, investment, and tax issues, including *US Taxation of International Business Income: Blueprint for Reform* (1992), *Economic Sanctions Reconsidered* (1990), *Europe 1992: An American Perspective* (1990), *The Free Trade Debate: Report of the Twentieth Century Task Force on the Future of American Trade Policy* (1989), *Trade Protection in the United States: 31 Case Studies* (1986), *Trade Policy for Troubled Industries* (1986), *Trading for Growth: The Next Round of Trade Negotiations* (1985), and *Subsidies in International Trade* (1984).

Jeffrey J. Schott is a Research Fellow at the Institute for International Economics. He was formerly a Senior Associate at the Carnegie Endowment for International Peace and an International Economist at the US Treasury. He is author or coauthor of several recent books on trade, including *Economic Sanctions Reconsidered* (1990), *Completing the Uruguay Round* (1990), *Free Trade Areas and U.S. Trade Policy* (1989), *The Canada–United States Free Trade Agreement: The Global Impact* (1988), *Auction Quotas and United States Trade Policy* (1987), and *Trading for Growth: The Next Round of Trade Negotiations* (1985).

Lee L. Remick was a Research Assistant at the Institute for International Economics and is now a candidate for a masters in international economics and finance at Brandeis University. She formerly worked as statistical assistant for The Economist Economic Intelligence Unit (1989).

Diana E. Clark is a Research Assistant at the Institute for International Economics. She received her Bachelors of Arts in International Studies and Foreign Languages from West Virginia University and her Masters in Public and International Affairs from the University of Pittsburgh. Her studies have concentrated in economic development in Latin America.

Rosa M. Moreira is a Research Assistant at the Institute for International Economics. She attended the Pontificia Universidade Católica in Rio de Janeiro and received her Bachelors of Science in Foreign Service from Georgetown University.

Joanna M. van Rooij was a Research Assistant at the Institute for International Economics during the completion of this study. She holds masters degrees from the Georgetown University School of Foreign Service and Nijenrode, the Netherlands Business School.

INSTITUTE FOR INTERNATIONAL ECONOMICS
11 Dupont Circle, NW
Washington, DC 20036-1207
(202) 328-9000 Telex: 261271 IIE UR
FAX: (202) 328-5432

C. Fred Bergsten, *Director*
Linda Griffin Kean, *Director of Publications*

Printed in the United States of America
94 93 92   3 2

Library of Congress Cataloging-in-Publication Data

Hufbauer, Gary Clyde.
    North American free trade : issues and recommendations / Gary Clyde Hufbauer, Jeffrey J. Schott. p.   cm.
    "March 1992."
    Includes bibliographical references and index
    1. Free trade—North America. 2. North America—Commerce. 3. North America—Commercial policy. I. Schott, Jeffrey J., 1949– . II. Title.
    HF3211.H84   1992
    382'.71'097—dc20   92-8

ISBN cloth 0-88132-145-1
ISBN paper 0-88132-120-6

Contents

References 345

Index 361

Tables

Preface

International trade negotiations have been one of the focal points of research at the Institute for International Economics throughout its history. At the request of then–United States Trade Representative Bill Brock, Gary Clyde Hufbauer and Jeffrey J. Schott developed one of the initial blueprints for the Uruguay Round in *Trading for Growth: The Next Round of Trade Negotiations* (1985). Schott subsequently offered a midcourse assessment in *Completing the Uruguay Round: A Results-Oriented Approach to the GATT Trade Negotiations* (1990). Paul Wonnacott prepared a blueprint for the Canada–US Free Trade Agreement in *The United States and Canada: The Quest for Free Trade* (1987), and Schott's *United States–Canada Free Trade: An Evaluation of the Agreement* (1988) was used extensively in the ratification debate in both countries. Schott's *Free Trade Areas and U.S. Trade Policy* (1989) examined the prospects for additional regional pacts, including one between the United States and Mexico.

Hufbauer and Schott drew on these previous analyses in preparing the current study, the most comprehensive to date of the proposed North American Free Trade Agreement (NAFTA). They address the aggregate economic effects of such an arrangement, its six key functional components, and the six sectors that would be most significantly affected. They draw implications for each of the three countries involved and for the world trading system as a whole, including how a NAFTA could affect the balance between globalism and regionalism in trade policy in the 1990s and beyond. Building on this analysis, Hufbauer and Schott will examine in a forthcoming Institute study the prospects for free trade in the Western Hemisphere along the lines proposed by President George Bush in his Enterprise for the Americas Initiative.

The Institute for International Economics is a private nonprofit institution for the study and discussion of international economic policy. Its purpose is to analyze important issues in that area, and to develop and communicate practical new approaches for dealing with them. The Institute is completely nonpartisan.

The Institute is funded largely by philanthropic foundations. Major institutional grants are now being received from the German Marshall Fund of the United States, which created the Institute with a generous commitment of funds in 1981, and from the Ford Foundation, the William and Flora Hewlett Foundation, the William M. Keck, Jr. Foundation, the Alfred P. Sloan Foundation, the C. V. Starr Foundation, and the United States–Japan Foundation.

Support for the present study was provided by the Charles R. Bronfman Foundation, the John D. and Catherine T. MacArthur Foundation, and The

Tinker Foundation. The Dayton Hudson Foundation supports the Institute's program of studies on trade policy.

A number of other foundations and private corporations also contribute to the highly diversified financial resources of the Institute. No funding is received from any government. About 12 percent of the Institute's resources in our latest fiscal year were provided by contributors outside the United States, including about 2 percent from Japan.

The Board of Directors bears overall responsibility for the Institute and gives general guidance and approval to its research program — including identification of topics that are likely to become important to international economic policy-makers over the medium run (generally, one to three years), and which thus should be addressed by the Institute. The Director, working closely with the staff and outside Advisory Committee, is responsible for the development of particular projects and makes the final decision to publish an individual study.

The Institute hopes that its studies and other activities will contribute to building a stronger foundation for international economic policy around the world. We invite readers of these publications to let us know how they think we can best accomplish this objective.

C. FRED BERGSTEN
Director
March 1992

For Sidney Weintraub,
pioneering analyst and advocate
of North American economic integration

Acknowledgments

The authors are indebted to Ann Weston of the North-South Institute in Ottawa and Gustavo Vega of El Colegio de México in Mexico City for organizing seminars to review earlier drafts of this study and to elicit views on North American free trade from government, business, and academia in Canada and Mexico. The authors would also like to thank C. Fred Bergsten, A. T. Halliday, Richard G. Lipsey, Clark Reynolds, Sidney Weintraub, and Ronald J. Wonnacott for their valuable comments on the entire manuscript; Michael Treadway for his thoughtful editing of the manuscript; Angela Barnes for typing it; and Linda Griffin Kean and Sharada Gilkey for shepherding the study through the publication process.

The Political Economy of a NAFTA

NAFTA: Overview and National Objectives

On 11 June 1990, US President George Bush and Mexican President Carlos Salinas de Gortari agreed to pursue the negotiation of a free trade agreement, or FTA, between their two countries. Exactly one year later talks began, with a third country, Canada, also taking a seat at the negotiating table. Even before the talks started, the process of crafting a North American Free Trade Agreement (NAFTA) was transformed from an incremental approach of melding separate bilateral FTAS between individual countries into a full-fledged trilateral negotiation.

The NAFTA negotiations represent a further step in a gradual process of economic integration that has been under way implicitly in North America for quite some time. The foundation stone was laid in 1965 with the Canada–US Auto Pact. A few years later, the maquiladora boom began to link the northern cities of Mexico with the US industrial economy.[1] Since 1985, extensive negotiations have produced a series of bilateral trade pacts that have lowered trade barriers in the region and provided institutional underpinnings for the prospective North American economic alliance. The most important accord has been the Canada–US FTA, which sets many useful precedents for the NAFTA.

In addition, both the United States and Canada have concluded bilateral framework agreements on trade and investment with Mexico. The United States and Mexico signed three major accords between 1985 and 1989:[2]

- The Understanding on Subsidies and Countervailing Duties (1985) was in essence a surrogate for Mexican participation in the subsidies code of the General Agreement on Tariffs and Trade (GATT). Mexico agreed to undertake reforms of its subsidy programs in exchange for an agreement by the United States to apply an injury test in countervailing duty cases involving Mexican products.

---

1. Maquiladoras are Mexican "in-bond" production facilities that process or assemble imported components for export, primarily to the United States (see chapter 5).

2. In addition, in 1986 the United States negotiated on behalf of other GATT signatories the Mexican protocol of accession. For a summary of these agreements see US International Trade Commission (1990b, chapter 2); and Morici (1991, 36–39).

- The Framework of Principles and Procedures for Consultation Regarding Trade and Investment Relations (1987) established a consultative and dispute settlement mechanism for bilateral trade problems and an "immediate action agenda" for negotiations on bilateral trade and investment issues in goods and services sectors; these negotiations resulted *inter alia* in sectoral accords on steel and textiles.

- The Understanding Regarding Trade and Investment Facilitation Talks (1989) initiated a bilateral round of negotiations on a broad range of issues, including difficult intellectual property questions.

Canada–Mexico trade negotiations have proceeded on a parallel but slower track, reflecting the smaller level of direct economic transactions between those two countries (only about $2 billion in total trade in 1989). In March 1990 Canada and Mexico signed 10 separate accords to improve bilateral consultations and data sharing on issues ranging from agricultural trade to environmental cooperation to such nontrade areas as extradition and drugs. The package also included a Framework for Trade and Investment Consultations that follows in many respects the 1987 US–Mexico accord.

Closer integration of the American, Canadian, and Mexican economies would yield a market as large and populous as the European Community (EC) and the European Free Trade Association (EFTA) combined: in 1989 the EC and EFTA countries had a combined GNP of $5,784 billion and a population of 358 million, compared with a combined Canada–Mexico–US GNP of $5,932 billion and a population of 357 million. Of course, the North American region is dominated by the US economy, which accounts for more than 85 percent of the regional output and nearly 70 percent of its population (table 1.1). By comparison, the largest single member of the European groups, the (combined) German economy, accounted for only 25 percent of combined EC–EFTA GNP in 1989, and 22 percent of the combined population. The appeal of a North American economic alliance is *not* that it would greatly embellish the existing trading bloc known as the United States, but rather that it holds open the prospect for substantial synergy among the three economies that could generate important income and employment gains and enhance the international competitiveness of firms throughout the region.

The last point is particularly important. All three countries run large current account deficits, have accumulated large foreign debts, and consequently need to pursue an export-led growth strategy. Clearly, each country cannot solve its problems on the backs of its neighbors; all three countries need to improve the efficiency and productivity of their labor forces and industries to compete more effectively against foreign suppliers in markets at home and abroad. This is the most important objective of the NAFTA.

Table 1.1 United States, Canada, and Mexico: selected economic indicators, 1980–89

	GNP 1989 (billions of dollars)	GNP per capita		Population		Average annual inflation rate 1980–89 (percentages)
		1989 (dollars)	Average annual growth rate 1980–89 (percentages)	1989 (millions)	Average annual growth rate 1980–89 (percentages)	
United States	5,201	21,057	1.9	247	1.0	4.7
Canada	530	20,385	2.1	26	1.0	5.8
Mexico	201	2,393	− 0.9	84	2.4	69.0

Sources: United Nations, *World Economic Survey,* 1989; International Monetary Fund, *World Economic Outlook,* April 1989; *International Financial Statistics,* Yearbook 1989 and September 1991; World Bank, *Social Indicators of Development,* 1989 and 1990. World Bank and International Monetary Fund data adapted with permission.

Moreover, the three economies are already closely linked by an extensive network of trade and investment, which makes the task of further negotiations somewhat easier. Both Canada and Mexico conduct between two-thirds and three-quarters of their trade with the United States, and the United States conducts about one-quarter of its trade with the two of them combined. The combined intraregional trade of the three countries represents about 40 percent of their total exports (by comparison, intraregional trade represents 60 percent of the exports of the EC member countries; Schott 1991). In addition, both Canada and Mexico host substantial US direct investment, while the United States benefits from substantial Canadian direct investment and hosts large sums of Mexican portfolio and real estate investment (much of which represents flight capital). The NAFTA reforms would further expand the trade and investment linkages among firms in the region.

Economic policies in the three countries are propelling closer economic integration, driven by common interests in deregulation and privatization on the domestic front, and common needs to deal with large current account deficits on the external front. A NAFTA would reinforce those existing trends. However, it would not result in the degree of deep integration already seen in the European Community. The implications of the prospective pact are significant, but they fall well short of a common market.

NAFTA: Integration of the Lesser Kind

Juxtaposed against the European Community, which is broadening and deepening the integration of its 12 member states and expanding the scope of its trade preferences with both the EFTA and the Eastern European countries, the NAFTA is often seen as North America's response to the European trading bloc. Such a comparison overlooks the idiosyncratic forces at work in Europe and North America and blurs numerous distinctions. Unlike in Europe, circumstances in North America have led the United States, Canada, and Mexico to pursue a free trade area rather than a more comprehensive economic union.[3]

A first major difference between the two forms of integration is that members of an economic union cede significant national sovereignty over economic affairs to a regional body. In the European Community, trade policy toward the rest of the world is implemented on a regional basis out of Brussels; the European Court of Justice handles internal commercial disputes arising from the implementation

---

3. A form of integration intermediate between a free trade area and an economic union is that of a customs union, with a common external tariff. In its early years the European Community was a customs union (often called the European Common Market). In our view, it will take many years before the NAFTA partners agree on a common external tariff.

of the Treaty of Rome; a single currency and a European central bank have been proclaimed as goals for 1999; and negotiations are proceeding toward closer political integration. Unlike the countries that have more recently joined the Community (Greece, Spain, and Portugal) or that now want to join (Austria and Sweden head the list), none of the three countries negotiating toward a NAFTA are willing to cede the requisite sovereignty to establish comparable regional bodies, or to provide large fiscal transfers among the members to cement the alliance.

Economic unions are rarely successful without the glue of intraregional subsidies, as the European experience amply demonstrates.[4] In contrast, the North American approach is one of "trade, not aid." Except for funds from the international financial institutions, direct subsidies to Mexico face substantial budgetary and political constraints in both the United States and Canada (witness the sharp criticism of alleged interest rate subsidies on the zero-coupon bonds offered to Mexico in 1989 by the US Treasury in the context of the Brady Plan).

Second, unlike the European Community, the NAFTA is likely to follow the precedent of the Canada–US FTA and not seek to provide a formal system of free labor mobility.[5] The FTA contained only sparse provisions that facilitate the temporary cross-border entry of business persons; coverage essentially is limited to the temporary entry of white-collar workers (who pose little immigration problem in any event). These limited provisions chart the outer boundary for the NAFTA talks. For the foreseeable future, immigration from Mexico to the United States will be dominated by illegal workers in search of better wages.

Large income disparities between prospective members make the process of economic integration more difficult and augment adjustment problems. The European Community spanned a wide divide when it incorporated Spain and Portugal, countries whose per capita GNP levels at the time of accession (January 1986) were $4,860 and $2,250, or 40 percent and 19 percent, respectively, of West German per capita GNP (World Bank 1989). By comparison, however, the inclusion of Mexico in the NAFTA poses an even greater challenge. Mexico's

---

4. In the Community, agricultural subsidies under the Common Agricultural Policy initially served this purpose. More recently, Greece, Spain, and Portugal received substantial regional aid for industrial development as part of the terms of their accession to the Community, and the former German Democratic Republic is receiving vast assistance in the context of German reunification.

5. Note, however, that labor mobility in North America is in many respects freer than in the European Community, for two reasons: European employment practices make it harder to hire workers because it is harder to fire them; and the limited availability and high cost of housing in Europe create implicit barriers to movement.

per capita GNP is only about 12 percent that of the United States and Canada combined.[6]

Furthermore, there were fewer people to accommodate at the lower income levels in the EC case, thus limiting the adjustment burden and simplifying the task of paying for adjustment assistance. The combined population of Spain and Portugal was 18 percent of the EC-10 total, whereas the population of Mexico is almost one-third the combined population of the United States and Canada.[7]

A third difference is that the NAFTA will follow the FTA precedent and will not deal with monetary and exchange rate issues, unlike the Community, where efforts are under way to build on the existing mechanism linking the members' currencies and to create a European central bank. Changes in real exchange rates will remain an essential adjustment mechanism of the three NAFTA economies. However, during the next decade Mexico may well decide to peg its currency even more closely to the US dollar and adjust its interest rate policies accordingly;[8] but that would be a unilateral decision, not a negotiated outcome.

Despite unsupported allegations by some FTA critics in Canada to the contrary, the FTA did not address exchange rates. The strengthening of the Canadian dollar after the agreement entered into force reflects the relative performance of the two economies and in particular the tight monetary policy followed by the Central Bank of Canada.[9]

These three large obstacles to broader economic integration in North America are compounded by a range of smaller difficulties. The Europe 1992 process demonstrates that meaningful economic integration requires tough new disciplines on member-state industrial subsidies and the removal of barriers created by product standards, different trucking requirements, wide differences in value-added and excise taxes, capital controls, differences in competition policy, and

---

6. Mexico appears more prosperous if one looks at real GDP levels derived by Summers and Heston (1991) for the UN International Comparison Program. Calculating purchasing power parities for hundreds of goods, they arrive at 1988 GDPs per capita of $19,851 (United States), $17,681 (Canada), and $5,323 (Mexico). However, these data ignore nominal money wage differences, which are often what motivate corporate decisions and migration flows, and they probably exaggerate the income of Mexico's impoverished rural population.

7. A closer analogue is the possible accession of Turkey to the European Community: Turkey's GNP per capita in 1989 was one-twelfth the EC average, and the Turkish population, at 52 million, was about one-seventh the EC total.

8. Since 1990, the Banco de México has tried to ratchet down the pace of its crawling devaluation of the peso against the dollar; this action can be seen as a prelude to a fixed exchange rate.

9. Even before the FTA was negotiated, analysis by John Williamson (appendix to P. Wonnacott 1987) predicted that the economic effects of freer US–Canada trade would lead *ceteris paribus* to some appreciation of the Canadian dollar.

so on (see Hufbauer 1990). To list these hurdles is enough to suggest that economic union in North America is well out of reach for the near future.

Free Trade Agreements: Some General Observations

It is important to emphasize three general points regarding FTAS.[10] First, FTAS result in freer trade, not free trade. Not all trade barriers are subject to elimination, and some nontariff barriers (NTBS) may be exempt from FTA obligations altogether. In the Canada–US negotiations, for example, all tariffs on bilateral trade are to be removed within 10 years, but several important NTBS, including domestic subsidies and agricultural quotas, remain intact. This is not necessarily inconsistent with the rules established by the General Agreement on Tariffs and Trade (GATT); indeed, the Canada–US FTA meets the GATT standards better than almost any other preferential trade agreement notified to the GATT in the past forty years.[11] The NAFTA negotiators thus have substantial flexibility to craft the provisions of the agreement to ensure that adjustment to freer trade is accommodated gradually and with a minimum of economic dislocation.

Second, FTAS serve an important function as an insurance policy against sudden changes in trade policies that may lead to increased discrimination against the trading interests of the partner countries and the imposition of new protectionist trade barriers. The ability to lock in existing levels of market access in the partner country is a major benefit of an FTA, and a very attractive feature to firms that are making investment and location commitments.

For example, in the Canada–US FTA an important US objective was to prevent a return to Canadian energy and investment policies that had sparked contentious bilateral disputes during the late 1970s and early 1980s. Similar considerations relative to recent Mexican economic reforms motivate US interest in the NAFTA talks. In turn, Mexico shares the Canadian concern about new US trade barriers, and in particular seeks insurance in the NAFTA against the abuse of US trade remedy laws that promote so-called process protectionism. In some respects, Canada receives preferential treatment under US contingent protection laws as a result of the dispute settlement provisions of the FTA, and Mexico will no doubt seek comparable treatment.[12]

---

10. For a detailed analysis of both the theory and the practical application of FTAS, see Schott (1989b).

11. Nonetheless, as with almost every agreement notified under GATT Article XXIV, the GATT working party reviewing the case noted concerns about specific aspects of the FTA and was unable to agree on whether the FTA was consistent with GATT obligations (see *Inside U.S. Trade*, 29 November 1991, S-1 to S-10).

12. In addition, Canada is accorded special treatment in safeguards cases under FTA Article 1102. The consistency of this provision with the GATT has not been put to the test, because no cases have been brought since the inception of the FTA.

l, there is little precedent for an FTA between developed and developing
.ies; most FTAS have been between countries at similar levels of economic
u. .opment.[13] Moreover, there have been few successful cases of FTAS solely
between developing countries, in part because of the high protectionist walls
that many poorer economies erected after World War II to insulate their industries from international competition. Protectionist policies, justified by appeals
to import substitution and infant-industry arguments, often cut developing countries off from valuable sources of foreign capital and technology. Many local
firms lost their ability to compete internationally, and free trade became politically difficult to achieve. Only in the 1980s did the policy mood in the developing
world swing away from the tenets of statism and protectionism.

Mexico, among the pioneers in this movement, turned toward free markets
and private enterprise in the mid–1980s.[14] Today, Mexico's trade regime fits the
Canadian and US mold more than that of the great majority of developing
countries. The breadth of its economic reforms since 1985 puts Mexico on solid
ground to pursue free trade with its northern neighbors.

National Objectives

The following sections examine the objectives of each prospective partner in a
NAFTA alliance.

United States

The United States has several fundamental objectives in pursuing negotiations
toward a NAFTA. At the broadest level, the United States has a strong and abiding
interest in promoting economic growth, political stability, and progress toward
greater democracy in Mexico. Such results would have important benefits for
the United States by reducing the risk of instability on its southern border. A
meaningful FTA could make a valuable contribution toward those goals.

At the same time, the United States has an important economic stake in trade
talks with Mexico. The first is simply to expand trade with Mexico, which is

---

13. The main exceptions have been the EC enlargement to include Greece and Portugal
and the EC and US FTAS with Israel; in the latter two cases politics dominated the economics,
and distance protected against major trade shifts in any event. One reason for the scant
number of FTAS between rich and poor countries, highlighted prominently in the US fast-
track debate, is concern about low-wage competition from developing countries in sensitive
manufacturing sectors.

14. In June 1985 the Mexican government initiated a drastic reform program. This excep-
tional episode of economic history has been ably recounted by Adriaan ten Kate (1990).

already its third-largest trading partner. Even more important, however, a NAFTA would promote the efficient use of natural and human resources in the North American region, and thus enable US firms and workers to compete more effectively in world markets.

In addition, a NAFTA would reinforce ongoing Mexican trade and investment reforms, which, along with reforms in Mexican laws relating to intellectual property rights, have generated substantial new opportunities for US firms. A NAFTA would contribute to increased economic growth in Mexico, which in turn would increase demand for US goods and services. If Mexico's recent strong growth performance can be maintained, net US exports to Mexico should expand substantially, generating net US employment gains in turn. Furthermore, growth in the Mexican economy will create new jobs and higher wages in Mexico and eventually slow the tide of illegal immigration (which, however, will remain a problem over the next decade or two).

In the aggregate, the direct, static benefits to the United States from the elimination of Mexican trade barriers will be small but not inconsequential. This reflects the fact that the Mexican economy today is relatively small, with a GNP less than 4 percent that of the US economy. In addition, US exporters have already reaped some of the benefits to be derived from lower Mexican trade barriers as a result of the substantial trade reforms that Mexico has embraced unilaterally since 1985.[15] However, the benefits of unilateral trade liberalization can be transitory; a NAFTA would secure and augment those reforms in an international accord and thus ensure that the benefits for US trading interests will be maintained.

The potential dynamic gains for US exporters from the NAFTA could be significant. The NAFTA would contribute to rapid growth in Mexican income and employment. Within four decades, Mexican per capita income could reach the same level that the United States attained in 1988—glowing prosperity compared with today's grinding poverty. A prosperous Mexico would become a thriving market for US exports.

To illustrate the potential dynamic trade gains, consider that Mexico now imports about $300 per capita annually from the United States; in contrast, Canada's annual imports from the United States run about $3,000 per capita.[16] Mexico already purchases about 70 percent of its imports from the United States; with strong growth in the Mexican economy, most of Mexico's additional purchases will also come from the US market. Although Mexico will not reach

---

15. Similarly, US tariff preferences for Mexico under the Generalized System of Preferences (GSP) and other programs have provided US firms access to low-cost, labor-intensive Mexican goods, which has strengthened their competitive position in the global economy.

16. Sidney Weintraub (1990c) originally put forward this line of argumentation in *The Washington Quarterly*.

the per capita import levels of industrialized Canada any time soon, annual US sales to Mexico could well increase from $28 billion in 1990 to nearly $60 billion by 1995 (see chapter 3).

Mexico

Mexican objectives in a NAFTA negotiation seem quite specific. First, an FTA with the United States would yield more open and secure access to a market that accounts for three-quarters of total Mexican exports. A NAFTA should reduce the threat of US protectionism and enhance Mexican export opportunities in the US market.

Second, international commitments under a NAFTA, together with prospective GATT accords, would help lock in domestic Mexican reforms instituted since 1985. In the initial wave of liberalization, licensing requirements were cut back for about 3,600 items, leaving 908 items under control. Since then, the maximum tariff level has been cut from 100 to 20 percent, the trade-weighted average tariff has fallen to just above 10 percent (table 1.2; data for production-weighted tariff averages are reported by sector in table 1.4), most licensing requirements have been eliminated (table 1.3), and the official reference prices for customs valuation purposes have been progressively removed. In addition, regulations regarding foreign investment and technology transfer have been liberalized and the intellectual property laws substantially revamped. These reforms have been complemented by substantial deregulation and privatization in key sectors including banking, telecommunications, and transport.[17]

The new trade regime was designed to confront Mexican industry with international competition and force greater efficiency. However, the impact was deliberately delayed by a severely depreciated peso. From early 1985 to the end of 1986, the Mexican peso was devalued by 27 percent in real terms (ten Kate 1990, table 1). As a result, the trade liberalization package did not immediately lead to an import surge, and Mexican industry was temporarily insulated from structural adjustments.

In 1987 the Mexican peso sharply appreciated, by 22 percent in real terms (ten Kate 1990, table 1). In addition, the Mexican government announced the Economic Solidarity Pact, which increased prices of public goods and services, cut back government spending, ended the indexation of wages to inflation, and continued the 1985 trade liberalization measures (tables 1.3 and 1.4). Imports

---

17. In September 1991 additional reforms were advocated by a group of 31 Mexican companies (including subsidiaries of major US firms), involving *inter alia* a doubling of infrastructure investment, pegging the peso to the US dollar, and cutting Mexico's marginal income tax rate (see *Journal of Commerce,* 9 September 1991, 1A).

Table 1.2 Mexico: trade policy reforms, 1985–90 (percentages)

	June 1985	June 1986	June 1987	June 1988	June 1989	June 1990
Coverage of import licenses[a]	92.2	46.9	35.8	23.2	22.1	19.9
Coverage of reference prices[a]	18.7	19.6	13.4	0.0	0.0	0.0
Maximum tariff	100.0	45.0	40.0	20.0	20.0	20.0
Production-weighted average tariff	23.5	24.0	22.7	11.0	12.6	12.5

a. With respect to tradeable output.

Sources: US International Trade Commission, *Review of Trade and Investment Liberalization Measures by Mexico and Prospects for Future United States–Mexican Relations* (USITC Publication 2275), April 1990, table 4-1 (original data from the Secretaría de Comercio y Fomento Industrial); Banco de México, *The Mexican Economy,* 1991.

Table 1.3 Mexico: shares of domestic production covered by import licensing, by industry, 1980–90 (percentages)

Industry	April 1980	June 1985	December 1985	June 1986	December 1986	June 1987	December 1987	June 1988	December 1988	June 1989	December 1989	June 1990
Agriculture	95	96	62	63	58	58	42	44	44	44	40	40
Crude oil and natural gas	100	100	100	100	100	100	100	100	100	100	100	100
Other mining	27	52	4	4	4	4	0	0	0	0	0	0
Foodstuffs	69	98	56	56	38	32	26	26	25	25	21	20
Beverages and tobacco	18	100	99	99	99	63	21	21	20	20	20	20
Textiles	80	91	10	10	10	10	7	2	3	3	3	1
Apparel and footwear	93	99	81	81	81	78	53	0	0	0	0	0
Wood products	77	100	47	47	12	12	0	0	0	0	0	0
Paper and printing	31	75	7	7	7	7	6	0	0	0	0	0
Petroleum refining	90	94	87	87	87	87	87	87	87	87	87	86
Chemical products	41	87	25	25	22	18	3	3	2	2	2	2
Nonmetallic mineral products	31	96	15	15	10	4	2	2	2	2	0	0
Basic metal industries	50	87	0	0	0	0	0	0	0	0	0	0
Metal products	22	74	8	9	3	2	1	1	1	1	1	1
Machinery and equipment	55	86	19	16	7	6	3	2	5	5	3	2
Electrical materials	51	97	41	37	32	24	0	0	0	0	0	0
Transport equipment	77	99	77	77	64	64	58	57	41	41	41	39
Miscellaneous manufacturing	52	92	23	23	18	17	0	0	0	0	0	0
Total production of goods	64	92	47	47	40	36	25	23	22	22	20	20

Source: Adriaan ten Kate, *The Mexican Trade Liberalization of 1985–1987: Lessons from Experience.* Reprinted with permission.

Table 1.4 Mexico: production-weighted tariff averages, 1980–90[a] (percentages)

Industries	April 1980	June 1985	December 1985	June 1986	December 1986	June 1987	December 1987	June 1988	December 1988	June 1989	December 1989	June 1990
Agriculture	9	9	13	12	13	13	7	6	9	10	9	9
Crude oil and natural gas	0	0	0	0	0	0	0	0	10	10	9	9
Other mining	12	19	19	18	18	16	8	8	11	11	11	11
Foodstuffs	24	23	32	29	29	26	14	12	12	12	12	12
Beverages and tobacco	73	77	77	41	40	37	20	20	20	20	20	20
Textiles	22	33	45	37	37	33	15	15	15	15	15	15
Apparel and footwear	32	47	48	41	41	37	19	19	19	19	19	19
Wood products	29	37	41	37	37	34	18	17	17	17	17	17
Paper and printing	22	20	22	19	19	18	10	5	7	7	7	7
Petroleum refining	2	2	3	2	2	2	1	1	10	10	4	4
Chemical products	31	29	32	27	28	26	13	13	14	14	13	13
Nonmetallic mineral products	33	32	39	33	33	30	15	14	15	15	15	15
Basic metal industries	12	15	22	20	20	19	8	8	11	11	11	11
Metal products	37	36	39	30	30	28	15	15	15	15	15	15
Machinery and equipment	24	22	33	29	31	28	15	16	16	16	16	16
Electrical materials	31	36	46	38	39	35	17	17	17	17	17	17
Transport equipment	42	39	42	29	32	29	14	15	16	16	16	16
Miscellaneous manufacturing	44	51	53	38	38	34	18	18	18	18	18	18
Total production of goods	23	24	29	24	25	23	12	11	13	13	13	13

a. Percentages ad valorem; these averages do not include the uniform surcharge that was abolished in December 1987.
Source: Adriaan ten Kate, *The Mexican Trade Liberalization of 1985–1987: Lessons of Experience*. Reprinted with permission.

ediately increased by more than 50 percent, from $12 billion in 1986 to $19
on in 1987, reflecting pent-up demand not only for consumer goods but also
for intermediate and capital goods that were in short supply in the Mexican
economy. This time, Mexican industry felt the full brunt of international competition and had no choice but to pursue a rigorous program of cost cutting and
retrenchment.

By securing and expanding Mexico's domestic economic reforms, a NAFTA
would send a positive signal that Mexico's current favorable climate toward trade
and investment will not easily be reversed. This added boost of confidence should
help encourage continued inflows of foreign direct investment, repatriation of
flight capital, and new lending from international financial institutions. These
are all needed to finance Mexican economic development in the years ahead.

Between 1987 and 1990, Mexico's current account balance shifted from a
surplus of $4.0 billion to a deficit of $6.3 billion (table 1.5); the Mexican government expects the deficits to rise further, to $11 billion and $13 billion in 1991
and 1992, respectively. In a sense, the current account deficits represent a vote
of confidence by the financial markets: instead of leaving Mexico, capital is
now returning to find new opportunities. Indeed, despite the mounting deficits,
Mexican reserves rose to almost $17 billion in November 1991 (*Financial Times,*
19 November 1991, 8).

Mexico's open trade policy depends importantly on its ability to sustain inflows
of foreign direct investment and the repatriation of flight capital needed to service
its external debt. Both require Mexico to maintain its economic stabilization
program to keep inflation under control and to avoid a sharp depreciation of the
peso.

Since the introduction of the economic stabilization and trade liberalization
programs in 1985, the stock of foreign direct investment in Mexico has more
than doubled, to a level of $30.3 billion at the end of 1990 (see chapter 4). The
rapid growth of this investment in Mexico is likely to continue. Mexico's strong
growth performance in 1989–90 and its prospective membership in a NAFTA
seem to have encouraged new investors; Japanese firms reportedly have already
committed $3 billion for future projects (*Business Week,* 3 June 1991, 20).

The major cloud on the Mexican economic horizon is its large foreign debt.
Mexico's total external debt is still about $98 billion, yielding a debt-export ratio
of 233 percent (table 1.6). Debt restructuring under the Brady Plan in 1989
contributed modestly to a reduction in both the aggregate debt burden and debt-
servicing requirements.[18] However, despite the relief afforded under the Brady

---

18. The 1989 debt accord affected $48 billion in medium- and long-term debt to foreign
banks and resulted in annual interest savings of about $1.5 billion. This resulted from a
reduction of $6.9 billion in the principal and lower interest charges on $25 billion in debt
through a conversion to fixed-interest bonds (the conversion was equivalent to another
$8.1 billion of debt forgiveness).

Table 1.5 Mexico: selected balance of payments accounts, 1980–90 and projected 1991–95[a] (millions of dollars)

Account	1980	1981	1982	1983	1984	1985	1986	1987	1988
Current account	−7,223	−12,544	−6,435	5,418	4,239	1,237	−1,671	3,966	−2,443
Trade	−3,700	−4,510	6,783	13,761	12,942	8,452	4,599	8,433	1,667
Nonfactor services[b]	n.a.[c]	n.a.[c]	−851	621	950	682	965	1,946	2,439
Factor services	−3,798	−8,323	−12,663	−9,265	−10,064	−8,899	−7,701	−7,062	−7,117
Transfers	275	289	296	301	411	1,002	466	649	568
Capital account (net)	11,948	21,859	6,754	−1,279	39	−1,527	1,837	−576	−1,448
Special drawing rights and other	74	70	0	0	0	0	0	0	−394
Errors and omissions	−3,648	−8,373	−5,271	−1,022	−924	−2,134	439	2,710	−2,842
Change in gross reserves	1,151	1,012	4,738	3,101	3,201	−2,328	985	6,924	−7,127

Account	1989	1990	1991	1992	1993	1994	1995	1996
Current account	−6,004	−6,349	−12,342	−16,950	−18,343	−20,626	−20,556	−20,952
Trade	−2,596	−4,140	−11,111	−15,993	−18,100	−21,398	−22,390	−24,011
Nonfactor services[b]	2,317	1,813	2,272	2,134	3,194	4,373	5,847	7,427
Factor services	−7,801	−7,577	−5,834	−5,772	−6,451	−7,023	−7,921	−8,817
Transfers	2,075	3,555	2,331	2,680	3,014	3,422	3,908	4,450
Capital account (net)	3,037	9,707	19,894	17,983	18,740	19,376	19,638	21,109
Special drawing rights and other	−125	181	219	81	221	866	882	548
Errors and omissions	3,362	−125	−636	890	550	1,087	1,194	821
Change in gross reserves	271	3,414	7,135	2,004	1,168	704	1,158	1,526

n.a. = not available.

a. Discrepancies are in the original data.

b. This includes various transactions at the frontier for which the method of calculation was changed in 1982.

c. Factor and nonfactor services not broken down separately.

Sources: Banco de México, The Mexican Economy 1991; Sidney Weintraub, A Marriage of Convenience: Relations Between Mexico and the United States (New York: Twentieth Century Fund, 1990), table 4.9, 88; CIEMEX-WEFA, Bala Cynwyd, PA (for 1988 to 1990 actuals, and 1991 to 1996 projections). Data reflect revisions through December 1991. CIEMEX-WEFA data reprinted with permission.

Table 1.6 Mexico: composition of external debt, 1985–90
(billions of dollars except where noted)

Year	Public sector	Commercial banks	IMF loans	Nonbank private sector	Total external debt	Total debt as a percentage of GDP	Total debt as a percentage of exports
1985	72	5	3	17	97	55	323
1986	75	6	4	16	101	78	421
1987	81	6	5	15	108	77	360
1988	81	8	5	7	101	58	316
1989	76	9	5	5	95	47	264
1990[a]	78	8	7	6	98	42	233

a. Preliminary.

Sources: Banco de México, *The Mexican Economy*, 1990 and 1991; International Monetary Fund, *International Financial Statistics*, 1990, various issues. International Monetary Fund data adapted with permission.

Table 1.7 Mexico: external debt service, 1985–90

Year	Total debt service (billions of dollars)	Exports of goods and services (billions of dollars)	Debt service ratio (percentages)	Interest payments as a percentage of exports
1985	13.0	29.7	43.8	34.1
1986	11.5	23.7	48.5	35.2
1987	12.8	29.9	42.8	27.1
1988	13.9	32.0	43.4	27.0
1989	13.0	36.0	36.1	25.8
1990[a]	12.2	41.6	29.3	21.7

a. Preliminary

Source: Banco de México, *The Mexican Economy*, 1990 and 1991.

Plan and increased oil export earnings, the annual interest payments on Mexico's external debt still consume almost 22 percent of total Mexican exports of goods and services (down from 35 percent in 1986; see table 1.7). Complacency is not in order.

Mexico conducts about three-fourths of its total trade with the United States; merchandise exports to the United States (including total maquiladora shipments) now account for about 13 percent of Mexican GDP (see table 3.1). The shift in the composition of Mexican exports—sharp growth in manufactures exports and a sharp drop in the share accounted for by oil—has, if anything, increased Mexico's trade dependence on the US market.[19]

To date, however, US protectionism has not been a severe problem for Mexican manufactured exports. The main restrictions affect textiles, apparel, steel, and some agricultural products (mainly fruits and vegetables); however, quotas in many of these areas have been liberalized as a result of agreements negotiated under the 1987 and 1989 bilateral framework accords.[20] Similarly, the number of antidumping and countervailing duty (CVD) cases has dropped considerably since 1985, with no new CVDs imposed since the bilateral accord on subsidies and CVDs in 1985, and only eight antidumping cases. However, the continued growth of Mexican nonoil exports to the United States could generate pressures for new US trade controls, which is one reason why Mexico has put so much emphasis on bilateral trade talks with the United States (see Trigueros 1989).

In sum, throughout the recent economic stabilization and reform program, trade policy has been the handmaiden of Mexican monetary and fiscal policy. Mexico's first task has been to slash the public deficit and to get inflation under control. Mexico's trade reforms have contributed to that end by opening the economy to greater import competition, which has helped dampen inflationary pressures (especially since 1988) while providing new competition in the marketplace. The reforms are already paying dividends: Mexico recorded solid economic growth in 1990 and 1991.

The key task of Mexican economic policymakers in the 1990s is to promote the restructuring and growth of the Mexican economy while keeping inflation under control. Investment, generated both from domestic savings and from foreign sources, will be the primary engine of growth. Trade policy can play an important role by ensuring the durability of the substantial measures already taken to open the Mexican economy to international competition, and by securing reciprocal trade concessions from Mexico's main trading partner.

Canada

In some respects, Canada is a reluctant partner in the NAFTA negotiations. It went through a wrenching national debate before ratifying the Canada–US FTA; critics

---

19. Oil accounted for about one-third of Mexican merchandise exports in 1989, compared with almost 69 percent in 1984; manufactured goods now account for 60 percent of total merchandise exports.

20. For example, in October 1989 the United States doubled Mexico's annual steel import quota from 400,000 to 800,000 tons; in February 1990 it agreed to eliminate quotas on 52 textile and apparel products and to expand quotas by an average of 25 percent for products that remain controlled (see chapters 12 and 13). These reforms took place after a period in which US quotas had been tightened or newly erected against the main exporters of these products to the US market.

of the FTA in Canada still loudly blame the trade pact for many of the ills that have befallen the Canadian economy over the past two years. Much of this criticism has been exaggerated and misplaced, but it does reflect legitimate sovereignty concerns first raised during the FTA debate.[21] In the NAFTA context, however, Canadian concerns seem to be much more focused on economic than on sovereignty issues.

To a significant extent, Canadian concerns about free trade with the United States and Mexico reflect discomfort with the prospect of structural adjustments in the economy and the implications such reforms may have for popular but expensive public programs. A system of free trade compels a country to examine carefully the costs its macroeconomic and microeconomic policies impose on individual firms. It does not *require* the convergence of national policies, but it does generate new competitive forces within the region and thus may increase pressure toward convergence.[22]

If Canada continues to run large fiscal deficits (3.4 percent of GDP in 1989) and to control inflation through tight monetary policy, it can expect high interest rates and a strong real exchange rate. Both of these macroeconomic policies put severe pressure on Canadian firms (just as similar policies under the first Reagan administration put US firms at a competitive disadvantage), as already evidenced by the growing traffic of Canadian shoppers across the US border, spurred by the strong purchasing power of the Canadian dollar and seeking to avoid high Canadian consumption taxes.[23]

Counterbalancing these economic concerns, Canada must consider its political position as one of the Big Four in international trade negotiations (together with the United States, the European Community, and Japan). For historical reasons, Canada has enjoyed a far larger role in shaping the international trading system than its economic position alone would merit; that role would be jeopardized if Canada were to sit out the NAFTA talks. Maintaining status was one important reason for Canada to seek a place at the table.

In addition, the Canadian decision to join the NAFTA negotiations rested importantly on the need to avoid a dilution of its FTA preferences in the US market and, to a lesser extent, to achieve access to the Mexican market comparable to

---

21. Given Conservative control of the sitting parliament, Canadian opposition to the NAFTA is not sufficient to derail Canadian participation. In any event, the NAFTA has been a much less strident political issue in Canada than the FTA. The political hot potato is the sovereignty of Quebec, not the current trade talks.

22. Of course, convergence pressures would exist even in the absence of a NAFTA, because of competition from foreign suppliers in both home and export markets.

23. Statistics Canada reported an almost 20 percent increase in cross-border shopping trips in May 1991 from a year earlier (*New York Times*, 9 August 1991, A1; see also *Wall Street Journal*, 20 June 1991, 1).

what its US competitors would enjoy. The Canadian decision thus can be read in economic terms both as a defensive move to safeguard the gains of the Canada–US FTA and as an effort to improve upon the FTA so as to create new export opportunities. Canada is particularly concerned to safeguard its position under the Canada–US FTA in areas such as trade in automobiles and energy, and to ensure that provisions that exempt Canadian cultural industries from FTA reforms remain intact.[24]

At the same time, Canada's chief negotiator, John Weekes, has indicated that Canada will seek improved access to the US and Mexican markets for Canadian banks under the financial services provisions of the NAFTA, and a further expansion of export opportunities for Canadian firms in the government procurement sector (*Inside U.S. Trade*, 7 June 1991, 6). Canada also has a growing export interest in agricultural trade with Mexico, especially field crops. Concessions in these areas will have to be significant for Canada to agree to changes in areas of concern to the United States and Mexico (e.g., energy investment, pharmaceutical patents, origin rules for automobiles, and agricultural trade barriers).

Canadian negotiators thus face an interesting challenge. They would be happy with the *status quo ante,* but they realize that reforms by the United States and Mexico will affect the Canadian position in the US market whether Canada participates or not. Thus, they will need to maximize the results in the financial services, procurement, and grains negotiations to achieve a balanced package from the Canadian perspective.

In addition, like the United States, Canada will need to rethink its labor adjustment assistance policies as it embarks on free trade with Mexico. In most cases, Canada is likely to face competitive pressures in the same sectors as the United States; some of these will involve industries that were only marginally affected by the Canada–US FTA (e.g., auto parts, textiles and apparel). Although the overall adjustment burden posed by a NAFTA will be much more limited than that posed by the FTA, it will be concentrated in these import-sensitive sectors. Canada, like the United States, will thus need to place greater emphasis on complementing income maintenance programs with retraining and placement services (chapter 6; see also Economic Council of Canada 1988).

In many instances, Canada is likely to be an impartial third party when the negotiations turn to issues that have a direct bearing only on the United States and Mexico.[25] However, issues will certainly arise where Mexico City and Ottawa

---

24. Both these concessions are likely to be challenged by the United States. In automobiles, ongoing discussions of North American trade pursuant to FTA Article 1004 have highlighted US–Canadian differences concerning whether to raise the rule of origin for automobile industry FTA benefits to 60 percent (see chapter 11); meanwhile, the exemption for cultural industries is a source of continuing bilateral friction.

25. Richard Lipsey (1991, 108) has made this point succinctly: "In most cases, Canada's less involved position is likely to leave it in its natural place: playing the part of honest broker between the two others, rather than being a major protagonist itself."

will find their common commercial interests conflicting with Washington's. In these cases, two coordinated voices may well have more impact than two distinct ones.

Plan of the Book

The prospect of an integrated North American market has intuitive economic appeal. However, because of large disparities in the countries' levels of development and in wage structures, a NAFTA will face much stronger political opposition from labor, agricultural, environmental, and manufacturing interests than did the Canada–US pact. Policymakers need to be fully apprised of both the opportunities and the adjustments that will arise from freer trade in North America.

The following chapters analyze both the substance and the form of a prospective NAFTA. Chapter 2 examines the potential shape and content of the agreement (including dispute settlement and institutional issues), its possible extension to third countries, and its implications for multilateral trade negotiations in the GATT.

The second part of the book examines the broad economic implications of a NAFTA for trade, investment, and employment. Chapter 3 analyzes the trade effects for both the NAFTA members and third countries of eliminating trade barriers on intraregional trade in North America. Chapter 4 looks at investment issues. Chapters 5 through 7 analyze the impact of the Mexican maquiladora program on bilateral and regional trade, and examine labor and environmental concerns that arise because of Mexico's lower level of economic development. Chapters 8 and 9 then cover the cross-sectional issues of rules of origin and intellectual property.

The third part of the book analyzes the implications of a NAFTA for selected industries and agriculture. Chapters 10 through 15 examine how producers of energy, automobiles, steel, textiles, agricultural goods, and financial services in the Mexican economy could be affected by a NAFTA and the implications for US and Canadian industries.

As Mexico is the prospective new member of the free trade club, much of the analysis is directed at that country and the effects of closer integration with its northern neighbors. The Mexican economic story has been dramatic but is not well understood. We therefore devote considerable effort to examining Mexican policies, recognizing that our treatment of the implications for Canada is less complete.

Each of the chapters contains its own conclusions and recommendations. The fourth and final part of the book summarizes the major conclusions and policy recommendations reached in the study.

2

The Substantive Agenda and Implications for Nonmember Countries

Although there are many historical examples of successful and unsuccessful attempts at bilateral and regional free trade agreements (FTAS), there is little precedent for a trilateral arrangement.[1] In part the explanation is simple: it is rare to find three countries with approximately balanced mutual trade interests; however, each country may have a more or less balanced relationship with the region as a whole.

A trilateral negotiation is inherently more unwieldy than the alternatives. But certain advantages compensate for the added complexity of initiating trilateral rather than bilateral negotiations. The accord can cover more issues (if at least two countries have an interest); compromises can be crafted among three countries in areas where the rift between two countries is too wide; and the negotiating outcome can reflect a variety of permutations and combinations.

Moreover, a trilateral negotiation is not wedded to a single document as the final outcome. Instead, the provisions can be applied on a selective basis, and the obligations can be phased in according to differential timetables.

Negotiators of a NAFTA start off with a blank page (or computer screen), which they can quickly transform into a variety of forms. This chapter examines some of the options available to the US, Canadian, and Mexican negotiators and the critical issues that will influence the shape of the final negotiating package. It also addresses the issue of extending NAFTA trade preferences to other countries in the future, either through accession to the NAFTA or through supplemental negotiations with one or more of the NAFTA signatories. It concludes with some thoughts on the interplay of the regional talks with ongoing multilateral negotiations in the GATT.

---

1. There have been only two examples in the postwar period: the Benelux Economic Union including Belgium, Luxembourg, and the Netherlands (which has been overshadowed by the participation of all three in the European Community), and the ill-fated East African Community (EAC), whose members were Kenya, Tanzania, and Uganda. The EAC was established in 1967 but soon broke down despite the countries' common colonial heritage and effectively came to an end in 1977.

The Road to a NAFTA

If one were to follow historical precedent, the road to a NAFTA would be likely to proceed first to a US–Mexico FTA before wending its way to a trilateral pact. Throughout the 1980s Mexico seemed to follow the Canadian model of pursuing closer economic integration with the United States in incremental steps. As Canada moved from sectoral talks to FTA negotiations, Mexico too entered into a series of negotiations with the United States, moving from specific issues such as subsidies and countervailing duties in 1985, to sectoral talks under bilateral framework agreements in 1987 and 1989, and finally to the pursuit of an FTA in 1990.

At the same time, Canada and Mexico began to pursue closer bilateral trade relations. In March 1990, Canadian and Mexican officials negotiated a series of framework accords that paralleled arrangements worked out between Mexico and the United States. Even then, however, Canadian Prime Minister Brian Mulroney did not anticipate trilateral negotiations in the near term: "Whether this emerges into a more formalized association with North America *over the next decade* [emphasis added], I don't know.... But I wouldn't be scandalized at the prospect" (as quoted by Canadian Press, 19 March 1990).

The announcement on 11 June 1990 that the United States and Mexico intended to negotiate a bilateral FTA, followed shortly by the launching on 27 June 1990 of the Enterprise for the Americas Initiative (EAI), raised the prospect of a series of new FTAs between the United States and other countries in the Western Hemisphere. These initiatives confronted Canada with the choice of either joining the "hub" (i.e., engaging in trilateral negotiations) or becoming just one of several "spokes" in the US FTA system.[2] After extensive cabinet debate in the second half of 1990, Canada opted for the negotiation of a regional trade pact, and on 5 February 1991 President Bush announced that the three countries would initiate negotiations on a NAFTA (*Wall Street Journal*, 6 February 1991, A8). Trilateral negotiations commenced in Toronto on 12 June 1991.

The Substantive Agenda

In principle, the NAFTA negotiators start off *tabula rasa*, but in fact the model of the Canada–US FTA will substantially influence the new agreement. Nineteen

---

2. Ronald J. Wonnacott (1990) has put forward an elegant discussion of the implications for Canada of a series of bilateral FTAs between the United States and third countries. In brief, he argues that most of the benefits accrue to the hub country (the United States) that negotiates FTAs with a number of countries; by contrast, the spoke countries continue to face barriers in each others' markets, while their trade preferences in the US market are undercut by increased competition from other spokes.

Table 2.1 NAFTA **negotiating groups**

Market access
    Tariffs and nontariff barriers
    Rules of origin
    Government procurement
    Agriculture
    Automobiles
    Other industrial sectors
Trade rules
    Safeguards
    Subsidies; countervailing and antidumping duties
    Standards
        Health and safety
        Industrial
Services
    Principles of services
    Financial
    Insurance
    Land transportation
    Telecommunications
    Other services

Investment (principles and restrictions)

Intellectual property

Dispute settlement

negotiating groups under six broad categories have been established (table 2.1). The type of agreements reached, however, will depend both on the extent to which the existing Canada–US FTA is augmented and on efforts to unravel present FTA obligations. For example, if one of the negotiating partners objects to proposed additions or deletions to the agenda, the negotiating process may proceed bilaterally in that area.

Augmenting the FTA Model

Both the United States and Canada agree that their FTA can be improved upon (indeed it has already been augmented twice to accelerate the implementation of tariff cuts), but they differ as to where and how. The NAFTA is likely to augment the FTA model in at least four specific areas: intellectual property, services, environmental issues, and subsidy-countervail and antidumping issues.[3]

Intellectual Property

The Canada–US FTA contains only two specific provisions relating to intellectual property issues: one resolves a bilateral dispute relating to copyrights on the retransmission of broadcasts; the other sets out a hortatory commitment by both countries to pursue a strong agreement on intellectual property in the Uruguay Round. A more extensive chapter setting out rights and obligations in this area was dropped from the agreement late in the negotiations, in large part because of US concerns about Canadian requirements for the compulsory licensing of pharmaceutical patents under law C-22. This area has also been a problem in US–Mexico relations but was substantially resolved by passage of new Mexican patent, trademark, and copyright laws in June-July 1991 (see chapter 9).

Given the prominence accorded intellectual property issues in the Uruguay Round talks, and the formation of a separate negotiating group on this set of issues for the trilateral negotiations, an intellectual property chapter will almost certainly be included in the NAFTA. At a minimum, it is likely to obligate the parties to accede to the prospective Uruguay Round agreement on intellectual property, or to accept obligations comparable to those currently under negotiation in the GATT.

The United States will seek to incorporate detailed obligations in the NAFTA that lock in the recent Mexican intellectual property reforms and that establish a model for both bilateral and regional accords in the Western Hemisphere (and in the GATT if the Uruguay Round is still in train). In addition, the United States will once again press Canada to modify its compulsory licensing practices. In contrast, Canada may well try to limit the NAFTA to general commitments and defer specific obligations to the multilateral negotiations. At the end of the day, however, Canada is likely to limit compulsory licensing to extreme situations, and thus remove the main obstacle to a NAFTA accord in this area.

Services

Trade in nonfactor services is an important component of the economic relationship among the North American countries. As table 2.2 shows, US–Canada trade

---

3. In the first session of the NAFTA talks in Toronto, the three countries agreed that intellectual property would be one of six broad areas under negotiation, and that subsidy issues would be dealt with under the rubric of trade rules (*Journal of Commerce*, 13 June 1991, 1A).

Table 2.2 United States: trade in nonfactor services with Canada and Mexico, 1988–90 (millions of dollars)

	Canada			Mexico		
	1988	1989	1990	1988	1989	1990
Exports						
Travel	3,986	4,852	5,690	2,652	3,398	4,004
Passenger fares	648	719	782	191	260	307
Other transportation	927	989	1,078	369	409	469
Royalties and license fees	795	938	1,102	134	150	217
Other private services	3,160	3,711	4,403	829	1,126	1,152
Total services	9,516	11,209	13,055	4,175	5,343	6,149
Imports						
Travel	−3,228	−3,390	−3,490	−4,828	−5,657	−5,999
Passenger fares	−254	−224	−260	−463	−518	−649
Other transportation	−676	−655	−877	372	−392	−362
Royalties and license fees	−222	4	−37	negl.	1	−13
Other private services	−1,985	−1,877	−1,840	−1,213	−1,420	−1,557
Total services imports	−6,365	−6,142	−6,504	−6,132	−7,986	−8,580
Trade balance	3,151	5,067	6,551	−1,957	−2,643	−2,431

negl. = negligible (less than $500,000).

Source: US Department of Commerce, *Survey of Current Business* 71, no. 6 (June 1991).

in nonfactor services totaled about $20 billion in 1990; US–Mexico nonfactor services trade reached almost $15 billion. Bilateral US–Canada trade has grown sharply since the FTA went into effect, primarily because of increased Canadian travel and tourism in the United States (bolstered by the appreciation of the Canadian dollar). Indeed, travel and tourism accounts for the predominant share of both US–Canada and US–Mexico bilateral trade in nonfactor services.

The Canada–US FTA broke new ground by establishing extensive rights and obligations relating to trade in services. FTA chapters 14 and 15 contain provisions regarding national treatment, right of establishment or commercial presence, licensing and certification procedures for service providers, and the facilitation of cross-border travel by business persons. Sectoral annexes to FTA chapter 14 on architecture, tourism, and computer and telecommunications network–based enhanced services address specific restrictions and regulatory issues in those areas. In addition, FTA chapter 17 contains specific commitments on financial services (see chapter 15 of this study; for a more detailed discussion of the FTA provisions on services, see Schott and Smith 1988, chapter 6).

In this area the NAFTA will follow the FTA model quite closely; new rights and obligations developed in the General Agreement on Trade in Services (GATS) in the GATT are likely to be incorporated as well. As in the FTA and GATS negotiations, the most contentious issues will involve sectoral coverage and commitments to regulatory reform and trade liberalization.

The NAFTA negotiations will have a dual focus. First, the talks will seek to fit Mexican policies into the network of rights and obligations already adopted by the United States and Canada in the FTA (a process that will be greatly facilitated if Mexico becomes a signatory to the prospective GATS). In this regard, the United States and Canada will be particularly keen on Mexican participation in agreements on financial services (see chapter 15) and tourism (which accounts for more than 60 percent of US–Mexico trade in nonfactor services). The United States will also push for reforms in the audiovisual sector, particularly if the GATS accord comes up short in this area.

Second, the NAFTA talks will attempt to extend the coverage of rules to service sectors not yet subject to FTA discipline. Notable omissions from FTA coverage include transportation services and most labor services, areas in which Canada and Mexico, respectively, have strong interests in US reforms. Incorporation of rules on transportation services are likely to turn on developments in the GATS; given the critical importance of land transport for Mexican trade, new provisions in this area are likely regardless of the results in Geneva. Provisions on labor services run up against immigration concerns and are thus less likely to be adopted by the NAFTA partners (see the discussion of immigration issues in chapter 6).

Environment

The "Action Plan" submitted by President Bush to the Congress on 1 May 1991, during the US debate on fast-track authority, commits the United States to dealing with a broad range of environmental concerns both in trade talks with Mexico and in parallel negotiations. The Canada–US FTA provides no precedent in this area, although both countries dealt with the acid rain problem in a separate bilateral forum.[4] Environmental issues are likely to arise primarily in the NAFTA

---

4. Title IV of the US Clean Air Act Amendments of 1990, signed into law on 15 November of that year, provides strict new guidelines for sulfur dioxide and nitrous oxide emissions and requires significant cuts in those emissions from 1980 levels. The United States and Canada subsequently entered into a framework agreement in March 1991 that dealt with acid rain and other air quality issues.

negotiating groups dealing with trade rules, health and safety standards, and agriculture.

Although many of the environmental problems cited during the fast-track debate are inherently bilateral, the NAFTA could set forth common provisions to guide national responses to trade-related environmental issues (involving, for example, minimum health and safety standards for products entering international commerce) and procedures for increasing the rigor of those standards throughout the region (see chapter 7). The environmental area seems amenable to the approach set out in the Canada–US FTA for financial services, in which both partner countries agreed on common principles supplemented by separate commitments by each to specific reforms of national policies and practices.

Subsidies, Countervailing Duties, and Antidumping Duties

The Canada–US FTA committed Canada and the United States to negotiate new substantive rules in the areas of subsidy-countervail and antidumping over a five- to seven-year period; however, those talks have been effectively frozen pending the outcome of the Uruguay Round (where negotiators are likely to achieve only modest results). In the interim, the dispute settlement provisions of FTA chapter 19 have been used to deal with bilateral problems regarding the implementation of existing national laws and regulations.[5]

The prospect of limited results in this area in Geneva puts the ball squarely back in the NAFTA court. Progress toward closer regional integration in North America will again focus attention on several key subsidy issues, especially regional aids (including subfederal subsidies), adjustment assistance programs, and investment incentives.[6] Given the shared interest of Mexico and Canada in greater discipline over the US use of countervailing duties, both may be amenable to subsidy reforms that go beyond what is achievable in the GATT round.[7] In particular, they may be willing to accept some limitations on purely domestic

5. Dispute settlement is discussed later in this chapter. For a more detailed discussion of the FTA provisions, see the introductory chapter by Jeffrey J. Schott and the chapter by Gary Horlick et al. (chapter 3) on dispute resolution mechanisms in Schott and Smith (1988).

6. In addition, the Canadian decision to abrogate the 1986 agreement with the United States on softwood lumber has resuscitated the contentious dispute over stumpage subsidies (*Journal of Commerce*, 4 September 1991, 1A).

7. During the period 1980–89, the United States initiated 15 countervailing duty cases against Canadian products and 26 against Mexican products. However, no new cases have been brought against Mexican products since the 1985 bilateral agreement on subsidies and countervailing duties. See Horlick and Steger (1990, 98), Weintraub (1990a, 81–82), and US International Trade Commission (1990b, 4–19).

subsidies in exchange for a different US approach to the issues of causation and injury, and perhaps the incorporation of a *de minimis* test (in which cases are terminated if the calculated subsidy effect is below a certain threshold—say, 2.5 percent).

In the antidumping area, however, the same obstacles that are limiting progress in the GATT are likely to surface in the NAFTA negotiations. US industries remain wary about predatory pricing practices of competing firms based in Mexico and Canada. With industrial lobbyists in mind, Congress is loath to consider reforms of US antidumping laws, even when limited to FTA partners.

In recent years there have been relatively few US cases applied against Mexican and Canadian firms; the Canadian and Mexican caseloads have also been moderate.[8] The relatively limited number of cases leads some to question whether reform of antidumping practices is worth the political fight.[9] We remain concerned, however, that resort to antidumping actions in the future (by all three countries) could threaten to unravel the gains from NAFTA reforms.

The first-best solution regarding antidumping rules in the NAFTA would be to introduce common competition policies to regulate predatory practices in intraregional trade rather than apply antidumping duties, but that approach seems beyond the pale of the present talks. Rather, the elimination of antidumping actions on intraregional trade (the approach adopted in the European Community) should be made a long-term goal of the NAFTA and considered in future trilateral (and multilateral) negotiations once the NAFTA is up and running. A companion long-term goal is to seek a closer approximation of competition policies among the NAFTA partners (see Feltham et al. 1991).

In the first stage, however, the NAFTA accord should work to extend the special dispute resolution rules and panel procedures of the Canada–US FTA to Mexico (see discussion below). As in the intellectual property area, NAFTA provisions may also supplement the GATT obligations of the three countries, and thus provide a building block for future multilateral negotiations.

Unraveling the FTA Model?

The risk that the NAFTA talks will unravel existing FTA provisions is most prominent in the energy sector and with regard to cultural industries; in both instances,

---

8. Since 1985, the United States has initiated 17 and 8 antidumping cases against Canadian and Mexican producers, respectively; Canada has brought 25 cases against the United States; and Mexico has initiated 15 cases against US firms.

9. Because antidumping cases affect only a fraction of a percent of bilateral trade in North America, Michael Stein, a former general counsel of the US International Trade Commission, has compared FTA attempts to proscribe antidumping cases to "trying to find a cure for which there is no known disease" (*International Trade Reporter*, 20 March 1991, 441).

exceptions from the FTA investment provisions could become targets for review.[10] In addition, the complex web of origin rules spelled out in FTA chapter 3 and its annexes will need to be revisited; pressures are already building to significantly increase local content requirements.[11]

Rules of Origin

Trilateral rules are essential for a NAFTA to work (see chapter 8). To be sure, as the gap between most-favored-nation (MFN) tariffs and the zero tariff for FTA partners is reduced, origin rules become less important. However, even in a world of zero MFN tariffs, rules of origin remain important to avert the circumvention of trade remedy laws (a key issue in some antidumping and countervailing duty cases). In the meantime, origin rules are particularly important in sectors where MFN protection remains high.[12]

Divergent national interests and sectoral protectionist pressures make this issue potentially contentious. The problem will be to balance competing goals: encouraging foreign investment in the region while preventing nonmember countries from using Mexico as a pure export platform to the US and Canadian markets.

The FTA origin rule provides an imperfect model for the NAFTA, but one that will be difficult to improve upon in the NAFTA negotiations. However, the FTA approach is complex; special sectoral rules provide a gold mine for accountants and lawyers. In some cases, firms have preferred to continue to pay MFN tariffs rather than undertake the paperwork necessary to qualify for FTA preferences (Hart 1990, 106; *Journal of Commerce*, 18 July 1991, 3A).

NAFTA origin rules are particularly important for the US automobile and auto parts industries. These firms are prepared to contest the entire agreement if the restrictive local content rule that applies uniquely to this sector is relaxed. Indeed, the US firms want the requirement tightened so as to slow down the entry of new Japanese firms (beyond Nissan) into Mexico (see Motor and Equipment Manufacturers Association 1991a).

---

10. At the initial NAFTA negotiating session, US Trade Representative Carla A. Hills stated that "the only thing that's off the table is the ownership of the mineral rights in Mexico and US immigration laws." Both Canada and Mexico contested the US position, adding to the list Canadian cultural industries and exploitation of Mexican energy resources, respectively *(Journal of Commerce*, 13 June 1991, 1A; 18 June 1991, 3A).

11. Hart (1990, 104) considers rules of origin "the most difficult and the most important chapter that will have to be tackled in negotiating Mexican accession."

12. That is why the general origin rule in the Canada–US FTA is supplemented by numerous industry-specific rules (usually of a more restrictive character) set out in the annex to FTA chapter 3.

Lipsey and Smith (1989, 328) have argued that "the rules of origin for duty-free treatment within an FTA should be made more liberal as the external tariffs of the parties are reduced either on an MFN basis or through negotiations of further regional FTAS." Following that logic, the enlargement of the FTA to include Mexico should lead to less-restrictive origin rules in the NAFTA. However, virtually all the political pressure coming from industry is to devise tighter rules. As explained in chapter 8, we believe the NAFTA negotiators should simply adopt the existing FTA origin rules with as few sectoral exceptions as possible. (The main exception that we think the negotiators should address is the problem of "roll-up" abuse in the automotive industry; see chapter 11.) But they should also create a trilateral mechanism to devise special rules when the general rules either prove too restrictive or are abused.

Energy

The Canada–US FTA already contains an extensive carve-out for energy industries from its investment provisions; Mexican officials are likely to seek to extend the carve-out *inter alia* to the obligations regarding supply access assurances, so as to maintain as much flexibility as possible for national policies in this area.

To encourage the development of Mexican energy resources and to promote regional energy security, the United States may try to narrow the energy carve-out from existing FTA disciplines on investment (see chapter 10). New investment in energy infrastructure (e.g., electricity grids, natural gas pipelines, and oil refineries) is critical for both objectives. In this case, the Mexican and Canadian position in the NAFTA negotiations differs from that of the United States. As discussed in chapter 10, however, Mexico needs to increase production in the energy sector to bolster its growth prospects, and it will need substantial foreign participation to fulfill Pemex's ambitious investment plans. The three countries are likely to follow pragmatic detours around the sovereignty land mines buried in Mexico and Canada.

Cultural Industries

FTA Article 2005 exempts specified cultural industries from most FTA obligations. As a result, trade and investment policies affecting particular goods and services (including *inter alia* the print media, film and music recordings, and radio and television broadcasts) can still discriminate against foreign suppliers. Nonetheless, a substantial share of Canadian sales of books, periodicals, and movies comes from the United States (Ryan 1991, 4A).

Canada considers Article 2005 critical to safeguard its cultural sovereignty and regards the FTA cultural exemptions as inviolable.[13] In contrast, the United States argues that the exemption should be narrowed to limit the scope of foreign investment restrictions and to allow the full exploitation of copyrights throughout the region. Mexico seems to be less sensitive than Canada to the need to protect so-called cultural industries;[14] its main sovereignty concern involves the energy sector, as noted above. The diverse set of attitudes toward cultural questions suggests an outcome that entails separate schedules of specific national practices that are excepted from the general disciplines of the NAFTA (following the FTA precedent).

NAFTA: Improving on the US–Canada Model

What kind of animal will this NAFTA be? Until the Canadian decision to join the negotiations in January 1991, the number of possible outcomes seemingly was limited only by the spirited imagination of the trade negotiators. As the talks began in June 1991, the form and substance of the eventual agreement were still unclear. However, the number of options for its basic form seemed to have been pared down to three: separate bilateral accords subsumed under a trilateral umbrella; a hybrid between a bilateral and trilateral pact; or a trilateralization of a new, improved Canada–US FTA.

Separate Bilateral FTAs

Until the Canadian decision to seek a trilateral pact, the negotiation of separate bilateral FTAS seemed to be the logical *modus operandi* for crafting a NAFTA. The United States would negotiate an FTA with Mexico, effectively implementing a hub-and-spoke policy; Canada and Mexico could then do the same with each other, building on their March 1990 Framework Pacts; over time the three separate bilateral FTAS then could be covered under a trilateral umbrella agreement.

---

13. For a thorough discussion of the cultural sovereignty issue and Canadian concerns, see Carr (1991).

14. Jaime Serra Puche, the Mexican Secretary of Commerce, has made this point quite starkly: "The free trade agreement does not threaten the Mexican cultural identity" (as quoted in *El Nacional*, 21 June 1991, 2). Similarly, Herminio Blanco, Mexico's chief NAFTA negotiator, has declared that "the cultural industries have to be negotiated as part of the services sector, which includes entertainment" (as quoted in the *Journal of Commerce*, 8 August 1991, 9A).

As Ronald J. Wonnacott (1990) has pointed out, the United States would come out ahead of its FTA partners under a hub-and-spoke approach, since it would benefit from freer trade with both countries (which in turn would make it the preferred market for new investment), while Canada would face increased competition in the US market and continued discrimination (compared with US firms) in the Mexican market. Moreover, Canada would not have the opportunity to influence the terms of the US–Mexico arrangement if it sat on the sidelines, even if Canada and Mexico worked out their own bilateral FTA. For those reasons among others, Canada opted to join the US–Mexico talks. The separate bilateral option thus seems to have been relegated to a fallback role, to be resurrected should the trilateral approach break down (or should Canada back out for domestic political reasons).

The Hybrid Trilateral Approach

The hybrid approach would mix trilateral obligations in a core agreement with separate bilateral commitments on specific issues. The larger the core, the more this approach parallels the straight trilateralization option discussed below.

The hybrid approach would set out an umbrella agreement among the three countries that would establish common administrative and dispute settlement provisions, as well as commitments regarding trade liberalization. The existing Canada–US FTA would remain intact. Each country would negotiate separate arrangements with Mexico regarding the extent to which Mexico would assume specific rights and obligations with regard to goods and services trade and perhaps investment and intellectual property; the schedule of those bilateral commitments would be annexed to the trilateral NAFTA framework.

Lipsey (1990, 1991) favors a hybrid approach combining a core agreement involving liberalization of trade in goods and services, as well as institutional provisions relating to dispute settlement and administration of the pact, with separate bilateral pacts between the partner countries. In essence, the core would be a diluted version of the Canada–US FTA that would be applied in its entirety by all three countries.[15] The Canada–US FTA would be preserved, and Mexico would negotiate side agreements with the United States and Canada to supplement its undertakings in areas not covered by the core agreement.

---

15. According to Lipsey (1991, 114), the core agreement would exclude FTA chapters 7 (agriculture), 9 (energy), 13 (government procurement), 16 (investment), and Article 2005 (cultural industries).

Trilateralization of the Canada–US FTA

The most straightforward approach to a NAFTA would be simply to trilateralize the Canada–US FTA by having Mexico accede to the existing agreement. Even better, all three countries could use the opportunity to improve the existing pact in the areas already noted. As a practical matter, some amendment would be necessary upon Mexican accession, because several of the FTA provisions involve separate national obligations on specific issues and would thus require complementary commitments relating to Mexican policies. Striking examples include financial services, insurance, and agricultural reforms.

The straight trilateral approach could have some drawbacks, however. Both Hart (1990) and Lipsey (1991) have surveyed the provisions of the Canada–US pact and found numerous areas where Mexico could have problems accepting FTA obligations; the most prominent examples involve energy, government procurement, and dispute resolution provisions. Both Hart and Lipsey conclude that a hybrid approach to a NAFTA would be more practical than the more ambitious trilateralization option.

However, their policy recommendation rests on two critical assumptions: that Mexico will accept only asymmetrical obligations because of its level of development, and that Mexico's different legal system will complicate the evolution of a common dispute settlement mechanism. On close examination, those assumptions do not stand up.

Symmetrical Obligations

The first assumption implies that developing countries start, by definition, at a competitive disadvantage in an FTA and therefore need to maintain their trade barriers longer than their industrialized partners. Indeed, there are few instances in history where developed and developing countries joined in an FTA. This may partly reflect the self-fulfilling prophecy of protection: trade barriers are frequently so high in developing countries that many firms fear they can not survive the shock of adjustment to open competition with an industrial economy.

Mexico seems to be an exception to the historical developing-country predilection for protection. The Mexican policy of *apertura* is based on a willing embrace of liberal trade and investment policies as the preferred path to economic growth. So far, the Mexican experiment has succeeded brilliantly: inflation has fallen sharply, distortions have been reduced, the stock market is booming, and growth has resumed. But Mexico needs to sustain and augment its recent reforms to encourage the new investment required to finance development over the long haul. Accession to the full obligations of the NAFTA would continue and solidify the ongoing reform process; differential and delayed staging of trade reforms would simply retard adjustment. Indeed, Mexico needs to *avoid* differential treatment in all but extreme circumstances. Differential treatment is usually rationalized as a crutch to prop up a weak economy; often, however, it becomes a handicap because it poses a sugar-coated obstacle to adjustment.

Mexico should be able to commit to reciprocal trade liberalization in the NAFTA. Mexico's average tariff is comparable to Canada's before implementation of the FTA, and it should be phased out over a similar 10-year time period.[16] Liberalization in the automobile and petrochemical industries will be more difficult, but the adjustment in Mexico should be facilitated by investment in new plant and equipment. In agriculture, the pace of reform will need to be slower, but even then Mexico should be able to keep up with the snail's pace of agricultural reform set out in the Canada–US pact (see chapter 14).

Of course, Mexico need not pursue obligations identical to those committed to by Canada and the United States, but it should be able to eliminate its tariffs as well as most import licensing requirements in a comparable time frame. Indeed, the United States and Canada may be more likely than Mexico to seek extended phase-out periods to ease the pain of reform in their most protected sectors (e.g., apparel; fruits and vegetables).

Mexico should be able to accept the full range of NAFTA obligations, including those pertaining to services, investment, and intellectual property (and, indeed, should accede to the accords under negotiation in the Uruguay Round). Mexico has already undertaken significant reforms (most recently with regard to protection of intellectual property) that are bringing many of its domestic regulations into conformity with the standards of the United States and other OECD countries. Moreover, Mexico is now seeking membership in the OECD to reinforce and further extend its economic reforms.

Furthermore, Mexico should be able to sign all of the GATT codes on nontariff barriers,[17] and to align its domestic procedures with the international norms established by those agreements (including antidumping, where despite Mexico's being a signatory to the GATT code, Mexican administrative practices remain somewhat arbitrary). Such action would make Mexican administrative procedures more transparent and consistent with US and Canadian norms and would establish a common basis for the review of antidumping and countervailing duty actions required to implement FTA chapter 19 procedures. Mexican willingness

---

16. As a result, Mexican imports would still be subject to some tariffs for a few years after the complete elimination of duties on US–Canada trade. One would expect, however, that after the NAFTA is signed, the tariff cuts would be accelerated (as noted above, this has occurred twice already in the US–Canada context).

17. Mexico is not yet a signatory to the GATT subsidies and government procurement codes. It signed the licensing, customs valuation, and antidumping codes in July 1987, and the standards code in January 1988 (US International Trade Commission 1990b, 2–3).

to sign the GATT codes, or to extend comparable rights to its NAFTA partners, should be a prerequisite for the inclusion of FTA chapters 18 and 19 dispute resolution procedures in the NAFTA. There is little reason to doubt that Mexico will take these steps. Thus, the legal differences between NAFTA partners may not be as hard to bridge as Hart and Lipsey imagine.

Dispute Settlement

The dispute settlement mechanisms in Canada–US FTA chapters 18 and 19 are among the most important benefits conferred by that agreement. For Canada, they provide an important binational check on the abuse of US trade laws. For the same reason, Mexico would like to see comparable provisions in the NAFTA. Canada is wary that a trilateralization of the dispute settlement process could dilute its positive influence on US trade policies. Both the United States and Canada are concerned that Mexico's different legal system and traditions will impede the enforcement of NAFTA rules.

The Canada–US FTA provides a bifurcated dispute settlement process. In most areas, disputes between the FTA partners are reviewed under the general procedures of FTA chapter 18. However, disputes concerning antidumping and countervailing duties, which have accounted for the vast majority of cases brought under the FTA, are handled under the provisions of FTA chapter 19.[18]

FTA chapter 18 establishes an alternative to GATT dispute settlement procedures (although both countries reserve their right to take cases to the GATT). Disputes raised by either country are examined by a panel of experts, who follow procedures adopted from US–Canadian legal experience. As in the GATT, findings of expert panels are subject to review by a senior political body (the Canada–United States Trade Commission).

In contrast, disputes brought under chapter 19 procedures are subject to binding panel rulings. Jean Anderson (1989, 15) succinctly describes the function of a dispute panel under chapter 19 of the Canada–US FTA: "the panel is to review a final determination, based on the administrative record, to determine whether the determination was in accordance with the AD [antidumping] or CVD [countervailing duty] law of the importing country, and must apply the standard of review and general legal principles of the importing country." In essence, FTA panels *substitute* for judicial review of trade actions. The fact that Mexico's nascent antidumping regime has not yet established a track record of

---

18. Neither process applies to disputes over financial services, which are handled separately by the US Treasury and the Canadian Department of Finance according to the provisions of FTA chapter 17.

judicial review is thus less troublesome, since the FTA provisions (if adopted in the NAFTA) would make that process redundant.[19]

By all accounts, the FTA dispute settlement process has worked exceedingly well. Only two cases (one involving Pacific coast salmon and herring, the other lobsters—both in 1989) have been reviewed under the general procedures of chapter 18. In contrast, as of June 1991, 15 cases had been brought under chapter 19, of which 7 were settled, 3 terminated, 2 consolidated with another panel, and 3 remain pending. In almost every case, the strict time limits of the FTA process have been kept. Panels have not acted as rubber stamps for national regulators; instead, some national actions have been overturned. Moreover, the decision by an extraordinary challenge committee to uphold the panel findings in the most contentious case to date—a dispute involving Canadian pork subsidies—seems to have bolstered the credibility of the FTA process.[20]

If Mexico aligns its administrative procedures with US and Canadian norms in terms of open proceedings and written opinions,[21] there should be no serious problem with regard to Mexican participation in dispute resolution provisions under the NAFTA. Mexican application of the general obligations of the NAFTA could be resolved in the context of a regional dispute settlement mechanism, modeled on FTA chapter 18 procedures. Panelists should continue to be drawn from the disputing parties. If all three countries are involved in a dispute, each should be represented, and the three should then select a fourth as chair.

Trilateralization of the chapter 19 process entails a few more complications, although none are insurmountable. The key concern involves Mexico's often opaque administrative procedures. Transparency can be achieved by Mexican adherence to the GATT Code on Subsidies and Countervailing Measures and adoption of the procedural obligations of the GATT Code on Antidumping. NAFTA panels could then function in the same manner, and subject to comparable procedures, as in the FTA.[22] In sum, the FTA chapter 19 process has worked

---

19. Until the US Trade Agreements Act of 1979, US companies had only limited resort to judicial review of antidumping and countervailing duty cases, so the US track record for such reviews is not that long either.

20. Bello et al. (1991) provide a good summary of each case brought under chapter 18 (general cases) and chapter 19 (subsidies and antidumping). For a report on the panel decision that ordered the rescission of US countervailing duties on Canadian pork, see also *International Trade Reporter*, 19 June 1991, 933.

21. US and Canadian negotiators have rightly argued that, without these changes, the FTA chapter 19 procedures would be unworkable with regard to Mexican cases.

22. Concerns about the lack of legal experience of Mexican panelists with these procedures seem to be exaggerated. Mexico has many fine jurists, a number of them schooled in the best US and Canadian law schools; panelists need not be lawyers (indeed, economists deserve more representation on panels); and Mexican officials already have experience with international dispute settlement processes.

surprisingly well for the United States and Canada and should be carried over into the NAFTA.[23]

Future Expansion

When the United States and Canada negotiated their FTA, the question of whether the agreement would be extended to third countries was more theoretical than real. Mexico was seen as a distant candidate; the pertinent issue seemed to be whether the FTA would be a building block for broader multilateral accords in the GATT or would be emulated by other countries in the event that the Uruguay Round faltered (Schott 1989b). Moreover, US fast-track procedures were designed to accommodate either bilateral FTAS or a multilateral trade pact in the GATT; they did not easily accommodate the notification of trilateral talks.[24]

Today, the prospect of future expansion of the NAFTA, or at least of additional FTAS between the United States and other countries, is enshrined in the Enterprise for the Americas Initiative (EAI). The United States has committed itself to negotiate FTAS with other countries in Latin America after the conclusion of trade talks with Mexico and Canada. The decision as to whether those negotiations will be conducted with individual countries or with groups of countries such as the Andean Pact (Bolivia, Colombia, Ecuador, Peru, and Venezuela) and Mercosur (Argentina, Brazil, Paraguay, and Uruguay) is as yet unsettled. To be eligible for FTA talks, however, US officials have indicated that a candidate country should be "committed to a stable macroeconomic environment and market-oriented policies" and should be making "progress in achieving open trade regimes" (Katz 1991, 7–8). The focus should be on recent trends rather than historical precedents.[25]

The hub-and-spoke issue thus again confronts Canada and Mexico, even as NAFTA negotiations unfold. Both countries are likely to insist that the NAFTA include provisions for how to deal with prospective new partners. Three options

---

23. This conclusion is reinforced if substantive agreements are eventually reached in the NAFTA on subsidies and countervailing duties and on antidumping rules. Even with NAFTA accords, initial decisions would presumably still be made by national authorities. Hence, there would be plenty of room for resort to a trilateral appeals process.

24. To be on the safe side, US officials notified their intent to use fast-track authorities for trilateral negotiations in February 1991, thus providing the House Ways and Means and Senate Finance committees an additional 60 legislative days to approve or deny the request. At that time, the 60-day period was about to expire for a similar notification that had been made in September 1990 with regard to bilateral talks with Mexico.

25. The authors have elsewhere (Hufbauer and Schott 1991) set out five preconditions for free trade talks: monetary stability, market-oriented policies, reduced budgetary reliance on import and export taxes, strong trade linkages, and a functioning democracy.

seem feasible: an accession clause could be added to the NAFTA; new FTAS could be negotiated between the NAFTA countries as a group and other countries or groups; or consultation clauses could be built into the NAFTA to ensure that Canadian and Mexican interests are not impaired as a result of US negotiations with other countries in the region.[26]

An accession clause (sometimes referred to as a docking clause), if adopted, would be modeled after current GATT practice. Prospective new entrants would apply for accession to the NAFTA and negotiate their entry terms with the existing membership. They would assume all the obligations of the NAFTA except as specified in their protocol of accession, which would also set the timetable for coming into conformity with NAFTA rules, agreed reservations, and specific national commitments as appropriate.[27] Acceptance of the terms of the protocol would be by consensus of the existing members.

The second option, joint negotiations, is a variant of the first. It would require the formation of a joint NAFTA negotiating team comprised of US, Canadian, and Mexican officials to work out the terms of a new FTA between the NAFTA members and the candidate country or group. Such an accord would be much less comprehensive than the NAFTA, perhaps covering only such "traditional" trade issues as tariffs, quotas, and licensing practices; otherwise it would make more sense to negotiate a protocol of accession to the NAFTA itself.

The third option, a consultation clause, presents the path of least resistance for the current NAFTA negotiators. It assumes that the United States will receive the bulk of requests for new FTAS,[28] and it provides a mechanism for keeping Mexico and Canada informed about those prospective negotiations so that they can consult with the United States about issues that affect their economic interests. It does not resolve the hub-and-spoke dilemma for Canada and Mexico, but it does make the process more transparent and tolerable.

Of the three options, the accession clause is by far the most desirable. It would encourage other countries in the region to continue to pursue trade and investment reforms so that they will become eligible to join the NAFTA, and it would provide the opportunity to build a common regime and thus avoid the patchwork quilt of inconsistent and discriminatory trade arrangements that could

---

26. Of course, this provision would also apply to bilateral or plurilateral FTA negotiations conducted by Mexico or Canada.

27. These protocols would also be subject to review under the provisions of GATT Article XXIV to ensure that the interests of nonmember countries are not adversely affected by the FTA trade preferences.

28. However, the consultation process would not necessarily be a one-way street to Washington. Mexico is already negotiating FTAS and preferential trading arrangements with other countries in the Western Hemisphere, including Chile, Venezuela, and the Central American countries.

arise if all three countries negotiate separately and establish different accords with fourth countries.

The main problem with an accession clause is whether the United States will be able to accept new members without new authority from the Congress. Current US trade law bars the extension of FTA benefits to fourth countries; moreover, fast-track authority (at least for bilateral FTA negotiations) is unlikely to be extended when it expires in June 1993. If an accession clause were included in the NAFTA and accepted by Congress in the NAFTA implementing legislation, there would seem to be no need for congressional approval of additional membership applications.[29] However, Congress is likely to want a bite at the apple each time a new member applies for NAFTA membership.

To address congressional concerns, the NAFTA should include a "nonapplication provision," akin to GATT Article XXXV, that allows member countries to deny the extension of the benefits of the NAFTA to any new member at the time of its accession. Under this provision, the President would seek congressional approval of new members under a newly designed bilateral fast-track provision and invoke the nonapplication provision if the Congress disapproved. As a practical matter, the United States would probably substantially influence the terms of the protocol of accession of new members (as it did with the Mexican protocol of accession to the GATT) and thereby seek to assuage specific congressional concerns *before* an applicant entered the club. Of course, other NAFTA members could also invoke the nonapplication provision.

Which countries should be eligible for membership in the NAFTA? In principle, if Canada, Mexico, and the United States are truly multilateral in their outlook, accession would be open to any GATT member. The process of regional liberalization could thus be extended to a broader group of countries—the more countries that join, the closer regional liberalization would come to parallel global liberalization.[30]

As a practical matter, however, membership should initially be limited to the Western Hemisphere. This constraint would serve two purposes: first, it would set geographical boundaries on the NAFTA and thus follow GATT practice, if not law, in accepting FTAS under GATT Article XXIV;[31] and second, it would avoid complications that could arise if countries sought to include restrictive provisions

---

29. Accession clauses are common in multilateral agreements; for example, Congress does not act when new signatories accede to the GATT or to the GATT codes negotiated during the Tokyo Round.

30. For a broader discussion of this general point, see Hufbauer (1989) and *Financial Times*, 14 June 1991, 18.

31. GATT Article XXIV does not contain a geographical proximity test, but almost all FTAS and customs unions that have been reviewed under its provisions (including the European Community) have limited membership to the immediate neighborhood.

in the NAFTA to guard against the future accession of East Asian trading powers, for example.

Over the medium to long term, the enlargement of NAFTA will depend importantly on the pace of multilateral trade liberalization in the GATT. The NAFTA should serve as a catalyst for continued trade and investment reforms in the Western Hemisphere and thus reinforce efforts to that end in the GATT. If the Uruguay Round comes up short, however, the NAFTA could become a "GATT–plus" agreement (as originally envisaged in the 1970s) that commits its members to broader rights and obligations than do existing GATT provisions. Under those conditions, there is no reason to restrict the geographic reach of the membership, which could then be open to all GATT members.[32]

The Interplay of Regional and Multilateral Negotiations

The negotiation of a NAFTA should be complementary to ongoing GATT negotiations in the Uruguay Round. The United States, Canada, and Mexico are all strong supporters of the GATT trading system and seek to build their North American alliance on the foundation of multilateral rights and obligations. This makes sound economic sense: each runs a large current account deficit and cannot solve its problems simply by exporting more to its neighbors; total regional exports to third markets need to expand as well. All three countries benefit from GATT rules and procedures that safeguard their access to overseas markets, and all three depend importantly on continuing progress on multilateral trade liberalization to increase their export opportunities.[33]

A NAFTA would be generally consistent with GATT provisions, even though the trade preferences would be applied only to its members and not on an MFN basis as prescribed by the GATT. Under GATT Article XXIV, however, exceptions to the basic MFN obligation are allowed for FTAs that remove barriers to "substantially all" trade among the partner countries and that do not raise barriers to third-country trade. These requirements are designed to preclude ad hoc discrimination

---

32. Given their reactions to the NAFTA talks so far, several East Asian countries may well be interested in joining a GATT–plus club if the GATT process should falter. In that event, the NAFTA could serve as a model both for the EAI in the Western Hemisphere and for closer trade relations among countries in the Pacific Basin.

33. Moreover, a successful GATT round would ensure that the European Community's internal market reforms maintain an outward orientation and do not discriminate against increasingly competitive North American suppliers. In that regard, the NAFTA objectives parallel those of the European Community at the start of its 1992 program.

through sectoral trade preferences that are likely to promote more trade diversion than trade creation.[34]

The NAFTA will be influenced by the timing of the conclusion of the GATT negotiations. If the Uruguay Round concludes before the NAFTA talks and achieves a substantive package of agreements, then the GATT outcome could significantly facilitate the negotiation *and ratification* of the NAFTA agreement. Problems in sensitive areas such as textiles, agriculture, and steel could be resolved—or at least partly mitigated—by GATT agreements. Simply put, the GATT results would relieve the NAFTA negotiators of the burden of negotiating and defending reforms in sensitive sectors, such as textiles and apparel, where entrenched political groups oppose the liberalization of longstanding trade barriers. In essence, a successful Uruguay Round could do the dirty work for the NAFTA negotiations.

If the pace of Uruguay Round talks is not accelerated, however, the NAFTA negotiation could well be given priority. That would pose a mixed blessing. US negotiators would probably be asked to address more issues and to resolve more problems, but they would also face stronger political resistance to trade reforms, since the "payment" for policy changes would come from only two countries (Canada and Mexico) rather than the 100-plus participating countries in the GATT round. (On the other hand, painful concessions in sensitive sectors would be limited to imports from Canada and Mexico.) The US task of negotiating and ratifying a regional pact would thus become more complicated—although *not* to the point of collapse.

At the same time, however, if the NAFTA proceeds faster than the GATT talks, the regional negotiation could be used, like the Canada–US FTA, as a prod for the multilateral process and as a model for GATT provisions in new areas such as intellectual property rights.[35] In addition, a NAFTA would provide the foundation for prospective negotiations in the Western Hemisphere under the EAI. However, for most countries in the region (except perhaps Chile), trade talks such as those now under way with Mexico are a bit down the road.

---

34. Efforts to extend benefits to Mexico while taking away quotas from other countries would violate the spirit, if not the letter, of GATT obligations. The unwritten obligation of Article XXIV is to promote more trade creation than trade diversion. For a full discussion of this issue, see Schott (1989a).

35. To do so, however, will require a strong push for a successful conclusion to the Uruguay Round. Otherwise, the NAFTA may scare countries away from Geneva rather than prod them to negotiate harder. Evidence of the latter is already starting to appear in the efforts of Southeast Asian nations to establish their own regional trading bloc.

II

Economic Implications

3

Trade Effects of a NAFTA: A Survey

Mexico's trade, like Canada's, exhibits a lopsided dependence on the United States (table 3.1). Mexican merchandise trade with the United States runs to about 75 percent of Mexican imports and exports; Mexican exports to the United States (including total maquiladora shipments) account for some 13 percent of Mexican GDP. In contrast, US merchandise trade with Mexico consistently runs between 5 percent and 7 percent of US imports and exports (table 3.1), and US exports to Mexico make only a small contribution to US GDP.

In 1980 the composition of Mexican exports was dominated by energy products (table 3.2). Crude oil exports peaked in dollar terms in 1982–84 and then fell off. Meanwhile, manufactured exports have tripled since 1980. Mexican merchandise trade statistics do not include maquiladora imports and exports; instead the value added through these processing operations is recorded under Mexican service exports. Maquiladora value added grew sharply in the 1980s, from $0.8 billion in 1980 to over $3.0 billion in 1990.

On the import side of the Mexican trade accounts, intermediate goods are the dominant component of merchandise trade (table 3.3). If, as expected, Mexican policy reforms continue to pay off in terms of larger domestic investment in the 1990s, capital-goods imports should grow sharply.

The Macroeconomic Effects of a NAFTA

Former Speaker of the House Thomas P. "Tip" O'Neill was fond of proclaiming that "All politics is local." In that spirit, the local repercussions of a NAFTA have already sparked heated debate: How will it affect the broom industry in Iowa or the citrus growers in Florida? What will be the consequences for sewage disposal in Nogales, Arizona, and Nogales, Sonora? Will it exacerbate "midnight dumping" of hazardous wastes at unsupervised Mexican landfills? In contrast with the impact of a multilateral tariff cut, which spreads more or less evenly across the vast reaches of the US economy, establishment of a free trade area sharply affects the profile of fewer activities.

Table 3.1 United States and Mexico: bilateral merchandise trade, 1980–90

Year	US exports to Mexico				US imports from Mexico				Bilateral trade balance (billions of dollars)
	Billions of dollars	As percentage of total US exports	As percentage of total Mexican imports	As percentage of US GDP	Billions of dollars[a]	As percentage of total US imports	As percentage of total Mexican exports[a]	As percentage of Mexican GDP[a]	
1980	15.1	6.9	69.7	0.6	12.8	5.0	69.3	6.9	2.3
1981	17.8	7.6	66.5	0.6	14.0	5.1	60.4	5.8	3.8
1982	11.8	5.6	67.0	0.4	15.0	6.2	62.5	9.0	−3.2
1983	9.1	4.5	72.1	0.3	17.0	6.3	62.0	11.9	−7.9
1984	12.0	5.5	74.8	0.3	18.3	5.4	61.3	10.7	−6.3
1985	13.6	6.4	73.7	0.3	19.4	5.4	66.7	11.0	−5.8
1986	12.4	5.7	73.6	0.3	17.6	4.5	72.4	13.5	−5.2
1987	14.6	5.8	74.0	0.3	20.5	4.8	69.2	14.6	−5.9
1988	20.6	6.4	75.6	0.4	23.5	5.1	73.4	13.5	−2.9
1989	25.0	6.9	73.4	0.5	27.2	5.7	74.7	13.5	−2.2
1990	28.4	7.2	74.8	0.5	30.8	5.8	78.6	13.1	−2.4

a. These figures somewhat overstate the importance of Mexican exports to the United States because they include total shipments from maquiladora plants, much of the inputs for which originated in the United States.

Source: International Monetary Fund, *Direction of Trade Statistics, Yearbook* 1987 and 1990, and March 1991; *International Financial Statistics, Yearbook* 1990; World Bank, *World Debt Tables,* 1989–90 and 1990–91; US Department of Commerce, Office of Mexico, "Data Sheet," January 1991; Banco de México, *The Mexican Economy,* 1991. World Bank and International Monetary Fund data adapted with permission.

Table 3.2 Mexico: composition of merchandise and nonfactor services exports, 1980 and 1989

	1980		1989	
	Billions of dollars	Percent of total	Billions of dollars	Percent of total
Total merchandise exports[a]	17.7	100.0	22.8	100.0
Agricultural products, livestock, and fisheries	1.9	10.5	1.8	7.7
Energy	11.3	64.1	8.5	37.3
Manufactures	4.5	25.4	12.5	55.0
Total nonfactor services exports	7.0	100.0	10.1	100.0
Tourism	5.2	74.2	4.8	47.5
Maquiladora operations	0.8	11.4	3.1	30.7
Total goods and nonfactor services	24.7		32.9	

a. Mexican merchandise trade statistics do not include maquiladora trade; instead, the value added through maquiladora operations is included in services exports.

Sources: Banco de México, *The Mexican Economy*, 1990; Business International, *Economic Risk Service: Mexico*, January 1991; International Monetary Fund, *Direction of Trade Statistics, Yearbook* 1987; United Nations, *Economic Survey of Latin America and the Caribbean*, 1988. International Monetary Fund data adapted with permission.

This sort of concentrated impact makes excellent newspaper copy, but thoughtful observers will want to step back and look at the big picture. The macroeconomic effects of a free trade area are largely captured by five variables:[1]

- changes in the volume of bilateral trade in goods and nonfactor services;
- changes in the balance of trade;
- the effect on jobs gained or lost in each country;
- the effect on wage rates in each country;
- the impact on the real exchange rate.

---

1. Other macroeconomic variables that are sometimes analyzed include induced changes in GNP and the price level. Later in this chapter we speculate on the impact on Mexican per capita income over a long period of time.

Table 3.3 Mexico: composition of merchandise and nonfactor services imports, 1980 and 1989

	1980		1989	
	Billions of dollars	Percent of total	Billions of dollars	Percent of total
Total merchandise imports	15.6	100.0	23.4	100.0
Consumer goods	2.0	12.8	3.5	14.9
Intermediate goods	9.1	58.4	15.1	64.7
Capital goods	4.1	26.6	4.8	20.4
Other	0.3	2.2	negl.	negl.
Total nonfactor services imports	6.5	100.0	7.6	100.0
Total goods and nonfactor service imports	22.1		31.0	

negl. = negligible.

a. Maquiladora imports are excluded from this table.

Source: Banco de México, *The Mexican Economy*, 1990; International Monetary Fund, *Direction of Trade Statistics, Yearbook* 1987; United Nations, *Economic Survey of Latin America and the Caribbean*, 1988. International Monetary Fund data adapted with permission.

The prospect of a NAFTA has already prompted extensive research on these variables in the three countries involved. Among the analytical tools available, the two current favorites are computable general equilibrium (CGE) models and econometric models. Although the two have many features in common, econometric models tend to be based on historical observations, whereas CGE models often rely on best guesses of unknown parameters.

In both frameworks an attempt is made to calculate the direct and indirect effects, sector by sector, of eliminating barriers to trade. These estimates can be based on the existing stock of capital and labor, or an allowance can be made for induced new investment and a higher capital stock. Once the trade effects have been computed, the number of jobs created or destroyed in each sector can be derived. The sectoral impacts can then be aggregated to calculate the economy-wide impact on trade and employment.

The final step (taken in some models but not others) is to compute the change in wage rates that would restore overall employment to its preexisting level. A simple example will illustrate the logic embodied in this final step. If US apparel workers lose their jobs on account of a NAFTA, they will seek alternative employment in local service establishments (restaurants, auto repair, etc.) and whatever manufacturing plants are nearby. These job-seekers will put downward pressure on wages generally and perhaps displace other workers. Given the huge size of the US economy, the models typically calculate that the laid-off workers will be employed elsewhere after a very small average decline in wages.

The CGE and econometric models are usually flexible enough so that they can be run under a variety of assumptions: for example, that employment rises or falls on account of the NAFTA; or that total US employment is fixed (by monetary policy); or that the Mexican real wage rate for unskilled workers is constant (because of surplus labor); or that each country's trade balance is fixed by macroeconomic conditions; or that additional Mexican investment is stimulated by the higher returns to capital that accompany an FTA.

The most advanced CGE and econometric models represent the state of the art in terms of internal consistency and mathematical elegance. However, these models contain a huge number of equations and entail many hidden assumptions about unknown parameters: elasticities of supply and demand, cross-elasticities of demand, substitution rates between capital and labor, expenditure functions, and so forth. The solutions require high-powered mathematical algorithms. Often the results look as if they came from a classic black box: only the authors of the models, and perhaps a few other scholars, understand all the ingredients.

As a reality check on the macroeconomic estimates derived in the various CGE and econometric models, we have drawn on the historical experience of other countries. Thanks to a recent seven-volume World Bank study (Papageorgiou et al. 1991) of 31 episodes of economic liberalization, it is now possible to generalize from a large number of cases.

The historical approach has its own strengths and weaknesses, however. Historical lessons can be applied to the NAFTA in a simple and easy-to-understand manner. These lessons capture the results of dynamic processes that are set in motion by policies of reform, including trade liberalization. However, the economic and political settings of prior cases obviously differ from each other and from that of Mexico. Further, the historical approach lacks the mathematical elegance and internal consistency of a general equilibrium model. Finally, although it illuminates the big picture, the historical approach does not readily lend itself to sectoral detail.

Notwithstanding its shortcomings, we think the historical approach has much to commend it for projecting the effects of a NAFTA. The simple historical model outlined in the following sections (which we call the "IIE" model) is designed to be "responsibly optimistic." From the experience with past liberalization episodes, parameters are chosen that lead to a projection of the rate of growth of Mexican exports and imports; everything else is then calculated as a function of the trade impact. The estimates presume that the entire package of Mexican reform is maintained in a NAFTA scenario: privatization across the board, stepped-up Mexican oil production,[2] fiscal and monetary restraint, and trade liberalization. Our

---

2. See chapter 10. The explicit assumption of stepped-up oil production and the implicit assumption of larger foreign participation in the Mexican oil sector are the most controversial components of a reform scenario.

figures are thus designed to portray the outer bound, in the medium term, of a successful free trade area and accompanying policy reforms; certainly it would be possible to achieve less.

The current episode of Mexican policy reform started in 1985, but liberalization did not actually take effect until 1988. Our projections therefore start from 1989, the first year of the Salinas administration. The terminal date is 1995; however, an optimistic outcome would still be achieved if the targets described below are not reached until 1997. In any event, our projections do not capture the very long run effects of the NAFTA, which could be quite substantial, especially for Mexico. The key assumptions and relations in the IIE historical model are outlined in the next few sections.

Mexican Export Growth

It is generally accepted that a NAFTA accompanied by continued policy liberalization will cause Mexican exports of goods and nonfactor services to grow at a faster rate than would otherwise have occurred. We assume that, in a liberalization scenario, Mexican exports will grow at the average rate experienced by the countries in the World Bank study that were characterized by "previous severe restrictions": 11.2 percent annual real growth (Papageorgiou et al. 1991, vol. 7, table 12.3, 191).[3] We assume that the growth spurt starts from the 1989 base of $32.9 billion of exports (table 3.2).[4] Hence, Mexican exports of goods and nonfactor services (principally tourism and maquiladora value added) are projected to reach $62.2 billion in 1995 (expressed in 1989 dollars).

This number depends heavily on Mexican investment reforms, especially to allow foreign participation in the energy sector. If Mexican oil production remains tightly controlled by the Pemex monopoly and only grows to 3.0 million barrels per day by the mid–1990s, rather than rising to at least 3.5 million barrels as our scenario requires, export revenues would be reduced. With crude oil valued at a constant nominal price of $20 per barrel, total exports might then be $3.6 billion less than our projection of $62.2 billion.

---

3. It should be noted that the World Bank table refers only to the first four years of sustained liberalization; we assume that the Mexican episode will enjoy a sustained impact for at least six years. By way of partial confirmation, Mexican merchandise exports to the United States grew by about 13.8 percent annually between 1987 and 1990.

4. Note that the 1989 figure in table 3.2 is somewhat lower than the 1988 figure for exports of goods and nonfactor services of $36.1 billion calculated by KPMG Peat Marwick (1991, table 13). The difference is purely a statistical anomaly: the KPMG figure includes exports from maquiladora plants of about $10.8 billion in 1988. However, maquiladora imports and exports are customarily excluded from official Mexican trade statistics, and likewise from table 3.2; instead, only the Mexican value added (about $3.1 billion in 1989) is reflected in the service sector of the Mexican balance of payments.

This 1995 export figure can be checked against the results of a cross-country regression (involving 91 countries) performed by Collins and Rodrik that examined the ratio of merchandise exports to GNP (Collins and Rodrik 1991, 32, with additional information supplied by the authors). Actual Mexican merchandise exports in 1988, as a share of GNP, were nearly identical to the value predicted by the Collins-Rodrik regression equation (13.75 percent predicted versus 13.96 percent actual). With a doubling of Mexican GNP, the predicted merchandise export–GNP ratio would increase from 13.75 percent to 16.14 percent. From these parameters it can be calculated that, with sustained 6 percent annual real GNP growth (doubling GNP in 12 years), Mexican exports of goods and nonfactor services could increase by a real multiple of 2.35 (2.00 × [16.14 ÷ 13.75]) between 1988 and 2000. Given 1988 Mexican goods and nonfactor services exports of $29.1 billion (Banco de México 1990, 135), this would indicate an end-of-century export level of $68.4 billion (2.35 × $29.1 billion). In this light, our figure of $62.2 billion for 1995 exports represents a responsibly optimistic projection of Mexican export performance.

We assume that, if the NAFTA talks fail, policy retrogression will also occur in other areas.[5] Mexican exports would then grow at the rate experienced by the World Bank panel of country episodes that were characterized by "collapsed liberalization," namely, 7.9 percent annual real growth. This figure is 3.3 percentage points less than the projection of 11.2 percent annual real growth under the continued reform scenario. Starting from the 1989 base, 1995 Mexican exports (expressed in 1989 dollars) would reach only $51.9 billion under a collapsed liberalization scenario (against $62.2 billion under the continued reform scenario).

Thus, additional Mexican exports of goods and nonfactor services in 1995, as a consequence of the NAFTA and accompanying reforms, are estimated at $10.3 billion ($62.2 billion minus $51.9 billion). At least $3.6 billion of this export increment depends on dramatic reforms in the petroleum sector.

Mexican Import Growth

Mexican imports of goods and nonfactor services in 1995 are assumed to equal the sum of Mexican exports in 1995, plus remittances from abroad (about $3.9 billion), plus the excess of capital inflows over net debt-service requirements (defined as interest on foreign debt plus dividends on foreign investment minus interest and dividend earnings from abroad, a total of about $7.9 billion in 1995; see table 1.5).

---

5. If the NAFTA talks fail, but instead Mexico continues on its post–1985 path of economic reform, then most of the adverse effects portrayed in this paragraph would not occur.

With a NAFTA and accompanying reforms, such "excess" capital inflows are assumed to reach $12.0 billion annually in 1995.[6] Hence, Mexican imports of goods and nonfactor services are assumed to reach $78.1 billion in 1995 ($62.2 billion in export revenues, plus $3.9 billion in remittances, plus $12.0 billion in "excess" capital inflows).

As Robert Z. Lawrence has pointed out,[7] this scenario implies some real appreciation of the Mexican currency. During the 1980s, each $830 million increase in capital inflows into Mexico was associated with a 2-percentage-point increase in the real peso exchange rate.[8] This relationship suggests that a $12.0 billion increase in capital inflows (by comparison with the non–NAFTA scenario described later) might lead to a 29 percent increase in the real peso exchange rate, above and beyond the level that would be reached without the additional capital. Indeed, between January 1990 and December 1991 the peso had already appreciated in real terms by 13 percent (*World Financial Markets*, January 1991 and February 1992).

Spain offers a precedent for large capital inflows and a real exchange rate appreciation following the entry of a small economy into a large trading area. Upon Spain's accession to the European Community, the Spanish peso appreciated in real effective terms from an index value of 97.3 in 1986 to an index value of 117.1 in 1990, an increase of 20 percent (Morgan Guaranty Trust Co., *World Financial Markets*, 1989, no. 1; 1991, no.2). During this period the Spanish current account position shifted from a $2.9 billion surplus to a $15.8 billion deficit (International Monetary Fund, *International Financial Statistics*, June 1991, 484).

We turn now to the alternative scenario in which a NAFTA does not come into being. We assume that without a NAFTA Mexico will experience policy stagnation or even retrogression. Mexico will then be a less attractive place in which to invest. Hence, in the alternative scenario, "excess" capital flows are assumed to

---

6. This corresponds to a current account deficit of about $20.0 billion, since net debt-service requirements will be about $8.0 billion. The forecast inflow of capital is not outlandish: in 1992, the projected Mexican current account deficit already reaches $17.0 billion, up from $6.0 billion in 1989 (table 1.5). The widening current account deficit represents a vote of confidence by the capital markets in Mexican policies.

7. At an ICI/UNCTAD/CEPAL conference in El Escorial, Spain, 8–11 July 1991.

8. The estimated regression equation, using data for the period 1980–89, is $XR = 71.4 + 0.2(CF)$, where XR is an index of the real peso exchange rate (1980 = 100), and CF is an index of capital inflows, including errors and omissions (with the 1980 level of $8.3 billion set to equal 100). Capital outflows have a negative sign in the equation. The R^2 statistic for this equation is 0.61, and the t statistic for the CF coefficient is 3.56 (data from ten Kate 1990, table 1).

be zero in 1995.[9] In this scenario, Mexican imports are assumed to be limited to export revenues plus immigrant remittances, or $55.8 billion in 1995.

Thus, additional Mexican imports in 1995, as a consequence of the NAFTA and accompanying reforms, are estimated at $22.3 billion ($78.1 billion minus $55.8 billion), an increase of 40 percent. Recall that a good part of the increment, some $12.0 billion, is financed by additional capital inflows attracted by the NAFTA.

Mexico–US Trade

In both scenarios, Mexico is assumed to purchase 75 percent of its imports of goods and nonfactor services from the United States, and to sell 75 percent of its exports of goods and nonfactor services to the United States. Slightly lower market shares have been experienced in recent years (see table 3.1). However, the experience of the European Community and the short record of the Canada–US FTA both suggest that trade between partners grows more rapidly than trade with the outside world.

Thus, the difference between the NAFTA and the no–NAFTA scenario is additional US exports of goods and nonfactor services to Mexico of $16.7 billion annually in 1995 (75 percent of $22.3 billion). Likewise the difference between the NAFTA and the no–NAFTA scenario is additional US imports from Mexico of $7.7 billion annually (75 percent of $10.3 billion).

Hence, the difference between the NAFTA and the no–NAFTA scenario is an improvement in the US trade balance of $9.0 billion annually ($16.7 billion minus $7.7 billion). Financed by "excess" capital inflows, the Mexican trade balance "worsens" by $12.0 billion annually under the NAFTA scenario. Of course this "worsening" translates into greater Mexican imports of much-needed consumer goods, industrial intermediates, and capital goods.

US Job Creation and Wage Rates

US jobs are assumed to be created at the rate of 14,500 jobs per billion dollars of net improvement in the US trade balance.[10] Thus, about 130,000 additional

---

9. The comparable figures were negative between 1981 and 1989; hence an assumption of zero net inflows is not unduly pessimistic.

10. This figure is based on *Statistical Abstract of the United States,* 1990, table 1311. In 1986 the manufacturers' shipment value of export goods (direct exports) was $159.4 billion, and export-related employment (direct and supporting) was 2,318,000 workers. These two figures indicate that each billion dollars of direct exports requires a total of 14,542 direct and supporting workers.

US jobs are created under a NAFTA scenario (9.0 times 14,500). This is an insignificant proportion of total US employment, and we assume that there is no impact on overall US real wage rates. There would, of course, be positive and negative impacts on specific industries and job types.[11]

Mexican Job Creation and Wage Rates

Mexican job creation is assumed to be determined by total Mexican export growth less Mexican import growth for consumer goods and services. It is assumed that imported foodstuffs, household appliances, and automobiles compete directly with Mexican products and thus subtract from Mexican jobs. Further, it is assumed that consumer-goods imports remain at 15 percent of total imports.

In both the NAFTA and the no–NAFTA scenarios, the increase in Mexican imports of intermediate and capital goods is assumed *not* to decrease Mexican employment, because the assumed constraint on Mexican economic activity is supply availability rather than domestic demand for intermediates and capital goods.

This is a crucial assumption of our analysis. It reflects our belief that the Mexican economy is limited neither by inadequate demand in a Keynesian sense, nor by labor shortages, but rather by supply constraints on capital equipment and intermediate goods.

We assume that employment creation in Mexico, per billion dollars of additional "net" exports (defined as additional exports minus additional consumer-goods imports), is on average six times the US parameter (the multiple of six is roughly based on the 1989 differential between US and Mexican average hourly compensation in manufacturing; see table 6.9). This works out to 87,000 new Mexican jobs per additional billion dollars of "net" exports.[12]

In the NAFTA scenario, the Mexican export figure is projected to increase by $10.3 billion by comparison with the no–NAFTA scenario. Further, in the NAFTA

---

11. See, for example, the calculations made by Interindustry Economic Research Fund (Clopper Almon, principal investigator; 1990). To illustrate the results of the Almon study, US apparel employment would decline by 6,000 jobs in 1995 (against a base of 515,700 jobs); US rubber and plastic products employment would increase by 41,200 jobs (from a base of 2,884,500 jobs); US professional and scientific employment would increase by 6,200 jobs; US service employment would decrease by 1,900 jobs. All these figures are vanishingly small compared with base levels of employment and annual turnover in the US work force.

12. Obviously, Mexican job creation would be much less than 87,000 employees for each billion dollars of gross maquiladora exports, since imported inputs loom so large in maquiladora trade (about 70 percent to 80 percent of export value). However, the statistical convention we have followed in this sketch (and the way the Mexican authorities state their trade data) only includes the value of maquiladora processing in Mexican exports.

scenario, Mexican imports of consumer goods and services are projected to be $3.3 billion higher than without a NAFTA (15 percent of $22.3 billion). Subtracting $3.3 billion from the projected export growth of $10.3 billion yields an employment stimulus of $7.0 billion from increased Mexican exports, net of increased Mexican imports of consumer goods and services. Calculated at 87,000 jobs per billion dollars, our arithmetic suggests that about 609,000 additional Mexican jobs will be created under the NAFTA scenario. This figure would represent about 2 percent of all Mexican jobs in 1995.

Because Mexico has an abundant supply of unemployed labor, we assume that there is no direct impact on the Mexican real wage rate for unskilled labor resulting from additional job creation. However, our NAFTA scenario entails an appreciation in the real peso exchange rate of 29 percent. On the assumption that a 1.0 percent appreciation in the real peso reduces the Mexican cost of living by 0.3 percent,[13] then a 29 percent real peso appreciation would translate into an 8.7 percent gain in real Mexican wages.[14]

Comparison with Other Models

Table 3.4 compares the results of the IIE historical model with those of several CGE and econometric models. The CGE and econometric models uniformly show a small impact on bilateral trade magnitudes in relation to established US trade levels. In 1989, total US exports of merchandise and nonfactor services amounted to $476 billion, while imports were $570 billion. Thus, a NAFTA increment of up to $10 billion in either magnitude practically disappears in statistical noise. On the other hand, the trade magnitudes are significant when compared either with 1989 Mexican exports of goods and nonfactor services ($32.9 billion) or with Mexican imports ($31.0 billion). Mexican export gains (that is, additional exports to the United States plus additional *net* exports to the rest of the world), for example, range up to 15 percent in the case of the CGE and econometric models devised by Almon, Baylor University, and Michigan-Tufts.

The IIE model suggests the possibility for larger trade gains in both directions than any of the CGE or econometric models predict. It should be stressed, once again, that the IIE model assumes that a successful NAFTA is only one part of a *package* of reforms, including sweeping privatization, significant liberalization of the Mexican oil sector, fiscal and monetary restraint, and other reform measures.

---

13. The coefficient of 0.3 implies that the effect of traded goods on the Mexican price structure is about twice the share of imports in Mexican GNP. In turn, the coefficient of 2 reflects the presumed impact on the prices of domestically produced goods.

14. This calculation assumes that nominal Mexican wages are not reduced on account of a real peso appreciation.

Table 3.4 United States and Mexico: alternative projections of changes in trade levels, employment, and wage rates as a consequence of a NAFTA[a] (billions of dollars except where noted)

	IIE	Almon[b]	KPMG[c]	Berkeley[d]	Baylor[e]	Michigan-Tufts[f]	El Colegio[g]
US exports to Mexico	16.7	8.5[e]	1.2	2.3	6.9	4.2	3.4
Mexican exports to US	7.7	2.7[e]	3.9	2.5	5.1	3.5	1.3
US net exports to ROW	0	0.2[e]	1.6	0.2	n.a.	-1.0	n.a.
Mexican net exports to ROW	-3	3.1[e]	1.3	-0.2	n.a.	0.5	-1.3
US trade balance	9	6	-1.1	0	1.8	-0.3	2.1
Mexican trade balance	-12	-2.7	4	0	-1.8	-0.2	0
US employment (thousands of workers)	130	44[f]	0	-234	n.a.	0.0	0.0
Mexican employment (thousands of workers)	609	-158[f]	1,464	273	n.a.	0.0	0.0
US wage rate (percentage change)	0	0.02	0.03	0.4[g]	0.01	0.10	n.a
Mexican wage rate (percentage change)	8.7	n.a.	0	2.27[g]	n.a.	2.90	16.0

ROW = rest of world.

n.a. = not estimated or not available.

a. The econometric and computable general equilibrium (CGE) models (all except the IIE model) generally assume elimination of tariffs and total or partial elimination of nontariff barriers. However, the Baylor model only eliminates tariffs. The IIE historical model assumes elimination of all trade barriers and continuation of major policy reforms, including liberalization of Mexican energy policy. The econometric and CGE models usually do not incorporate the effects of policy reforms, outside of trade liberalization. The dollar figures are expressed in terms of 1988 or 1989 price levels. The Berkeley, Michigan-Tufts, and El Colegio models assume fixed levels of employment and hence generate relatively large wage gains in Mexico. The wage gain in the IIE model reflects real appreciation of the peso.

b. The trade figures in the Almon report are based on 1977 price levels. They were adjusted to 1988 price levels by applying a multiple of 1.70 (based on the US producer price index for industrial commodities). The employment figures in the Almon model are for the year 1995.

c. The KPMG model summarized here assumes that the FTA spurs an additional $25 billion of investment in Mexico. The model is specified so that the change in the US employment level and the change in the Mexican wage rate are both zero.

d. The Berkeley model summarized here is described as the pro-competitive trade liberalization model. It reflects reduced distortions in US and (especially) Mexican capital allocation, together with complete trade liberalization. The wage rate figures in the Berkeley model are weighted averages for various skill categories. The decline in US employment largely reflects a return flow of illegal immigrants to Mexico.

e. The percentage change figures in the Baylor study are applied to 1989 trade flows to produce these estimates.

f. The Michigan-Tufts results summarized here are roughly calculated as the difference between the reported NAFTA results with investment liberalization that leads to a 10 percent increase in Mexico's capital stock, and the Canada–US FTA results. The NAFTA results in the Michigan-Tufts model reflect a partial rather than a total relaxation of agricultural and textile nontariff barriers.

g. The El Colegio results summarized here are from Version Three, which specifies zero change in Mexican employment, but allows the Mexican capital stock to increase.

Sources: The IIE historical model is described in this chapter; KPMG CGE model: KPMG Peat Marwick, Economic Policy Group, *The Effects of a Free Trade Agreement Between the U.S. and Mexico* (Washington: KPMG Peat Marwick, May 1991), tables 21 through 30; Almon econometric model: Interindustry Economic Research Fund, *Industrial Effects of a Free Trade Agreement Between Mexico and the USA* (Washington: US Department of Labor, September 1990), 3, VII-A-9, IX-A-1; Berkeley CGE model: Raul Hinojosa-Ojeda and Sherman Robinson, *Alternative Scenarios of U.S.–Mexico Integration: A Computable General Equilibrium Approach* (Berkeley: University of California, Division of Agricultural and Resource Economics, 1991), tables 1, 5, 7, and 8; Baylor CGE model: Roy G. Boyd, Kerry Krutilla, and Joseph A. McKinney, *The Impact of Tariff Liberalization Between the United States and Mexico: A General Equilibrium Analysis* (Waco, TX: Baylor University, Hankamer School of Business, 1991), 13 and table 3; Michigan-Tufts econometric model: Drusilla K. Brown, Alan V. Deardorff, and Robert M. Stern, *A North American Free Trade Agreement: Analytical Issues and Computational Assessment* (Ann Arbor, MI: University of Michigan, and Medford, MA: Tufts University, 27–28 June 1991), table 4; El Colegio de México CGE model: Horacio E. Sobarzo, *A General Equilibrium Analysis of the Gains from Trade for the Mexican Economy of a North American Free Trade Agreement* (Mexico City: El Colegio de México, June 1991), table 7.

The values reported are for the full package, not just the NAFTA component. The possible gain in Mexican exports to the United States is calculated at $7.7 billion, while the possible gain in US exports to Mexico is figured at $16.7 billion. The Mexico export gain is 50 percent larger than the most optimistic alternative model, while the US export gain is more than twice as large. In rough terms, the difference between the IIE model and the CGE and econometric models is the difference between examining trade liberalization as an isolated phenomenon and viewing it as a necessary component, but only a component, of a broader reform process that attracts very substantial capital inflows.

Turning to other macroeconomic magnitudes, all the models agree that the gross effect on US jobs and on US wage rates will be small. These numbers are good news, for they imply that targeted programs, not requiring large budget expenditures, can be deployed to address the work force adjustment problems that will arise in the United States. Assuming that each billion dollars of additional US imports from Mexico displaces 14,500 workers,[15] then the IIE model indicates that the gross number of US workers displaced would be 112,000 ($7.7 billion times 14,500). This calculation does not take into account US workers employed to produce additional exports. Moreover, it exaggerates the public adjustment burden, since some displaced workers will find alternative employment without assistance. Public assistance will be most in demand for workers living in isolated communities (e.g., apparel towns in the Carolinas) and workers with limited skills.

Assuming that adjustment programs are budgeted at $8,000 per dislocated worker (a figure that is comparable with recent US experience),[16] a special appropriation of $900 million could handle up to an additional 112,000 workers that might be dislocated over a period of several years by North American trade liberalization.

On the Mexican side of the border, the models suggest that a large number of jobs could be created: some 609,000 jobs in the IIE model and as many as 1.5 million new jobs in the KPMG model. These figures range between 2 percent and 5 percent of total Mexican employment. Faced with rapid population growth, Mexico's foremost gain from NAFTA reforms over the short term should be the payoff in jobs.

---

15. This figure assumes that job displacement associated with manufactured imports is about the same as job creation (direct and supporting) associated with manufactured exports (see *Statistical Abstract of the United States,* 1990, table 1311).

16. Unpublished US Department of Commerce data show that the Trade Readjustment Allowances (TRA) paid in fiscal 1989 amounted to about $5,300 per worker ($125.4 million for 23,680 workers). In addition, Trade Adjustment Assistance training payments have averaged about 50 percent of TRA payments in recent years.

On the implausible assumption that Mexican employment remains fixed, a NAFTA would instead cause Mexican real wages to increase—by 2 percent to 3 percent in the Berkeley and Michigan-Tufts models, and by a surprising 16 percent in the El Colegio model. The IIE historical model also suggests an 8.7 percent gain in Mexican real wages, but this result reflects a NAFTA–induced appreciation of the real peso, not a fixed level of employment in Mexico.

The models generally project modest changes in Mexican net exports to the rest of the world. One exception is the Almon econometric model, which indicates a big gain in Mexican net exports to the rest of the world, owing to increased Mexican competitiveness through lower input costs.

Finally, the models portray very different outcomes for the overall trade balance. The IIE model assumes that successful reform draws large amounts of capital to Mexico, thereby financing a significant trade deficit. The CGE and econometric models, for the most part, either see the capital account as accommodating the impact of sector-by-sector trade outcomes, or assume a one-shot addition to the Mexican capital stock and then calculate the trade position after the new investment has been digested. Based on the accommodating-capital-account framework, the Almon econometric model foresees the NAFTA adding modestly to the Mexican trade deficit; based on the one-shot framework, the KPMG model shows a big increase in the Mexican trade surplus, once the Mexican economy has adjusted to its larger capital stock.

Mexican Per Capita Income Growth Over the Long Term

None of the models purports to forecast the impact of a NAFTA on Mexican per capita income over long periods of time. However, as a speculative exercise, it is worth applying the empirical findings of Barro and Sala-i-Martin concerning income convergence. These scholars examined experience within the United States over the period 1880 to 1989, and within Europe between 1950 and 1985 (Barro and Sala-i-Martin 1991; summarized in *Wall Street Journal,* 3 May 1991, A10). In both cases, Barro and Sala-i-Martin found that, within these economic unions, about 2 percent of the income gap between poor regions and rich regions vanished each year. Roughly speaking, the poor regions grew at a rate about 2 percentage points faster than the rich regions over long periods of time.[17]

---

17. In a similar exercise, Ben-David (1991) found that the number of years required to cut per capita income disparities in half (the "half-life of convergence") was 25.9 years for the original six members of the European Community between 1960 and 1985, and 19.8 years for the states of the United States between 1960 and 1984. Our assumption of 2 percentage points faster Mexican growth suggests that the ratio of Mexican to US per capita GNP would increase from 26.8 percent in 1988 to 53.7 percent in 2023. In other words, our projected half-life of convergence (35 years) is rather long compared to the recent experience of the European Community and the United States.

Let us assume that, as a consequence of the NAFTA, Mexican per capita income converges in accordance with the historical experience of poorer regions in the United States and Europe. What would this entail? Assuming that, with a renewed national emphasis on productivity, US real income grows at a rate of 2 percent per year over the next 35 years, then US GDP per capita, expressed in 1988 dollars, would double to about $39,700 in 2023, compared with a level of $19,851 in 1988. Following the Barro–Sala-i-Martin model, Mexican real income might correspondingly grow by 4 percent per year, and thus quadruple to a level of $21,300 in GDP per capita in 2023, compared with a figure of $5,323 in 1988.[18]

This speculative exercise suggests that, by 2023, Mexican living standards would surpass the level that the United States reached in 1988—a very long march indeed from the grinding poverty that Mexico experienced in the 1980s.

Mexico-Canada Trade

Bilateral Mexico–Canada trade is, of course, much smaller than bilateral Mexico–US trade. Table 3.5 summarizes the structure and importance of bilateral trade between Canada and Mexico. If the trilateral free trade area were to exert about the same proportional impact on Canadian imports as on US imports, the CGE and econometric models suggest that Mexican exports to Canada would grow by 7 percent to 11 percent over the base level, while the IIE model suggests additional Mexican exports, as a result of the NAFTA, of about 20 percent of the base level. Correspondingly, the IIE model suggests additional Mexican imports, as a result of the NAFTA, of about 40 percent of the base level.

If the high IIE figures are realized, the jump in Canadian imports from Mexico occasioned by the NAFTA could be as much as $350 million (a NAFTA–induced growth of 20 percent). By similar arithmetic, additional Canadian exports to Mexico could exceed $250 million (a NAFTA–induced growth of 40 percent).[19] These are not trivial magnitudes, but they are small compared with total Canadian exports of $122 billion and imports of $120 billion in 1989. A large part of the increment in bilateral Mexico-Canada trade would probably stem from Mexican assembly operations that import Canadian equipment and parts and export fabricated items. Trade in automobiles and parts, and in textiles and apparel, would be particularly enhanced by the NAFTA accord.

---

18. The data on 1988 real per capita GDP are taken from Summers and Heston (1991). Using current exchange rates, the nominal per capita GDP for Mexico in 1988 was much lower: $1,820.

19. We assume that in the absence of a NAFTA Canadian imports from Mexico would reach $1,750 million in 1995 and that Canadian exports to Mexico would reach $630 million.

Table 3.5 Canada: composition of trade with Mexico, 1989
(millions of US dollars except where noted)

	1989 Canadian imports	1989 Canadian exports
Food and live animals	97	130
Beverages and tobacco	13	0
Inedible crude materials, except fuel	20	39
Mineral fuels, lubricants, and related materials	43	0
Animal and vegetable oils and fats	negl.	2
Chemicals and related products	12	7
Manufactured goods	287	140
Machinery and transport equipment	951	185
Miscellaneous manufactured articles	37	4
Other	8	15
Total	1,468	522
As percentage of total Canadian merchandise trade	1.2	0.4
As percentage of total Mexican merchandise trade	2.4	1.8

negl. = negligible.

Sources: Michael Hart, *A North American Free Trade Agreement: The Strategic Implications for Canada* (Ottawa: Centre for Trade Policy and Law, and Halifax: Institute for Research on Public Policy, 1990), table 9, 67; International Monetary Fund, *International Financial Statistics*, July 1990; *Direction of Trade Statistics, Yearbook* 1990. International Monetary Fund data adapted with permission.

From a Canadian perspective, an important trade consequence of the NAFTA will be the rediversion of US imports from Canadian sources to Mexican sources. According to unpublished estimates prepared at the World Bank by Sam Laird, the Canada–US FTA may have cost Mexico about $100 million in diverted exports.[20] Conversely, in a context that entailed total elimination of tariffs and nontariff barriers, adding Mexico to the Canada–US FTA could lead to the rediversion of some $150 million in Canadian exports.

---

20. An unpublished Mexican report (Mexico, Ministry of Trade and Industry 1990) estimated that gross trade diversion of the Canada–US FTA, in terms of 1988 trade flows, was $662 million, of which $421 million was in the automotive sector and $102 million in consumer electronics. Offsetting the gross diversion was $257 million of trade creation for Mexico, of which the largest component was $123 million for knitting mills. A more recent estimate by the Michigan-Tufts team (Brown et al. 1991, table 4) suggests that the Canada–US FTA decreased Mexican exports by $11 million and decreased Mexican imports by $61 million.

Again, these are not trivial numbers, but even if they understate the rediversion effect by a factor of two or three, they are not of great commercial importance—except in the few sectors where rediversion would be concentrated, such as automobiles and parts. More important to Canada than outright rediversion is the precedent set by rules in particular sectors and topics: notably automobiles and energy, subsidies and dumping, intellectual property, and dispute settlement. Moreover, for Canada as for the United States, the NAFTA talks provide an opportunity to reopen Canada–US issues that were not satisfactorily resolved in the 1988 agreement.[21]

Sectoral Effects of a NAFTA

The CGE and econometric models attempt to estimate the sectoral impact of a free trade area. Although the models broadly agree on the winning and losing sectors in each country, their estimates of sectoral magnitudes differ greatly. Moreover, the CGE and econometric models generally suggest much smaller trade impacts in key sectors than the results implied by our own examination, reported in chapters 10 through 14.

With these caveats, it is worth doing a quick survey of the sectors where large positive or negative impacts can be expected. As a foundation for this survey, we rely on the KPMG Peat Marwick analysis, summarized in table 3.6. In the remarks below, we note the sectors where their estimate of the impact significantly differs from our own judgments. Sectors where there are important negotiating issues and large prospective trade impacts are further examined in part III of this study.

Sectors with Prospective Large US Export Gains

The sectoral composition of Canadian export gains will probably parallel the US experience, but since the absolute magnitudes will be much larger for the United States, we concentrate on that story.

In the agricultural sector, US exports of field crops (corn, wheat, and soybeans) and processed foods should expand dramatically. The KPMG figures (under $100 million for both subsectors together) seem to grossly understate the size of the prospective trade gains, both because the trade-inhibiting consequences of

---

21. On balance, however, many Canadians fear rather than welcome a reopening of "settled" FTA issues. Ronald Wonnacott (1991b), among this group, takes a strong position against any recontracting of FTA provisions. We do not share his sentiment that the terms of the FTA are set in concrete.

Mexican agricultural subsidies are not reflected in the KPMG estimate of a 4.6 percent tariff-equivalent rate for field crops (reported in table 3.6), and because the size of formal trade barriers does not capture the scope for large-scale penetration of the Mexican processed food market by efficient US producers. These issues are explored in chapter 14.

Chemical intermediates, rubber goods, plastics, and pharmaceuticals represent another area with potentially large US export gains, again well beyond the KPMG estimates ($183 million). Mexican tariff barriers to these products are only modest, and there should be little resistance to a fast phaseout of tariffs. As recently as 1990 the most serious policy issue affecting these goods was the Mexican stance on intellectual property rights, but that issue has now been satisfactorily resolved (see chapter 9).

The metals group—iron and steel, nonferrous metals, and fabricated metal—is one in which large two-way trade expansion can be expected. In particular, as chapter 12 explains, US exports of high-grade steel goods should expand dramatically with a faster pace of Mexican development, while Mexico should sell more commercial-grade and construction steel.

Likewise, as a consequence of increased Mexican capital spending, US exports in the equipment group of industries should be exceptionally strong. US firms already command a dominant share of the Mexican capital-goods market, and the current Mexican emphasis on investment promotion should make it easy to dismantle the remaining barriers.

Another star sector for US exports should be transportation equipment—both assembled automobiles sold into the protected Mexican market and components for assembly. This sector poses a number of interesting and complex policy questions, which are addressed in chapter 11.

Sectors with Prospective Large Mexican Export Gains

Dwarfing all other sectors will be additional Mexican exports of crude and refined petroleum—if Mexico chooses to liberalize foreign participation in the energy sector. In the near term, additional Mexican petroleum exports could reach $3.6 billion, and the gains could be twice as large early in the next century. But this happy outcome will require a drastic revamping of nationalistic priorities. The KPMG model, driven as it is by tariff-equivalent barriers, shows no increase in petroleum exports and misses the potential impact of investment liberalization in the energy sector. This subject is taken up in chapter 10.

Mexican exports of fruits and vegetables and minor crops are likely to be far larger than the KPMG figures ($62 million together). As discussed in chapter 14, Mexican agricultural gains depend both on liberal Mexican attitudes toward investment by the large-scale growers that control distribution networks in the

Table 3.6 Hypothetical impact of a NAFTA on bilateral US–Mexico trade, by industry, 1988

Industry	Mexican imports from United States				Mexican exports to United States			
	Millions of 1988 dollars	As percentage share of Mexican consumption	Tariff rate plus tariff equivalent of quotas (percentages)	Additional Mexican imports with NAFTA (millions of 1988 dollars)	Millions of 1988 dollars	As percentage of Mexican production	Tariff rate plus tariff equivalent of quotas (percentages)	Additional Mexican exports with NAFTA (millions of 1988 dollars)
Animal products	242	2.9	1.7	-1	263	3.2	3.4	30.4
Field crops	869	14.4	4.6	30.8	768	13.1	9.0	152.7
Fruits and vegetables	245	4.2	4.8	4.7	216	3.7	7.1	32.9
Other agriculture	0	0.0	0.0	0	365	17.4	0.0	29
Mining	89	2.0	2.1	2.4	210	4.5	0.5	25.8
Crude oil and gas	0	0.0	0.0	0	2,854	74.5	0.6	-9.8
Construction	0	0.0	0.0	0	0	0.0	0.0	0
Sugar	17	1.2	5.3	-0.7	81	5.5	102.0	213.3
Food products	870	2.9	10.4	65.7	559	1.9	7.9	92.5
Tobacco manufactures	1	0.1	35.7	0.4	5	0.5	0.0	0.4
Textiles	335	6.7	3.9	13.5	133	2.8	30.1	62
Apparel	242	6.4	17.3	30	506	12.5	49.1	399.8
Lumber and wood	180	11.6	8.7	14.8	208	13.2	0.5	20.8
Furniture and fixtures	125	5.9	0.9	-1.4	461	18.3	2.2	51.8
Paper	733	17.0	2.4	13.6	342	9.2	2.6	42.7
Printing and publishing	64	2.3	0.9	-0.5	24	0.9	0.0	1.9
Chemicals	1,722	16.6	6.8	116.7	613	6.5	1.3	71.3

Rubber and misc. plastics	779	17.7	9.6	62.6	324	8.2	5.9	48.3
Drugs	68	3.4	7.8	3.4	27	1.4	0.0	2.1
Cleaning and toilet preps.	28	1.0	13.0	3.2	31	1.1	0.0	2.2
Petroleum refining	319	5.5	5.1	15.7	204	3.6	0.5	18.7
Leather	68	2.7	3.9	1.1	184	6.8	7.1	30.8
Glass	45	5.1	2.1	0.5	200	18.0	3.0	29.1
Stone and clay	139	3.1	5.4	5.4	286	6.1	3.1	35.2
Iron and steel	341	4.4	1.0	7.5	283	3.9	4.8	48
Nonferrous metals	525	31.5	0.9	18.4	834	41.6	1.6	123.3
Fabricated metal	703	14.8	8.3	57	469	11.3	2.8	58.6
Machinery and equipment	2,306	51.2	11.1	189.4	919	39.2	2.7	113.1
Computing equipment	557	43.3	11.1	42.1	550	53.9	1.8	60.5
Electrical equipment	2,157	53.0	11.1	165.2	2,296	54.7	4.5	370.1
Household appliances	516	39.7	11.5	46	1,368	63.8	4.3	228
Electronic components	1,283	59.4	12.4	119.3	1,801	67.2	4.1	312.5
Motor vehicles and bodies	29	0.5	21.5	7.1	1,870	24.1	2.5	191.1
Motor vehicle parts	1,680	30.7	5.3	103.1	1,331	29.8	3.1	204
Transportation equipment	321	28.9	13.0	32.3	71	10.3	2.8	6.4
Miscellaneous manufactures	988	38.9	12.7	89	864	38.1	4.4	117.4
Transportation	443	2.5	0.0	-8.8	835	4.6	0.0	65.1
Communication	253	11.2	0.0	-5.6	639	24.2	0.0	51.6
Utilities	0	0.0	0.0	0	0	0.0	0.0	0
Wholesale and retail trade	0	0.0	0.0	0	0	0.0	0.0	0
Finance and insurance	141	1.8	0.0	-2.5	0	0.0	0.0	0
Hotels and restaurants	2,652	23.2	0.0	-56	4,828	35.5	0.0	418.7

continued next page

Industry	Mexican imports from United States				Mexican exports to United States			
	Millions of 1988 dollars	As percentage share of Mexican consumption	Tariff rate plus tariff equivalent of quotas (percentages)	Additional Mexican imports with NAFTA (millions of 1988 dollars)	Millions of 1988 dollars	As percentage of Mexican production	Tariff rate plus tariff equivalent of quotas (percentages)	Additional Mexican exports with NAFTA (millions of 1988 dollars)
Other business services	494	3.6	0.0	−10.2	1,325	8.9	0.0	109.6
Health, education and government	0	0.0	0.0	0	0	0.0	0.0	0
Total tariff average	22,569	7.1		1,174.2	29,147	9.1		3,862.9
Overall			8.5				4.8	
Excluding maquiladora			11.1				8.0	

Source: KPMG Peat Marwick, Economic Policy Group, *The Effects of a Free Trade Agreement between the U.S. and Mexico,* (Washington: KPMG Peat Marwick, May 1991), tables 13, 14, 15, 29, and 30, commissioned by the US Council of the Mexico–US Business Committee. Data reprinted with permission.

United States, and on liberal US attitudes toward seasonal tariffs. The United States has already indicated a willingness to enforce its phytosanitary standards on-site within Mexico rather than through time-consuming border checks.

Textiles and apparel are another area of potentially large Mexican export growth. Here everything depends on continued relaxation of bilateral quotas; moreover, additional US investment is needed to cement relations between the US and the Mexican textile and apparel industries. In the KPMG model, Mexican export gains in textiles and apparel approach $500 million; for reasons spelled out in chapter 13, we think the gains could be several times as large. Moreover, the competitive US textile industry could greatly increase its shipments of so-called flat goods (carpets, sheets, blankets, curtain material, and industrial fabric) to Mexico.

Mexican durable-goods exports will be propelled by two-way trade in transportation equipment, various machinery items, and electronic components. Finally, with better organization of its facilities, Mexico should renew its attraction as a travel destination, leading to significant gains in tourist receipts, and reversing the experience of the 1980s when tourism in Mexico languished.

4

Investment

In the European Community, intraregional investment drove the process of economic integration and the Europe 1992 agenda. The same is happening in North America. US–Canada direct investment was already substantial before the negotiation of the Canada–US FTA, but two-way flows increased substantially once the FTA talks had begun, as companies positioned themselves to operate in a larger and more competitive regional market.[1] By 1990, Canadian foreign direct investment (FDI) in the United States had reached an estimated $43 billion at market values; US FDI in Canada also grew sharply during this period to about $106 billion at market values (table 4.1). In turn, the extensive US and Canadian holdings in each other's economies spurred a sharp increase in bilateral trade, particularly between parent and subsidiary.

A similar pattern now seems to be emerging in US–Mexico economic relations. Domestic economic reforms in Mexico and the series of bilateral accords leading to the NAFTA negotiations have prompted a sharp growth in both bilateral trade and bilateral investment. To date, much of the investment has been concentrated in the automobile and electronics industries, and among manufactured goods these have become the largest and fastest-growing areas of bilateral trade. In 1990, half of Mexican manufacturing exports consisted of intrafirm trade, and just five companies were responsible for 20 percent of Mexico's exports.[2] These same firms were responsible for much of the growth in FDI.[3]

As discussed in chapter 1, the sustainability of the Mexican economic reforms depends importantly on inflows of foreign investment and the repatriation of

---

1. For an examination of US–Canada investment flows during this period and how they influenced the FTA negotiations, see Schott and Smith (1988, chapter 6).

2. The five are IBM, Ford, Chrysler, General Motors, and Nissan. General Motors is Mexico's biggest private-sector employer, with a work force of 55,000 (*Financial Times*, 3 June 1991, 16).

3. A recent study by A.T. Kearney found that 65 percent of foreign companies in Mexico interviewed were expanding their operations there. The companies surveyed gave cost and quality of the work force, access to markets, and size of the internal market as their main reasons for investment. Pollution in the metropolitan and industrial areas and the high cost of capital were cited as the main deterrents to expansion (*Journal of Commerce*, 29 August 1991, 5A).

Table 4.1 United States and Canada: bilateral direct investment, by sector, 1982–90[a] (billions of dollars)

Year	Total	Petroleum	Manufacturing	Services[b]	Other	Total at market value
Canadian investment in the United States						
1982	11.7	1.5	3.5	1.1	5.6	n.a.
1983	11.4	1.4	3.3	1.0	5.7	n.a.
1984	15.3	1.5	4.1	1.1	8.5	n.a.
1985	17.1	1.6	4.6	1.5	9.4	n.a.
1986	18.3	1.4	5.4	1.5	10.0	n.a.
1987	24.7	1.1	8.1	2.2	13.3	29.6
1988	26.6	1.2	9.7	2.1	13.5	33.0
1989	28.7	1.2	9.9	2.1	15.4	44.3[c]
1990	27.7	1.4	9.3	2.4	14.6	42.8[c]
US investment in Canada						
1982	43.5	10.4	18.8	6.1	8.2	n.a.
1983	44.4	10.4	19.3	6.5	8.2	n.a.
1984	46.7	11.2	21.0	6.6	7.9	n.a.
1985	47.1	10.5	21.8	6.3	8.5	n.a.
1986	50.6	10.9	23.8	7.0	8.5	n.a.
1987	57.8	11.1	27.1	10.6	13.3	73.3
1988	62.7	11.5	28.9	11.9	13.5	81.9
1989	65.5	10.7	31.6	12.7	15.4	101.3
1990	68.4	10.7	33.2	13.1	14.6	106.3[d]

n.a. = not available.

a. Figures in the first five columns are at historical cost.

b. In the case of Canadian investment in the United States, the data are for wholesale trade; in the case of US investment in Canada, the data are for banking and finance.

c. The market value figures for Canadian investment in the United States are estimated from the US ratios between market value and historical cost.

d. Estimated from the 1989 ratio between market value and historical cost.

Source: US Department of Commerce, *Survey of Current Business,* August issues, 1985–91.

flight capital. To that end, Mexican policy toward FDI has been reoriented toward actively encouraging foreign investors in most sectors of the economy. Until the mid–1980s, foreign investment played a small role in the Mexican economy and was concentrated mainly in the maquiladora sector (see chapter 5). As recently as 1985, foreign investment amounted to only about 5 percent of Mexican gross fixed investment (US International Trade Commission 1991a, I-5).

Table 4.2 Mexico: foreign direct investment from all countries, 1980–90 (billions of dollars)

Year	New investment	Accumulated investment
1980	1.6	8.5
1981	1.7	10.2
1982	0.6	10.8
1983	0.7	11.5
1984	1.4	12.9
1985	1.9	14.6
1986	2.4	17.1
1987	3.9	20.9
1988	2.2	24.1
1989	2.5	26.6
1990	3.7	30.3

Source: Banco de México, *The Mexican Economy*, May 1991.

After the introduction of the economic stabilization and trade liberalization programs in 1985, the stock of FDI in Mexico more than doubled to $30.3 billion at the end of 1990 (table 4.2).[4] About 20 percent of that total was invested in just the last two years of the period. Moreover, Mexico's rapid growth in 1989–90 seems to have encouraged new investors; for example, Japanese firms reportedly have committed $3 billion to future projects.[5] In addition, cheaper labor, proximity to the US market, and the prospect of a NAFTA all reinforce the investment allure of Mexico.[6]

---

4. These data reflect current market values. On a historical-cost basis, total foreign investment in Mexico equaled $15 billion. According to President Salinas's deputy press secretary, in 1991 Mexico received about $14 billion in new foreign investment (new FDI of about $8.3 billion and new securities bought by foreigners of about $5.1 billion; *Journal of Commerce*, 17 December 1991, 1A).

5. See *Business Week*, 3 June 1991, 20. Rising wages in Southeast Asia and Mexico's proximity to the US market are seen as the main advantages. But the shift to Mexico should not be overstated, since rapid growth in Southeast Asia will continue to attract investment on a large scale, while weak infrastructure in Mexico will remain an inhibiting factor.

6. An illustration of this trend was the recent announcement by Zenith that it would relocate its last US assembly plant to Mexico and move 600 jobs from Taiwan to Mexico. These shifts represent an attempt to reduce costs while still retaining easy access to the US market. (*Journal of Commerce*, 31 October 1991, 1A; *Wall Street Journal*, 22 November 1991, 7A).

Table 4.3 Mexico: geographic and sectoral composition of accumulated foreign direct investment, 1990[a]

	Billions of dollars	Share of total (percentages)
Geographic distribution		
United States	19.1	63.0
Germany	2.0	6.6
United Kingdom	1.9	6.3
Japan	1.5	5.0
Switzerland	1.3	4.3
Other	4.5	14.9
Total	30.3	100.0
Sectoral distribution		
Industry	18.9	62.3
Services	8.8	29.0
Commerce	2.1	6.8
Extractive industries	0.5	1.6
Agriculture	0.1	0.3

a. As of the end of the year. The official US figure for US foreign direct investment in Mexico at the end of 1989 was $21.0 billion (*Survey of Current Business*, October 1991, 51).

Source: Banco de México, *The Mexican Economy*, May 1991.

Table 4.3 indicates the geographic and sectoral distribution of FDI in Mexico. About 63 percent of the total comes from the United States; Germany, the United Kingdom, Japan, and Switzerland account for most of the rest, although none had a significant stake in the Mexican economy.[7] From 1985 levels, cumulative US FDI in Mexico doubled to $19.1 billion in 1990; although much smaller, Canadian FDI in Mexico also almost doubled during the same period to $0.5 billion and accounted for 1.4 percent of total FDI. The bulk of foreign investment in Mexico (62 percent) has been in the industrial sector, although foreign holdings in the services sectors have grown significantly in recent years and in 1990 accounted for almost 30 percent of total Mexican FDI (table 4.3).

7. According to an official of the Mexican Board of Investment, the countries expected to increase their investment include Germany (in automobiles and chemicals), Korea (in electronics), France (in electronics and automobiles), Sweden and Canada (in food processing), and Italy (in capital goods). Investment from the United States will remain around 63 percent of the total, and investment from Japan will continue to be small (*Journal of Commerce*, 17 December 1991, 1A).

In sum, the process of integrating the North American economies is well under way through the investment channel. Already possessing substantial holdings in each other's economies, US and Canadian firms have increased their stakes in Mexico as recent reforms have taken root and revitalized the economy.

Continued inflows of FDI are critical if Mexico is to sustain its economic recovery. Investment is the engine propelling Mexican development, and Mexican policy needs to build on recent reforms to continue to attract foreign capital. In that regard, the NAFTA should pose a welcome challenge to Mexican policymakers, since the United States and Canada are likely to press Mexico to adopt FDI policies compatible with the obligations set out in the Canada–US FTA.

Conforming to FTA standards on investment would raise a number of important and politically sensitive issues for Mexico in key sectors such as energy; the FTA standards would also raise more general concerns relating to the national treatment principle. Although recent Mexican reforms relating to FDI have brought Mexican policy closer to that of the United States and Canada, significant restrictions still exist, affecting foreign participation in the Mexican industrial, agricultural, and services sectors. This chapter examines Mexican investment policies and discusses how these issues need to be addressed in the NAFTA negotiations.

Mexican Regulations on Foreign Investment

Mexican regulations on foreign investment reflect the strong constraints incorporated in the 1917 Constitution. Article 27 of the Mexican Constitution states that:

> To the Nation corresponds the direct ownership of all the minerals or substances which in veins, layers, masses, or beds constitute deposits whose nature is distinct from the components of the lands, such as the ores from which are extracted metals and metaloids used in industry, petroleum and solid, liquid, or gaseous hydrocarbons...the ownership of the Nation is inalienable and imprescriptible, and only concessions may be made by the Federal Government to individuals or civil or commercial companies constituted in conformity with the Mexican laws, upon the condition that there be established regular works for the exploitation of the elements to which reference is made and that the requisites for which the laws provide be complied with.

Furthermore, Article 28 reserves what it calls "strategic" sectors for exclusive control by the Mexican government. These sectors now include oil exploration, oil refining and pipelines, other hydrocarbons, radioactive materials, electricity, basic petrochemicals, mail, satellite telecommunications, and railways. In the 1920s and 1930s these articles prompted a series of expropriations in the energy, transportation, and agricultural sectors, which deterred most foreign investment in the Mexican economy for many years.

In 1973, Mexico amalgamated its foreign investment decrees and rulings into a single Law to Promote Mexican Investment and Regulate Foreign Investment (often shortened to Law on Foreign Investment, or LFI). The LFI established a general maximum limit of 49 percent for foreign participation in Mexican companies, classified certain sectors as subject to greater restriction on or outright prohibition of FDI, and created the National Foreign Investment Commission (Comisión Nacional de Inversión Extranjera, or CNIE) to administer the FDI law, screen applications, and issue implementing regulations.

During the 1970s and up to the debt crisis of the early 1980s, FDI continued to be sharply restricted under the LFI, since abundant oil revenues seemed to preclude the need for foreign capital. However, the Mexican approach toward FDI became more accommodating during the administration of President Miguel de la Madrid, as alternative sources of funds from commercial banks and international financial institutions dried up. The LFI remains the basic statute governing FDI, but its implementing regulations were modified during the administration of President José López Portillo to gradually open selected sectors to increased foreign participation.

In 1984, Mexico adopted new guidelines for the promotion of foreign investment in specific sectors of the economy, including the ability to hold majority interests in certain activities.[8] Subsequently, the Mexican government adopted further modifications of the LFI, *inter alia* eliminating the requirement of prior approval by the CNIE for foreign investment in maquiladoras and, in 1988, providing automatic approval (i.e., no prior screening by the CNIE) for foreign participation of up to 49 percent of the shares of an established Mexican company.

It was not until May 1989, however, that the Mexican government announced sweeping reforms in the regulations that implement the 1973 law.[9] The 1989 regulations include guidelines indicating those activities subject to foreign investment restrictions ("classified activities," consisting of six broad categories) and

---

8. The 1984 guidelines aimed at those sectors that generated positive foreign-exchange balances, produced competitive exports or import substitution, contributed to national scientific and technological development, advanced Mexico's further integration into the international community, involved large investments, and created employment and geographic decentralization of industry (US International Trade Commission 1990b, 5–6).

9. The May 1989 regulations entail interpretations of the 1973 LFI, rather than an outright change in the statutory provisions. Since regulations are more easily changed than laws, the United States and Canada are likely to seek commitments from Mexico in the NAFTA to make regulatory reform more permanent.

those covered by less restrictive rules ("unclassified activities"). The six "classified" categories are:[10]

- Activities reserved exclusively to the Mexican state (e.g., extraction of petroleum and natural gas; petroleum refining; the generation, transmission, and supply of electrical energy; telegraph services; railways)

- Activities reserved to Mexican nationals (e.g., private broadcast of television programs; road freight and passenger transportation)

- Activities in which foreign investment is limited to 34 percent (e.g., coal mining; extraction and refining of sulfur, phosphoric rock, and ferrous minerals)

- Activities in which foreign investment is limited to 40 percent (e.g., secondary petrochemical products; the automotive industries and related activities)

- Activities in which foreign investment is limited to 49 percent (e.g., fishing, mining activities except those listed above, telephone services, insurance, and finance leasing companies)

- Activities in which prior approval by the CNIE is required for foreign investors to hold a majority interest (e.g., agriculture, livestock and cattle, printing, publishing and associated industries, industrial and other construction, and educational services).

The new policy provides automatic approval for foreign direct investments of up to $100 million and allows 100 percent foreign control in companies in "unclassified" economic activities. The CNIE grants automatic approval for foreign investment provided the following conditions are met: capital investment does not exceed $100 million; all financing is external; if an industrial facility, the project is located outside Mexico City, Guadalajara, and Monterrey; there is "equilibrium" in the project's balance of foreign exchange over the first three years; permanent employment is generated and training given to Mexican personnel; and adequate technology is used to satisfy environmental requirements (US International Trade Commission 1990c, 2–13). The "unclassified" category has since been broadened to include the previously restricted glass, iron, steel, and cellulose industries. As a result, unclassified industries and sectors now cover approximately two-thirds of Mexico's GDP (Husband et al. 1991).

The 1989 regulations introduced a trust mechanism that allows temporary foreign investment in classified sectors (including shares in publicly traded Mexi-

---

10. This section draws on Banco de México, *The Mexican Economy*, 1991.

can stocks in those sectors). The trust has a maximum life of 20 years, after which the trust shares must be sold to a Mexican investor. The trust provision applies to those classified industries subject to percentage foreign investment restrictions as well as to three industries normally reserved for ownership by Mexican nationals: air and maritime transportation and gas distribution. Other important sectors affected by the trust mechanism include mining,[11] secondary petrochemicals, automotive parts, fishing, and financial leasing (normally restricted to a maximum foreign ownership of 34 percent or 49 percent).

Any trust established under the new provisions must meet CNIE approval. Approval generally requires that the companies demonstrate that an infusion of foreign capital is needed "for new export projects, or to overcome extreme financial imbalances resulting from foreign-denominated liabilities incurred prior to the issuance of the regulations or a drastic decline in sales" (US International Trade Commission 1990b, 5–9). Further, it must be shown that domestic financing was not available, that Mexican investors have waived their rights of first refusal, and that the investment is in the form of either cash or a capitalization of the company's liabilities.

The trust mechanism has introduced a significant degree of flexibility into the administration of the Mexican FDI law. In certain instances, it has provided a detour around constitutional roadblocks when foreign investment was needed to advance important industrial priorities, while ensuring that foreign shares would eventually revert to Mexican hands. To date, however, the trust mechanism has not been used extensively in the energy sector, where arguably its potential usefulness and need are greatest.

The 1989 regulatory reforms maintain a broad range of restrictions on foreign investment. However, the combination of the 1989 reforms and extensive privatization efforts have created significant new opportunities for foreign investors in Mexico, particularly in such sectors as telecommunications, which previously was reserved exclusively to the state; insurance, in which foreign investment had been limited to only 15 percent; banking, in which foreign participation of up to 30 percent is now allowed (see chapter 15); petrochemicals, where broad reclassification of basic and secondary products has enabled greater foreign participation (see chapter 10);[12] and mining, in which some of the land previously reserved to the state has been opened to foreign exploitation.[13] Privatiza-

---

11. New regulations affecting FDI in the mining sector became effective 10 December 1990. These regulations introduce new trust provisions that are specific to the mining sector.

12. In the petrochemical sector, 14 petrochemical products have been reclassified from "basic" (reserved exclusively to the state) to "secondary" (minority foreign participation permitted); a further 539 petrochemicals have been reclassified from "secondary" to "tertiary" (open to 100 percent foreign participation).

13. One million hectares (nearly 2.5 million acres) of land are now open to foreign exploration and development. Foreign participation in this activity was formerly limited

tion has been an important component of the economic reforms undertaken under the Salinas administration. Through privatization, Mexico has reduced its fiscal deficit, consolidated or disbanded inefficient enterprises, and encouraged inflows of foreign capital, technology, and management skills. Of the 1,155 enterprises controlled by the government in December 1982, only 280 remained in government control at the end of 1990 (Banco de México, *The Mexican Economy*, 1991. Between January 1989 and November 1991, the government sold 160 enterprises for nearly $11 billion; the offerings included some of the crown jewels of Mexican industry: the state telephone company Telmex, the banking group Banamex, Aeroméxico, and the steel company SICARTSA).[14]

Illustrative of the privatization process was the successful sale of the state telephone company Telmex (Compañía de Teléfonos de México), made possible by the 1989 reforms allowing up to 49 percent foreign investment in telecommunications firms. The privatization of Telmex involved the sale of Telmex common stock to an international consortium made up of the Carso group, Southwestern Bell Corp., and France Telecom;[15] the sale of 4 percent of the stock to company employees; and then, on 13 May 1991, the sale of 14 percent of the company's stock on the New York Stock Exchange. Following the New York placement, Telmex was valued at $14.4 billion, compared with $1.2 billion in 1988. With the proceeds of the stock sale, Telmex plans to invest $7.7 billion over the next three years to upgrade phone lines and switches (*Washington Post*, 3 September 1991, E1).

The transition from public to private ownership in the banking industry has been equally promising. In May 1990 a constitutional amendment overturned the 1982 nationalization of the Mexican commercial banks. On 18 July 1990 the Law on Credit Institutions determined the criteria for ownership of, and extent of foreign participation in, Mexican banks (see chapter 15). Foreign investors can participate in the banking sector through so-called "C" shares upon authorization by the Ministry of Finance, and subject to a maximum of 30 percent of bank capital. In addition, foreign banks can hold a minority stake in the holding companies of financial groups.

From June to mid-August 1991, six Mexican banks were privatized; the proceeds of $1.35 billion represented three to four times the banks' book value.

---

to 34 percent or 49 percent, depending upon the category of mineral. The new regulations allow temporary 100 percent ownership in the 49 percent category, through the medium of a trust mechanism (for both exploration and exploitation activities).

14. *Financial Times*, 25 October 1991, IV. Mexico expects to finish the privatization program by the end of 1992. The Mexican government does not plan to privatize the state oil company Pemex, the electric power monopoly, the postal services, or the railroads.

15. The deal involved a 20.4 percent controlling stake in Telmex, half of the full voting shares.

In late August 1991 the government of Mexico sold 50.7 percent of Banamex for $2.3 billion to a group of 800 investors led by the brokerage firm Accival (Acciones y Valores de México). Roberto Hernández, president of the brokerage firm, plans to make an international offering of 19 percent of the company (*New York Times*, 27 August 1991, D1).

A further example is the case of Aeroméxico, privatized in October 1988. Since privatization, Aeroméxico has cut its staff by half, to 6,000 workers, yet upgraded its service and gained market share. The fact that Aeroméxico was bankrupt at the time of privatization facilitated its restructuring. In contrast, following its privatization in August 1989, Mexicana de Aviación was unable to cut staff significantly because of union resistance.[16]

Other reforms by the Mexican government in the areas of intellectual property and technology transfer have also encouraged FDI inflows. New protections for intellectual property rights holders remove a major disincentive to foreign investment, particularly where patented technology is involved, by reducing the risk of piracy or misappropriation of proprietary know-how. In January 1990 the Mexican government revised the Technology Transfer Law of 1973.[17] This action was complemented, in June–July 1991, by the revision of the 1976 Law of Inventions and Trademarks (LIT) and the Mexican Copyright Act of 1956 (see chapter 9).

Foreign Participation in the Stock Market

Since 1990, the Mexican stock market (the Bolsa de Valores) has been one of the world's best performing markets. Participation by international investors has pushed the market to historical highs: the Bolsa increased by 99 percent in dollar terms between January and early December 1991 (*Financial Times*, 18 December 1991, 36). Total foreign investment in Mexican stocks in August 1991 reached $13.6 billion out of a total market capitalization of $59 billion (excluding govern-

---

16. George Santana, an analyst with DA Campbell Co., estimated that Aeroméxico would earn a profit of $15 million on revenue of $781 million in 1991. Mexicana, on the other hand, was expected to incur losses of $43 million on revenues of $995 million in 1991 (*Wall Street Journal*, 22 November 1991, A8).

17. The Technology Transfer Law of 1973 imposed standards and prior registration requirements for patents, trademarks, and technological and managerial services, and provided discretionary powers over the revision and approval of all royalty and licensing agreements. The 1990 revisions reduced onerous requirements and protection for technology licensors (see US International Trade Commission 1989a, 2–3; Investment Canada 1991, 76–77).

ment holdings), three times the level of January of that year.[18] Telmex, the supermarket chain Cifra, and Cemex are largely responsible for the Bolsa's recent gains, accounting for 69 percent, 7 percent, and 6 percent of the increase, respectively (*Financial Times*, 18 December 1991, 36).

As already noted with respect to Telmex, Mexico has also been successful in raising foreign capital through international equity issues. By the end of August 1991, investment in New York in American depository receipts (ADRs) amounted to $9.8 billion, of which $8.9 billion was invested in Telmex (*Financial Times*, 25 September 1991, 42).

There are three avenues for foreign portfolio investment in Mexican equities:

- By purchasing nonvoting "B" shares, foreigners can participate in 550 of 754 scheduled economic activities. The maximum percentage share available to foreigners in each activity is regulated by the CNIE.

- Within the "neutral trust" framework, foreigners can purchase Certificates of Ordinary Participation (CPOs). These certificates confer ownership rights except for voting rights; a Mexican trust takes custody of the shares and exercises voting rights. By this mechanism, normal "A" shares are transformed into so-called neutral shares. A major neutral trust fund managed by Nacional Financiera (Nafinsa) started with $300 million in 1989, and by August 1991 had increased its assets to $1.34 billion.[19] However, half of all foreigners investing in Mexican equities prefer ADRs because of the trust's high custodial fees and the relatively short hours of the Bolsa—ADRs are traded on the New York exchanges (*Wall Street Journal*, 22 April 1991, C12).

- Finally, foreign investors can acquire ADRs. The ADRs of 10 Mexican companies were listed on the New York and American stock exchanges at the end of April 1991.[20] In addition, three Mexican investment funds are traded on the New York Stock Exchange: the Mexico Fund (market value in April 1991,

---

18. Salomon Brothers, Inc., a New York securities firm, has estimated that, in 1990, half of the $8.4 billion in new capital that came into Mexico through equity investment, bond issues, and other issues consisted of capital being repatriated by Mexicans (*Wall Street Journal*, 24 May 1991, A1).

19. Interview with Timoteo Harris, Representative of Nacional Financiera, in Washington, 17 April 1991; *Financial Times*, 25 September 1991, 25.

20. The 10 companies were Compañía de Teléfonos de México S.A. (Telmex; telecommunications), Cifra S.A. (retailing), Tubos de Acero de México S.A. (TAMSA; seamless pipes for the oil industry), Grupo Sidek S.A. (consumer goods); Internacional de Cerámica S.A. (a tile maker); Tolmex (building materials), FEMSA (beer and soft drinks), Equipos Petroleros Nacionales S.A. (manufactures of valves for the oil industry); Vitro S.A. (a glass and plastics company); and Corporación Industrial Sanluis S.A. (a mining company). *Wall Street Journal*, 1 October 1990, B8; *Latin Finance*, June 1991, 32. See also chapter 15.

$362 million), the Mexico Equity and Income Fund ($71 million), and the Emerging Mexico Fund ($65 million; Shearson Lehman Brothers 1991).

As of August 1991, total foreign investment in Mexican equities was estimated at about $13.6 billion. This total should increase significantly as Mexican companies increasingly float international stock offers.[21] These efforts to raise equity internationally come at a time when the Bolsa is putting pressure on companies with difficult-to-trade shares to improve liquidity.

Mexican Energy Sector Regulations

Since the ratification of the 1917 Constitution, foreign participation in the oil sector has been reserved to the Mexican state. Between 1917 and 1938, however, foreign companies could operate in Mexico under special concessions (see chapter 10). On 18 March 1938, President Lázaro Cárdenas expropriated all foreign oil companies operating in Mexico, provided compensation, and consolidated their holdings under Pemex, which was totally controlled by the government (Manke 1979, 76–77). Since the 1938 expropriation, foreign companies have been hired to run drilling rigs but have never been given the right to keep a percentage of the oil discovered. Control of energy resources has been considered part of the national patrimony.[22]

The limits to change are as much political as legal. Since 1917, the Mexican Constitution has been amended more than 400 times. However, unlike in the banking sector where President Carlos Salinas was willing and able to amend the Constitution in 1990 to advance his privatization objectives (see chapter 15), the Mexican government has closed the door to amendments affecting the petroleum sector. In his second annual state of the nation address, Salinas declared that Mexico's state-run oil industry would not be subject to NAFTA negotiations, saying, "I want to confirm the fact that Mexico will maintain its

---

21. In the fall of 1991 some 11 companies were expected to make stock offerings (expected amounts are in parentheses): Televisa (between $400 million and $500 million); G-Carso ($250 million); Desc, a chemical and mechanical-metals company ($200 million); Vitro ($200 million); TMM, a transportation company (between $50 and $100 million); Alfa (between $50 million and 150 million); TAMSA (between $60 million and $70 million); Grupo Troika, a bottle maker, and Bachoso, an agroindustrial company (between $40 million and $80 million each). *El Nacional* (Mexico City), 23 September 1991, 25.

22. Moreover, after the boom-and-bust cycle in the oil industry of the past 15 years, some Mexicans are reluctant to depend on oil as the mainspring of economic growth. The ban on foreign equity is seen by this faction as a mechanism for regulating the pace of development.

ownership and complete dominion over hydrocarbons" (*New York Times*, 2 November 1990, A6).

The burden of history thus acts as a major barrier to Mexican economic progress. Without substantial foreign investment, Mexican oil resources are likely to be developed at an exceedingly slow pace. And without faster oil development, Mexico will miss the opportunity for rapid economic growth. Some compromise will be necessary between economic realities and political rhetoric if Mexico is to attract the foreign investment and proprietary technology held by major oil companies needed to further develop its oil fields (see chapter 10).

The Maquiladora Program

From the start of the maquiladora program in 1965 until 1989, foreigners were allowed 100 percent ownership of maquiladora subsidiaries with the approval of the CNIE, under an exemption from the LFI. (The maquiladora program is discussed in detail in chapter 5). Article 6 of the May 1989 Foreign Investment Regulations abolished prior CNIE authorization requirements on foreign participation in maquiladora enterprises, including foreign acquisition of established maquiladoras (US International Trade Commission 1990b, 5–16). The 100 percent foreign ownership exception was also extended to textile and apparel operations, which had previously required CNIE approval.[23]

The December 1989 Maquiladora Decree, enacted by the Secretaría de Comercio y Fomento Industrial (SECOFI), is designed to ensure the continued rapid growth of the maquiladora industry. Changes from the 1983 decree are aimed at deregulation and simplification, which will mostly benefit captured (foreign-owned) maquiladoras. The administrative process at SECOFI has been streamlined to a "single window" in which one office is authorized to handle all administrative details relating to new investment applications (previously, applications could involve up to nine different government agencies). Applications can now be processed at local SECOFI offices as well as in Mexico City.

Maquiladora licenses have been adapted to accommodate long-term investment. Licenses are now issued for an open-ended period instead of the previous limit of two years (at which point the license was reviewed for renewal, suspension, or termination).

---

23. When Mexican exports to the United States were strictly limited by quotas under the Multi-Fiber Arrangement, the right to export was a license to print money. The CNIE naturally favored Mexican apparel producers rather than foreign-owned maquiladoras. However, the underlying US quota system with respect to Mexico was significantly modified in 1988 (see chapter 13). To take advantage of these changes, it proved sensible for Mexico to permit 100 percent foreign ownership of textile and apparel maquiladoras.

A new governmental work group has been established to improve infrastructure and provide urban services needed by the maquiladora industry. Other relevant changes allow for a greater level of domestic sales (33 percent) by the maquiladoras and easier regulations on those sales (see chapter 5).

In 1989, 55 percent of the 1,800 Mexican maquiladoras were wholly or majority US–owned; 40 percent were wholly or majority Mexican-owned, mainly in the furniture and textile sectors; about 4 percent of maquiladoras were directly owned by Japanese or Korean firms.[24] But these statistics are misleading because the majority of Japanese and Korean maquiladoras are controlled through US subsidiaries. Taking indirect ownership into account, perhaps 30 percent of maquiladoras are owned or controlled by Japanese or Korean parent firms; these operations are concentrated in electrical and electronic products and transportation equipment.

The question of "third country" maquiladora ownership has taken on greater importance with rising Japanese and Korean interest in Mexico. The concern over third countries using Mexican maquiladoras as an export platform has led to calls for stricter rules of origin in the NAFTA (see chapter 8). However, if Mexico's current in-bond policies are revoked, third-country maquiladoras could be worse off than under current law (see chapter 5).

Transportation Regulations

Most commerce between the United States and Mexico passes overland, either by road or rail. Between 1,500 and 2,000 trucks cross the border at Nuevo Laredo each day, representing 45 percent of Mexican foreign trade.[25] While Mexican carriers can operate in the US market, Mexican trucking regulations reserve transportation of most cargo within Mexico exclusively to Mexican carriers (the only exception to the rule is the transport of dangerous substances such as explosives, toxins, or chemicals). Obtaining free access and reciprocal treatment on cargo transportation is likely to be a key issue for the NAFTA talks.

There are two major impediments to foreign participation in the trucking business in Mexico: trucking permits are only issued to Mexican citizens, and a commercial driver's license is a federal license reserved to Mexicans. Despite

---

24. The ownership percentages greatly overstate the importance, in terms of sales volume, of Mexican-owned maquiladoras. Further, the number of Mexican companies could be overestimated because of the difficulty of determining the true nationality of beneficial owners. As of mid–1989, European participation in the maquiladora industry totaled about eight plants (US International Trade Commission 1990b, 5–14, 5–15; Grant 1991, 12)

25. *Journal of Commerce*, 3 October 1991, 3A. This section draws on Giermanski et al. (1990) and US General Accounting Office (1991b).

efforts since 1987 by the US Department of Transportation and Mexico's Secretaría de Comunicaciones y Transporte to open the sector to foreign participation, Mexican unions have blocked reform. Nonetheless, an informal agreement between the twin cities of Nuevo Laredo, Mexico, and Laredo, Texas, allows tractors from each side to deliver trailers across the border as long as they return home empty.

Since 1989 Mexico has deregulated its trucking industry to some extent. As a result, maquiladora plants are allowed to use their own fleet of motor carriers to transport their own intermediate components and final products back and forth across the border. Similarly, in December 1990 an agreement was reached allowing US tourist buses reciprocal access to Mexico, the same as Mexican tourist buses have in the United States (US General Accounting Office 1991b, 22).

The United States has reacted to Mexican restrictions by imposing retaliatory measures on Mexican access to the US transportation market. Provisions of the 1984 Motor Carrier Act require foreign carriers to register with the Interstate Commerce Commission (ICC) and limit the access of Mexican carriers to the US market to specific commercial zones designated along the border by the ICC. To obtain a certificate of registration to operate in the US market, Mexican motor carriers must provide proof of insurance and payment of US highway taxes to the Internal Revenue Service and must operate equipment that meets US safety standards. Enforcement of these requirements, however, has proven to be impractical. US enforcement actions often have led to countermeasures by Mexico. Reciprocal access for commercial motor carriers in both countries remains a major obstacle to normalizing transborder commercial traffic between the United States and Mexico.[26]

North American Taxation of Foreign Corporations

Mexico, Canada, and the United States have broadly similar corporate tax systems.[27] As table 4.4 illustrates, total (federal plus subfederal) corporate income

---

26. Enforcement of the problematic trucking regulations rests in the hands of the even more problematic customs facilities on the Mexican side of the border. Inefficient, corrupt, and overstaffed facilities create a backlog of trucks entering the country. One step in the right direction has been taken with the new customs building in Nuevo Laredo: sophisticated computer equipment was installed on both the US and the Mexican sides to speed up the process, and the staff has been selectively cut with a view to weeding out corrupt officials. The "red light–green light" system will be tried; if all goes well, the system will then be implemented at the California and Arizona borders (*Journal of Commerce*, 3 October 1991, 3A).

27. Emilio Romano of the Embassy of Mexico in the United States provided useful information for this section.

Table 4.4 United States, Canada, and Mexico: taxation of business income, 1991[a]

	Mexico	United States	Canada
Corporate income tax rate: general (percentages)			
Federal	35	34	28
Subfederal[b]	4	6	15
Total	39	40	43
Indexation of deductions	Full	No	No
Loss carryforward years	5	15	7
Loss carryback years	0	3	3
Capital gains taxation			
Coverage	Full	Full	Two-thirds
Indexation	Full	No	Full
Rate (percentages)	35	34	28
Deduction for dividends received	No	Yes	Yes
Full expensing of investment	No	No	No
Investment tax credits	Regional and priority sectors	Energy investment, rehabilitation of real estate, targeted job credit, R&D	Regional and R&D
Statutory withholding tax rates			
Interest	35	30	28
FDI dividends	0	30	25
Portfolio dividends	35	30	25

Technology transfer fees	15	30	25
Royalties	35	30	25
Illustrative treaty withholding rates[c]			
Interest	15	0	15
FDI dividends	10	5	10
Portfolio dividends	15	15	15
Royalties and technology fees	15	0	10

a. Information for Canada is for 1990.

b. State, provincial, and other tax authorities. For Mexico, the figure given is the profit-sharing rate; in the United States, the average state tax rate; in Canada, the average provincial tax rate.

c. The treaty rates refer in the case of Mexico to the Canada-Mexico tax treaty, in the case of the United States to the US–Germany tax treaty, and in the case of Canada to the US–Canada tax treaty.

Source: Anwar Shah and Joel Slemrod, "Do Taxes Matter for Foreign Direct Investment?" *World Bank Economic Review,* 5, no. 3 (September 1991): 473–91, table A-1. Adapted with permission.

tax rates vary only slightly, from 39 percent in Mexico, to 40 percent in the United States, to 43 percent in Canada. Corporate capital gains tax rates are also similar: 35 percent in Mexico, 34 percent in the United States, and 28 percent in Canada. To be sure, differences exist in loss carryover rules, investment tax credits, and indexation features (Mexico's more extensive indexation was inspired by the country's bout of high inflation in the 1980s), but the broad contours of corporate taxation are much the same. This broad similarity is important because it answers anxieties about a flood of tax-induced investment reaching Mexico from Canada or the United States.

The major problem in the corporate tax realm is high statutory Mexican withholding taxes on interest and royalties paid by Mexican subsidiaries to their foreign parents (see table 4.4 for US, Mexican, and Canadian withholding tax rates). These taxes deter new foreign investment in Mexico. The withholding tax is the tax analogue of a tariff: just as a tariff restricts trade flows, the withholding tax restricts investment and technology flows.[28]

Mexican statutory withholding taxes on interest paid to foreigners are 15 percent for payments to financial institutions and up to 35 percent in other cases (Mexico, Secretaría de Hacienda y Crédito Público 1991). Royalties for the use of patents, trademarks, and trade names are taxed at 35 percent; payments for technical assistance fees and copyright royalties are taxed at 15 percent. But in one respect Mexican taxation is quite liberal: Mexico does not impose withholding taxes on dividends paid by Mexican subsidiaries to their foreign parent companies (FDI dividends) when those dividends are paid out of the earnings and profits that have already been subject to regular corporate taxation.[29]

The general US statutory withholding tax rate is 30 percent, while Canadian rates are 25 percent to 28 percent (table 4.4). However, in contrast with Mexican practice, US and Canadian statutory rates are reduced in nearly all cases through bilateral tax treaties.

Mexico is now negotiating a tax treaty with the United States that should reduce the statutory withholding rates on income flows in both directions. One possible precedent for the US–Mexico negotiations is the Mexico-Canada tax treaty, which sets reciprocal royalty, interest, and portfolio dividend tax rates at 15 percent and nonreciprocal FDI dividend rates at 10 percent for dividends flowing from Canada to Mexico and zero for dividends from Mexico to Canada.[30]

---

28. Anwar Shah and Joel Slemrod (1991) provide empirical confirmation: they find that FDI in Mexico is sensitive to the tax regime in Mexico, the credit status of multinationals, country credit ratings, and the regulatory system.

29. If, for some reason, the dividends are paid out of corporate income that escaped the normal corporate tax, a withholding tax of 35 percent is imposed.

30. Nonreciprocal withholding rates are highly unusual; in this case Mexico insisted on its zero withholding rate policy as a spur to inward foreign investment.

Another possible precedent is the US–Canada tax treaty, which sets the reciprocal withholding tax rate on royalties and interest at 10 percent, on portfolio dividends at 15 percent, and on FDI dividends at 10 percent.[31]

Most US firms do not look favorably at either precedent. Both the US–Canada and the Canada-Mexico treaty rates are well above the rates in most US tax treaties with industrial countries. For example, the new US–German treaty provides a reciprocal withholding rate of zero percent on royalties and interest, 15 percent on portfolio dividends, and 5 percent on FDI dividends.[32] A major US negotiating objective is to achieve zero rates on royalties and interest paid within North America.

In this spirit, the Mexico–US Business Committee has called for cuts in Mexican withholding tax rates on royalties and interest in the context of comprehensive Mexican income tax treaties. But since Mexico depends heavily on withholding tax revenue, it is reluctant to reduce its rates.[33] To accommodate Mexican revenue concerns, a phaseout period will be required. At the end of 10 years, the goal for all of North America should be zero withholding taxes, backed up by special features to ensure adequate tax reporting (see Hufbauer 1992, chapter 4).

In the Canada–US FTA negotiations tax issues were not covered, largely because a revised tax treaty had been signed as recently as August 1984. The situation between the United States and Mexico is quite different, since the existing tax treaty has very limited scope. Active negotiations are under way between the United States and Mexico to forge a comprehensive tax treaty, and an agreement will probably be initialed in early 1992.

The Canada–US Free Trade Agreement

Chapter 16 of the Canada–US FTA establishes rights and obligations regarding investment. The most important aspect of these provisions is that they include a national treatment obligation under which Canada and the United States agree to treat foreign investors in the same manner as local investors. In addition, the FTA mandates the phaseout of export and production-based performance requirements, once a standard entry ticket for foreign companies seeking to

---

31. Canada does not levy a withholding tax on royalties in respect of copyrights, other than motion pictures and television films. See Price Waterhouse (1990).

32. Within the European Community the withholding tax on FDI dividends will soon be abolished. This precedent should be followed in North America.

33. According to a Mexican source, revenues from withholding tax on FDI interest, royalties, and technology fees represent 10 percent of Mexican corporate tax revenue and about 3 percent of total government receipts; the United States accounts for 70 percent of the withholding tax figure.

invest in Canada. The FTA also eliminates screening by Investment Canada of all new greenfield and most other direct investment in Canada; as of 1992, reviews will only apply to individual investments above C$150 million (FDI by other countries remains subject to lower review thresholds: C$5 million for direct acquisitions and C$50 million for indirect acquisitions).[34] In effect, the new threshold limits only screen US acquisitions of the largest Canadian companies.[35] Since the entry into force of the FTA, screening has not been the subject of bilateral dispute, even in sectors such as energy that were exempted from most of the FTA obligations.

Recommendations

The 1989 Mexican reforms on foreign investment have brought Mexican practices more in line with US and Canadian obligations under the FTA. However, significant differences remain, including Mexico's lack of commitment to national treatment; numerous performance requirements (banned by the Canada–US FTA); technology transfer restrictions; high Mexican withholding tax rates on interest and royalties; and, most important, the prohibition of foreign participation in the oil and gas sector and in the production of certain petrochemicals.[36]

Outright changes in the Mexican Constitution of 1917 are out of the question. But substantial reforms can be achieved by amending the Mexican LFI, by other statutory changes, and by a new US–Mexico tax treaty. The task for the NAFTA negotiators in drafting the investment chapter is to achieve in Mexico the degree of liberalization already reached between Canada and the United States.

---

34. Mandatory review requirements for all new investment were eliminated in 1985 with the adoption of Investment Canada.

35. For a discussion of services and investment in the Canada–US FTA, see Schott and Smith (1988, chapter 6).

36. Although the Canada–US FTA exempts energy investment from most of the new obligations, it does extend reciprocal rights regarding pricing and supply access that are more liberal than current Mexican policies (see chapter 10).

5

The Maquiladora Phenomenon

Maquiladoras are in-bond production facilities engaged in processing or secondary assembly of imported components for reexport, primarily to the United States.[1] The term "maquiladora" derives from the Spanish word *maquilar*, which means to retain a portion of the flour in payment for milling wheat—by analogy, a *maquiladora* is thus any processor of goods to be returned to the original producer for resale. Under the "in-bond" arrangement, imported inputs enter Mexico duty-free, but the importer posts a bond to guarantee that the finished products will indeed be exported rather than sold on the domestic market; otherwise, appropriate duties are collected from the posted bond.

Traditionally, maquiladora operations have been highly labor-intensive, combining abundant low-wage Mexican labor with foreign capital and technology. In two respects, the US–Mexico maquiladora program has worked for Mexico much as the US–Canada Auto Pact worked for Canada: both allowed duty-free imports of components as an incentive for national production, and both served as foundation stones for wider free trade arrangements.

The first maquiladoras were established in 1965 under Mexico's Border Industrialization Program. In that year, 12 plants were opened; by March 1991 more than 1,900 plants were in operation (table 5.1; Giermanski 1991). The initial purposes of the program were to attract foreign investment and manufacturing facilities to the US–Mexico border region and to provide employment for Mexican farm workers disemployed by the end of the US Bracero Program.[2]

The maquiladora program was initially limited to the border zone, but with expanded authorization in 1972, maquiladoras have spread throughout Mexico. Nevertheless, about 80 percent of maquiladora operations remain in the border zone (Chrispin 1990, 78–79). The greatest maquiladora employment is in the border cities of Ciudad Juárez and Tijuana (table 5.2).

---

1. This introductory section draws on US International Trade Commission (1990b) and Weintraub (1990b).

2. The Bracero Program (1942–64) allowed migrant Mexican workers to enter the United States on a seasonal basis. An estimated 4 million Mexican laborers worked in the United States under this program between 1942 and 1960.

Table 5.1 Mexico: maquiladora employment and net exports, 1970–90

			Net exports[a]	
Year	Number of plants	Total employment	Millions of dollars	As a percentage of total Mexican merchandise exports
1970	120	20,327	83	6
1975	454	67,213	332	11
1980	578	119,546	772	5
1981	605	130,973	976	5
1982	585	127,048	851	4
1983	600	150,867	818	4
1984	722	199,684	1,155	5
1985	789	211,968	1,268	6
1986	844	249,833	1,295	8
1987	1,432	305,253	1,598	8
1988	1,441	369,489	2,337	11
1989	1,699	429,725	3,047	13
1990[b]	1,924	472,000	3,635	14

a. Figures reflect value added in Mexico.

b. Preliminary.

Sources: Sidney Weintraub, *A Marriage of Convenience: Relations Between Mexico and the United States* (New York: Twentieth Century Fund, 1990), 159; *The Maquiladora Industry in Mexico: Its Transitional Role* (Commission for the Study of International Migration and Cooperative Development, June 1990); Gabriel Székely, ed., *Manufacturing Across Borders and Oceans* (San Diego: University of California Center for US–Mexican Studies 1991), 121; Banco de México, *The Mexican Economy*, 1991.

Because of their proximity to the US market, which reduces transportation, managerial, and inventory costs by comparison with comparable low-wage operations in Asia, nearly all maquiladora output is destined for the US market. Maquiladoras are exempted by Mexico from duty on any raw materials or components that are processed for reexport (these imports are defined as "temporary importations under bond"). In addition, maquiladoras are exempted from duty on imported machinery and parts used in their export operations.

Maquiladora industries, like other industries in Mexico, receive favorable treatment both under the US Generalized System of Preferences (GSP) and under special provisions of the Harmonized Tariff System (HTS). Under the GSP, US duties are eliminated on certain imports from developing countries (in several sectors these benefits are sharply limited by "competitive need" tests and exemptions for sensitive industries). But in the aggregate, HTS benefits are much more important to the maquiladoras than the GSP. HTS items 9802.00.60 and

Table 5.2 Mexico: cities with the largest maquiladora employment, 1991

City	Number of maquiladoras	Number of employees
Ciudad Juárez	321	134,838
Tijuana	634	69,472
Matamoros	94	38,268
Reynosa–Rio Bravo	82	30,000
Chihuahua	61	29,229
Mexicali	160	22,000
Nogales	80	21,084
Nuevo Laredo	93	21,000
Monterrey	80	14,853
Ciudad Acuña	45	13,342

Source: Twin Plant News, September 1991, 68. Reprinted with permission.

9802.00.80 (formerly items 806.30 and 807.00 of the Tariff Schedules of the United States, TSUS) exclude from US customs valuation that portion of the imported article's value that is US–made. As a consequence, for eligible products, US duty is levied only on the value of Mexican processing and of Mexican and third-country components.[3]

---

3. HTS 9802.00.60 covers metals of US origin processed in a foreign location and returned for further US processing. HTS 9802.00.80 covers goods containing US–made components; this is by far the more important provision.

Metal Processing: Item 806.30 (old TSUS)—"Any article of metal (except precious metal) manufactured in the US or subjected to a process of manufacture in the US, if exported for further processing, and if the exported article as processed outside the US, or the article which results from the processing outside the US, is returned to the US for further processing... (there shall be levied)... A duty upon the value of such processing outside the US."

Assembly: Item 807.00 (old TSUS)—"Articles assembled abroad in whole or in part of fabricated components, the product of the US, which (a) were exported in condition ready for assembly without further fabrication, (b) have not lost their physical identity in such articles by change in form, shape, or otherwise, and (c) have not been advanced in value or improved condition abroad except by being assembled and except by operations incidental to the assembly process such as cleaning, lubricating and painting... [There shall be levied] a duty upon the full value of the imported article, less the cost or value of such products of the US."

A recent ruling by the US Court of International Trade held that the painting of automobile components does not disqualify them from item 807.00 treatment. This ruling, if it survives on appeal, will enlarge the range of permitted automotive processing, thus providing considerable additional benefit to Mexico (*Journal of Commerce*, 7 August 1991, 1A).

Characteristics of Maquiladora Operations

Employment

The majority of the early maquiladoras were established by US textile firms that moved certain of their operations to Mexico to take advantage of lower wages, and other firms whose production involved simple subassembly and required little skilled labor. The number of maquiladoras grew rapidly in the 1980s, mainly because real Mexican wages (in dollar terms) decreased in those years while wage rates in other developing countries rose.

Labor-intensive industries were attracted to Mexico's northern border region as a means of keeping pace with growing competition in the US market from other newly industrializing countries. As a result of several peso devaluations, the national average Mexican wage rate declined from a peak of $3.71 per hour in 1981 to $1.50 per hour in 1986. Thus, by 1986 Mexico's average wage rate was below those of Taiwan, Hong Kong, and Singapore (see table 6.9).

By 1990, maquiladora plants employed a total of 470,000 workers (table 5.1), representing about 26 percent of total manufacturing employment in the six northern Mexican states and about 11 percent of the national total.[4] The maquiladora work force is predominantly female: 62 percent in 1989 according to estimates of the Secretaría de Comercio y Fomento Industrial (SECOFI). However, this ratio has declined from about 80 percent in 1980, coincident with the emergence of labor shortages in the border area.

Maquiladoras located on the border currently experience annual turnover rates of 200 percent to 300 percent,[5] probably because their US owners prefer the advantage of low wage rates to the disadvantage of an unstable labor force. However, with the increasing sophistication of many plants and the higher costs of retraining the labor force, this calculus should change.

Maquiladoras can no longer all be lumped together as labor-intensive operations utilizing low technology. In many cases a higher level of technology is reflected in a wage bill that comprises only 10 percent to 25 percent of total costs, owing to advances in automated production techniques and microtechnology.[6]

---

4. These percentages are based on 1986 data cited in US Department of Labor, Bureau of International Labor Affairs (1990b, 57).

5. George (1990, 223). According to Alejandro Paz, Director of the Asociación de Maquiladoras de Chihuahua, turnover rates in that state range from 4 percent monthly to as high as 20 percent monthly (some of the highest rates are experienced by Japanese-owned firms). In Paz's opinion, wage levels are not the main factor affecting turnover rates.

6. Weintraub (1990b, 5). The emergence of a strong maquiladora motor vehicle industry, characterized by plants requiring sophisticated, up-to-date technology, has reinforced this trend. See also Fatemi (1990, 27).

Table 5.3 Mexico: maquiladoras and their employment, by industry, 1989

	Number of maquiladora plants	Share of maquiladora production (percentages)	Thousands of workers	Share of total maquiladora employment (percentages)
Total	1,699	100	444	100
Electrical and electronic goods	472	28	171	39
Textiles and apparel	255	15	42	9
Furniture	228	13	21	5
Transportation equipment	143	8	90	20
Other	601	35	120	27

Source: US International Trade Commission, *Review of Trade and Investment Liberalization Measures by Mexico and Prospects for Future United States-Mexican Relations* (USITC Publication 2275), April 1990, 5-13.

Moreover, maquiladora plants often require Mexican professionals (lawyers, consultants, accountants, and managers) in support and administrative positions.

At the end of 1989, maquiladora plants were concentrated in the manufacture of electrical and electronic goods (39 percent of maquiladora employment), textiles and apparel (9 percent), furniture (5 percent), and transportation equipment (nearly 20 percent of employment; table 5.3). In recent years, maquiladora growth has been somewhat faster in the medium- and high-technology end of the product spectrum (Chrispin 1990, 79–80).

Ownership

The maquiladora program is overseen by SECOFI, which reviews applications and issues the necessary licenses. Formally, there are three types of maquiladoras: captured, sheltered, and subcontracting. Captured maquilas are majority foreign-owned; sheltered maquilas are Mexican-owned but managed by a foreign corporation; subcontracting maquilas, also Mexican-owned, may or may not be foreign-managed and may have contracts with several foreign firms. Maquiladoras may be established in any industry except those reserved for state ownership (e.g., energy, air and maritime transportation). Since the start of the program, foreigners have been allowed 100 percent ownership of maquiladora subsidiaries (with the approval of the Comisión Nacional de Inversión Extranjera, or CNIE), under an exemption from the general requirement of a minimum 51 percent Mexican ownership under the Foreign Investment Law (see chapter 4).

US firms have been a major presence since the inception of the maquiladora program. More than half of the 100 largest US companies operate assembly plants in Mexico (*Financial Times*, 22 July 1991, 2). Mexican-owned maquiladoras, although large in number, tend to be relatively small and concentrated in the apparel and furniture industries. There are only six Canadian firms, operating eight plants, participating in the maquiladora program.[7] Most of their activity is in the auto parts sector, and they employ approximately 3,000 people. The main reasons that Canadian companies cite for moving to Mexico are much the same as those cited by US firms: inexpensive labor, preferential tariff treatment, and proximity to key markets (Grant et al. 1991, 57–59). European and Asian maquiladoras generally operate through US subsidiaries, and their production is typically destined for the US market. Some studies suggest that about 50 percent of new applications for establishing maquiladoras are being submitted by non–US manufacturers (Fatemi 1990, 10; for more information on ownership of the maquiladoras see chapter 4).

Exports

Growth in US imports from Mexico under HTS items 9802.00.60 and 9802.00.80 was rapid during the 1980s (table 5.4). Imports from Mexico under these HTS items increased from $5.6 billion (29 percent of total US imports from Mexico) in 1985 to $11.9 billion (45 percent of the total) in 1989.[8] Duty-free imports from Mexico under the GSP system were $2.5 billion in 1989, and GSP imports were often in the same product categories that enjoy HTS benefits.

Broadly speaking, the main industries benefiting from HTS and GSP preferences are automobiles and parts, electronic components, furniture, and textiles and

---

7. Canadian involvement is sometimes thought to be larger because a number of Canadian companies have joint ventures with Mexican firms, and because there is some confusion between Canadian companies and Canadian subsidiaries of US companies. For example, Mitel Corp. has a joint venture with Telmex in Guadalajara, and Woodbridge Foam Corp. has a joint venture with a Mexican foam company. In addition, some Canadian companies enter into joint operating agreements, which are similar but not identical to a maquiladora operation. Under such an agreement, the foreign company provides inputs and leases capital equipment to a Mexican company; this gives the foreign firm access to the Mexican market while also reducing its Mexican tax liability (Grant et al. 1991, 7, 18–21).

8. In 1989 total US imports under HTS from all countries amounted to $74.2 billion (16 percent of all US merchandise imports). In addition to Mexico, other large HTS suppliers were Canada ($26.5 billion), Japan ($16.9 billion), and Germany ($4.0 billion; US International Trade Commission 1991b, B-6 and B-14). Practically all the HTS imports are in HTS item 9802.00.80 (table 5.4).

apparel. In 1988 the breakdown of imports under HTS 9802.00.60 and 9802.00.80 was as follows: motor vehicles, 16.3 percent; electrical conductors, 9.9 percent; television receivers, 7.2 percent; motor vehicle parts, 5.8 percent; articles for making and breaking electrical circuits, 5.6 percent; internal combustion engines, 5.4 percent; and textiles and apparel, 5.3 percent (US International Trade Commission 1990b, 5–14).

Under HTS provisions, third-country (and other) maquiladoras receive duty-free treatment for the US content of their exports to the United States, regardless of the third-country content of the product. This benefit should be reconsidered in the determination of NAFTA rules of origin. Under Mexican in-bond provisions, third-country (and other) maquiladoras avoid Mexican duties on imported components, provided the final products are exported. This incentive, too, should be reconsidered: as in the Canada–US FTA, Mexico should eventually eliminate its in-bond provisions (see chapter 8).[9]

Maquiladoras are only a small part of the Mexican economy: in 1987 the gross output of maquiladora plants was equivalent to 5 percent of Mexican GDP, but their value added accounted for only about 1 percent (table 5.5). However, maquiladoras account for about 60 percent of Mexico's nonoil exports to the United States. They are Mexico's second-largest source of foreign exchange behind petroleum. In 1989 the value added in Mexican maquiladoras reached $3 billion (Banco de México, *The Mexican Economy,* 1991, 139). The wage bill accounts for 45 percent to 49 percent of the value added, operating expenses for 45 percent to 51 percent, and less than 6 percent of value added represents other Mexican inputs and packaging (Weintraub 1990, 4–5; Schoepfle 1990, 5).

The maquiladoras have successfully promoted industrial development at the border, but they remain something of an export enclave. From the standpoint of Mexico, an important question for the 1990s is how to strengthen the purchasing links between the maquiladoras and the rest of the Mexican economy.[10] Greater sourcing within Mexico is a logical, but elusive step. Even low-technology components such as plastic cases for electronic goods are still imported (Wilson 1990, 4).

---

9. In other words, duty drawback would only be allowed on a product that was trans-shipped, without physical alteration, say from Guatemala to Mexico, and then to the United States ("same-condition drawback"). However, during the transition period while North American tariffs are being phased out, duty drawback should be allowed on components shipped from one North American country to another, then processed and exported to a fourth country.

10. Weintraub (1990b, 10) argues that "[t]he export processing zone must increasingly become a productive operation fully part of Mexico's industrial and technical structure. Failing this, the great long-term opportunity of the maquiladora will be lost."

Table 5.4 United States: imports for consumption from Mexico under HTS 9802.00.60 and 9802.00.80 and GSP, 1985–89

	Total US imports from Mexico	GSP from Mexico	HTS 9802.00.60 from Mexico	HTS 9802.00.80 from Mexico	Total HTS from Mexico	Total HTS from all countries
1985						
Value (millions of dollars)	18,938	1,240	30	5,537	5,567	30,535
Percent of total		6.5	0.2	29.2	29.4	
Average tariff rate (percentages)						
Nominal			4.0	4.7		
Effective			2.8	3.6		
1986						
Value (millions of dollars)	17,196	1,443	90	6,367	6,457	36,497
Percent of total		8.4	0.5	37.0	37.5	
Average tariff rate (percentages)						
Nominal			4.9	4.3		
Effective			1.7	3.6		
1987						
Value (millions of dollars)	19,766	1,721	112	8,576	8,689	68,549
Percent of total		8.7	0.6	43.4	44.0	
Average tariff rate (percentages)						
Nominal			2.2	2.6		
Effective			1.2	2.1		

	22,617	2,192	131	10,654	10,785	73,733
1988						
Value (millions of dollars)	22,617	2,192	131	10,654	10,785	73,733
Percent of total		9.7	0.6	47.1	47.7	
Average tariff rate (percentages)						
Nominal			2.2	2.5		
Effective			1.1	1.9		
1989						
Value (millions of dollars)	26,557	2,471	181	11,767	11,948	74,173
Percent of total		9.3	0.7	44.3	45.0	
Average tariff rate (percentages)						
Nominal			2.2	2.4		
Effective			0.9	1.8		

Sources: US International Trade Commission, *Production Sharing: U.S. Imports Under Harmonized Tariff Schedule Subheadings 9802.00.60 and 9802.00.80, 1985–1988* (USITC Publication 2243), December 1989, 7-1; *Review of Trade and Investment Liberalization Measures by Mexico and Prospects for Future United States–Mexico Relations* (USITC Publication 2326), 1990, D-6; *Production Sharing: U.S. Imports Under Harmonized Tariff Schedule Subheadings 9802.00.60 and 9802.00.80, 1986–1988* (USITC Publication 2365), March 1991, 1–7, 1–8, B–2.

Table 5.5 Mexico: product composition of maquiladora output and value added, 1987 (millions of dollars)

	Output	Imported inputs	Mexican value added	Mexican value added as a percentage of total output
Total	7,105	5,507	1,598	22
Food	44	28	16	36
Textiles and apparel	410	308	101	25
Leather	78	58	20	25
Furniture	255	177	78	31
Chemicals	18	8	10	56
Transportation equipment	2,086	1,705	382	18
Nonelectronic machinery	116	87	28	24
Electrical machinery	1,309	1,025	283	22
Electronic components	1,847	1,454	393	21
Toys and sporting goods	152	108	44	29
Other manufacturing	681	490	192	28
Services	111	60	51	46

Source: Economic Development Corporation of San Diego County, *Maquiladora Industry: The Economic Impact on San Diego's Economy* (San Diego: Economic Development Corporation of San Diego County, June 1989), table 5, based on data from WEGI. Reprinted with permission.

Performance Incentives

Initially, a maquiladora's entire output had to be exported for the plant to enjoy duty-free importation of components from the United States or third countries. A 1983 decree authorized up to 20 percent of maquiladora production to be sold on the domestic market, but approval had to be granted on an item-by-item basis. Strict conditions regarding domestic content, technology transfer, and foreign-currency availability limited such authorizations; by early 1988, only 15 maquiladoras were authorized to sell their output in the domestic market.

A 1989 decree somewhat liberalized regulations governing domestic sales. A maquiladora may now qualify for duty remission if it sells locally an amount equal to 50 percent of the preceding year's total export sales, provided the local sales are additional to established exports. In effect, the new maximum level for domestic sales is now 33 percent of production (the previous limit was 20 percent). Approval to sell on the domestic market is now subject to less restrictive conditions: the plant must simply maintain a positive foreign-currency account, meaning that the value of imports used in the production of goods sold on the domestic market must be more than offset by expenditures of foreign currency in Mexico for operating expenses, purchases of supplies, wages, and the like (US International Trade Commission 1990b, 5–17).

When maquiladora goods are sold in the domestic market, the duty on the imported content may be calculated in one of two ways:

- The maquiladora may pay duties on the foreign content of the products according to the tariff rate applicable to the final good (a less onerous requirement now that the average Mexican tariff has been sharply reduced); or

- The maquiladora may opt to pay the duties applicable to the individual imported components; these rates are usually lower than the rate applicable to the final product.

Maquiladoras and the NAFTA

Maquiladoras have generated criticism from factions within both the United States and Mexico. Mexican critics contend that the maquiladora phenomenon has made their economy more dependent on the rest of the world, because maquiladoras are not really an integral part of Mexico and their control remains in the hands of foreigners. The follow-on accusation is that maquiladora employment offers no job insurance: if Mexican wages rise relative to those in other semideveloped countries, the operations may leave. Moreover, external conditions such as a prolonged US recession or the financial health of the parent company, can adversely affect maquiladora operations. Finally, there are various sociopolitical implications, especially the perception that border towns will become estranged from Mexico City and draw nearer to the United States in cultural and political terms (Weintraub 1990b, 6).

In the United States, criticism focuses on the export of American jobs[11] and exploitation of Mexican workers, the majority of which are young and female: examples of abuse of child labor laws and sweatshop conditions have been widely reported (*Wall Street Journal,* 8 April 1991, A1). Because of such concerns, US organized labor fought for the elimination of duty exemption under HTS 9802.00.60 and 9802.00.80, well before it took up the battle against a NAFTA.

Recent US Department of Labor econometric analysis (based on 1986 data for TSUS 807.00) suggests, however, that the elimination of HTS 9802.00.80, which is by far the larger of the two HTS categories, would have a fairly small effect on the level of US employment (Schoepfle and Pérez-López 1990; see also table 6.2

---

11. The leading Canadian study (Grant 1991, 32) suggests that the impact on Canada has been minimal—a loss of about 200 Canadian jobs.

of this study). The elimination of item 807.00 imports from all sources could result in a gain of 18,000 jobs if the goods were replaced by US–made products; on the other hand, 16,000 jobs could actually be lost if the goods were replaced by products from other sources. The elimination of item 807.00 imports from Mexico alone could increase job opportunities by 6,000 or reduce them by 5,000, depending on the source of the replacement goods (see table 6.2).

The Labor Department study suggests that changes in the distribution of US employment among various industries would be more dramatic than the aggregate net gain or loss of jobs within the US economy. For example, US employment in textiles and apparel, and electrical and electronic goods, would likely grow significantly following the removal of HTS benefits.[12] In the same spirit, one econometric study reports that a NAFTA with Mexico—which can be interpreted as a wholesale extension of the maquiladora concept—would result in the loss of 1,000 US jobs in the textile industry, 4,400 US jobs in the apparel industry, and 5,200 US jobs in the electrical equipment and electronic components industries (KPMG Peat Marwick 1991, 19–20). Organized labor believes that estimates such as these vastly understate the maquiladoras' effect on "exporting jobs."[13]

Labor's criticism is countered by the argument that US jobs inevitably face competition from low-wage countries, whether from Mexico or Malaysia or elsewhere, and that a shift of this competition to Mexico is the better outcome because of the spin-off benefits to the US economy. Indeed, some new Mexican jobs will come directly from Asia, where several US companies earlier moved in search of lower wages. A few companies are already planning to relocate. InterAmerican Holdings Co., for example, is moving 2,000 jobs from China to Mexico (*Business Week*, 1 July 1991, 43). Hugh McCaffrey, president of San Diego Alta, which operates an industrial park in Mexico, said that his company already has six clients that are planning to move from Taiwan, Korea, China, and Hong Kong to Mexico (*El Nacional*, 28 June 1991). Arguably a major effect on the automobile and auto parts industry will be a relocation of activity from East Asia to North America (see chapter 11).

In addition, small and medium-sized US firms that might otherwise have been driven out of the market by foreign low-wage competition may be able to stay

---

12. Elimination of HTS imports from all sources could increase job opportunities by almost 13,000 in the textile and apparel industries and by 2,000 in the electronics industry, if the imports are replaced by US products (Schoepfle and Pérez-López 1990, table 1).

13. In the debate over extension of the fast-track authority of US trade law in the spring of 1991, organized labor did not release specific figures for potential job losses, but it did make some qualitative statements: "The one thing we do know is that some 500,000 Mexican workers produce goods destined almost solely for the US market. If our market was being serviced by domestic production, even taking productivity differences into account, US employment would clearly be hundreds of thousands higher" (American Federation of Labor and Congress of Industrial Organizations 1991, 4).

in business by acquiring cheap components made by maquiladoras. Finally, increased sales in Mexico practically fall into the lap of US firms. As Under Secretary of State for Economic Affairs Robert B. Zoellick has noted, "for each dollar of growth in Mexico, about 15 cents is spent on US goods. As Mexico grows, it will import more. Seventy cents of each Mexican-import dollar is spent on goods from the United States" (*Washington Post*, 20 April 1991, C7). In contrast, US firms must engage in concerted marketing efforts to reach booming markets in Thailand or Malaysia.

Other US critics point to a different set of potential problems stemming from increased maquiladora activity. Environmental groups and others describe the border region as a potential ecological disaster zone because of pollution, buried toxic chemicals, and sludge. A report for the American Medical Association labeled the region "a virtual cesspool" and found "the environmental health problems of the US–Mexico border to be of major magnitude" (Council on Scientific Affairs, American Medical Association 1990). So-called dirty industries allegedly set up in Mexico because environmental controls there are less strict, or are less well enforced, than US and other countries' standards.

Under Mexican legislation and a US–Mexico binational agreement signed in 1983 (the La Paz Agreement), waste generated by US maquiladoras is supposed to be transported back to the United States. However, loopholes have been used to avoid this requirement, because the cost of disposing of hazardous waste in Mexico is about one-tenth the cost in the United States.[14] Illegal dumping of waste also occurs because Mexico's environmental regulatory agency, the Secretaría de Desarrollo Urbano y Ecología (SEDUE), is short-staffed and under-funded. According to one US nonprofit environmental group, The Border Ecology Project, the maquiladoras cannot account for 95 percent of the waste they generated between 1969 and 1989.[15]

Recommendations

Maquiladora operations have served as a lightning rod for larger social issues—principally labor and environmental conditions—that permeate the Mexican economy.[16] Solutions to these issues will not be found by focusing on the

---

14. Data reported by Roberto Sánchez, from a Tijuana-based research institute, cited in *Journal of Commerce*, 7 August 1990, 5A. See also *Financial Times*, July 1991, 2.

15. *Journal of Commerce*, 7 August 1990, 5A. See also the testimonies of Mark A. Anderson, an economist with the AFL-CIO, and Steve Beckman, an economist with the United Auto Workers, in US Congress, House Committee on Ways and Means, Subcommittee on Trade (1990), and Giermanski (1991, 13).

16. This section draws on Giermanski (1991, 7–17).

afflictions of the maquiladora sector. Instead, the answers will come through continuing Mexican reform, and through NAFTA and other accords that encompass the entire North American economy, as we discuss in chapters 6 and 7.

The questions specific to the maquiladoras are much narrower. How will the system of duty-free treatment for imported components destined for reexport be meshed with the larger framework of a free trade area? And how will the Mexican policy of conditioning maquiladora sales to the domestic market on maquiladora exports be phased out?

A major competitive advantage of maquiladora production—favorable tariff treatment under HTS 9802.00.60 and 9802.00.80 and the GSP—will slowly merge into the greater elimination of all tariffs. Under the Canada–US FTA, import duties are being phased out incrementally and will terminate in 1998; if a similar tariff phaseout schedule is applied to US and Canadian trade with Mexico, preferences under HTS 9802.00.60 and 9802.0080 and the GSP will cease to have practical relevance by 1998 and can be abolished.

However, the broad merger of maquiladora and NAFTA benefits does not resolve all the issues. One important question is how NAFTA rules of origin will affect maquiladoras. Currently, maquiladoras can benefit from HTS 9802.00.60 and 9802.00.80 regardless, for example, of how many Korean components are installed in a piece of electronic gear. That same piece of gear might not qualify under NAFTA rules of origin, and its entire value, including any US components, would then be subject to US duty, once the NAFTA-supersedes HTS benefits.

Our recommendation, set forth in detail in chapter 8, is that generally applicable NAFTA rules of origin should be applied to maquiladora shipments after a short transition period—say, by January 1996. In other words, after 1995 the benefits of HTS 9802.00.60 and 9802.00.80 would be withdrawn if the goods in question do not meet the NAFTA rules of origin.

Provided that a liberal change-of-tariff-heading (CTH) rule of origin is adopted as the basic rule in the NAFTA (as recommended in chapter 8), we see no merit in granting special benefits to maquiladora activities that cannot meet the CTH test. The more difficult problem arises in the automotive, textile, and apparel industries, where more demanding rules than the CTH test are likely to be adopted. Even in these areas our general position is to oppose more demanding rules of origin; but if special rules are adopted, they should be applied to maquiladora production just like any other production.

A more pressing question is the status of Mexican in-bond provisions. In-bond treatment really amounts to duty-free entry of foreign components into the NAFTA area, provided that the assembled item meets the NAFTA rules of origin test. From the standpoint of the rest of the world, this is an extremely liberal provision. However, from the standpoint of US politicians who worry about Asian countries converting Mexico into an "export platform,"[17] and of economists who worry about efficient location of production within a free trade area,[18] the in-bond provisions are unsustainable. Reflecting similar (if more muted) concerns, duty drawback will be eliminated on all US–Canada trade under the FTA by 1994. The same prohibitions should apply within the NAFTA by 1996.[19]

The most serious issue relating to the maquiladora phenomenon is the force-feeding of maquiladora exports by linked access to the increasingly rich domestic Mexican market. Under the 1989 decree, maquiladora access to the internal Mexican market is conditioned on earning an equivalent amount of foreign exchange through exports. This distortion, which essentially amounts to an export subsidy, should come to an end. The issue is one of phasing, particularly for automotive products. As we explain in chapter 11, Canada conditions its benefits, both under the Auto Pact and under the FTA, on produced-in-Canada tests. However, Mexico should not be able to prolong indefinitely its linked export incentives under the maquiladora program by pointing to Canadian practices. These Canadian practices were grandfathered as part of the overall FTA bargain, not because they represent model commercial policy.

Our recommendation is twofold. First, all Mexican linked export incentives, outside the automotive sector, should be swiftly eliminated—say, within three years. Maquiladoras should be perfectly free to sell within Mexico, upon payment of duties at the appropriate rate (NAFTA or otherwise) on imported components. Second, for the automotive sector, linked Mexican export incentives should be phased out over a longer period of, say, five years (see chapter 11).

With these reforms the distinctions between maquiladoras and other industries will gradually disappear. In conjunction with NAFTA rules of origin, these reforms should assuage concerns that Mexico could become an export platform into the US market for third-country suppliers.

---

17. See, for example, the remarks of House Majority Leader Richard A. Gephardt (D-MO) at the Institute for International Economics (Gephardt 1991).

18. To illustrate the efficiency problem, consider a manufacturing operation that uses components from Asia. Continuation of the in-bond practice would favor production in Mexico over production in the United States. In the case of Mexican production, the components would escape all duty once tariffs between the United States and Mexico are eliminated; in the case of US production, the components would still pay the US duty on imports from a fourth country.

19. Contrary to this recommendation, the National Customs Brokers and Forwarders Association insists on the retention of duty drawback in its present form, arguing that "those incentives play only a minimal role in a company's decision to invest in Mexico" (*Journal of Commerce*, 12 December 1991, 5A).

6

Labor Issues

During the US debate on fast-track authority for trade negotiations with Mexico, much of the opposition to a NAFTA focused on potential US job losses. Two principal fears were expressed: low-wage competition from Mexico, and inadequate Mexican enforcement of labor standards. Together these two factors are seen as an incentive for investment to flow into Mexico at the expense of the United States. Opponents of a NAFTA also maintain that disparities in working conditions between the two countries would provide Mexico with an unfair trade advantage.[1] Similar concerns have been raised in the Canadian debate over the NAFTA. (Table 6.1 compares the US, Canadian, and Mexican labor forces.)

Proponents of a NAFTA concede that Mexican wages are low and that enforcement of labor standards has been lax, but contend that the best way to improve Mexican living standards is to stimulate trade and investment through freer trade.

The Jobs Debate in the United States and Canada

Various empirical studies have attempted to predict the positive and negative consequences for US labor of a free trade agreement with Mexico. A US Department of Labor study (1990) predicts a net US gain from a NAFTA of 64,000 jobs

---

1. Issues related to working conditions include minimum wages, working hours, and occupational health and safety. Since the inclusion of a workers' rights provision in the 1983 Caribbean Basin Initiative there has been a growing interest in using US trade law to promote international labor standards. The Generalized System of Preferences was modified to include workers' rights provisions, and the Omnibus Trade and Competitiveness Act of 1988 defines workers' rights as an objective of US trade policy: section 1301(d)(B)(iii) labels violations of workers' rights as an unfair trade practice, actionable by the President (see US Department of Labor, Bureau of International Labor Affairs, 1990a, 1, 8–10).

Diana E. Clark helped draft this chapter.

Table 6.1 Sectoral composition of the US, Canadian, and Mexican labor forces, 1989

Sector	United States	Mexico[a]	Canada
Total employment (millions)	117.3	26.3	13.6
Sectoral distribution (percentages)			
Agriculture	2.7	26.0	4.5
Mining	0.7	1.3	1.5
Construction	4.4	9.5	2.2
Manufacturing	16.5	12.8	17.5
Services	70.8	50.4	66.5
Transportation and public utilities	4.8	5.1	6.3
Wholesale and retail trade	22.0	13.9	21.3
Finance, insurance, and real estate	5.7	—[c]	5.7
Other services	23.1	31.4[b]	33.2
Government	15.1	—[c]	6.7

a. The reported total Mexican labor force may be understated by these estimates. According to the Mexican Secretariat of Labor and Social Welfare, the total labor force numbered 29.8 million in 1990.

b. Includes finance, insurance, real estate, and government.

c. Included in other services.

Sources: Economic Report of the President, February 1991, table B-43; US Department of Labor, Bureau of International Labor Affairs, Foreign Labor Trends, 90-32; OECD Economic Survey—Canada, 1990; US Department of State, Background Notes: Mexico, May 1990.

(88,000 jobs added and 24,000 jobs lost) over 10 years.[2] This estimate lies near the middle of the range of studies published to date.

Estimates done by or for labor unions tend to project much more dramatic US job losses. Indeed, union officials argue that a large number of jobs have *already* been lost from factories moving to Mexico (the estimates range from 25,000 on up; *The Oregonian [Portland],* 5 May 1991, S1). Jeff Faux, president of the Economic Policy Institute, believes that "no one can accurately predict the outcome of this proposition with any accuracy. It is a question of judging risk" (statement in US Congress, Senate Committee on Finance 1991, 2). He points

---

2. The study was conducted by groups from the University of Maryland (INFORM) and the University of Guanajuato, Mexico (CIMAT). Clopper Almon of the University of Maryland was the project director. Of the 64,000 net increase in jobs, 48,000 would be in the manufacturing sector and nearly 12,000 in agriculture (see White House 1991, table 1, 6).

out, however, that most US job losses will occur among non-college-educated workers, who tend to be at the lower end of the wage scale.

According to a study by the Cato Institute (Salinas-León 1991, 9), a NAFTA would negatively affect several labor-intensive manufacturing industries in the United States, particularly in the northern states. Those industries represent 23 percent of America's GNP and employ 18 percent of the US labor force.

Drawing on results of a computable general equilibrium (CGE) model, Raul Hinojosa-Ojeda and Sherman Robinson (1991) suggest that US job losses could reach 350,000 under a scenario that included a comprehensive elimination of all trade barriers and a NAFTA that was completely porous to Asian trade and investment. Their model assumes that Mexican capital stock is increased by $25 billion (a 7.6 percent increase), and that productivity increases in both countries.

Other studies predict a small but positive impact on the US labor force. A study commissioned from KPMG Peat Marwick by the Mexico–US Business Committee (KPMG Peat Marwick 1991) estimates job gains similar to those in the Labor Department study. In sectors and industries likely to face strong competition from Mexico (textiles, apparel, sugar, fruits and vegetables), the projected job losses total 7,000; many other sectors stand to gain, however, yielding a net increase of 61,000 jobs. Finally, at the higher end of optimistic estimates, Rudiger Dornbusch of the Massachusetts Institute of Technology has projected that an FTA could show a net gain of "at least 150,000 good US jobs" over its first five years.[3]

The potential impact of a NAFTA on the US labor force can also be gauged by reviewing the employment effects of tariff preferences under former item 807.00 of the Tariff Schedules of the United States (TSUS), the US legal umbrella for the maquiladora program.[4] A recent US Department of Labor study estimated that the repeal of TSUS item 807.00 preferences would have a fairly small net effect on the level of US employment, ranging from a gain of 18,000 jobs to a loss of 16,000 jobs, depending on whether maquiladora goods were replaced by US

---

3. Testimony in US Congress, Senate Committee on Finance (1991). Researchers at the Economic Strategy Institute (Prestowitz and Cohen 1991, table 1, 60) also foresee large US job gains, in the range of 225,000 to 264,000, but only if NAFTA trade is appropriately "managed" to displace third-country imports (especially Asian imports) from the North American market. The explicit "management" of North American trade with an eye toward displacing Asian imports could violate the GATT obligations of the NAFTA partners and could well spur a similar bout of "management" on the part of the Asian countries affected.

4. TSUS item 807.00, in effect since 1963, provides for duty-free treatment of US–made components used in the assembly of products for the US market. The present version is HTS 9802.00.80. An importer into the US market can take advantage of TSUS item 807.00 without operating a maquiladora plant in Mexico, but in practice the vast preponderance of 807.00 imports come from maquiladora plants. (See chapter 5 for details on the maquiladora program.)

products or by imports from third countries (table 6.2). These results seem to rebut the oft-repeated contention that repeal of TSUS item 807.00 would lead to a substantial return of lost jobs to the United States. If the NAFTA exerted an employment effect four times the size of the maquiladora program (probably an outside estimate), its net impact would range from a loss of 69,000 jobs to a gain of 72,000 jobs. Our own view, spelled out in chapter 3, is that about 112,000 US workers would be dislocated by a NAFTA and that these gross job losses would occur over a period of years, thereby moderating the adjustment burden. On balance, we think that a NAFTA will lead to a net gain of new jobs both in the United States (130,000 net new jobs created) and in Mexico (609,000 net new jobs; see table 3.4).

A second and related concern for labor is whether a NAFTA will exert a dampening effect on real wage rates in the United States. A US International Trade Commission study predicts that "all classes of [US] workers find their real income [will] increase as a result of a free trade agreement."[5] Most of the CGE models predict very small average wage gains, generally less than 0.1 percent in the United States (table 3.4).

One study took a nuanced look at various segments of the labor market. McCleery and Reynolds (1991) calculated the wage impact by the year 2000 under four scenarios: free trade only, free trade with capital movement and increased investor confidence, free trade with more efficient resource allocation in Mexico, and free trade with productivity gains in the United States (table 6.3). Under all four scenarios, the United States experiences a net increase in high-wage incomes and a net decrease in low-wage incomes.[6] The study assumes that productivity levels in the United States and Mexico will begin to converge with or without a free trade agreement, and the authors find that free trade will accelerate the convergence process. With free trade, McCleery and Reynolds estimate a "positive convergence" of productivity levels and wages in the high end of the job market (i.e., Mexico catches up slightly relative to the United

---

5. Internal US International Trade Commission memorandum of 8 March 1991, as reported in *Inside U.S. Trade,* 22 March 1991. An earlier commission report acknowledged the possibility that "unskilled workers in the United States would suffer a slight decline in real income," although under certain circumstances, such as limited substitutability between Mexican imports and US import-competing products, all workers would benefit (US International Trade Commission 1991a, 2–6). The March 1991 memorandum clarified the earlier statement and incorporated a new round of estimates, using lower cross-elasticities of substitution between US and Mexican products.

6. McCleery and Reynolds estimate that the US low-wage sector has 14 million workers out of a total US labor force of 140 million, of whom 130 million are employed. Their findings reflect a theoretical expectation that free trade between Mexico (with its abundant low-skilled labor and scarce high-skilled labor) and the United States (with less abundant low-skilled labor and more plentiful high-skilled labor) will, to a small extent, drive up US wages for high-skilled workers and drive down US wages for low-skilled workers.

Table 6.2 Hypothetical impact of the elimination of TSUS 807.00 on US employment, by industry, 1986 (work years)[a]

Industry	All imports under 807.00 replaced by US products		All imports under 807.00 replaced by other imports	
	From Mexico	From world	From Mexico	From world
Textiles and apparel	3,810	12,567	-3,065	-9,163
Footwear	430	1,100	-590	-819
Furniture, mattresses, and pillows	40	40	-10	-59
Industrial papers and packaging	35	46	-5	-47
Chemicals	35	67	-25	-70
Fabricated metal products	50	130	-45	-143
Internal combustion engines	50	88	-15	-92
Office machines	10	127	-5	-178
Motors, generators, and transformers	90	119	-65	-132
Television apparatus	140	170	-50	-278
Radio and telephonic equipment	100	258	-50	-316
Tape recorders and record players	60	75	-20	-180
Semiconductors	10	90	-7	-115
Other electrical articles	830	1,341	-600	-1,449
Motor vehicles	5	137	-3	-163
Motor vehicle parts, rail locomotives, rolling stock, industrial vehicles, and motorcycles	30	199	-40	-223
Other machinery and equipment	10	66	-15	-73
Scientific instruments	150	274	-145	-303
Miscellaneous manufactures	180	669	-170	-1,742
Total	6,065	17,563	-4,925	-15,545

a. Negative numbers indicate a decline in US employment. The calculations in the first two columns assume that 807.00 imports are replaced dollar-for-dollar by domestic products; the calculations in the next two columns assume that 807.00 imports are replaced by finished products from from third countries that do not incorporate US-made components.

Source: US International Trade Commission, The Use and Economic Impact of TSUS Items 806.30 and 807.00 (USITC Publication 2053), January 1988, table 7-19.

Table 6.3 Simulation estimates of the impact of a NAFTA on US wages, for the year 2000 (billions of dollars)

Group	Basic free trade scenario	Scenario 2[a]	Scenario 3[b]	Scenario 4[c]
High-wage earners	2.9	4.0	2.9	5.5
Low-wage earners	−0.7	−2.9	−0.7	−0.5

a. Free trade with capital movement.

b. Free trade with more efficient resource allocation in Mexico.

c. Free trade with productivity gains in the United States.

Source: Adapted from data in Robert K. McCleery and Clark W. Reynolds, "A Study of the Impact of a US–Mexico Free Trade Agreement on Medium-Term Employment, Wages, and Production in the United States: Are New Labor Market Policies Needed?" Paper presented at a conference at the Center for Strategic and International Studies, Washington, 27–28 June 1991.

States, but both countries gain). At the low end of the labor market, however, McCleery and Reynolds estimate that free trade will lead to "negative convergence" (i.e., a slight fall in US labor productivity and wages in low-skilled jobs relative to the status quo without free trade; McCleery and Reynolds 1991, 2).

Another estimate of the effects of a NAFTA on US wage rates comes from Edward E. Leamer of the University of California, Los Angeles (1991). Leamer believes that real wages for unskilled workers in the United States will be depressed from their baseline levels over the next several decades as a result of the global integration of production and competition from hundreds of millions of unskilled workers in the developing world. This will happen regardless of whether a NAFTA is implemented. However, in Leamer's view, the NAFTA can only accelerate the pressure on unskilled wages.[7]

Pessimism about the wage outlook for unskilled workers also emerges from a study by George Borjas, Richard Freeman, and Lawrence Katz (1991). They find that US high school dropouts experienced a 10 percent relative wage decline between 1980 and 1988. They attribute 30 percent to 50 percent of the decline to the combined impact of the US trade deficit and increased migration; they

---

7. Leamer (1991, 9). This pressure is reflected in Zenith's announcement that it would shift the last of its US television assembly to Mexico, taking away about 1,200 semiskilled American jobs. According to chairman Jerry Pearlman, the move "is a necessary component of Zenith's programs to reduce costs and improve profitability." But Zenith's production relocation also reflects comparative advantage, as Pearlman declared, "all of our knowledge workers" will remain in the United States (*Journal of Commerce,* 31 October 1991, 1A; *Financial Times,* 6 December 1991, 26).

Table 6.4 Government expenditures on labor market programs in selected industrialized countries, 1988–90 (percentages of GDP)

Country	Training	Unemployment compensation	Total labor market programs
France	0.28	1.34	2.87
Germany	0.23	1.30	2.32
Canada	0.22	1.58	2.09
United Kingdom	0.22	0.94	1.62
United States	0.10	0.38	0.62
Japan	n.a.	0.36	0.52

n.a. = not available.

Source: Organization of Economic Cooperation and Development, *Labor Market Policies for the 1990s* (Paris: OECD, 1990), table 14.

attribute another 30 percent to 50 percent to the fall in the number of unionized workers in the United States.

We agree that the long-term outlook for unskilled US and Canadian workers is bleak. But we think it is wrong to commingle this general outlook with the specific impact of the NAFTA. Over the long term, US and Canadian wage gains will reflect US and Canadian productivity gains. Even the most robust possible free trade area will be a small part of the productivity story in the United States and Canada. Productivity will be far more affected by investment in private equipment and public infrastructure, by technological factors, and by the education and training of the US and Canadian work forces, than by commerce with Mexico. The main factor determining the relative wage prospects of unskilled workers is whether public and private programs enable them to shed their unskilled status. We are skeptical that even ten years after the NAFTA has been in force it will be possible to detect a specific adverse effect on the wages of unskilled US and Canadian workers—even though this segment of the work force will continue to suffer declining relative wages.

US Adjustment Programs

US expenditures on labor market programs are lower, and benefits are provided for shorter time periods, than in most other industrialized countries (table 6.4). By comparison with Canada and Europe, the United States provides substantially less assistance through unemployment compensation, retraining, job search, and redevelopment programs for people and communities dislocated by various forms of economic change, including foreign competition.

Meager US labor adjustment programs probably serve to lengthen the period of transitional unemployment in the US economy and contribute to the pool of hard-core "discouraged" workers. (On the other hand, the limited duration of unemployment compensation in the United States may encourage laid-off workers to find new jobs quickly.) A recent national survey of dislocated workers (reported by Jeff Faux) found that, in January 1986, approximately one-third of workers who had lost their jobs in plant closings during the early 1980s were still unemployed.[8] The absence of effective labor programs also has political consequences. According to Howard F. Rosen (see statement in US Congress, House Committee on the Budget 1991, 183) of the Institute for International Economics, "Inadequate programs feed the sense of insecurity which targeted workers experience as they face the prospect of economic change, strengthening their opposition to such change."

The United States has three major labor market programs. The economy-wide unemployment insurance program provides unemployed workers with income maintenance payments; the Job Training Partnership Act (JTPA) provides dislocated workers (whatever the cause of their dislocation) with job search and training assistance programs;[9] and the Trade Adjustment Assistance (TAA) program provides targeted assistance for trade-impacted workers.

By far the largest program is the unemployment insurance program; in 1988, for example, benefits paid out amounted to $13.2 billion. In 1990, unemployment insurance covered 37 percent of unemployed workers, reaching a total of 2.5 million people (statement by Howard F. Rosen in US Congress, House Committee on the Budget 1991, table 1, 5). The main goal of unemployment insurance is to offset income loss for up to six to nine months while a worker is unemployed.[10] Payments are based on the worker's previous wage experience; more emphasis is given to paying benefits during temporary layoffs than to providing retraining and relocation assistance when job losses are permanent.

---

8. See page 4 of the statement by Faux cited above. This bleak picture is contested by a more recent study of a sample of 20,000 displaced workers in North Carolina during the three-year period ending in 1989. The results of the North Carolina study, reported by Alfred S. Field and Edward M. Graham, showed that some 92 percent of manufacturing workers dislocated by plant closings found alternative employment after about 2.0 quarters, at the same or lower wages. (See Southern International Policy Network, *Clearinghouse on State International Policies*, June 1991, 6.)

9. Dislocated workers are defined as "those people laid off and who are unlikely to return to their previous industry or occupation, including those workers who lost their jobs as a result of a permanent plant closing, and long-term unemployed who have substantial barriers to employment, such as age or lack of skills" (statement by Howard F. Rosen in US Congress, House Committee on the Budget 1991, 187).

10. Although there is a wide variation among states, payments average 35 percent to 40 percent of the previous year's wages for 26 weeks. Benefits can be extended for 13 weeks in case of a severe economic downturn. Congressional efforts during the 1991 recession to extend the normal 26-week period were sidetracked by the Bush administration, which cited the impact on the huge US budget deficit (*Wall Street Journal*, 5 August 1991, A14) but a 13-week extension was eventually approved.

Table 6.5 Participation in and expenditures of the US Job Training Partnership Act program, 1984–89 and projected 1990–92[a]

Year	Participants[b]	Expenditures (millions of dollars)
1984	173,002	162
1985	209,873	190
1986	219,622	193
1987	186,052	177
1988	207,575	256
1989	234,843	307
1990[c]	n.a.	427
1991[c]	n.a.	515
1992[c]	n.a.	527

n.a. = not available.

a. Based on program year (July to June).

b. Includes participants continuing from the previous year.

c. Based on fiscal-year budget projections.

Source: US Department of Labor, unpublished data.

Indeed, the unemployment insurance program contributes to the tendency of displaced workers to seek work in the declining industries from which they have been laid off rather than to retrain for new jobs (McCleery and Reynolds 1991, 5).

In 1989 the JTPA program provided benefits to 235,000 participants at an average cost per participant of $1,308. The budget for the JTPA program has grown steadily from $162 million in 1984 to a projected $527 million in fiscal 1992 (table 6.5). The program empowers local officials to allocate federal funds. This approach has proven to be an effective way of providing training assistance to targeted populations: according to a survey, 70 percent of JTPA participants found new jobs (statement by Rosen in US Congress, House Committee on the Budget 1991). However, this success rate must be tempered by the fact that, between 1985 and 1989, only 18 percent of all dislocated workers participated in the program. In its present form, the program is much too small to address the overall labor adjustment pressures in the US economy.[11]

---

11. There have been at least two evaluations of the effectiveness of the JTPA: one, by the US General Accounting Office (1987), estimated that fewer than 10 percent of eligible displaced workers benefitted from the program; the other, by Margareth Simms (cited by Rosen in US Congress, House Committee on the Budget 1991, 188), reported that those workers with the greatest need for assistance (i.e., older and less-educated workers) were inadequately served by the program.

The TAA program was established in 1962 to provide income support and job retraining and relocation assistance for workers displaced by import competition. Until the mid–1970s, the TAA program was relatively inactive because of strict eligibility requirements. The Trade Act of 1974 loosened the requirements; easier eligibility tests, coupled with a slowdown in the automobile sector, resulted in a dramatic increase in the number of petitions for TAA benefits (statement by Rosen in US Congress, House Committee on the Budget 1991). In 1980–81, total TAA expenditures exceeded $3 billion, and the program became a target of the Reagan budget cuts. Thereafter annual outlays ranged from $35 million to $208 million during the 1980s (table 6.6).

In 1989, income maintenance payments (called trade readjustment allowances, or TRAS) under the TAA totaled $125 million (primarily outlays for job retraining); expenditures for job search and relocation were minuscule (statement by Howard F. Rosen in US Congress, House Committee on Ways and Means, Subcommittee on Trade 1991, 9). About 24,000 workers received TRAS, for an average payment per worker of $5,300 (table 6.6). The TAA budget is scheduled to rise to $154 million in fiscal 1992, but in its 1993 budget the Bush administration has proposed abolishing TAA and transferring its appropriations to JTPA programs (*Budget of the United States Government, Fiscal Year 1993*, Appendix One-676).

In its May 1991 Action Plan, the Bush administration argued that labor adjustment problems arising from a NAFTA could be dealt with through existing programs that emphasize retraining more than income maintenance, such as the 1988 Economic Dislocation and Worker Adjustment Assistance Act (EDWAA; Title III of the JTPA). According to the US Department of Labor, EDWAA costs $1,200 per worker, and its training programs have succeeded in placing 70 percent of those enrolled in new jobs. This compares favorably with the TAA program, which costs about $7,000 per worker (taking into account TRA, training, and other benefits) and has a placement rate of only 35 percent.[12] This comparison, however, is misleading; EDWAA benefits are focused on a segment of the unemployed population who are much easier to place than TAA clients.

Canadian Adjustment Programs

Canada faces many of the same labor adjustment problems that confront the United States but has developed a broader array of programs to address them.[13]

---

12. *New York Times*, 6 May 1991, D2. As an additional comparison, the average benefits of the unemployment insurance program per worker for the period from September 1990 to August 1991 were $2,400 (figure supplied by Cindy Ambler, Bureau of Labor Statistics, October 1991).

13. This section draws on Economic Council of Canada (1988).

Table 6.6 Participation in and expenditures of the US Trade Adjustment Assistance programs, 1975–89

| | Number of workers | | | | | Outlays (millions of dollars) | | | |
Year	Certified workers	Receiving TRAs	Entered training	Job search	Relocation	TRA[a]	Job training	Job search	Relocation
1975	34,879	47,000	463	158	44	71	n.a.	n.a.	n.a.
1980	684,766	531,895	9,475	931	629	1,622	5	negl.	1
1981	51,072	281,426	20,366	1,491	2,011	1,440	2	negl.	2
1982	19,456	30,463	5,844	697	662	103	33	n.a.	1
1983	56,173	30,032	11,299	696	3,269	37	17	n.a.	3
1984	19,688	15,821	6,821	799	2,220	35	30	negl.	2
1985	25,339	20,300	7,424	916	1,692	40	29	n.a.	n.a.
1986	93,132	42,000	7,743	1,384	1,089	119	n.a.	n.a.	n.a.
1987	103,805	55,289	22,888	1,709	1,537	208	n.a.	n.a.	n.a.
1988	60,920	46,882	9,528	1,156	1,347	186	n.a.	n.a.	n.a.
1989	89,021	23,681	17,042	863	989	125	n.a.	n.a.	n.a.

TRA = trade readjustment allowance.

n.a. = not available.

negl. = negligible (less than $500,000).

a. Projected outlays for 1990–92 are $101 million, $170 million, and $154 million.

Source: US Department of Labor, Office of Trade Adjustment Assistance, unpublished data.

As in the United States, the largest form of Canadian support is unemployment insurance, which in 1985 provided C$10 billion in income maintenance to 3.2 million claimants.[14] The Canadian unemployment insurance system covers a larger percentage of the unemployed than the US system, and the replacement rate (the ratio of benefits to prior wages) is usually higher. To limit regional imbalances, the Canadian system offers more generous insurance to unemployed workers in high-unemployment provinces,[15] thereby reducing the incentive to look for a job in another province or even in another sector. These regionally selective benefits tend to subsidize declining activities, diverting attention from efforts to improve labor mobility (Organization for Economic Cooperation and Development [OECD] 1990, 96).

On the other hand, recent reforms within the Canadian unemployment insurance system have reallocated funds from straight benefits to training and reemployment programs. To free up resources, the reforms tighten the eligibility criteria, shorten the duration of benefits, and impose penalties on those who quit their jobs without a valid reason.[16]

The Canadian government maintains an Industrial Adjustment Service (IAS). Its main function is to make information available to both employers and employees about the full range of Canadian Employment and Immigration Commission (CEIC) and Labor Canada programs, and about developments in the labor market. In its broad outlines, the Canadian program provides services similar to those available from the employment security systems of several US states.

In addition, Canada has a program that provides income maintenance and other preretirement benefits for older workers. The Program for Older Worker Adjustment (POWA), announced in 1986, applies to "older workers who lost their jobs through major layoffs or plant closures and who have no immediate prospects for re-employment" (Economic Council of Canada 1988, 36). The program is designed to be both a federal and a provincial endeavor, with an initial allocation of C$125 million for its first four years. POWA supersedes the preretirement program adopted in the 1970s and 1980s for workers in trade-sensitive industries. But overall, neither POWA nor other Canadian programs

---

14. Both the United States and Canada have historically applied only 20 percent to 30 percent of unemployment insurance funds to non–income maintenance programs (McCleery and Reynolds 1991, 6).

15. The four Western provinces and the Atlantic provinces are thought to be more vulnerable to shocks because of the high sectoral concentration of their economies.

16. OECD (1990–91, 117). Many of the reforms reflect the recommendations of the Advisory Council on Adjustment (1989).

have answered the adjustment problems facing trade-sensitive industries such as textiles, clothing, and footwear.[17]

Mexican Labor Law and Practices

As written in law, current labor standards in Mexico are comparable to those in the United States. The Mexican Constitution guarantees worker rights and provides a framework for trade unionism (White House 1991, tab 3, 1). The key statute is the Federal Labor Law (Ley Federal del Trabajo) of 1 May 1970, with its subsequent amendments. The law regulates labor contracts, minimum wages, hours of work and legal holidays, paid vacations, employment of women and minors, labor unions, collective bargaining, strikes, labor courts, occupational safety, apprenticeship, profit sharing, compensation upon dismissal, and conditions of work in specified fields (US Department of Labor, Bureau of International Labor Affairs 1990b, 46).

In certain formal respects, Mexican labor standards exceed those in the United States. The Mexican social security system, for example, provides medical and maternity care, pensions, and payment for temporary and permanent disability (Zoellick 1991, 8). As of January 1991 Mexico had ratified 72 International Labor Organization (ILO) conventions dealing with worker health and safety standards, whereas the United States had ratified only 10.[18]

Labor abuses are widespread in Mexico, however. Weak enforcement of Mexico's labor laws has been cited as a strong argument against freer US trade with the country. Mexican resources for enforcement are scarce; workplace inspections are infrequent, particularly for maquiladora operations; and only in rare cases are sanctions applied by inspectors. Inadequate safety conditions contribute to industrial accidents in smaller firms and at construction sites.[19] In

---

17. In fact, according to a statement by the Economic Council of Canada (1988), the POWA program could have perverse effects on labor market adjustment. For example, troubled industries usually lay off younger workers first because of seniority rules. However, because of programs such as POWA, older workers may be asked to take early retirement voluntarily. The program could thus give younger workers an incentive to stay in declining industries.

18. Some of the Mexican ratifications apply to ILO conventions that superseded earlier conventions. One important ILO convention *not* ratified by Mexico (or by the United States or Canada) is the Child Labor Convention.

19. See, for example, the survey of three Mexican border cities and their twin US border cities from 29 June to 18 July 1989, conducted by the US Department of Labor's Bureau of International Labor Affairs (1990b).

addition, a large part of the labor force operates outside the organized economy and hence outside the framework of formal labor standards.[20]

Child Labor Laws

Child labor laws are observed in large and medium-sized manufacturing and commercial establishments in Mexico. They are not well observed in small shops and factories, and they are virtually ignored in the informal sector (e.g., street vendors). The statutory minimum age for employment is 14 years. Mexican children between 14 and 16 years of age may work but are subject to special legal protection and shorter working hours.[21] According to a study by the Cato Institute (Salinas-León 1991, 12), an estimated 10 million children work at least part-time in Mexico, supplementing an adult labor force of about 30 million. The huge number of child workers reflects generalized poverty and inadequate enforcement of child labor laws.

As a rule, the minimum age requirements specified in Mexican labor legislation are observed by maquiladora employers. But abuses are frequent and well documented. Approximately 5 percent of the workers hired in the maquiladora sector are between 14 and 16 years old (according to information obtained by the US Labor Department in Ciudad Juárez), and it is this pool that creates the greatest opportunity for child abuse (US Department of Labor, Bureau of International Labor Affairs 1990b, 2).

Minimum Wages and Maximum Hours

By law, Mexican production workers are guaranteed a minimum wage stated in terms of pay for an eight-hour workday. However, stated in dollar terms, the average hourly compensation is presently below its 1980 level (table 6.7). Moreover, some employers fail to pay even the minimum wage; noncompliance is highest in rural areas (US Department of Labor, Bureau of International Labor Affairs 1990b, 49). But among the urban labor force, over 80 percent of the workers earn more than the minimum wage (White House 1991, tab 3, 11).

---

20. According to a survey by the National Chamber of Manufacturing Industries, the underground economy employed 22.5 percent of the labor force in 1990, mostly in retail commerce. The National Chamber also noted that 60 percent of all business firms in Mexico claim to have no employees, creating a major tax collection problem *(Journal of Commerce,* 9 October 1991, 9A).

21. For more details see White House (1991, tab 3, 10).

Table 6.7 Mexico: average hourly compensation rates, 1980–89

	1980	1985	1986	1987	1988	1989
National industries[a]						
Hourly compensation in pesos	68	538	919	2,168	4,522	5,702
Consumer price index (1985 = 100)	9.3	100.0	186.2	431.7	924.6	1,109.6
Hourly compensation in 1985 pesos	731	538	494	502	489	514
Exchange rate (pesos per dollar)	23	257	612	1,378	2,273	2,461
Hourly compensation in US dollars	2.96	2.09	1.5	1.57	1.99	2.32
As percentage of average US hourly compensation	30	16	11	12	14	16
Maquiladora industries[b]						
Hourly compensation in pesos	33	276	490	1,114	2,238	2,820
Hourly compensation in 1985 pesos	355	276	263	258	242	254
Hourly compensation in US dollars	1.42	1.07	0.80	0.81	0.98	1.15

a. Average of selected manufacturing industries, excluding all maquiladora plants. The industries covered represented only 25 percent of the total manufacturing employment in 1985. Average compensation in the industries covered was about 30 percent higher than that for total manufacturing in 1985. The compensation figures for 1988 and 1989 are preliminary estimates using an index of hourly compensation for all employees.

b. Average of selected maquiladora manufacturing plants. Figures cannot be directly compared to the national industries average because of substantial differences in the industries included.

Sources: US Department of Labor, Bureau of Labor Statistics, Office of Productivity and Technology, unpublished data sheets, July 1990 (updated March 1991).

Table 6.8 Mexico: average hourly compensation in the maquiladoras, by industry, 1980–88[a] (dollars)

Industry	1980	1985	1986	1987	1988
Food and related products	1.45	0.85	0.69	0.65	0.75
Apparel and other textile products	1.27	0.92	0.66	0.66	0.76
Footwear and leather products	1.62	1.10	0.82	0.78	0.89
Furniture and fixtures	1.59	1.09	0.84	0.85	1.01
Chemicals and chemical products	n.a.	1.33	0.82	0.74	0.98
Machinery and equipment[b]	1.31	1.33	1.02	1.01	1.15
Electrical and electronic equipment	1.43	1.06	0.80	0.83	1.02
Transportation equipment	1.49	1.18	0.88	0.86	1.09
Toys and sporting goods	1.55	1.08	0.75	0.82	1.12
Other manufacturing	1.47	1.03	0.74	0.74	0.85
Average	1.42	1.07	0.80	0.81	0.98

n.a. = not available

a. Production workers in manufacturing maquiladoras.

b. Except electrical.

Source: US Department of Labor, Bureau of Labor Statistics, Office of Productivity and Technology, unpublished data sheets.

In 1989 the average wage (including fringe benefits) for production workers in manufacturing, as reported by the Bureau of Labor Statistics (BLS), was $2.32 per hour in Mexico and $14.31 in the United States. According to these data, Mexican industrial wages were about a sixth of the US wage level (table 6.9). The White House report (1991, tab 3, 11) suggests that Mexican hourly compensation is lower than the reported BLS figure. As of December 1990, the average manufacturing-sector cash wage including fringe benefits was said to be only $1.23 per hour. The comparable figure for maquiladora workers was $1.26 per hour (US Department of Labor, Bureau of International Labor Affairs 1990b, 49). If these numbers are correct, the Mexican industrial wage is about one-eleventh the US level (tables 6.7 and 6.8).[22] The disagreement over Mexican wage levels may reflect the large role of fringe benefits in the Mexican compensation system, in the form of transportation, housing, food at work, and health care. According to Alejandro Paz, Director of the Asociación de Maquiladoras de

---

22. A similar comparison among European countries in 1989 reveals that the dispersion in labor costs within the European Community between the richest and poorest members was generally less than in North America. Labor costs per hour in manufacturing in Germany were $17.53, Spain's were a little over half the German level, Greece's were less than a third, and Portugal's were less than a sixth (table 6.9).

Table 6.9 Average hourly compensation costs for production workers in manufacturing, selected countries, 1982–89[a] (dollars)

Country	1982	1983	1984	1985	1986	1987	1988	1989
United States	11.64	12.10	12.51	12.96	13.21	13.40	13.85	14.31
Germany	10.28	10.23	9.43	9.56	13.29	16.91	18.11	17.53
Japan	5.70	6.13	6.34	6.43	9.31	10.83	12.80	12.63
Singapore	1.96	2.21	2.46	2.47	2.23	2.31	2.67	3.09
Hong Kong	1.67	1.52	1.58	1.73	1.88	2.09	2.40	2.79
Taiwan	1.22	1.27	1.42	1.50	1.73	2.26	2.82	3.53
Brazil	1.86	1.26	1.07	1.12	1.47	1.38	1.50	1.72
Mexico	2.54	1.85	2.06	2.09	1.50	1.57	1.99	2.32
Korea	1.13	1.20	1.31	1.35	1.45	1.78	2.50	3.57
Greece	4.12	3.76	3.74	3.66	4.07	4.61	5.22	5.48
Portugal	1.88	1.62	1.45	1.53	2.08	2.51	2.67	2.77
Spain	5.35	4.64	4.58	4.79	6.43	7.86	8.81	9.10

a. Hourly compensation includes all payments made directly to the worker, before payroll deductions, but including employer expenditures for legally required insurance programs and contractual and private benefit plans.

Source: US Department of Labor, Bureau of Labor Statistics, *International Comparisons of Hourly Compensation Costs for Production Workers in Manufacturing, 1975–89* (Report 794), October 1990, 8.

Chihuahua, these fringe benefits add about 180 percent to the average cash wage.

In Mexico, the maximum length of the work week is 48 hours; in practice the work week is usually 44 to 48 hours in maquiladoras and 42 to 43 hours in other firms (White House 1991, tab 3, 12). Overtime must be paid at higher rates. In addition, all employees are entitled to six days of paid vacation and seven paid official holidays, plus a Christmas bonus.

Health and Safety

In 1978 the Mexican government instituted a major revision of the Federal Labor Law of 1970, to deal with occupational safety and health problems and to carry out its obligations under the ILO conventions. The revisions stipulate that the safety of the workplace is the direct responsibility of the employer, who must report accidents, create health and safety committees to review working conditions, and train workers to prevent job-related injuries. Firms employing more than 300 workers are required by law to set up their own health clinics, at company expense, to supplement the social security health care system (White House 1991, tab 3, 13 and 15).

At the same time that the government revised the Federal Labor Law, it enacted regulations for occupational health and safety. These cover virtually all aspects of occupational health and safety for industries.

Two official bodies are responsible for enforcing the occupational health and safety regulations: the Directorate General of Federal Labor Inspection and the Directorate General of Medicine and Safety in the Workplace, both located in the Secretariat of Labor and Social Welfare. In practice, the enforcement of Mexican workplace health and safety laws and regulations depends on the vigilance of local workplace safety committees, which generate most of the inspections. These committees tend to be most effective in large firms with strong union representation. Small and medium-size firms often do not have workplace safety committees.

Most US and Japanese firms probably bring high industrial safety standards to their Mexican plants. The Bureau of International Labor Affairs report (1990b, 67), based on a visit to a few industrial sites, found that workplace safety notices and hazard signs were posted and safety masks or goggles were provided; that lighting and ventilation were adequate; and that good industrial safety and health conditions were maintained. However, in cases related to the handling of toxic chemicals, other reports maintain that workers are often neither alerted to nor trained to deal with potentially hazardous conditions.[23]

The most pervasive problems arise outside the workplace. With the rapid growth of maquiladoras there has been a large migration of people to the border. Public facilities and housing have not kept pace, and many workers endure miserable living conditions. Public water and sewer services are inadequate. Many workers live in cardboard hovels with no running water or sanitation facilities (*Wall Street Journal,* 18 April 1991, A17). Government housing funds often get diverted; private investors have not built apartments, since most workers (who often are supporting large families) cannot afford the rent for even very modest dwellings (US Department of Labor, Bureau of International Labor Affairs 1990b, 68).

Mexican Trade Unions

In a letter to US Trade Representative Carla A. Hills, Congressman John D. Dingell (D-MI) pointedly asked whether the Mexican maquiladora workers can form unions of their own choosing and bargain a contract with the employer (*Inside U.S. Trade,* 1 March 1991, 9). The answer is "yes" in theory and "maybe" in practice.

---

23. See, for example, a study by Leslie Kochan (1989) of the Oregon Department of Environmental Quality.

Approximately 9.5 million Mexican workers are unionized, out of a total work force of 25 million to 30 million (table 6.1 and US Department of Labor, Bureau of International Labor Affairs 1990b, 47). The vast majority of Mexican trade unions are affiliated with the ruling Partido Revolucionario Institucional (PRI) and tend to support the government and the PRI. Their freedom of maneuver is limited, since most union leaders are also PRI officials and may occupy PRI elective office.

The Congress of Labor serves as the umbrella organization for some 36 PRI–affiliated labor confederations and independent unions. It has some 8 million members—over 85 percent of Mexico's total union membership (US Department of Labor, Bureau of International Labor Affairs 1990b, 47). Excluding the maquiladoras, more than 90 percent of industrial production workers in establishments employing over 25 workers are unionized (White House 1991, tab 3, 6). By comparison, only about 10 percent to 20 percent of maquiladora workers are unionized (*Journal of Commerce*, 16 May 1989, 4A).[24] Nearly all the maquiladoras in the northeastern region are organized by the CTM, but in the north-central region (Juárez) only 15 percent are organized, and in the northwestern region (Tijuana and Mexicali) only a few are openly organized.

The lower union rates in Juárez, Tijuana, and Mexicali reflect a combination of forces: anti-union sentiments held by maquiladora operators, the absence of effective attempts by established unions to organize the maquiladora work force, the perception on the part of maquiladora workers that trade unions have little to offer, and the high turnover of workers. In some cases, "company unions" are set up by management, usually as a shield to protect the company against the entrance of authentic unions (*Journal of Commerce*, 16 May 1989, 4A)

Illegal Immigrants

The number of illegal immigrants dwelling in the United States rose from an estimated 2.5 million to 3.5 million in 1980 to an estimated 3.0 million to 5.0 million in 1986. Since 1986, however, the number of illegal aliens in the United States has dropped; estimates now range from 1.8 million to 3.0 million (*Urban Institute Policy and Research Report*, Winter-Spring 1991, 13).

Mexico is the largest source of immigration into the United States. Although Mexicans accounted for only 12 percent of the total pool of legal immigrants

---

24. The Mexican government and the Confederation of Mexican Workers (Confederación de Trabajadores Mexicanos, or CTM) allegedly reached a tacit understanding at the start of the maquiladora program in the 1960s that the CTM would not actively seek to organize the maquiladora sector so as not to frighten away potential foreign investment. Both government authorities and CTM leaders publicly deny this charge.

admitted in 1987, they accounted for 50 percent to 60 percent of the annual flow of illegal immigrants entering the United States (US Department of Justice, Immigration and Naturalization Service 1987, 7; Weintraub 1990a, 185). Considering the number of border apprehensions, about 1.0 million in 1990, the current estimate of 1.8 million to 3.0 million illegal aliens dwelling in the United States may seem too small. However, much of the inflow from Mexico consists of temporary migrants.[25] Consequently there is a large unreported reverse flow from the United States back into Mexico (*Urban Institute Policy and Research Report,* Winter-Spring 1991, 13).

The 1986 US Immigration Reform and Control Act (IRCA), also known as the Simpson-Rodino Act, enabled 2.7 million illegal immigrants to attain legal status.[26] Subsequently, Border Patrol apprehensions dropped from 1.6 million in 1986 to 1.1 million in 1987.[27] The reason seems to be that, once legal status was granted, many Mexicans no longer had to sneak back and forth across the border.[28]

In a recent study, Michael Fix questioned whether employer sanctions—a major feature of the Simpson-Rodino Act—have significantly limited the hiring of illegal immigrants.[29] Fix cites the fact that in 1990 the number of apprehensions rose by 22 percent. Rewriting legislative history, US Ambassador to Mexico Charles Pilliod, Jr., even asserted that the Simpson-Rodino Act "was not conceived to eliminate the movement of Mexican workers to the United States. The US needs these workers—not only in the farm area but also in the many service

---

25. See Weintraub (1990a, 186). Weintraub points out that the figure of 90 percent Mexicans among apprehensions may disproportionately undercount non-Mexicans (who enter on tourist visas) and is not adjusted for the fact that many Mexicans are caught more than once. According to the San Diego Sector Patrol, during September 1990–91 apprehensions numbered 542,000, up from 473,000 the previous year. It is estimated that about half of all illegal immigrants enter through the San Diego Sector (*San Diego Union,* 31 October 1991, C-6).

26. Legalization was extended only to those who could prove they had lived in the United States without interruption since 1982. Congress enacted a new Immigration Act in 1990. The most notable change between the 1986 and 1990 acts was a slight shift in emphasis away from the social goal of family unification to the economic goal of meeting the labor requirements of employers.

27. *Washington Post,* 24 June 1991, A13. Apprehensions are estimated to account for between 10 percent and 40 percent of illegal border crossings.

28. This explanation is offered by Jorge Bustamante, of the Tijuana-based Colegio de la Frontera Norte, who conducted research on migration along the US–Mexico border (*Washington Post,* 24 June 1991, A13).

29. For a more elaborate discussion on employer sanctions see Fix (1991) and Bean et al. (1990). According to the Chief of the US Border Patrol's San Diego Sector, the answer to illegal immigration is stronger enforcement at the border—double the number of officers— and stronger enforcement of employer sanctions (*San Diego Union,* 31 October 1991, C-6).

sectors such as food outlets, hotels, etc." (*Journal of Commerce*, 9 June 1988, 10A).

The root cause of illegal immigration from Mexico is obviously the search for better-paying jobs. As a 22-year-old Mexican woman put it: "by working in the US for a week and saving enough to send $100 back to Mexico, a person can eat for a month" (*New York Times*, 30 June 1991, 12). In our view, illegal immigration on a large scale will be a fact of economic life between the United States and Mexico for decades to come, whether or not a NAFTA is created. The Mexicans who emigrate are usually not the poorest;[30] moreover, as the number of Mexicans living in the northern cities rises, the temptation to cross the border will increase.[31] Economic prosperity in Mexico will gradually ease the pressure on Mexican workers to seek US jobs,[32] but an abrupt end of illegal immigration is neither feasible nor desirable.

Recommendations

The impact of a NAFTA on the US labor force will be small but not inconsequential. For years to come, the average Mexican income ($2,393 per capita in 1989) will continue to be just a fraction of the average US income ($21,057 in 1989, according to table 1.1; the difference is somewhat smaller when differences in purchasing power are taken into account). But the gap will gradually close over time with Mexican growth and productivity gains (see chapter 3). Rising US exports to Mexico under a NAFTA should generate new, generally high-wage jobs in the United States. Overall, the new jobs should offset losses of mostly low-wage jobs. With or without a NAFTA, low-wage workers in many sectors of the US economy will continue to face strong competitive pressures from abroad, including from Mexico. Given Mexico's high propensity to import US goods,

---

30. A survey found that only 3.2 percent of emigrants were unemployed in the month prior to leaving Mexico (Weintraub 1990a, 191). The survey was conducted by the Centro Nacional de Información y Estadísticas del Trabajo (CENIET).

31. As Weintraub (1990a, 191) points out, "It takes money to immigrate, thereby mostly excluding the unemployed. And as income rises, one's appetite for still more income is whetted. As incomes rise, so do aspirations... [A]s Mexican wages rise, emigration may increase temporarily, implying that increased employment in Mexico is unlikely to have much deterrent effect on emigration in the short term, say for the rest of this century. Over a longer term, if incomes in Mexico continue to rise, emigration will eventually decline."

32. McCleery and Reynolds (1991) argue that free trade could reduce the flow of illegal immigration over a period of 5 to 10 years by increasing Mexican employment opportunities and wages. We think their outlook is too sanguine; but based on our projected long-term convergence of per capita income between the United States and Mexico (see chapter 3), the flow of illegal immigration might be reduced in 15 or 20 years.

there is some validity to the argument that "losing" those jobs to Mexico entails a smaller adjustment burden than "losing" them to East Asia.

Moreover, many US firms benefit from production and trade linkages with their Mexican subsidiaries. A US International Trade Commission (1988b, appendix L) survey of US firms reported that the vast majority of 323 respondents stated that their Mexican assembly operations increased the competitiveness of their US production.

The real problem that a NAFTA poses for the United States is not a net loss of jobs but the transition from old jobs to new jobs. Compared with other industrialized countries, the United States spends rather little on labor market adjustment programs. As the United States reaps the benefits of freer trade, dislocated US workers should be offered more generous and more effective job retraining and income maintenance programs.[33] The government should also support efforts by individuals to retrain for and relocate to new jobs. A good example would be encouragement for apprenticeship programs that enhance the role of private business in training efforts (OECD 1990–91, 101).

In our view, the United States should budget at least $900 million over a period of five years to handle up to an additional 112,000 US workers that might be dislocated by North American trade liberalization. Funds allocated toward adjustment should have a large component of retraining outlays.

In fact, a worker training bill that partly answers this need was introduced in Congress in October 1991.[34] The total federal outlay envisaged is $580 million annually; part of the funding would come from a 1 percent payroll tax paid to state-administered training funds.

In the same spirit, Canada should seize on the NAFTA as an opportunity to restructure its adjustment programs away from income maintenance and toward retraining.

Mexico must confront its inadequate enforcement of labor standards. With a growing economy, companies will be able to provide better working conditions, and government officials will find it easier to enforce labor standards. These trends can be accelerated through the NAFTA: Mexico should commit itself to enforcing its labor laws, to allowing meaningful trade union representation among maquiladora workers, and to a progressive upgrading of labor standards.[35]

---

33. Jack Sheinkman, President of the Amalgamated Clothing and Textile Workers Union, insists on assurances that "workers displaced by freer trade with Mexico will receive both adequate unemployment benefits and retraining for new jobs" (*Journal of Commerce*, 9 October 1991, 1A).

34. The bill (S. 1790, H.R. 3470) is sponsored by Senators Edward M. Kennedy (D-MA) and Mark O. Hatfield (R-OR), House Majority Leader Richard A. Gephardt (D-MO), and Congressman Ralph Regula (R-OH; *Journal of Commerce*, 3 October 1991, 12A).

35. Just such commitments were advocated by author and former Mexican Ambassador to France Carlos Fuentes and former Secretary of Finance Jesús Silva Herzog, in a letter to the US House of Representatives in November 1990.

Public debate on labor relations between the United States and Mexico will be strongly colored by continuing immigration from Mexico. Even assuming rapid economic growth until the end of the century, Mexico will not be able to provide jobs at attractive wages to all those entering the labor market.[36] Illegal immigration into the United States will thus continue on a large scale, unless the United States erects an electronic Berlin Wall along the border. In our view, the best policy toward this thorny problem has three components: leave the US immigration law as it is and not discuss immigration in the NAFTA talks; keep US border enforcement outlays no higher than present levels; and allow economic prosperity in Mexico to ameliorate the flow of immigrants over the next several decades.[37]

Joint US–Mexico-Canada reports should be issued biennially on labor conditions and adjustments in each country, including a review of illegal migration. These reports would facilitate a timely assessment of the impact of the NAFTA in each country's labor market and would serve as a catalyst for effective adjustment measures.

Finally, the United States should give Canadian and Mexican performers relief from the new US immigration law that tightens restrictions on foreign professionals allowed to work in the United States on a temporary basis.[38] Planned rules for implementing the new law would especially restrict performers who have not yet gained "national or international acclaim," and performers who have not been associated with a group or team for a year or more. These rules will bear harshly on young Canadian performers, who often get their start by touring the United States (*Journal of Commerce*, 16 August 1991, 5A). The rules could also act as a bar to aspiring Mexican performers. Special provisions for Canadian and Mexican performers should thus be a US concession in the services agenda.

---

36. Weintraub (1990a, 195) estimates that, to slow down illegal immigration, Mexico would have to create 1 million jobs per year between now and the year 2000—an enormously difficult task.

37. For a discussion of US policy toward Mexican immigration see also Weintraub (1983, 185–214).

38. The new law establishes an annual quota of 65,000 for workers in occupations that require highly specialized knowledge. Previously there was no quota, but the number of workers who arrived in this category was estimated at 45,000 per year. The new law also establishes a quota of 25,000 for entertainers, other artists, and athletes (*Wall Street Journal*, 27 September 1991, 1B; Maryland Chamber of Commerce, *International Trade Advisor*, 1991, 6).

7

Environmental Questions

The 1991 congressional debate on extension of fast-track authority for the NAFTA negotiations pushed environmental issues front and center. At one point, many prominent environmental groups were arrayed with organized labor in a broad coalition against the US–Mexico talks, but in the last weeks of the debate, the National Wildlife Federation announced its support of the NAFTA negotiations as the best way to make progress on a range of difficult questions.[1] The National Audubon Society, the Environmental Defense Fund, and the Natural Resources Defense Council remained quiet on the issue, while other groups such as the Sierra Club and Friends of the Earth voiced strong opposition (*Inside U.S. Trade*, 24 May 1991, 7).

Before plunging into the details of the controversy, it must be observed that neither Canada nor Mexico sees the NAFTA as an appropriate forum for sorting out environmental questions. They fear that the United States, catering to domestic environmental lobbies, will use the NAFTA to impose its environmental views throughout North America. Canadian and Mexican officials agree that North American solutions are needed for regional problems such as acid rain in the Great Lakes region and air pollution in the Tijuana–San Diego basin. But they do not accept that North American solutions are required for local pollution problems, for example the emissions of petroleum refineries in Houston or Mexico City. From the Canadian and Mexican vantage point, local pollution problems should be addressed locally, according to a timetable that reflects income levels and national priorities,[2] and not become a subject of NAFTA standards dictated by the United States.

---

1. Just days before the fast-track vote, the group endorsed the NAFTA negotiations in a *New York Times* op-ed (19 May 1991, 17).

2. Gene Grossman and Alan Krueger (1991), in a study of the relationship between air quality and economic growth, found that at low levels of national income, for some pollutants, concentrations increase with per capita GDP; but at higher levels of per capita GDP concentrations decrease with GDP growth. According to their findings, Mexico has reached the turning point at which further growth will prompt the country to invest more in solving its environmental problems. A similar study done by Ishac Diwan and Nemat Shafik (1991) likewise found a turning point at approximately the Mexican level of real per capita GDP. Robert Lucas, David Wheeler, and Hemamala Hettige (1991) also found an inverse U-shaped curve for the relationship between manufacturing emissions and GDP,

In the congressional deliberations, no sharp distinction was drawn between continental, regional, and local pollution issues. Instead, three major reasons were offered for covering a broad range of environmental issues in the NAFTA talks. The first and broadest reason is concern about sustainable development. Environmental degradation is already a severe problem in Mexico. As barriers to trade and investment are removed, increased industrialization will strain the environmental infrastructure—not only along the border (Tijuana, Juárez, Nuevo Laredo) but also in major industrial cities far from the United States (Mexico City, Monterrey, Guadalajara).

A second and more specific reason, cited by US environmentalists and worker groups and some industrialists, is the fear that some US and Canadian plants cannot compete against Mexican-based enterprises that escape tough and expensive pollution standards. The specter of "environmental dumping" was frequently raised in the congressional debate: the fear that polluting Mexican plants, perhaps located far from the border, would sell goods more cheaply than clean US plants, with the result that "good" production in the United States would shut down while "bad" production in Mexico would start up.[3] This fear is not allayed by the supposed distinction between regional pollution and local pollution. Many environmentalists are just as concerned with local pollution in Guadalajara as in Portland. In their view the environment, like human rights, is a proper concern of all mankind. In our view, the huge disparities in income between the United States and Mexico argue for tolerance toward Mexican priorities in addressing local pollution problems (i.e., problems that do *not* spill across the border).

A third concern was that a NAFTA might directly and indirectly undercut environmental standards within the United States. Mexican economic growth stimulated by a NAFTA might give rise to ever-larger volumes of polluted Mexican air blowing north to San Diego and El Paso and more raw sewage contaminating the Pacific coast waters and the Rio Grande; a reduction in trade restrictions might lead to pesticide-laden Mexican vegetables being sold in supermarkets across the nation. At a more subtle level, it was feared that the prospective shift of industrial plants to Mexico and the attendant loss of jobs would undercut US political support for tough environmental standards at the state and federal levels; in the worst case, it was feared that NAFTA mechanisms would be invoked to overturn those stateside environmental standards that could be characterized as nontariff trade barriers.

The Bush administration responded to the concerns of various environmental groups (and others) in its May 1991 Action Plan (White House 1991). To

---

but they argue that the turning point is due to a change in the sectoral composition of output and not to changes within individual manufacturing industries.

3. The threat of environmental dumping reinforces a parallel concern of environmentalists that Mexico might become a pollution haven.

ensure that environmental concerns remain front-burner issues during the NAFTA negotiations, the House of Representatives passed the so-called Gephardt-Rostenkowski resolution (H.Res. 146), parallel to its vote extending fast-track negotiating authority. This resolution binds the administration to its outlined commitments in the NAFTA talks regarding labor, environmental, and health concerns. The resolution also requires the President to report to Congress on progress toward meeting the objectives of the Action Plan; in addition, private-sector committees that advise the US Trade Representative (USTR) are asked to submit their own assessments.[4]

Several environmental groups are seeking further "clarifications and assurances" (Inside U.S. Trade, 17 May 1991, 11–12). Fundamentally, these groups would like to link parallel environmental negotiations, proposed in the Action Plan, with the NAFTA negotiations, so that the fruits of the negotiations are brought to Congress in conjunction with the NAFTA. More broadly, they seek institutional reforms that would ensure that environmental interests are incorporated in the formulation of trade policy, and they seek a new dispute settlement mechanism, accessible by private parties, for dealing with environmental issues.

As its first step, the USTR has coordinated an interagency review of US–Mexico environmental issues to assess the effects of free trade, drawing on past experience at the border (USTR 1991), and has established the new position of Assistant US Trade Representative for the Environment. As trade talks get under way, environmental concerns will be dealt with in parallel negotiations. In addition, "a representative of the non-governmental environmental organizations" will be added to the Advisory Committee on Trade Policy and Negotiations (ACTPN) to ensure that environmental concerns are reflected in the formulation and conduct of overall US trade policy.[5]

On 1 August 1991, Public Citizens, the Sierra Club, and the Friends of the Earth filed suit against the USTR, charging a violation of the National Environmental Policy Act. This act requires the filing of an environmental impact statement (EIS) whenever a federal agency proposes major legislation or makes a recommendation on a major federal action that would significantly affect the environ-

---

4. *Congressional Record*, H 3589–90, 23 May 1991. Reports are to be submitted from "the Labor Advisory Committee for Trade Negotiations and Trade Policy, the Industry Policy Advisory Committee, and, where appropriate, other policy, sectoral, and functional advisory committees...."

5. White House (1991, tab 4, 7). Environmental representatives will also be included in the following committees: the Inter-Governmental Policy Advisory Committee, the Services Policy Advisory Committee, the Investment Policy Advisory Committee, the Industry Policy Advisory Committee for Trade and Policy Matters, and the Agricultural Policy Advisory Committee. In addition, the Environmental Protection Agency has created its own Advisory Group on Trade and Environment with some 50 participants from the private sector.

ment.[6] The USTR contends that trade negotiations are outside the purview of the act.[7] In January 1992 a US District Court dismissed the suit; the decision has been appealed (*Inside U.S. Trade*, 17 January 1992, 11).

Meanwhile, a good deal of political sparring is under way. Senator Max Baucus (D-MT) has declared that the NAFTA will not be approved by the Congress unless it includes, or is accompanied by, environmental protection provisions (Baucus 1991). In stark contrast, Mexican Secretary of Commerce Jaime Serra Puche has insisted that "labor and environmental issues are not part of the treaty that will create NAFTA" (*Inside U.S. Trade*, 1 November 1991, 14).

US–Mexico environmental problems existed long before the concept of a North American market became popular, and many of them will endure long after the trade agenda is worked out. Nevertheless, three topics on the environmental agenda seem particularly appropriate for "tight" inclusion in the negotiations: transborder pollution problems; the definition of admissible standards for restricting imports from another NAFTA party; and a determination of when different national environmental standards (including different degrees of enforcement) can act as an objectionable industrial incentive or, conversely, as an undesirable trade barrier.

Recent Environmental Efforts in Mexico

Mexican President Carlos Salinas has said that Mexico will not become a pollution haven for companies seeking low environmental costs, nor will it tolerate investment that has been rejected by the United States and Canada for environmental reasons.[8] In the face of severe environmental degradation, Mexico has recently constructed a solid legal framework for protecting the environment. Mexico also has a policy of "directed development," which encourages development in those Mexican cities better able to absorb increased industrial activity.

---

6. *Journal of Commerce*, 5 August 1991, 3. Precedents for an EIS for the NAFTA are impact statements filed in connection with the Panama Canal Treaty and for several fishing conventions in the 1970s (*Inside U.S. Trade*, 2 August 1991, 12).

7. According to administration attorneys, the requirement of an EIS "would interfere with the formulation of foreign policy and would also violate the separation of powers doctrine and run contrary to presidential authority to carry out international negotiations." They also argued that it is a matter of speculation whether environmental damage would result from a NAFTA without an EIS and that "many of those injuries could not be redressed because they are not site-specific" (*Inside U.S. Trade*, 29 November 1991, 8).

8. This section draws on the Bush administration's Action Plan (White House 1991, tab 4); the statement by Robert B. Zoellick in US Congress, Senate Committee on Foreign Relations (1991, 8–10); and Kamp and Kelly (1991).

Private firms are also taking up the cause. Recently, the Mexican Chemical Industry Association voted to emulate the US Chemical Manufacturers Association "Responsible Care" program, which calls for companies to adopt safe and environmentally responsible measures when dealing with chemical products (*Journal of Commerce*, 29 October 1991, 7A). Private Mexican producers in all branches of industry spent some $150 million on environmental programs during 1989–91, and the government-owned petroleum monopoly Pemex has spent even more (*Journal of Commerce*, 29 October 1991, 7A). The Mexican government has announced that, over the three years beginning in 1992, it will spend nearly $500 million to protect the environment along the border, including an extra $223 million to build sewage plants, $26 million for solid waste disposal, and $44 million to create border-area nature preserves (*Journal of Commerce*, 25 October 1991, 1A).

As to global environmental issues, Mexico was the first country to ratify the Montreal Protocol, an international treaty to stop the use of chemicals that harm the ozone layer. Mexico will halt the use of ozone-depleting substances (primarily chlorofluorocarbons, or CFCs) by the same deadline as the United States—10 years ahead of the treaty schedule for developing countries.[9] However, Mexico was slow to sign the 1975 Convention on International Trade in Endangered Species of Wild Fauna and Flora (CITES), only acceding in October 1991.

The General Law for Ecological Equilibrium and Environmental Protection, enacted in March 1988, serves as the cornerstone of Mexico's commitment to address domestic environmental problems. Much of the law is drawn from US legislation and experience. The 1988 Protection Law covers air, water, and soil pollution; contamination by hazardous waste; pesticides and toxic substances; the conservation of ecosystems; ecology reserves; and the rational use of natural resources. There is also a provision for administrative sanctions, and there are judicial penalties for noncompliance.

A key element of the statute is the requirement that new investments in Mexico (both public and private) be accompanied by an environmental impact assessment if they involve hazardous risk activities or dangerous substances. This requirement is more stringent than US environmental law, which generally demands an EIS only as a condition of public spending or other public action (e.g., allowing mining or forestry, or changing land use from agricultural to residential). The Mexican provision, covering as it does all new investment that poses an environmental hazard, could affect private plants established to take advantage of the NAFTA.

---

9. *Journal of Commerce*, 8 May 1991, 7A. In 1988, Mexican production of CFCs was 9.5 thousand tons (less than 1 percent of world production), primarily by foreign firms such as Du Pont. In exchange for signing the Montreal Protocol, Mexico will receive $9 million over the next three years to cover the incremental cost associated with the discontinuation of CFC production.

Enforcement

Mexico's strong legislation is impaired by weak enforcement. Mexico's environmental agency, the Secretariat of Urban Development and Ecology (Secretaría de Desarrollo Urbano y de Ecología, or SEDUE), lacks resources to hire and train new people and to keep up with rapid changes in pollution control and monitoring technology. SEDUE has traditionally relied on industry to comply voluntarily with its regulations. SEDUE currently has 140 enforcement personnel, a seemingly large number compared with the enforcement staff of the US Environmental Protection Agency (about 300), given that the US economy is 20 times as large as the Mexican economy (Kamp and Kelly 1991, 9; communication with the EPA's Office of Enforcement, 7 June 1991). However, SEDUE operates with far fewer technical resources, and its salaries are extremely low.

President Salinas has made stricter enforcement a priority: from 1989 to 1991 SEDUE's budget was increased from $5 million to $39 million (compared with $2,313 million in 1991 for the EPA; *Budget of the United States Government, Fiscal Year 1992*, Part Two-87, table E-1). The agency is also seeking an $84 million loan from the World Bank (*El Nacional*, 21 October 1991, 23). Demonstrating its resolve, SEDUE recently shut down some 980 industrial sites temporarily, and 82 sites permanently, because of noncompliance with the 1988 Protection Law.

In parallel with the NAFTA talks, the EPA and SEDUE have intensified their efforts to improve all dimensions of enforcement. The EPA is providing SEDUE with technical assistance on field enforcement, pesticides regulation, hazardous wastes regulation, and standards setting. The program includes the exchange of modern monitoring and surveillance equipment. In addition, the public is invited to submit information to the agencies on noncompliance in the border area. At the border, the EPA and SEDUE will continue their practice of "exchange" training, in which inspectors from SEDUE participate in EPA inspections on the US side of the border and vice versa. In addition, the US Department of Commerce has been charged with helping small to medium-sized Mexican businesses in meeting environmental standards. Mexico will also double the number of environmental inspectors in the border area from 100 to 200 and will set up a computer system to monitor pollution by border-area factories (*Journal of Commerce*, 25 October 1991, 1A).

Mexico is negotiating an $84 million loan from the World Bank that is primarily designed to increase inspection of industrial sites; Mexico has already allotted funds to add 50 new inspector positions for Mexico City and 50 for the border area. Finally, SEDUE has been negotiating "environmental compliance agreements" with Mexican industry; for example, the Maquiladora Association has agreed to encourage its members to adhere to regulations. SEDUE's cooperative approach will be bolstered by the creation of an Office of Environmental Inspection for Industry, which will have the power to oversee, control, and impose punitive sanctions against industries that violate environmental standards.

Mexico City

The magnitude of the air pollution problem in Mexico City is well known (see, for example, *Financial Times*, 7 March 1991, 6; *The Economist*, 18 May 1991, 50). In 1990 the Salinas administration took significant and costly steps to reduce the city's air pollution. Most of the pollution is generated by some 3 million motor vehicles in Mexico City. To combat this, proposals have been introduced to limit traffic and industrial activity when pollution in Mexico City reaches dangerous levels. Meanwhile, Pemex is cutting the lead content of Mexico's cheapest gasoline by half,[10] and all new cars are required to have catalytic converters, including over 40,000 new taxis. In October 1990 the Salinas administration committed $2.5 billion for a range of pollution control projects, including improving and encouraging the use of public transportation; upgrading old buses with clean engines; buying new, low-pollution buses; increasing supplies of unleaded gasoline; and banning the use of private cars one day per week.[11]

Mexico City's 16,000 factories are also major polluters. In response, the government has shut down all 24 military industrial factories in the region, together with 120 of the dirtiest private factories. President Salinas's most dramatic step thus far has been the closure in March 1991 of Mexico's largest oil refinery, the Azacapotzalco refinery, which provided 8 percent of Mexico's distillation capacity but contributed 15 percent of Mexico City's industrial pollution.[12] The closure action cost $500 million in annual output and 5,000 jobs.

Since 1989, the EPA and SEDUE have developed joint technical and training assistance programs to address air and water pollution, hazardous waste, and environmental health issues in Mexico City. In addition, the US Department of Energy is working with the Mexican Petroleum Institute to develop a computer model of Mexico City's air pollution, and the Inter-American Development Bank

---

10. *Journal of Commerce*, 10 June 1991, 2A. Pemex has invested $2 billion in its production of unleaded gasoline and low-sulfur fuels. Japan has contributed $750 million in loans for these projects (*The Economist*, 18 May 1991, 50).

11. However, the number of cars in Mexico City increased by 275,000 from 1989 to 1990. About 10 percent of the increase is attributed to the purchase of second cars to evade restrictions under the "day-without-a-car" program (*New York Times*, 31 January 1991, A4).

12. Other dramatic schemes have been proposed for the air pollution problem, including digging huge "wind tunnels" through the Ajusco mountains southwest of Mexico City (*The Economist*, 18 May 1991, 50).

has worked out debt-for-nature swaps amounting to $75 million to plant trees around Mexico City to replace those dying from environmental stress (International Monetary Fund, *Morning Press*, 5 March 1991).

The Border

The environmental problems of the US–Mexico border region (defined in the 1983 Border Environmental Treaty as the area within 100 kilometers of the border on either side) are associated with overdevelopment, rapid population growth, and the maquiladoras. The problems include water contamination from raw sewage and toxic waste; air pollution; a disappearing habitat for endangered species; daily gridlock at border crossings; and the threat of sudden emergencies.[13] A major concern is that the Mexican regulatory and physical infrastructure will not be able to accommodate the added strain from increased industrialization when trade barriers are removed under the NAFTA.[14]

In fact, US–Mexican cooperation on environmental issues has been the strongest on transborder questions.[15] The forerunner to the present International Boundary and Water Commission (IBWC) was established over 100 years ago. The IBWC is charged with addressing all border sanitation problems; so far, most of its work has concerned cross-border water pollution.[16]

More recently, the La Paz Agreement of 1983 committed the EPA and SEDUE to formulate and oversee "work programs" in the border area under the following categories: air and water pollution, hazardous waste, and accidental spills. Under

---

13. A Bhopal-style chemical disaster, for example, becomes ever more likely with growth at the border. One answer has been the creation of an Inland Joint Response Team (USTR 1991). To strengthen its emergency response capability, the Mexican government has established a $4 million revolving fund (Embassy of Mexico in the United States 1991).

14. The interagency review of US–Mexico environmental issues coordinated by the USTR points out that, in a non–NAFTA scenario, the economy of the border area is expected to grow by 5 percent to 15 percent annually. This implies that, with or without a NAFTA, "the environmental problems of the border region will require priority attention" (USTR 1991). However, with the NAFTA, industry is more likely to move deeper into Mexico, partially offsetting the pressures on the border region, but increasing the pressures in the interior.

15. Rogelio González García from SEDUE points out that "for the past several years the work done on air pollution between Juárez and El Paso has shown that our countries can work together while maintaining sovereignty and respect" (*New York Times*, 22 December 1991, 18).

16. The IBWC was preceded by the International Boundary Commission (IBC), founded in 1889. In 1944 the IBC joined with the International Water Commission (IWC) to form the IBWC. The IBWC is divided into an American and a Mexican section. As part of its responsibilities, the IBWC administers any treaties concerning water pollution and sewage between the United States and Mexico (Weintraub 1990a, 168; US General Accounting Office 1991e, 13).

the agreement, hazardous waste from US chemicals imported by the maquiladoras must be returned to the United States for disposal in approved sites. However, the La Paz Agreement has been criticized for lax enforcement: SEDUE only has five inspectors in Tijuana and three in Mexicali, while the EPA has 63 investigators nationwide. Little is known about the exact amount of hazardous waste generated in the northern border area, but in Tijuana alone the known figure is 5,500 gallons of waste per week, and only about 25 percent of that amount makes its way back to the United States. The reason is expense: the average cost of retransportation runs about $300 per barrel. Faced with these charges, many maquiladoras look for legal ways around the law, for example, buying their chemicals from Mexican firms or paying the duties on imported chemicals to cancel the requirement that wastes be reexported. In addition, some maquiladoras simply cheat or store waste on-site for indefinite periods (*San Diego Union*, 16 June 1991, B-1, B-4, B-5).

On 1 August 1991 the EPA and SEDUE released a draft proposal to clean up the border (US EPA and SEDUE 1991). The proposed Border Environmental Plan will be a parallel to the NAFTA and will address all topics under the La Paz Agreement as well as those of pesticides and enforcement. In the first phase, the goal is "To protect human health and natural ecosystems along the U.S./Mexican border in an integrated, comprehensive, long-term manner" (US EPA 1991). The objectives would be achieved through cooperative enforcement, protection of transboundary environmental resources, strengthened financing of environmental protection, private-sector support, and joint emergency planning and response capabilities (US EPA and SEDUE 1991, VI-28 and VI-29). Most important, the proposal added a Work Group on Enforcement to the four work groups established under the 1983 La Paz Agreement.

In September 1991, public hearings on environmental concerns were held in 10 US and 7 Mexican cities. On the basis of those hearings, SEDUE announced a three-year plan to address environmental problems along the border. The total Mexican commitment will amount to approximately $460 million.[17]

Hazardous Waste Disposal

Mexico's capacity to dispose of hazardous waste is inadequate. Currently, only maquiladora factories are required to return hazardous waste to the country of

---

17. Sewage and waste water treatment will cost about $220 million; municipal solid waste, $25 million; transportation and roads, $168 million; territorial reserves, $43 million; and contingency funds, $4 million. For 1992, public works spending on the border region will amount to $147 million. The largest sums will be spent in Tijuana ($28 million), Ciudad Juárez ($26 million), Mexicali ($17 million), and Nuevo Laredo ($16 million). See Embassy of Mexico in the United States (1991).

origin. Under the proposed Border Environmental Plan, SEDUE will work with industry to develop a Mexican hazardous waste treatment facility.[18]

In 1987 US hazardous waste disposal costs were running about $7 per person per year; this figure is projected to rise to about $35 per person per year by 1995 (US EPA 1990, table 2-1, pages 2-2 and 2-3). If the lower figure is applied just to the Mexican urban population (38 million), annual costs of $270 million are suggested as the price tag for dealing with hazardous waste generated in Mexico.

Besides hazardous waste, there is a severe problem of disposing of Mexico's nonhazardous solid waste. It is estimated that 65 percent of municipal solid waste is currently disposed of in open dumps, with attendant air and water pollution. To address this problem, Mexico is currently designing ordinary landfills for waste disposal (USTR 1991).

Water

Water shortage and contamination are both problems at the border. Border cities are extracting groundwater at a rate 20 times faster than the aquifers can recharge; water shortages have already occurred throughout the area (for example, in the Nogales and Agua Prieta–Douglas areas of the states of Arizona and Sonora); in Ciudad Juárez there is enough water for current needs but not for future expansion. A transborder regime remains to be negotiated for groundwater deliveries. Water scarcity may lead to improvements in water treatment to make waste water available for other uses (USTR 1991).

Long-established treaties have defined the flow of surface water that the United States must deliver to Mexico (principally via the Rio Grande and Colorado rivers).[19] The quality of water entering Mexico has deteriorated because of development in the United States; both surface water for agricultural use and groundwater for home use have been affected. US irrigation projects (particularly the Wellton-Mohawk project in Arizona) raised the salinity of the Rio Grande and Colorado rivers to levels that make the water unusable for Mexican agriculture (Kneese 1990; National Wildlife Federation 1990, 8). As the downstream riparian state, Mexico is the injured party so far as surface water is concerned. However, in 1973, the United States and Mexico entered an agreement by which the United States would provide to Mexico, under the 1944 treaty, water of the

---

18. The United States and Mexico are also signatories of the Basel Convention regulating transboundary movement of hazardous and municipal wastes (USTR 1991).

19. The apportioning of the Rio Grande and Colorado rivers has been governed by treaties dating from 1906 and 1944, respectively. The treaties are administered by the IBWC (Weintraub 1990a, 168).

same salinity as the United States delivered to the US Imperial Dam (Hayes 1991, 1–3).

Whatever the transborder regime, it is clear that substantial expenditures will be required to provide adequate amounts of good-quality water for use in Mexican cities. EPA data suggest that, in the United States, water pollution control costs run about $150 per person per year (US EPA 1990, table 2-1, pp. 2-2 and 2-3). Such a figure, applied just to the urban population in Mexico, suggests total annual costs of $5.7 billion. Mexican states and municipalities may already be spending some money to control water pollution, but it is easy to imagine that additional outlays of $1.0 billion to $2.0 billion annually are required.

The most striking component of the overall water pollution problem is the extensive raw sewage in the northern border cities.[20] The Council on Scientific Affairs (1990, 3320) of the American Medical Association found that "46 million liters of raw sewage daily flows into the Tijuana River. Another 76 million and 84 million [liters] are dumped into the New River and Río Grande respectively." The IBWC is coordinating a response to this high-profile problem through projects with the EPA and SEDUE. Meanwhile, the Mexican government is calling on private enterprises to do more. In Ciudad Juárez, major US companies have announced their participation in a new water treatment plant.[21] By 1992, all existing maquiladora plants must be recertified, and all new ventures must submit an EIS (Embassy of Mexico in the United States 1991).

Air Quality

The EPA and SEDUE are planning an "air basin control plan" for El Paso–Juárez, an urban area that fails to meet EPA ozone, carbon monoxide, and inhalable particulate standards. Further, under Section 815 of the Clean Air Act, the EPA will provide Mexico with considerable technical training assistance on air quality regulation in the border area. Predictably, the tough questions will come down to cost: what automobile emission standards will be required, and how quickly?

---

20. This raises concern about the spread of the South American cholera epidemic to the United States. Cholera is spread through unsanitary water supplies, unsanitary food preparation, and shoddy sewage systems. At the end of August 1991, Mexican officials reported 696 cases of cholera, 9 of them fatal. However, no cholera cases related to US–Mexico water issues have been reported (*Wall Street Journal*, 16 August 1991, 5B; *New York Times*, 14 September 1991, 2).

21. Embassy of Mexico in the United States (1991). Recently General Motors announced plans to build water treatment facilities at its 35 manufacturing plants in Mexico (parallel to its practice in the United States). This announcement was prompted by SEDUE border inspectors, who found that GM's maquiladora facilities were dumping raw sewage into rivers and streams (*Journal of Commerce*, 15 May 1991, 1A).

Enforcement of California-style air pollution standards in Mexico would doubtless mean high costs. A rough estimate of the vehicle-related air pollution bill can be made. According to EPA data (1990, table 2-1, pp. 2-2 and 2-3), air pollution control costs in the United States averaged about $42 per vehicle per year in 1987. The Mexican vehicle fleet numbers about 7.8 million. Hence a very conservative estimate suggests an annual charge of some $330 million.[22]

In addition, there is the problem of point-source industrial air pollution. Again according to EPA data, in the United States, point-source air pollution cleanup costs are about 0.8 percent of sales for manufacturing corporations (US EPA 1990, table 3-2, p. 3-2). Applying this figure only to maquiladora plants in Mexico implies a pollution charge of about $60 million per year. Applied to all Mexico, the suggested cost is at least $800 million per year.[23]

The impact of a NAFTA on air quality was studied in the USTR draft review of US–Mexico environmental issues (USTR 1991). The effects of a NAFTA depend on the level of US–Mexico policy cooperation. If the NAFTA is coupled with policy coordination, a favorable scenario emerges under which emissions growth ranges from − 20 percent to + 85 percent over 10 years. In contrast, a no–NAFTA scenario combined with growth in the maquiladora sector and lessened policy cooperation leads to an unpleasant scenario: emissions growth of + 40 percent to + 225 percent over 10 years.

Conservation

The United States and Mexico have cooperated on broad-based conservation projects since 1936. Joint projects have been undertaken in several areas: wildlife conservation; international wildlife trade (in 1991, as noted above, Mexico ratified the CITES, an international convention for the protection of endangered species); preservation of parks, forests, and indigenous wildlife; control of pollution in the Gulf of Mexico; and the protection of marine life (mostly dolphins and sea turtles) from harmful practices of the fishing industry (*Journal of Commerce*, 5 November 1991, 8A).

Recent reforms in land tenure of forest property could have a positive environmental impact. Under the reforms, it will no longer be necessary for individuals

---

22. This is no doubt an understatement because the age of the average Mexican vehicle is over 11 years, compared with 7.6 years in the United States; automobile maintenance on average is poorer in Mexico; and there is greater use of leaded gasoline (*The Economist*, 18 May 1991, 50; *Statistical Abstract of the United States 1990*, table 1027).

23. In 1987, industrial output accounted for 30 percent of Mexican GDP, or $51 billion. Assuming that the sales to value-added ratio is two to one, Mexican industrial sales would be $102 billion annually.

to "work" their land in order to maintain property rights (the "working" require-ment encouraged deforestation, since clearing jungle or forest to grow crops met the legal test). In addition, companies will be allowed to convert forest conces-sions into private property. The harvesting of timber on public lands under concessions from the government had encouraged short-term planning and irresponsible exploitation of these resources. Both changes should promote con-servation, since they will give individuals and private firms a long-term stake in forest property (*El Nacional,* 9 November 1991, 8; 19 November 1991, 10).

The major outstanding conservation issue is the US—Mexico dispute over dolphins. Under the 1988 Marine Mammal Protection Act (MMPA) the United States prohibits the import of yellowfin tuna from countries whose vessels have an incidental marine mammal taking rate 1.25 times that of the US vessels. ("Taking" includes animals killed and those caught in the nets and released.) Mexican tuna are banned under this provision.

Mexico challenged the US import prohibition as a violation of the GATT, pointing out that its practices were consistent with international standards and that it had already reduced its incidental dolphin take by 70 percent.[24] In August 1991 the GATT dispute panel ruled that the US ban was inconsistent with US obligations under the GATT (*Journal of Commerce,* 22 August 1991, 3A; 13 Septem-ber 1991, 1A; *Inside U.S. Trade,* 6 September 1991, Special Report). In September 1991 Mexico deferred action on the GATT ruling and issued a 10-point plan to further reduce its dolphin kills, in exchange for a promise by US administration officials to seek repeal of parts of the 1988 MMPA. But changes to the MMPA face overwhelming opposition in Congress. Adding to the debate, in January 1992 a federal judge invoked the MMPA to ban more than half of US tuna imports: $266 million in imports from 30 countries (*New York Times,* 15 January 1992, D16). The tuna case has become a political metaphor for the broader "battle" between environmental objectives and trade objectives.[25]

---

24. The Earth Island Institute claimed that Mexican fishing fleets would kill 50,000 dolphins in 1991, but Mexico claimed that its fleet would kill fewer than 15,000. Mexico asserts that it has one of the world's lowest incidental kill rates. US law allows the US tuna fleet to kill 20,500 dolphins annually. In 1988, the US fleet caught 70,000 tons of yellowfin tuna and killed 19,000 dolphins; in 1990, the Mexican fleet caught 120,000 tons of yellowfin tuna and killed only 16,000 dolphins. (*Journal of Commerce,* 28 October 1991, 5A; 5 November 1991, 8A).

25. One GATT—legal solution to this ongoing dispute would be to impose an excise tax on all tuna sold in the United States that was not caught in a dolphin-safe way (see Palmeter 1991, 12A). However, it is not clear that the more strident environmentalists would accept a clever technical solution that would deprive them of a public relations triumph.

Recommendations

Public and Private Money

The big environmental question is how much money for additional environmental protection the parties are willing to bring to the table.[26] So far the negotiators have ducked this critical question. Most of the problems are all too obvious. Many of them belong squarely within the responsibilities of the public sector: for example, ensuring an adequate supply of clean water for urban areas and proper sewage treatment. Others are clearly private-sector responsibilities: for example, the construction of hazardous waste facilities and the curtailment of point-source air pollution. Other problems require the establishment of a property rights regime before cleanup costs can be allocated. This is particularly true of groundwater.[27]

All these problems have a common denominator: the need to find money for appropriate cleanup and prevention programs. In any environmental accord that accompanies the NAFTA, each country should commit itself to meeting realistic physical targets of pollution abatement. Both the US and the Mexican federal governments will need to loosen their pursestrings to find money to meet these commitments. In its fiscal year 1993 budget the Bush administration proposed $201 million in expenditures for environmental projects along the Mexican border (*Budget of the United States Government, Fiscal Year 1993,* Part-One-216), almost double the amount for 1992 but still well short of requirements. The demands on Mexico will be even greater. In addition, the two federal governments will need to enforce standards on private industry, even when those standards are costly to meet.

Additional Mexican outlays to ensure adequate water quality and proper sewage disposal, for example, could easily run to $2.0 billion annually. The United States should probably spend up to $1.0 billion annually to mitigate saline surface and groundwater deliveries to Mexico. Private industry in Mexico

---

26. The US Congress is particularly concerned about Mexican funding for environmental efforts. In a 29 July 1991 letter to US Trade Representative Hills, legislators argued that the increased prosperity afforded by a NAFTA would provide Mexico with the resources to bolster its environmental programs (*Inside U.S. Trade,* 2 August 1991, 5–6).

27. In parallel with the NAFTA talks, a groundwater treaty should be negotiated that would cover rights to the customary groundwater flow, establish quality standards, and manage groundwater flows in times of water shortage (see Hayes 1991). A more general question, explored by Lawrence Herzog (1991, 7), is the design of a transfrontier policymaking framework to address a range of environmental problems at the Mexico–US border. According to Herzog, "transfrontier cooperation" has enjoyed some success in Western Europe but so far rather little in the Mexico–US case.

should spend at least $0.3 billion per year to deal with hazardous waste, and another $0.8 billion annually to address point-source air pollution.

Some commentators have suggested that environmental cleanup money can be extracted from the benefits expected to flow from a NAFTA. One suggestion is that foreign investors should pay a surcharge on their Mexican corporate tax. The Environmental Protection Fund, for example, has suggested a "green tax" for goods manufactured in Mexico by US companies and exported to the United States (*El Nacional*, 21 October 1991, 23). Another idea is to establish a temporary environmental fund with a percentage of tariff revenue from North American trade.[28]

In our view, earmarked taxes and tariffs are not the right way to fund environmental improvement. Over time, as tariff rates drop and corporate profits fluctuate, the total amount raised from such charges will be mismatched with environmental needs. Equally important, the *incidence* of such charges will fall too heavily on some activities that are not responsible for pollution, and too lightly on others that are responsible. If nonpolluting activities are made to pay for environmental cleanup, they will be less competitive in world markets, thereby defeating a major goal of NAFTA. A better approach is to set minimum physical targets for pollution abatement, backed both by budget commitments from the respective federal governments,[29] and by specific user fees charged for hazardous waste, air emissions, sewage, and other sources of environmental pollution.[30]

For private firms, this prescription amounts to application of the "polluter-pays" principle, advanced by the Organization for Economic Cooperation and

---

28. Morici (1991, 86) estimates (based on the 1990 volume of trade) that $1 billion could be generated by earmarking 25 percent of the tariff revenue on US, Canadian, and Mexican imports in the first year.

29. William K. Reilly, EPA administrator, and Congressman E. "Kika" de la Garza (D-TX) have proposed forgiving part of Mexico's external debt in exchange for Mexican expenditure on environmental undertakings (*El Nacional*, 21 October 1991, 23). Timothy Atkeson, EPA assistant administrator, has identified additional financial sources: "An environmental infrastructure financing facility in Mexico, US government monies, Mexican appropriations for SEDUE, funds from multilateral banks such as the World Bank and the Inter-American Development Bank" (*Inside U.S. Trade*, 18 October 1991, 2).

30. House Majority Leader Richard A. Gephardt (D-MO), speaking at the Institute for International Economics, proposed that stockholders be allowed to bring derivative suits against US companies if their foreign subsidiaries fail to meet Mexican, Canadian, or other host-country environmental and labor standards (*Inside U.S. Trade*, 13 September 1991, 3). The Gephardt approach raises the specter of extraterritorial enforcement: using US courts to adjudicate offenses arising under Mexican or Canadian laws and perpetrated by Mexican or Canadian corporations. This is anathema to Mexico and Canada, and it recalls a rich history of past quarrels over efforts by the United States to apply its laws extraterritorially to the foreign subsidiaries of US corporations. Clearly, the burden of enforcing environmental standards in Mexico and Canada must be primarily discharged by authorities in those countries.

Development in the 1970s and since accepted by most economists. To be sure, difficult problems of measurement and administration remain (see Robertson 1991, 3). What is the appropriate standard for "tolerable" sulfur emissions? Should user fees be set at flat rates, or should pollution rights be auctioned and traded? It would take us well beyond the scope of this chapter to answer these important questions. We only insist on two key points: public environmental responsibilities should be met from general budget resources rather than earmarked taxes and tariffs; and private responsibilities should be addressed by progressive implementation of the polluter-pays principle.

Environmental Standards

Inevitably, federal and subfederal jurisdictions will set their own environmental standards, either as the conclusive answer to health and safety issues or as a component of enforcing the polluter-pays principle. The international issues raised by the application of environmental standards to private-sector activity can be grouped under two headings: preemption and harmonization. Preemption issues principally concern foodstuffs and consumer goods; harmonization issues mainly affect industrial production.

Preemption occurs when national standards (federal, state, provincial, or local) are overridden by the workings of an international accord. The possibility of a preemption clause in the NAFTA juxtaposes two deeply held but ultimately conflicting values. On the one hand, jurisdictions do not want to lower their environmental and public health standards for any reason; further, most environmental groups want their state and local governments to retain unfettered freedom to set standards. On the other hand, standards can be deliberately designed or can inadvertently work as nontariff barriers (NTBS), which most business firms and trade policy analysts regard as a harmful form of clutter in the path of world commerce.

In a sense, preemption is the inverse of the "environmental dumping" issue. Lax standards can be used as a means of subsidizing production, but overly rigid standards can be used as a device to protect the local market. For example, the United States and Canada ban or strictly limit the use of certain pesticides, such as DDT and heptachlor, and they test Mexican vegetables for minute traces of these chemicals. Mexican producers, noting that some scientists condone the use of these pesticides, might argue that the DDT and heptachlor restrictions act as NTBS.[31]

---

31. See the remarks of a representative of the Illinois Consumers for Safe Food, as quoted in *Journal of Commerce*, 14 May 1991, 10A. Mexico allows the use of DDT, which is banned in the United States and Canada, and allows about 20 times the dosage of heptachlor permitted by the United States.

Such disputes are not just a theoretical possibility. GATT Article XX allows countries to establish any measures deemed necessary to protect human, animal, and plant life as long as they do not constitute a "disguised restriction" on international trade.[32] In the agricultural sector, the United States and Mexico, both GATT members, have already accused each other of using pesticide, safety, and sanitation regulations as GATT–inconsistent barriers to agricultural trade. In 1989, Mexico required that US swine be vaccinated for hog cholera 30 days before export, even though the United States has been free of hog cholera since 1978. Conversely, the United States requires that Persian limes grown in Mexico undergo a chlorine-based treatment before export because of citrus canker, which Mexican growers claim has been eradicated. Similarly, all Mexican avocados are banned by the United States because of the danger that some might carry the seed weevil (US General Accounting Office 1990, 14–15).

The EPA is responsible for establishing the levels of pesticide tolerance on domestic and imported food under the Federal Food, Drug and Cosmetic Act (FFDCA). Monitoring programs by the US Department of Agriculture and the Food and Drug Administration (FDA) enforce the tolerance levels. The Agriculture Department pesticide data program involves regular monitoring of contamination on 600 different food samples (*Journal of Commerce*, 27 September 1991, 1A).[33] The Bush administration has said—and Mexico and Canada have agreed—that established tolerance levels and enforcement functions will not change under a NAFTA but will only be changed on the basis of scientific review (USTR 1991).

In the United States, individual states and even localities can set environmental standards that are stricter than federal standards.[34] Likewise, under Mexico's 1988 General Law, states and local governments can devise their own standards in some areas, and the Canadian provinces enjoy similar powers. Thus the

---

32. For an authoritative analysis of the intersection between trade law and environmental law, see Charnovitz (1991). Twenty years ago, the GATT created a working group on trade and the environment, but the group never met until recent environmental issues prompted its revival in October 1991 (*Financial Times*, 9 October 1991, 3).

33. The FDA reports that food imports from Mexico have gradually improved their compliance levels over the years (USTR 1991, 183).

34. For example, California has more stringent air emissions and toxic waste standards than apply either at the federal level or within most other states. In *Wisconsin Public Intervenor v. Mortier* (case no. 90-1905), the US Supreme Court upheld the power of localities to impose pesticide regulations more stringent than federal standards. This decision leaves open the door for continued litigation between states and localities as to proper pesticide use. The State of California has already been at odds with towns in the Los Angeles metropolitan area that have tried to block state-mandated spraying against the Mediterranean fruit fly (*New York Times*, 22 June 1991, 9).

preemption question, which was not addressed in the Canada–US FTA,[35] will almost certainly arise, given the foreseeable thicket of state, provincial, and local standards. Federal environmental standards adopted in the three NAFTA countries will also be subject to challenge, for they too could act as NTBs.

In this looming debate, all parties concede that food safety standards higher than those set forth by the internationally accepted Codex Alimentarius Commission do not per se constitute an NTB.[36] The UN Codex standards have already been criticized in the United States for being less stringent as to pesticide residue on fruits and vegetables than US law. A precedent for extending the US position to the NAFTA has been set by the European Community, which allows member states to impose standards tougher than the Codex if the European Commission determines that they are not NTBs.

Beyond the proposition that international standards do not automatically settle the preemption question, much remains to be decided. US and Mexican states, and Canadian provinces, have asserted their own strong interest in environmental matters. Hence, we recommend a three-pronged approach that accords maximum deference to subfederal rules:[37]

■ Health, safety, and environmental standards that are enumerated by the Codex Alimentarius Commission and by other recognized international bodies may be enforced by each of the NAFTA countries on an even-handed basis that does not act as a "disguised restriction" on NAFTA commerce. That is to say, internationally recognized standards may be used to bar imports, or to require special sanitation measures, provided that goods produced locally are treated in a similar fashion. The new twist would be the use of NAFTA dispute settlement

35. In the Canada–US FTA, technical standards were not harmonized. Instead, both countries reaffirmed their obligations under the GATT Agreement on Technical Barriers to Trade and promised "to make their respective standards-related measures and procedures more compatible and thus reduce the obstacles to trade and the costs of exporting which arise from having to meet different standards." Mexico acceded to the GATT Standards Code in 1988 (Hart 1990, 112).

36. "[The] Codex, jointly administered by the UN Food and Agriculture Organization (FAO) and the World Health Organization, is a scientific body that sets regional and worldwide advisory pesticide regulations and provides technical assistance among other activities related to food safety" (Overseas Development Council and World Wildlife Fund 1991, 14).

37. An alternative proposal by Uimonen and Whalley (1991) would seek to solve disputes by linking international trade and environmental organizations. Initially, the "link agency" would arbitrate disputes, but eventually it would initiate efforts to modify trade and environmental regulations.

procedures to resolve complaints that internationally recognized standards are being applied in a discriminatory fashion.[38]

■ The existing federal standards of each party should be accepted in their current form.[39] However, when *new* federal standards are adopted by any one of the NAFTA members, other members should have a right of consultation. Once adopted, federal standards could only be challenged as NTBs if they acted as a "disguised restriction" on NAFTA commerce. The question for a NAFTA dispute settlement panel would be the presence or absence of discriminatory design or application, not whether the rationale for the standard is valid on its own terms. The challenger would need to show that the offending standard was designed or in fact acts as an impediment to NAFTA commerce. A party could defend against the challenge by showing that the standard is neither designed nor applied in a discriminatory fashion. In the event the standard cannot be defended, the other trade partner would be entitled to trade "compensation," in the GATT sense of permission to withdraw an equivalent trade concession.[40] The standard itself, however, would continue to have full force and effect unless withdrawn or modified.

■ The existing subfederal standards of each party should also be accepted as is. Again, however, *new* state, provincial, and local standards that come into place after the NAFTA is approved, and that are more stringent than both the appropriate international standard and the federal standard, could also be challenged as to their discriminatory design or application. The dispute procedure and remedies would be the same as for new federal standards that come under challenge.

■ The NAFTA parties would agree to use the NAFTA dispute settlement mechanisms exclusively to resolve disputes over new, post–NAFTA standards, but the parties would retain their right to take disputes over pre–NAFTA standards to the GATT.

The harmonization issue concerns two related questions. First, will standards be harmonized "up" or "down"? Second, when should differences in environmental and public health standards be regarded as an objectionable subsidy?

---

38. The GATT Standards Code contains a dispute settlement mechanism for issues such as food safety. However, not all GATT members have signed the code, and its effectiveness has been questioned by those that have signed (Smith 1991, 7).

39. For NAFTA purposes, the MMPA, which led to the tuna dispute, would thus be accepted as is. The tuna dispute would thus play out under GATT auspices, rather than be carried over into the NAFTA.

40. In the case of subfederal standards, the compensation would be exacted overall from the partner country, not necessarily from the state or province with the offending standard. This remedy parallels the US response to the EC ban on beef fed with hormones: a 100 percent tariff on $100 million in food imports from the Community.

Table 7.1 United States: Pollution abatement expenditures in selected industries, 1988

Industry	Percent of value added
Hydraulic cement	3.17
Pulp mills	2.42
Wood buildings and mobile homes	2.39
Primary nonferrous metals	2.35
Industrial inorganic chemicals	2.21
Industrial organic chemicals	2.13
Paperboard mills	2.08
Papermills	1.97
Agricultural chemicals	1.94
Iron and steel foundries	1.83
Petroleum refining	1.62
Blast furnaces and basic steel	1.39
Miscellaneous nonmetallic mining products	1.28
Metal services not elsewhere specified	1.18
Miscellaneous wood products	1.17
Ordnance and accessories	1.15
Secondary nonferrous metals	1.07
Miscellaneous primary metal products	1.03

Source: Patrick Low, "Trade Measures and Environmental Quality: The Implications for Mexico's Exports," preliminary draft, 1991, annex table A. Reprinted with permission of the author.

Weak standards or lax enforcement can give industries a cost advantage when they relocate (Morici 1991, 43). For example, a recent study by the US General Accounting Office (1991f) found that, over the period 1988 to 1990, between 11 and 28 furniture manufacturers in the Los Angeles area relocated all or part of their manufacturing operations to Mexico, adversely affecting between 960 and 2,547 American workers. The study (which covers too few firms to have much statistical significance) found that "the high costs for workers' compensation insurance and wages, and stringent air pollution emission control standards were major factors in their decision to relocate."[41]

However, table 7.1 shows that the cost of pollution abatement as a percentage of output is relatively low for most US industries.[42] In 1988, US industry spent

---

41. Since 1986 Mexican furniture exports to the United States have doubled. By 1990 Mexico had replaced Italy as the third-largest furniture exporter to the United States, behind Canada and Taiwan (*Journal of Commerce,* 24 June 1991, A1).

42. Low (1991). More than 85 percent of US companies incur pollution abatement costs of less than 2 percent of value added (USTR 1991).

on average only 0.5 percent of output on pollution abatement. High spenders included the hydraulic cement industry (3.2 percent); the pulp mill, wood buildings and mobile homes, and primary nonferrous metals industries (all at 2.4 percent); and the inorganic chemicals industry (2.2 percent).

According to the review supervised by the USTR, those firms that might consider relocation under a NAFTA for environmental reasons are firms that enjoy relatively high US trade protection. Otherwise they would have already taken advantage of low US trade barriers to relocate environmentally hazardous operations abroad. The review indicates that, out of 442 US industries, only 11 have "both significant environmental costs and relatively high trade barriers in the United States."[43] These "target sectors" include steel, petroleum refining, and chemicals— all capital-intensive industries that are not easily relocated. Moreover, the multinational firms that dominate these sectors generally adhere to worldwide standards, since the reputation of the firm can be damaged by the adverse events of a single subsidiary (the Bhopal experience of Union Carbide is the outstanding illustration). Ford Motor Company, for example, states that, even where not required by Mexican law, "Ford environmental practices in the US are also applied at [their] Mexican Maquiladora facilities" (USTR 1991, 142).

As noted earlier, environmentalists are concerned that a lowest-common-denominator approach will be accepted by the NAFTA negotiators. Industries would then be free to locate in Mexico, take advantage of lower standards or relaxed enforcement, and incur no penalty when they shipped goods to the United States or Canada. Conversely, Mexican producers (particularly small, locally owned firms) fear that they will be put out of business by the sudden application of stiff US pollution control standards. They argue the case for environmental sovereignty: when the pollution impact is strictly local, it should be a concern for Mexicans alone. Many Canadians sympathize with the concept of environmental sovereignty over local pollution issues. On this point, there is sharp disagreement between the US environmental groups and most Mexicans and Canadians.

One solution, often discussed in Washington, would entail countervailing duties on imports from NAFTA partners, equal to industry-average pollution abatement costs, in response to privately initiated petitions and upon a showing that international shipments from the polluting firms caused "material injury"

---

43. USTR (1991). Buttressing this conclusion, Gene Grossman and Alan Krueger (1991) of Princeton University studied the determinants of the pattern of US imports from Mexico. They found that intensive use of unskilled labor is a key determinant and that a variable reflecting pollution abatement costs in the US industry adds no further explanatory power.

to the nonpolluting industry.[44] However, a countervailing duty approach would have uneven and highly questionable consequences:

- Duties equal to average pollution abatement costs as a fraction of sales might be small (see table 7.1) and thus ineffective;

- Duties to redress lax environmental enforcement could be challenged under the GATT Code on Subsidies and Countervailing Measures, since lax enforcement in other dimensions of public policy (tax collection, labor standards) are not enumerated in the Code as an impermissible subsidy;

- Duties that depend on privately initiated petitions could be imposed haphazardly, since firms that produce both in the United States and in Mexico would have little incentive to mount legal action (Low 1991, 16).

- The US countervailing duty statute is regarded with great hostility in both Canada and Mexico, despite its limited use against both countries.

Rather than extend the countervailing duty statute to embrace an environmental cause of action, we believe that a better solution is for the NAFTA parties to accept new environmental obligations in staged fashion, with enforcement a public rather than a private matter. Underlying this approach is our belief that over time Mexico, like Canada and the United States, will advocate harmonization "up" rather than "down." All three countries want a cleaner environment, and all three must consider the likely prospect of accession to the NAFTA by other Western Hemisphere countries. Mexico, for example, would not welcome environmental dumping from neighboring Guatemala.

The following is one possible staging scenario:

- In stage 1, to last three years, from 1992 to 1995, all NAFTA parties would commit themselves to strict enforcement of their own standards, and trinational reports would be submitted annually on enforcement practices in each country.

- In stage 2, to commence after 1995, each party could put on notice those standards that it wanted the others to elevate within their own jurisdictions. The standards so notified would become the subject of NAFTA negotiations. When one party could establish, to the satisfaction of a trinational panel, that

---

44. A bill sponsored by Senator David L. Boren (D-OK) advocates the use of countervailing duties. The proceeds from these duties would be used mainly for two purposes: to subsidize the sale of pollution equipment to developing countries and to finance new environmental technologies in the United States. Senator Max Baucus (D-MT) has also suggested the use of countervailing duties (*Financial Times*, 5 December 1991, 7).

it was losing an industry to its NAFTA partners as a direct consequence of its own higher standards, the first resort under the treaty would be to an upward harmonization of standards within the NAFTA. Only if a satisfactory degree of harmonization could not be negotiated within a reasonable period of time (say, one year) would the country applying the higher standards be entitled to apply a special "compensating duty" to its imports of the products in question. For obvious reasons, this special duty should not be labeled a countervailing duty. To make the distinction even sharper, the proceeds of the compensatory duty should be paid over to the exporting country.

■ Also in stage 2, the failure of a country to enforce either its own minimum standards or agreed NAFTA standards would be subject to dispute settlement and trade compensation, using NAFTA mechanisms.

8

Rules of Origin

Free trade areas are by nature discriminatory: lower tariff and nontariff barriers are enjoyed only by the partner countries. To ensure that other countries do not evade the barriers still applied to nonmembers, FTAS necessarily adopt rules of origin to determine which goods actually were produced within the member countries and therefore qualify for preferential treatment.

Rules of origin are designed to ensure that significant economic activity goes into the production of a good in a particular country before an importer can claim that country as the source of the good and thereby take advantage of preferential trade rules. The rules guard both against the transshipment of goods through a member country with relatively low external trade barriers, and against "trade deflection," which occurs when products are only slightly altered or repackaged in order to mask the real country of origin.

The Canada–US FTA provides for the elimination of all US and Canadian tariffs on each other's goods by the end of 1998, and for the reduction or elimination of many nontariff barriers. The United States and Canada have already negotiated detailed rules (explained below) for determining what goods and services, if not wholly US or Canadian, qualify for FTA benefits.

Both Canada and the United States are concerned that a NAFTA might inadvertently facilitate the transshipment of third-country goods through Mexico, bypassing both US and Canadian trade barriers. Indeed, many critics feel that the NAFTA will become an "export platform" for Asian manufacturing firms. To the extent that strict North American rules of origin are agreed upon, the risk that Mexico will serve as an entry point for third-country goods is minimized. At the same time, however, the attractiveness of Mexico as an alternative site of production to Malaysia or the Philippines, for example, will be diminished.

We recommend a middle course between strict and liberal rules. This will be accomplished if the NAFTA rules of origin are closely based on existing Canada–US FTA rules: in fact, this starting point has been accepted by the NAFTA negotiators (see *Inside U.S. Trade,* 26 July 1991, 3; *El Nacional,* 7 September 1991, 25). Two alternative approaches should be mentioned, if only to be rejected: the EC "discretionary" approach, and the distant possibility that global rules of origin will be negotiated under the GATT.

The Canada–US Free Trade Agreement

General Rules of Origin

Rules of origin are important for other purposes besides the creation of preferential trade areas.[1] For example, rules of origin come into play in determining the source of goods that might be subject to antidumping duties, quota limitations, or limitations under voluntary restraint agreements, or for determining the source of goods eligible for special treatment under the Generalized System of Preferences (GSP). The framework for establishing rules of origin to which the European Community and most industrial countries (but not the United States) subscribe is set out in annex D.1 of the International Convention on the Simplification and Harmonization of Customs Procedures (the Kyoto Customs Convention). Annex D.1 was agreed to in 1973 and entered into force in 1977.

Annex D.1 defines a good's country of origin as the country where the good was "wholly produced," or, when two or more countries supply components, the country where the last "substantial transformation" occurred. "Substantial transformation" is qualitatively described as the process that gives the product its "essential character."[2] Specifically, substantial transformation is achieved when:

- the tariff heading under which the inputs are classified is different from that of the output, with exceptions for where a change in tariff heading (CTH) is not decisive;

- certain specified manufacturing or processing operations are undertaken; or

- a specified minimum amount of value is added.

Although the United States subscribes to the concept of substantial transformation as the general rule of origin, it has not agreed to the specifics of annex D.1. In any event, the decision as to whether substantial transformation has occurred is often made on a case-by-case basis, leading to the criticism that the general standard is subjective and unpredictable and promotes needless litigation. In

---

1. This section draws on Hart (1990), US Department of Commerce (1988, 1989b), US General Accounting Office (1988), US Council of the Mexico–US Business Committee (1990), and Motor and Equipment Manufacturers Association (MEMA; 1991).

2. According to the substantial transformation test, a product claims the origin of the last country in which it was transformed into a "new and different article of commerce...[with] a name, character, or use distinct from that of its components..." (US International Trade Commission 1987, 14).

negotiating their FTA, both the United States and Canada were resolved to provide a higher degree of certainty in this murky area.[3]

Rules of Origin Under the Canada–US FTA

The Canada–US FTA explicitly defines substantial transformation by requiring either that the product undergo a CTH under the nomenclature established in the Harmonized Tariff Schedule (HTS),[4] or that the product meet certain value-added tests, or both.[5] The value-added tests are often difficult to implement, but the CTH test can be applied more or less mechanically. This provides an administrative benefit for the Customs Service and a predictability benefit for producers. The rules of origin for preferential treatment under the Canada–US FTA can be summarized as follows:

- Goods are of US–Canada origin if they are wholly obtained or produced in the United States or Canada (e.g., minerals, agricultural and fish products, live animals). Goods in this category may not contain components or ingredients from a third country, nor may they have been added to or undergone any manipulation or assembly in a third country.

- Goods are of US–Canada origin even if they contain imported materials, provided that the imported materials are changed in ways that are physically and commercially significant. The processing or assembly of the imported

3. US International Trade Commission (1987, 14). In September 1991 the US Customs Service proposed new regulations related to rules of origin. Part of the proposal includes certain special guidelines for imported base metals. Eventually these guidelines will be extended to all imported products. The Customs proposal would change the current definition of country of origin to that used in the Canada–US FTA (see the next section). Meanwhile, the Customs Service is contemplating a tougher definition of substantial transformation to require a new "name, character, *and* use." This would be more difficult to demonstrate than the old standard of "name, character, *or* use" (*Journal of Commerce,* 25 November 1991, 8A).

4. The CTH standard includes changes both at the four-digit HTS classification level (usually referred to as "headings") and at the six-digit level (usually referred to as "subheadings").

5. It has been claimed that the FTA rules of origin are really "rules of preference" and that the substantial transformation test still applies to Canada for purposes other than granting preferential tariff treatment. According to this argument, a good may enter the United States and not qualify for duty-free or reduced-duty treatment, yet still be considered of Canadian origin for other purposes, such as quotas, country-of-origin marking, or status under a voluntary restraint agreement (Palmeter 1989, 42). If accepted, this contention would occasionally lead to different origin determinations for the same goods, causing much confusion; hence the United States is developing a proposal that would govern origin for all purposes (*United States–Canada Free Trade Agreement: Biennial Report,* 30 January 1991, 11).

goods must have caused a change in tariff classification under the HTS,[6] and that transformation must have occurred entirely in the United States and/or Canada.

■ With respect to some goods (generally products that can be assembled from parts) the designation of US–Canada origin is conferred only if a specified change in the HTS classification has occurred *and* at least 50 percent of the value of the originating materials plus the direct cost of processing is US, Canadian, or a combination of the two (this is the so-called factory cost test).[7] This means, for example, that if a part classified under HTS heading 8708 (e.g., a steering box) is assembled into a product classified under HTS heading 8703 (motor vehicles for the transport of persons), the finished vehicle must meet the 50 percent test in order to qualify under the FTA.[8]

■ In cases where there is no change in the HTS classification, the 50 percent factory cost test can still confer US–Canada origin. This criterion applies, for example, to automotive products assembled in the United States or Canada from third-country components that were imported in unassembled form, and to textile goods made from fabric listed in the same tariff subheading.

Goods do not qualify for FTA tariff relief if the processing in the United States and/or Canada consisted only of one or more of the following steps:

■ packaging, unless expressly provided for in the HTS;

---

6. The HTS is based on the Brussels Tariff Nomenclature and its successor, the Customs Cooperation Council Tariff Nomenclature. Canada introduced the HTS in 1988; the United States in 1989. Mexico also uses the HTS tariff nomenclature. The HTS is divided into 21 sections and 99 chapters. The US version of the HTS identifies about 15,000 statistical line items. Sections and chapters are arranged according to levels of processing, with primary commodities classified first, followed by more complex products. The HTS classification number consists of six digits; any additional digits are country specific. For example, 0101 is identified as a heading; 0101.19 as a subheading; 0101.19.90 as a tariff item; and 0101.19.90.00 as a classification number (Hart 1990, 195; US Department of Commerce 1989, 2–3).

7. "Factory cost" is defined as the cost of materials, the direct cost of processing or assembling, and factory overhead. The direct cost of processing or assembling is defined to include costs that are either directly incurred in, or can be reasonably allocated to, the production of the good in the United States and/or Canada, namely, labor costs; inspection and testing of the goods; energy, fuel, and machinery costs (including depreciation and maintenance); and development, design, and engineering costs (provided these activities are performed in the United States and/or Canada). The term "direct cost" excludes general business expenses: general administration, debt service, legal fees, and marketing costs. A similar 50 percent factory cost standard has historically been used for US imports of steel products from countries other than Canada. However, the US Customs Service has proposed to adopt a CTH test instead (*Journal of Commerce*, 10 October 1991, 1A).

8. The example is supplied by MEMA (1991, 3).

- dilution with water or any other substance that does not materially alter the characteristics of the goods;

- any alteration or process that was undertaken for the sole purpose of circumventing the rules of origin under the FTA.

Goods that are further processed in a third country before being shipped to their final destination in the United States or Canada do not qualify for FTA treatment. For example, auto parts assembled in US or Canadian maquiladora plants located in Mexico do not qualify, regardless of the degree of US and/or Canadian content. However, component parts built or assembled in Mexico may be transformed sufficiently in the United States to gain US origin status, and then be exported to Canada under FTA tariff preferences (Canada, Standing Senate Committee on Foreign Affairs 1990, 61).

The rules of origin under the Canada–US FTA largely rely on CTH tests to remedy the ambiguities associated with the concept of substantial transformation. However, simple CTH tests do not always work. The HTS nomenclature was not designed to determine the significance of production processes (Palmeter 1989, 47). Most assembly operations produce a CTH, but the change is not always significant. To address these anomalies, products at certain classification levels have been excepted from the general CTH test, which looks to changes in the four-digit heading or the six-digit subheading. In some cases, only designated tariff heading changes confer origin.[9] In other cases (which are far more important in terms of trade coverage), the CTH test is used together with a value-added test. It is worth noting that the 50 percent value-added test in the Canada–US FTA is more demanding than the value-added tests in predecessor arrangements. The GSP, the US–Israel FTA, and the Caribbean Basin Initiative all establish 35 percent value-added tests (MEMA 1991, 5–6). The 35 percent test can be rationalized partly on the ground that the agreements in question had a concessional flavor, but more importantly on the ground that the partner countries are small and must rely heavily on imported components.

---

9. For example, within heading 6812 (fabricated asbestos fibers, etc.) only a change to subheadings 6812.60 through 6812.90 (which includes paper, millboard, felt, and compressed asbestos fiber jointing) from a subheading outside the group (e.g. 6812.20, 6812.30, 6812.40, etc.) will confer origin (Harmonized Tariff Schedule of the United States, 1990, Supplement 1, 21). The requisite CTH to confer US–Canadian origin at specified classification levels has been identified for all irregular cases. The specifications are contained in FTA chapter 3: annex 301.2, which consists of 21 sections (some 20 pages and 1,498 separate rules). In some cases, notably textiles and apparel, the FTA rules are particularly strict where third-country materials are involved.

Many US and Canadian business firms want to modify the FTA rules of origin in the context of the NAFTA negotiations.[10] Some business firms find that the cost of meeting the FTA rules is not worth the benefits of duty-free tariff treatment under the FTA. Other firms, particularly in the automobile industry, see their Japanese competitors taking unfair advantage of the FTA rules. These problems are illustrated by taking a closer look at the rules applied in the textiles and apparel industries and in the automobile industry.

Rules of Origin for Textiles and Apparel

The rules of origin for textiles and apparel were tightly drawn to minimize third-country transshipments. Special exceptions were then created to accommodate "customary" trade. Even with these special exceptions, many textile and apparel firms, together with some electronics firms, complain that FTA benefits are out of reach because of burdensome value-added tests.

FTA rules generally specify that apparel made from foreign fabric must undergo a two-step process to be considered of US or Canadian origin. For example, imported fabric needs to be cut and then sewn. A similar two-step rule applies to textiles: for example, imported wool needs to be spun into yarn and woven into fabric. Analogous rules were devised for steel products made from imported steel. However, a special quota was created so that designated quantities of apparel and fabric that do not undergo a two-step process can nevertheless qualify for FTA preferential treatment.[11]

Most complaints involve the burden of meeting the value-added criterion in cases where processing operations do not change the HTS classification (Toni Dick, US Department of Commerce, International Trade Administration, personal communication, 30 January 1991). Producers in the textile and apparel industries and the electronics industry often complain that there are insufficient tariff headings to account for all product variations; hence, under the general CTH rule, resort must be made to the value-added test. Some companies find the

---

10. Under existing FTA procedures, changes in administrative procedures to implement the rules do not require congressional or parliamentary approval. However, any change in the language of the rules of origin must go through a bilateral review process and be approved by both the US Congress and the Canadian Parliament. Changes made as a result of a NAFTA will obviously be submitted for legislative approval with the rest of the NAFTA package.

11. The FTA establishes the following preferential quotas (in millions of square-yard-equivalents, or SYE): 50 million SYE in nonwoolen apparel and 6 million SYE in woolen apparel imports from Canada, and 10.5 million SYE in nonwoolen apparel and 1.1 million SYE in woolen apparel imports from the United States. Imports above these levels that do not meet the FTA rule of origin pay the normal MFN duty rates.

value-added test either too difficult to meet or too complicated from a bookkeeping standpoint; instead, they choose simply to forgo FTA benefits. Nevertheless, US textile and apparel industry organizations such as the American Textile Manufacturers Institute and the American Apparel Manufacturers Association initially recommended a "down to the cotton ball" rule of origin for the NAFTA— in other words, they advocate "a *100 percent* North American content rule" (*Journal of Commerce,* 25 October 1991, 3A). This was later modified to a "yarn forward" rule, which would allow importation of non–North American fibers.

Automobiles and Parts

Under the US–Canada Auto Pact of 1965, 95 percent of bilateral automotive trade is duty-free. Under the FTA, tariffs and nontariff barriers on all automotive products will be phased out by 1 January 1998;[12] by that time, a new rule of origin will have replaced the rule of origin in the Auto Pact. The new FTA automotive rule of origin will apply to *all* US imports of automotive products from Canada, but it will apply only to Canadian imports of US automotive products *not* entering Canada under the Auto Pact.[13]

The hybrid rules of origin created by the Auto Pact and the FTA may be summarized as follows:

■ For imports of automobiles and parts into the United States from Canada, the FTA rule of origin will replace the current rule of origin under the Auto Pact. Those imports that qualify under the Auto Pact and meet the FTA rule of origin will enter duty-free; those that do not qualify under the Auto Pact but meet the FTA rule of origin will pay the FTA tariff until it is eliminated;[14] imports that

---

12. Tariffs on motor vehicles and original-equipment parts will be phased out over 10 years. Tariffs will be phased out over five years on aftermarket automotive parts that are not eligible under the Auto Pact. The FTA also provides that Canada's export-based duty waiver program will be eliminated in all cases by 1 January 1998 (it has already been eliminated on shipments to the United States), and its special production-based duty waivers (applicable to Honda, Hyundai, Toyota, and the General Motors–Suzuki joint venture CAMI) will end by 1 January 1996. Canada will phase out its embargo on the importation of used cars over five years.

13. Since Canada limits Auto Pact benefits to producers that meet Canadian production tests, it does not need to wrestle with two sets of rules of origin. The US Customs Service would like to accelerate replacement of the Auto Pact rule of origin with the FTA rule, to avoid having to administer two rules of origin for the same category of goods.

14. The phaseout period is 10 years for vehicles and original-equipment parts (to be eliminated in 1998) and 5 years for aftermarket parts (to be eliminated in 1993).

do not qualify under the Auto Pact and do not meet the FTA rule of origin will pay the MFN rate.[15]

- For imports of automobiles and parts into Canada from the United States, Canadian rules of origin for firms that qualify under the Auto Pact will not change; however, no new firms may qualify for Auto Pact or similar benefits.[16] Imports that do not meet Canadian Auto Pact rules but do meet the FTA rule of origin will pay the FTA tariff until it is fully eliminated; imports that do not meet Canadian Auto Pact rules and do not meet FTA rules will pay the MFN rate.

The general FTA rule calls for a change of classification under the HTS. The FTA also requires a special and tougher 50 percent US–Canadian factory cost test for vehicles and assembled parts that embody imported intermediate components. Only labor, materials, and direct processing costs are included in the factory cost version of the value-added test. The old Auto Pact value-added test was more liberal in that it encompassed advertising and overhead.

The new FTA method effectively increases the amount of US and Canadian-sourced parts needed to meet the origin requirement for Auto Pact companies. Nevertheless, US and Canadian parts manufacturers continue to lobby for a 75 percent or higher rule of origin, so as to provide even greater protection against imported parts.[17] They argue that the 50 percent rule enables automobile firms to import an "essential" component, namely, the power train (the engine and transmission), yet still qualify under the FTA. The push for a stricter rule of origin is warmly supported by the United Auto Workers (UAW), which sees jobs at stake (the union seeks an 80 percent rule of origin; *Journal of Commerce*, 24 September 1991, 3A); but it is resisted by the Big Three, at least for their own operations.[18]

---

15. MFN rates for the United States are as follows: automobiles, 2.5 percent; trucks, 25 percent; parts, 3 percent to 6 percent. For Canada the rate for all automobiles and parts is 9.2 percent. Mexico's MFN rates are as follows: automobiles, 15 percent; parts, 13.2 percent. The United States has preferential duty rates under the GSP and HTS 9802.00.60 and 9802.00.80. Canada allows automobile manufacturers that qualify under the Auto Pact to import auto parts duty-free, both from the United States and from third countries (US International Trade Commission 1991a, 4–19).

16. The FTA froze Auto Pact membership, limiting it to the firms that either qualified on 1 January 1988 or were able to qualify by the end of the 1999 model year; those firms must continue to meet both a special Canadian value-added test and a Canadian production-to-sales ratio test (see chapter 11). The major automobile firms that qualify are General Motors, Ford, Volvo, Chrysler, and CAMI (see MEMA 1991, 5).

17. MEMA (1991, 6–12). This is an old issue, carried over from the FTA debate; see Schott (1988, 28–29).

18. Chrysler Corp. et al. (1991, 8–9). The Big Three would, however, apply a 60 percent to 70 percent rule of origin to new entrants. General Motors opposes a higher than 50 percent rule of origin for its own operations because CAMI might be adversely affected.

Instead, the Big Three are most exercised by another issue, namely, the "roll-up" issue. The Canada–US FTA rules attribute origin to the country of majority content. Thus, a part shipped from the United States to Canada that contains $49 worth of third-country content and $51 worth of US content is regarded as entirely of US origin and enters Canada duty-free. If the part is combined in Canada with another third-country component worth $80 and then reenters the United States, all $180 will be regarded as of Canadian origin and thus will enter the United States duty-free. The Automotive Parts Manufacturers' Association (1990, 111) argues, "In this manner, a vehicle could be considered North American despite the fact that far less than 50 percent of its value actually originated there." The Big Three automakers strongly object to roll-up techniques used by Japanese transplants, and they fear that including Mexico in the NAFTA will lead to even more roll-up abuses.[19]

The European Community

The European Community's approach to rules of origin entails greater discretion than the mechanical tests applied in the Canada–US FTA.[20] To some extent the Community has used this discretion as a tool of industrial policy. In our view, the discretionary flavor of the EC approach should be avoided in the NAFTA rules of origin. Opaque protection implemented by tailored rules of origin is far more offensive—just because it is hidden and hard to quantify—than transparent protection implemented by tariffs.

In 1968 the European Community established Regulation 802/68 to determine the origin of goods that are not eligible for Community preferences. Article 5 of this regulation relates to goods that contain products of two or more countries and ascribes origin to "the country in which the last substantial process or operation that is economically justified was performed, having been carried out

---

19. According to the US Customs Service and a study by the University of Michigan, the Honda case illustrates roll-up techniques. Honda claims that its Civics made in Japanese transplant factories have a 75 percent North American content; Customs says the North American content is 15 percent, while the University of Michigan says it is 16 percent. Part of the problem seems to be that overhead has been included by Honda in its calculations, violating the rules of the FTA. But the gap in the figures is mainly due to the exclusion by Customs and the University of Michigan of items that may not violate the FTA but seem to fall in a gray area; these items include depreciation charges (most of the machinery is from Japan) and parts that undergo relatively little processing in the United States and are supplied by US subsidiaries of Japanese companies (*Business Week*, 18 November 1991, 107).

20. This section draws on Winter et al. (1989), US International Trade Commission (1985 and 1990a, chapter 14, 3–9), and US Council of the Mexico–US Business Committee (1990, 12–16).

in an undertaking equipped for the purpose, and resulting in the manufacture of a new product or representing an important stage of manufacture" (US International Trade Commission 1990a, 14–4). Much the same language was later incorporated in annex D.1 of the Kyoto Customs Convention, which entered into force in 1977.

However, the term "substantial process," even when qualified by "economically justified," obviously leaves a great deal to the imagination of the EC Customs Union Service. In order to avoid creating a thicket of qualitative rules, the European Community adopted a CTH standard as its basic rule. The Community requires a change in HTS classification at the four-digit level: origin is ascribed to the last country where the CTH occurred; if that country is an EC member state, the goods are regarded as of EC origin.

Up to this point, the EC rules anticipate the Canada–US FTA approach, which primarily relies on the CTH.[21] However, the Community soon judged that the basic four-digit CTH rule was too strict in some cases and too liberal in others. Hence, extensive exceptions to the CTH test were established by the EC Customs Union Service.[22] It is often contended that the discretionary exceptions amount to an *ad hoc* industrial policy for certain sectors (Winter et al. 1989, 89; Greenwald 1990, 372–73). Three cases are notable: semiconductors, photocopiers, and automobiles.

In 1989, the European Community defined origin for semiconductors as the location of the "*most* substantial process" rather than that of the "*last* substantial process" (*International Trade Reporter,* 18 January 1989, 72; emphasis added). In turn, the most substantial process was defined as "diffusion," the highest-value-added part of the semiconductor manufacturing process. Diffusion must now occur in the European Community for the chip to be considered of EC origin. In the view of most observers, the purpose of this change was to promote semiconductor production in Europe.[23]

In the case of photocopiers, the Community devised a negative rule of origin. In this strange case, the Community defined certain additional operations that do *not* confer origin: "assembly of photocopiers accompanied by manufacture of certain standard parts such as the harness, drum, roller, and side plates." This

---

21. Recall that the Canada–US FTA rule can require either a four-digit or a six-digit change in the tariff heading, or more complex permutations.

22. The exceptions are contained in three lists: items in List A require further changes before EC origin is conferred (affirmative specific processing operations, negative specific processing operations, and value-added tests); List B specifies operations that qualify a good for origin without changing the tariff classification; List C contains rules for determining the origin of petroleum products.

23. The EC diffusion test actually finds precedent in the Canada–US FTA. See Flamm (1990, 273–76).

rule, announced in the context of an antidumping case, was designed to deny a US–origin determination to Japanese-made Ricoh photocopiers assembled in California. Once the goods were deemed not of US origin, they could be subjected to an outstanding EC antidumping order against the same Japanese manufacturer (*International Trade Reporter*, 8 February 1989, 185).

EC proposals for a 1992 automobile rule of origin are based on a value-added standard, somewhat akin to the Canada–US FTA rule. However, the Community is still split over the specifics: the United Kingdom and Germany favor a low threshold, while France, Spain, and Italy favor a high threshold (Randy Miller, US Department of Commerce, Office of Automotive Industry Affairs, personal communication, 21 February 1991). Higher value-added thresholds are widely seen as a way of pressuring Japanese vehicle manufacturers to increase the sourcing of parts within Europe.

The Proposed GATT Agreement on Rules of Origin

To date there is no accepted international standard for determining origin. The closest proxy is annex D.1 of the Kyoto Convention, which leaves important details to national authorities. The benefit of harmonized GATT rules, stated at a high level of specificity, would be simplified customs procedures and increased transparency of trade policies. By the same token, some countries resist the formulation of GATT rules that would apply to preferential trading areas, for they wish to retain a discretionary tool for restricting imports (Toni Dick, US Department of Commerce, International Trade Administration, personal communication, 30 January 1991).

Efforts are under way to negotiate harmonized rules within the GATT. The GATT talks are more likely to make progress in defining rules of origin that apply on an MFN basis than in defining rules that apply to preferential trading areas. But even MFN results will not be seen in the near future: at best the GATT will produce a framework agreement calling for several years of technical work, in conjunction with the Customs Cooperation Council, to address the details.

As a first step, a technical committee would negotiate harmonized definitions in the following areas: goods that are to be considered wholly obtained in one country; and minimal operations that alone do *not* qualify the good for origin. Then, for goods produced by more than one country, the proposed rule of origin would be based on the principle of substantial transformation, with origin conferred on the last country where this occurred.

The technical committee would be charged with elaborating upon the specific use of a CTH rule for each product sector. Where a change in tariff classification is not appropriate, supplementary criteria—value-added and manufacturing process requirements—would be established by specifying the operations that confer origin and by indicating the method for calculating the required value-added percentage. According to the framework draft, the technical committee would have up to two years and three months to complete its work.

The GATT timetable is clearly too leisurely to provide results that might be useful in the NAFTA talks. Later in the decade, however, it may be necessary to reconcile the NAFTA rules with their GATT counterparts.

Recommendations

The major US concern in negotiating rules of origin for the NAFTA is that Mexico will become an "export platform" for Japanese, Brazilian, or other third-country goods seeking duty-free access to the North American market.[24] The focal point of concern is automobiles and auto parts, but other industries ranging from textiles and apparel, to electronics, to steel products are also worried. Meanwhile, these same industries and others (telecommunications, chemicals, and personal care product manufacturers) want to use the NAFTA talks as an opportunity to revisit the value-added tests incorporated in the Canada–US FTA.

Canada and Mexico see the problem differently. They do not want to cut themselves off from investment by Asian and European firms. Canadian Minister of International Trade Michael Wilson, reflecting the position of Honda, Hyundai, and Volkswagen, has thus insisted that Canada will not increase the North American content requirement for cars beyond 50 percent.[25] Mexico is even more adamant. Low Mexican wages make it harder for Mexican processing operations to meet any given North American value-added test. Mexican Commerce Secretary Jaime Serra Puche states the Mexican position: "...[origin rules] have to be designed with enough intelligence so that they do not reduce the competitiveness of Mexico's industries" (*Inside U.S. Trade*, 23 August 1991, 19). Soichi Amemiya, head of Nissan Mexicana, has called a 70 percent rule of origin "totally out of the question" (*Financial Times*, 7 October 1991, 8).

---

24. This section draws on Hart (1990, 37–38)

25. *Inside U.S. Trade*, 29 August 1991, 1. As a general proposition, according to John Simpson, Deputy Assistant Secretary of the Treasury, while the United States and Mexico see themselves as "integrated economies that manufacture goods with domestically sourced raw and intermediate materials," Canada views itself as "an assembly point for goods made with imported parts." Canada thus wants liberal rules of origin (*Journal of Commerce*, 5 December 1991, 1A).

A Trinational Commission

If the US–Canada negotiating process in the FTA were to serve as the model, NAFTA negotiations on a product-by-product basis would be required to devise rules for products of special interest to Mexico. Our first recommendation is that, with very few exceptions, the negotiators should *not* engage in a product-by-product exercise. Instead, they should simply incorporate the existing US–Canada rules into the NAFTA. Product-by-product negotiations invite protectionism to creep into the NAFTA, ushered in by "industry specialists," the only people familiar enough with the mind-boggling technical details of tariff classification (Palmeter 1989, 47).

In making this recommendation, we are aware that the negotiators have already embarked on product-by-product talks, with a view to designing stricter rules of origin than the Canada–US FTA provides.[26] We are concerned that a good deal of disguised protectionism will creep into this exercise, setting a bad precedent for Asia and, in a sense, ratifying the protectionist inclinations of the European Community.

In October 1991, trade officials from the three countries agreed that the CTH test will be used for the majority of products and that a specific "percentage of regional content" will be negotiated for sensitive areas.[27] Whatever details are worked out in these talks, the NAFTA negotiators should devise a workable process for changing an FTA rule when it can be shown that the rule is overly burdensome, or that it invites abuse, or that new products require new tariff headings.[28]

To manage the process of change, we recommend the creation of a permanent trinational commission. In response to petitions, the commission would hold open hearings modeled after those of the US International Trade Commission and the Canadian Import Tribunal. The commission would then determine whether the rules should be altered to avert an abuse or to answer some other problem. Its recommendations, by majority vote, would take effect within 120 days, unless specifically overruled by the Canadian Parliament, the Mexican Congress, or the US Congress.

---

26. According to press reports, as of September 1991 the negotiating group had already examined 50 of the 99 chapters of the HTS (*El Nacional,* 7 September 1991, 25; *Inside U.S. Trade,* 13 September 1991, 18–19).

27. Further, it has reportedly been agreed that "the rules governing regional content might differ from product to product but not from country to country" (*Financial Times,* 7 October 1991, 8). According to John Simpson, content-value tests are likely to be used in chemicals and automobiles (*Journal of Commerce,* 5 December 1991, 1A).

28. Some of the issues that may arise, as pointed out by John Simpson, include potential conflicts over the purchase of imported components at artificially low prices; fluctuations in the market prices of those components; and foreign-exchange fluctuations (*Journal of Commerce,* 5 December 1991, 1A).

We would assign the commission a second task as well: that of initiating the gradual transformation of value-added tests into CTH tests.[29] Value-added tests are undesirable for two reasons. They require detailed and expensive bookkeeping, and, more important, they discriminate against Mexico. Because of its lower wages, Mexico may incur smaller labor costs than Canada or the United States in carrying out exactly the same processing operations; thus, under a value-added test, the Mexican component would be disqualified as a North American product, whereas the US and Canadian components would qualify.

If the trinational commission succeeds in its work, and if later in the 1990s the GATT should design harmonized international rules of origin, the commission could then be assigned the task of with conforming the NAFTA rules to those of the GATT. Alternatively, the commission could open talks with the European Community to harmonize or at least approximate NAFTA and EC rules of origin.

Although our major recommendation is the formation of a trinational commission, not all issues can be consigned to this body. Two specific issues require the immediate attention of the NAFTA negotiators. The first involves the intersection of Mexican duty drawback provisions and NAFTA rules of origin in the context of maquiladoras that use large quantities of third-country components (see chapter 5). The second involves the immediate need for new rules to address the roll-up problem in the automobile sector (discussed above).

HTS Benefits

The HTS production-sharing provisions (HTS 9802.00.60 and 9802.00.80) exclude the US portion of the imported good from US tariffs. As a consequence, US duty is levied only on the value of foreign components and processing. Currently, maquiladoras can benefit from HTS 9802.00.60 and 9802.00.80 preferences for the US component of their products, regardless of the extent of third-country content in the final product. Moreover, under the current maquiladora arrangement, no Mexican duties are charged on third-country imports of components provided that the finished product is exported. This in-bond provision is functionally equivalent to the rebate, or drawback, of duty on imported components when the product is exported.

Under NAFTA rules of origin, Japanese- and Korean-owned maquiladoras might find that their shipments to the United States do not qualify for duty-free treat-

---

29. New HTS subheadings will sometimes be required to accomplish this result. The NAFTA negotiators have already indicated a preference for CTH tests rather than value-added tests (*Inside U.S. Trade*, 13 September 1991, 18–19). The US Customs Service also prefers CTH tests for administrative reasons, as evidenced by its proposals (*Journal of Commerce*, 10 October 1991, 1A).

ment. Moreover, application of the Canada–US FTA provisions would prohibit duty drawback when goods with third-country components are shipped from one NAFTA partner to another ("same-condition drawback" would, of course, still be permitted). The combined result is that third-country maquiladoras could lose not only existing US HTS benefits on their US components, but also Mexican in-bond benefits.

In the Canada–US FTA, Canadian use of production-based duty remissions will be phased out by 1996.[30] We recommend that the Mexican maquiladora incentives be treated according to a similar timetable.[31] Thus, HTS benefits would be temporarily continued, whether or not the goods meet the NAFTA rules of origin, but only until January 1996. After that, HTS benefits would be denied to goods that do not meet NAFTA rules of origin. Likewise, in-bond processing would be abolished for intra–NAFTA trade by January 1996, well before the NAFTA duty-free provisions take full effect.

Rules of Origin for Automobiles

In President Bush's biennial report on the Canada–US FTA, the Automotive Select Panel offered an answer to the roll-up problem. It recommended increasing the origin rule from 50 percent to 60 percent for an auto part or vehicle to qualify for purposes of the Auto Pact or the FTA.[32] In the context of the NAFTA, the penalty for not complying with the rule would be continued application of the MFN tariff rates by each of the countries, both to auto parts and to automobiles.

The reason for a 60 percent figure seems to be that Asian transplant manufacturers could not then import power trains and still meet a 60 percent test for the assembled automobiles. For the same reason, Canada has so far refused to increase the origin rule, fearing that transplant producers located in Canada would be disadvantaged. As negotiations proceed, the Canadian position may shift under pressure from organized labor and Canadian parts markets. Moreover, if a distinction is drawn between established producers and new entrants, as the Big Three suggest, Canada will find it easier to modify the FTA rule.

---

30. All export-based duty remissions to the United States were immediately ended under FTA Article 1001:2(a) except for products exported from Canada in exactly the same form as they were imported into Canada (same-condition drawback).

31. The important question of Mexican and Canadian production-to-sales ratio tests, applied under the Mexican Auto Decree of 1989 and the Auto Pact, is discussed in chapter 11.

32. *United States–Canada Free Trade Agreement: Biennial Report*, 30 January 1991, 24; *Financial Times*, 12 March 1991, 3. Senator Donald W. Riegle, Jr. (D-MI) suggested a 75 percent North American content provision. US Trade Representative Carla A. Hills has said that the administration will try to negotiate in the NAFTA a new rule of origin higher than the rule contained in the Canada–US FTA (*Inside U.S. Trade*, 3 May 1991, 1).

The Big Three announced a new position in September 1991 (Chrysler Corp. et al. 1991). They recommend that the 50 percent standard be retained for existing Auto Pact companies, but that a higher standard of 60 percent (the General Motors suggestion) or 70 percent (the Ford and Chrysler suggestion) be applied to new entrants. In addition, the Big Three want special provisions to address the roll-up issue.

In contrast with the Big Three, the auto parts manufacturers want a rule of origin that amounts to at least 75 percent. Indeed, this is the overriding goal of the auto parts manufacturers in the NAFTA negotiations. They argue that a 75 percent or higher rule would encourage automobile firms to source "essential" components within the North American region. The MEMA (1991, 7) has produced the following illustrative calculation. For a $10,000 automobile (f.o.b. factory price basis), some $1,445 represents items that are not included in "factory cost," namely, indirect labor, nonproduction overhead, and markup. Of the remaining $8,555, about $2,113 is the cost of a power train. This means that factory cost excluding the power train is $6,442, or 75.3 percent. On the basis of these figures, the MEMA contends that, to ensure that power trains are produced within the NAFTA, the rule of origin should be 75.3 percent or higher.

We have three responses to the recommendations of the Big Three and the auto parts manufacturers. First, as to the two-tier idea advanced by the Big Three, we oppose the use of rules of origin, which are understood only by lawyers and technicians, to discriminate between new entrants and existing market players. The only plausible justification for such opaque discrimination is that the European Community has, in different but reminiscent ways, discriminated against Japanese firms. We do not think that the United States should borrow the worst features of EC commercial policy. Opaque protection has invisible costs that get buried from public view; hence the protective measures are hard to dislodge.[33]

If a decision is made that established North American automakers are to be sheltered for a period of years from head-to-head competition with new Japanese firms operating in the North American market, we strongly prefer that the decision be implemented through transparent forms of protection (see chapter 11) rather than by two-tier NAFTA rules of origin.

Second, we do not warm to the idea of using rules of origin as a mini–industrial policy to encourage the production of power trains or other "essential" auto parts in North America. Instead we would like to see the 50 percent "factory cost" test of the Canada–US FTA retained and applied to all NAFTA producers. The tariff-equivalent of raising this value-added test from 50 percent to 70 percent could be very steep. For example, if an automobile firm is just over the 50 percent

---

33. An example is the extraordinarily long life of the American Selling Price (ASP) tariff system, a highly protective device that lasted from the Fordney-McCumber Tariff of 1922 until the Tokyo Round reforms of 1979.

threshold, and if it stands to lose all its NAFTA tariff benefits on 100 percent of its shipments unless it now raises its North American content to 70 percent, then the implicit tariff equivalent rate on the extra 20 percent of auto parts could work out to between 15 and 100 percent.[34] In our view, the NAFTA should not be launched by imposing a disguised tariff of 15 percent or more against third-country suppliers of power trains or other auto parts. That said, we recognize that the auto parts firms, working through Washington and Ottawa, might well be rewarded with some increase in the 50 percent rule of origin. As a fallback concession, we strongly prefer a 60 percent rule to a 70 percent rule. The higher rule, if enacted, should apply to all firms, not just newcomers. North America should not set a visible precedent for Europe and Japan to discriminate against "foreign" multinationals.

Third, we recommend that new anti-roll-up provisions be imposed as an overlay test—but only on the largest automotive manufacturers, namely, the Big Three and their European and Japanese counterparts. For example, each of these manufacturers could be required to show, as a qualifying overlay test for NAFTA benefits, that their overall sales within North America meet a 50 percent value-added test (defined in factory cost terms). At the option of the manufacturer, the firm could either include or exclude its vehicle and parts exports to countries outside North America from the overlay test. With this flexibility, exports would not be discouraged by the new test. The administrative burden of imposing this overlay test, coupled with the lesser ability of small manufacturers to engage in roll-up games, argues that it should only be applied to the largest firms.

---

34. Tariffs between NAFTA partners, by comparison with MFN tariffs, will entail preferences of 3 percentage points to 20 percentage points of *ad valorem* tariff, depending on the direction of intra–NAFTA shipments. A tariff saving of 3 percent on $100 of shipments is $3; this $3, expressed as a percentage of an extra $20 of auto parts, works out to a 15 percent tariff-equivalent. This calculation illustrates the situation for shipments from Mexico or Canada to the United States. The impact on shipments to Mexico could be much larger. A tariff saving of 20 percent on $100 of shipments is $20; this $20 expressed as a percentage of an extra $20 of auto parts works out to a 100 percent tariff-equivalent.

9

Intellectual Property Issues

The United States, Canada, and Mexico are all members of the most important international conventions on patents, trademarks, and copyrights, including the World Intellectual Property Organization, the Lisbon Agreement for Protection of Appellations of Origin, the Universal Copyright Convention, the Berne Convention for the Protection of Literary and Artistic Works, the Brussels Satellite Convention, the Geneva Phonograms Convention, and the Rome Convention. However, because of a combination of inadequate standards for the protection of intellectual property in some areas (especially with regard to new technologies), lax enforcement, and national reservations, problems relating to intellectual property rights (IPRS) have posed a serious obstacle to improved North American economic relations.

In the NAFTA talks, the three countries have established a separate negotiating group on intellectual property issues. The group is likely to have a dual focus: first, to augment the meager results of the Canada–US Free Trade Agreement (FTA) in this area and to tackle anew the longstanding US–Canada dispute over the compulsory licensing of pharmaceutical patents; and second, to lock in recent changes in Mexican intellectual property laws and regulations and resolve the remaining problems with Mexican intellectual property protection.

US industries have long been concerned about inadequate protection and lax enforcement of IPRS in Mexico. The US International Trade Commission (1988a) ranked Mexico fourth-worst in the world in the overall protection of these rights: Mexico scored the worst ranking for inadequate patent protection and for trademark problems, second-worst for trade secret problems, and fifth-worst for proprietary technical data problems. In 1989 Mexico was placed on the "priority watch" list under the United States' Special 301 provisions regarding intellectual property, but it was removed from the list in 1990 when the Mexican government introduced draft legislation designed to strengthen intellectual property protection.

Enactment of new Mexican intellectual property legislation in June and July 1991 eliminates the vast majority of problems cited by US industries relating to

---

Lee L. Remick and Joanna M. van Rooij helped draft this chapter.

patents, copyrights, and trademarks. If adequately enforced, the legislation will remove a significant irritant to the bilateral trade relationship. The reforms are so comprehensive that, in many respects, the new Mexican legislation will serve as a standard against which the United States gauges the intellectual property regimes of other countries.

Mexican Protection of IPRs

Until recently, Mexican laws and regulations afforded little effective protection for IPRS. The base legislation governing IPRS in Mexico was the 1976 Law of Inventions and Trademarks (LIT) and its 1987 amendments. The Mexican system reflected nationalistic concerns that foreign firms would gain an undesirable degree of control over the Mexican economy if they enjoyed liberal access to patent, copyright, and trade secret protection.

In January 1990 the Mexican government published a comprehensive plan to modernize its intellectual property regime; new industrial property protection legislation was sent to the Mexican Congress in December 1990. In May 1991, the Mexican Senate approved the comprehensive patent and trademark law, and the Chamber of Deputies followed suit in late June 1991. In light of these developments and the pending NAFTA negotiations, Mexico was not placed on the 1991 Special 301 "watch list," despite recommendations from the International Intellectual Property Alliance that it be listed (see the testimony of US Trade Representative Carla A. Hills in US Congress, Senate Committee on the Judiciary, Subcommittee on Patents, Copyrights and Trademarks 1991, 12; and *Inside U.S. Trade*, 7 June 1991, 1–2). In parallel fashion, the Mexican government introduced legislation in May 1990 to revise the 1956 Copyright Act. The legislation, which expands both the coverage and enforcement of copyright protection, was enacted in early July 1991 (see Hills's testimony, cited above, 12–13; and *Journal of Commerce*, 11 July 1991, 3A).

The passage of adequate intellectual property legislation prior to the commencement of formal NAFTA talks was seen as an acid test of Mexico's ability to deliver on the commitments it will make in future negotiations. Mexico passed the test with distinction: US pharmaceutical manufacturers, computer software producers, and the recording industries had conditioned their support for the talks on substantial reforms in the Mexican intellectual property laws (*Journal of Commerce*, 20 February 1991, A1), and informal soundings indicate that these groups were well satisfied with the legislative outcome and that their attention has now shifted to the enforcement details.

Patents

The 1976 LIT did not afford patent protection for a wide variety of products and processes, including pharmaceutical products. The 1987 amendments increased the scope and coverage of patent protection and extended the life of a patent from 10 years to 14 years. The period within which a patent must be worked in order to obtain protection was extended from one to three years.[1] However, some key products such as pharmaceuticals and chemical products, beverages and food for animal consumption, fertilizers, pesticides, herbicides, fungicides, and biologically active products and the biotechnological processes used to produce them, would not be covered until 1997.

As with Canada, the main US concern in this area involved compulsory licensing provisions. The Mexican Patent and Trademark Office (MPTO) had the authority to grant compulsory licenses if a patent had not been worked within three years of its issuance. Justifiable nonuse—for example, too small a prospective scale of production within Mexico—was no defense against a compulsory licensing order.

The new Mexican legislation on IPRs addresses most of the specific US concerns. For example, the prohibition of unrestricted parallel imports addresses the concern of the US pharmaceutical industry that Mexico would allow the importation of a patented pharmaceutical product that was manufactured anywhere in the world—including countries without patent protection. The 1991 legislation also restricts compulsory licensing of patents to special circumstances (importation of a product is sufficient to meet "working" requirements so that the foreign patentholder can avoid compulsory licensing; this contrasts sharply with Canadian policy, under which pharmaceutical companies are still required to license their products to other manufacturers if the Canadian government judges that the prices charged are too high; *Journal of Commerce*, 2 August 1991, 3A; 7 November 1991, 1A). In addition, the Mexican law extends immediate coverage of patent protection to previously unprotected products, including pharmaceutical and beverage and food products; and it increases the life of the patent to 20 years.[2]

---

1. "Working" or exploitation usually requires that the local manufacture of the invented product, or the use of the invented process, occur within some specified time period. This requirement is designed to facilitate technology transfer. In Mexico, exploitation must be on an "industrial scale and on satisfactory conditions as to quality and price" (*Manual of Industrial Property* 1990, Supplement no. 61, March 1990, 7).

2. *Inside U.S. Trade*, 7 June 1991, 1–2. Harvey Bale, senior vice president of the Pharmaceutical Manufacturers Association, states that, with its new law, Mexico offers US companies "far better protection than Canada."

Trademarks

The 1976 LIT granted trademark protection for renewable five-year periods. However, the trademark was automatically canceled if there was no proof of use within three years after registration. The 1987 amendments strengthened trademark protection by banning the use of identical or similar trademarks, by hearing objections before registration of a trademark, and by eliminating "linking."[3]

The United States had three major concerns with Mexican trademark legislation after the 1987 reforms. First, Mexico could grant a compulsory license if the trademark was not used within three years. Second, Mexico required that a trademark must be used exactly as registered; any other form would result in cancellation of the trademark. Third, Mexico allowed no exceptions regarding its policy to cancel the trademark if there was no proof of use within three years after registration.[4] All three concerns have been mitigated under the new law, which increases trademark protection to 10 years; allows variations in the manner and form in which a trademark is used; and permits justifiable nonuse (Draft Law for the Development and Protection of Industrial Property, Title Four, Chapter I, 18–21).

Copyright

The 1956 Mexican Copyright Law provided stronger and broader protection for copyrights than applies to patents and trademarks under the 1976 LIT. However, the United States has had four concerns with Mexican copyright protection. First, Mexico did not provide statutory protection for computer software (however, 1984 regulations administering the LIT extended copyright protection to software).[5] Although the 1984 regulations prohibited copying software for profitable resale, the regulations permitted copying for nonprofitable use—for example by universities, government agencies, and corporations (testimony of Karen Casser, Director of Public Policy and Legal Affairs, Software Publishers Association, in

---

3. Linking is the requirement that every foreign trademark must be used in conjunction with a Mexican trademark owned by the licensee. See the testimony of D. Michael Clayton, Samsonite Corporation, in US Congress, Senate Committee on the Judiciary, Subcommittee on Patents, Copyrights, and Trademarks (1991).

4. In that respect Mexico did not conform to Article 5 of the Paris Convention, under which a registration may only be cancelled if the owner does not justify its nonuse.

5. The US Business Software Alliance found no evidence that, under these regulations, software protection has ever been upheld in any judicial decision. See US International Trade Commission (1990b, 6–12).

US Congress, Senate Committee on the Judiciary, Subcommittee on Patents, Copyrights and Trademarks 1991).

Second, Mexican copyright law did not protect sound recordings, but only the underlying composition.[6] To establish a case, proof of infringement was required from several US parties—the US author, the publisher, the record company, and, finally, the foreign licensee—rather than from the record company alone (Neil Turkowitz, Recording Industry Association of America, Inc., personal communication, 10 May 1991). This requirement hindered the prosecution of infringement cases.

Third, Mexico allowed retransmission of international satellite signals for "public performances." Under this loophole, Mexican cable systems retransmitted US broadcasting material without payment to the US copyright owner (US International Trade Commission 1990b, 6-12 and 6-13).

Fourth, Mexican law was geared to the payment of royalties to authors, composers, directors, and performers, whereas the US law is oriented to the payment of royalties to film studios and producers. Under the 1956 law, Mexico suspended royalty payments claimed by US producers because Mexican performers did not receive royalties for films and sound recordings distributed in the United States (US International Trade Commission 1990b, 6-13).

The 1991 legislation adds computer software programs to Article 7 of the Copyright Law (but does not provide explicit protection for computer programs as literary products as under the Berne Convention); prohibits private copying of software; and strengthens enforcement by increasing the financial penalties to $30,000 and by extending the maximum prison term to 6 to 12 years. In addition, the 1991 legislation extends protection for sound recordings to 50 years and resolves the impasse on copyright royalties.

However, the problem of pirated satellite retransmissions remains, since the new law does not clarify the definition of "public performance" (US International Trade Commission 1990b, 6–12; testimony of Karen Casser in US Congress, Senate Committee on the Judiciary, Subcommittee on Patents, Copyrights and Trademarks 1991). A similar issue arose in the Canada–US context and resulted in a provision being added to the FTA (Article 2006) that commits both countries to provide "a right of equitable and non-discriminatory remuneration for any retransmission to the public of the copyright holder's program where the original transmission of the program is carried in distant signals intended for free, over-the-air reception by the general public." The same formula could also be applied to deal with this remaining US–Mexican problem.

---

6. The piracy rate for records and cassettes in Mexico is estimated to exceed 50 percent. The Recording Industry Association of America has estimated that foreign companies lose $250 million a year in Mexican sales, of which US producers account for $75 million (US International Trade Commission 1990b, 6–11 and 6–14).

Trade Secrets

While patent protection confers a legal monopoly for a definite period of time, trade secrets are protected indefinitely until they are properly discovered by outsiders. Trade secret protection is particularly important in high-technology industries where the commercial half-life of new products is often shorter than the time needed to process a patent application.

The 1987 amendments to the 1976 LIT provided intellectual property protection for trade secrets. However, the Mexican statute required proof that another party had obtained the trade secret through illicit means or used the secret while knowing that it was stolen; this was often very difficult to determine (US International Trade Commission 1990b, 6–16).

Here again the 1991 legislation fits Mexican law into the US mold. The new law broadly defines trade secrets in a way that parallels US concepts; provides for trade secret protection against appropriation without consent of the owner, and provides a mechanism for preliminary relief.

Enforcement

Inadequate enforcement has long been a major problem relating to the protection of intellectual property in Mexico. The agencies responsible for intellectual property protection—the MPTO, the Mexican Copyright Office, and the Federal Policy and Prosecutors Office—lack the human and technical resources to adequately administer and enforce the intellectual property laws. For example, 30 MPTO examiners (compared with 1,500 in the United States) are responsible for processing applications and enforcing Mexican patents and trademarks; 10 Copyright Office examiners (compared with 200 in the United States) are responsible for copyrights (US International Trade Commission 1990b, 6–4 and 6–7). The cost, duration, and uncertainty of proceedings have led to few infringement cases being brought in Mexico, and most cases are settled out of court (US International Trade Commission 1990b, 6–10).

In August 1988, new regulations strengthened the enforcement powers of the MPTO, the Copyright Office, and the Federal Police and Prosecutors Office. The regulations gave the authorities the right to seize goods, impose fines, and close businesses engaged in piracy.[7] However, there still was no preliminary relief for

---

7. To further strengthen the protection and enforcement of IPRS, the Mexican government announced in January 1990 that "the infrastructure of the Patent and Trademark Registry will be modernized and measures for simplified administration will be introduced to expedite services to individuals. Industrial property infractions or crimes...will be energetically combatted" (US International Trade Commission 1990b, 6–7).

intellectual property infringement before the completion of legal procedures; and low criminal penalties, applied per case and not per copy, provided little economic disincentive for infringers. Arrests, fines, and imprisonments were rare. Mexican prison terms ranged from one month to six years; prison terms for less than six months were avoided by payment of a small fine. The maximum fine for infringement was $4.00. In contrast, the 1991 legislation provides for prison terms of 6 to 12 years and fines of up to 10,000 times the daily minimum wage in Mexico City (or about $30,000) for the violation of patents, trademarks, and trade secrets (Draft Law for the Development and Protection of Industrial Property, Article 224, 46).

Protection of IPRs in the Canada–US FTA

Despite extensive negotiating efforts, the Canada–US FTA does not include a chapter on IPRs. The dispute over broadcast retransmissions was satisfactorily resolved, but the dispute over pharmaceutical patent protection led to a breakdown of talks in the bilateral working group on intellectual property (Hart 1989, 120). Instead, Article 2004 was added to the FTA, committing the United States and Canada to "cooperate in the Uruguay Round of multilateral trade negotiations and in other international forums to improve the protection of intellectual property rights."

From the US perspective, the major outstanding issue is Canada's patent law, which permits the compulsory licensing of pharmaceutical products. The Canadian government can compel patent holders to license their pharmaceutical know-how to Canadian manufactures at a low royalty rate. The Canadian justification for this provision (known as law C-22) is that pharmaceutical patents often give foreign firms excessive profits while limiting consumer access to drugs (Maskus 1989, 70). Obviously US pharmaceutical firms disagree. The Pharmaceutical Manufacturers Association (PMA) has flagged other objectionable provisions in the Canadian patent law:

> [a] discriminatory patent term of seven or ten years for products not researched and discovered in Canada versus twenty years for those products researched and discovered in Canada; automatic compulsory licenses for export; market exclusivity (not patent term) of seven years if a Canadian generic company plans to produce the active ingredient in Canada versus market exclusivity of ten years if the active ingredient is imported; and, linkage of patent protection to prices through compulsory licensing. (Testimony of Gerald Mossinghoff, President of the Pharmaceutical Manufacturers Association, in US Congress, Senate Committee on the Judiciary, Subcommittee on Patents, Copyrights and Trademarks 1991)

In response, the PMA recommended in 1991 that the USTR initiate a Section 301 case against Canadian practices (*Inside U.S. Trade,* 22 February 1991, 3). Canada was placed on the USTR Special 301 watch list in 1989, 1990, and again in 1991 because of its continued policy of compulsory licensing for pharmaceutical products.

A second problem relates to Canadian restrictions on foreign investment in "culturally sensitive" sectors such as publishing, television, and cinema (Maskus 1989, 71). The restrictions hinder US firms from exploiting copyrights, especially through the use of lucrative TV channels. US industry has strongly argued that "culture is frequently merely a convenient, if thinly veiled, disguise for economic protectionism, and has little to do with content, but a great deal to do with who will profit in the marketplace from the exploitation of American copyrighted material" (testimony of Jason S. Berman, President of the Recording Industry Association of America, in US Congress, Senate Committee on the Judiciary, Subcommittee on Patents, Copyrights and Trademarks 1991). While the Canadian restrictions are permissible under the "cultural exemption" provisions of the Canada–US FTA, US industry is likely to lobby hard to delete that exemption from the trilateral agreement.[8] Following their lead, US Trade Representative Carla A. Hills has argued that both the cultural exemption and compulsory licensing issues need to be revisited in trilateral negotiations (US Congress, Senate Committee on the Judiciary, Subcommittee on Patents, Copyrights and Trademarks 1991 11).[9]

Recommendations

As a result of the new Mexican legislation, trilateral negotiations on IPRS will focus more on Canada than Mexico. The primary objective of the intellectual property talks should be to resolve the longstanding US–Canada dispute relating to Canadian compulsory licensing practices, if adequate arrangements have not by then been worked out in the GATT negotiations.

There are still outstanding issues with Mexico, however. For example, the US Council for International Business recommends that the Mexican government give patent protection to biotechnology and computer program inventions, improve the protection accorded to semiconductor mask works, clarify the protection of trade secrets, and ensure comprehensive protection of all classes of literary works, particularly computer software (*Inside U.S. Trade*, 15 November

---

8. Supporting the inclusion of cultural issues in the NAFTA talks, Herminio Blanco, chief negotiator for Mexico, said that "cultural industries have to be negotiated as part of the services sector which includes entertainment" (*Journal of Commerce*, 8 August 1991, 9A).

9. Jack Valenti, President of the Motion Picture Association of America, has stated that his association will oppose any agreement that does not adequately address the cultural exemption issue (speech at Georgetown University, 2 October 1991).

1991, 5). In addition, the NAFTA should include a surveillance mechanism to monitor the patent licensing practices and the enforcement of intellectual property laws (an issue of particular relevance in Mexico), and to ensure compliance with NAFTA obligations.

Canada can be expected to exact a high price for accepting obligations regarding compulsory licensing comparable to those legislated by Mexico. In return for those concessions, the United States should agree that future intellectual property disputes involving firms in the region will be handled within the trinational framework of the NAFTA dispute resolution procedures, thus preempting recourse to remedies under section 337 and the Special 301 provisions of US trade law.

Finally, an intellectual property agreement within the NAFTA should lock in reforms in Mexico and commit the NAFTA partners to adhere to the prospective GATT accord on intellectual property, or undertake equivalent obligations if the GATT talks fail. Together, these various actions should dramatically reduce the incidence of intellectual property disputes within North America.

Sectoral Analyses

10

Energy

The energy sector is the anomaly of the NAFTA negotiations. It accounts for the largest share of US trade with Canada and Mexico, yet neither country is willing to commit to open trade and investment policies comparable to the prospective liberalization in other sectors. The reason is their overriding concern about sovereignty over national resources.

The Canada–US FTA contained important provisions relating to the pricing of, and access to, energy resources, but in general it exempted the energy sector from obligations to liberalize investment policy. Mexico would like an even broader carve-out for the energy sector in the NAFTA so that its ability to regulate production and exports in keeping with its national security and industrial policy objectives remains unconstrained (see Vega 1991).

However, Mexico faces a strong challenge in its effort to strengthen and modernize its energy sector. Revenues from the oil boom of the late 1970s were unwisely spent and left a legacy of debt. Since the 1982 debt crisis, investment in oil and gas exploration and development has been inadequate, both because of debt constraints and because of Mexico's desire to foster diversification of the economy away from its heavy dependence on petroleum. Moreover, despite a diet of reform since 1988, the state energy monopoly, Petróleos Mexicanos (Pemex), remains one of the world's least efficient energy companies.

During the period 1988–90, Mexico's production of crude petroleum averaged about 2.5 million barrels per day, allocated almost equally between domestic demand and exports. In 1990 oil revenues accounted for 5.2 percent of Mexican GDP, and oil accounted for about one–third of Mexican export earnings (Banco de México, *The Mexican Economy*, 1991). As the Mexican economy grows, however, domestic demand will claim a larger share of total output and reduce the supplies available for export. Unless production increases markedly, Mexico is on a trajectory to become a net oil importer shortly after the year 2000.[1] Only major

---

1. According to energy consultant Rafael Quijano, domestic demand alone could consume all of Mexico's petroleum output by the year 2004, unless there is a big boost in exploration and development.

Rosa M. Moreira helped draft this chapter.

Table 10.1 Mexico: energy production, 1970–90
(thousands of barrels of crude oil equivalent per day)

	1970	1975	1980	1985	1988	1989	1990
Coal	19	32	33	55	59	n.a.	n.a.
Hydrocarbons	756	1,103	3,390	3,390	3,274	3,210	3,260
Crude oil	426	697	1,933	2,687	2,596	2,513	2,548
Gas	330	406	703	703	678	697	712
Associated	79	201	602	602	595	n.a.	n.a.
Nonassociated	251	204	100	100	84	n.a.	n.a.
Hydroelectric	86	84	125	125	96	n.a.	n.a.
Geothermal	0	3	8	8	22	n.a.	n.a.
Firewood, etc.	141	155	171	171	178	n.a.	n.a.
Total	1,001	1,376	3,749	3,749	3,628	n.a.	n.a.

n.a. = not available.

Source: Secretaría de Energía, Minas, e Industria Paraestatal, *1990–1994 National Energy Modernization Plan.* (Mexico City: SEMIP).

new oil field investments, coupled with a diversification of energy resources for domestic consumption, can reverse these trends.

To meet the energy needs of its growing economy, and to forcefully address its burgeoning environmental problems (see chapter 7 and US Trade Representative 1991, 166–72), Mexico needs both to increase its production of oil and natural gas and to alter its demand mix so that a larger share of domestic consumption is met by natural gas and electricity. Resources can come largely from domestic production; however, Mexican supplies will need to be complemented (especially in the short run) by increased imports of natural gas and electricity from the United States.

The NAFTA negotiations provide an opportunity to rebuild the Mexican energy sector, to expand trilateral energy trade, and thus to use the energy resources of the entire North American continent more effectively. Both Canada and the United States have declining oil reserves but a well-developed energy infrastructure (pipelines, refineries, power-generating plants, etc.) and substantial production of crude and refined petroleum, natural gas, coal, and electricity. US and Canadian companies have advanced exploration and production skills and technologies that could be tapped for Mexican projects. In contrast, Mexico has abundant reserves of oil and gas but inefficient production and an inadequate energy infrastructure (for a product breakdown of Mexico's energy output, see table 10.1). All three countries could gain from further integration of North

American energy markets. However, any attempt to negotiate an energy chapter in the NAFTA will run up against a long history of antagonism between US oil companies and the Mexican government, and the entrenched position of Pemex.

The Historical Basis of Mexican Energy Policy

Historically, Mexican energy policy has been hostile to foreign equity participation.[2] Restrictions on foreign participation in the energy sector were set out in the 1917 Mexican Constitution, Article 27 of which reserves subsoil rights exclusively to Mexican citizens. In addition, the Constitution prohibits foreign participation in "strategic" sectors of the economy such as oil exploration, refinement, and pipelines, other hydrocarbons, radioactive materials, electricity, and basic petrochemicals (see chapter 4).

Between 1917 and 1938 these constitutional provisions were enforced haphazardly. No decision was made as to whether the Constitution required confiscation of foreign property or whether firms already established in Mexico could continue to operate. American, British, and Dutch oil companies actually increased their investments in Mexico in the 1920s and transformed the country into a major oil producer and exporter.

The 1925 Petroleum Code was the first attempt to enforce the constitutional constraints. The code established the National Petroleum Agency (NPA) in 1925 to compete in production and refining operations with the foreign companies then operating in Mexico. In addition, the code limited new concessions to a maximum of 50 years. Adverse reaction from foreign oil companies and the American government brought about an amendment in 1928 that reaffirmed perpetual concessions to companies that had acquired their subsoil concessions before May 1917.

In 1934 Petróleo de Mexico (Petrómex), a semiprivate, fully integrated oil company, assumed the functions of the NPA. The government controlled 40 percent of the equity of Petrómex and barred foreign participation. The Pemex organization of today is an outgrowth of Petrómex.

On 18 March 1938, President Lázaro Cárdenas expropriated the foreign oil companies operating in Mexico and consolidated their holdings under Pemex, which was totally controlled by the government (Manke 1979, 76–77). The expropriation reinforced the constitutional provision that declared control of energy resources to be part of the national patrimony. Grayson (1988, 3) described the expropriation as:

---

2. This section draws on Manke (1979), Ronfeldt et al. (1980), and Weintraub (1990a).

the last major act of the Mexican revolution. This event, which is still celebrated every year as a "day of national dignity," imbues the oil industry with a sense of importance unknown in any other sector of the economy. The 1938 take-over fulfilled one of the salient goals of the revolution—that is, reestablishing national control over subsoil mineral rights claimed by North Americans and Europeans.

Since the 1938 expropriation, foreign companies have been hired to run drilling rigs but have never been given the right to keep a percentage of the oil discovered.

From 1938 to 1976, Pemex was charged with promoting energy self-sufficiency for Mexico and encouraging industrial development through subsidized energy prices. By statute, Pemex does not operate for profit but for the achievement of social goals such as employment and low prices. During this period, Pemex kept exports to a minimum, partly because it lacked the technical capability and the capital to become a major exporter, and partly because nationalist sentiment opposed the prospect of any entanglement with "imperialist" foreign oil companies.

Immediately following nationalization, the expropriated foreign oil companies boycotted the purchase of Mexican oil; the result was a fall in Mexico's petroleum exports from 2 million barrels in February 1938 to only 331,000 barrels in April 1938. The boycott was ended in 1940 because of wartime necessity.

Following World War II, the Mexican government realized that the domestic market for petroleum products could not generate the level of investment needed to upgrade Pemex's increasingly outdated oil field equipment. Pemex negotiated a few technology transfer agreements and exploration contracts with foreign companies, but insisted that they waive rights to any petroleum that might be discovered (Manke 1979, 84–85).

In 1949 Pemex tried to negotiate a $500 million loan from the US Export-Import Bank (Eximbank), but the attempt failed because US oil companies, hoping to gain access to the Mexican oil industry, argued that private capital, not public funds, should be used to develop Mexico's oil industry. In the 1950s technological advances in offshore exploration reopened the issue of foreign participation. US investors offered to supply the equipment necessary for exploring and producing Mexico's maritime oil deposits in return for modification of Mexico's position on subsoil rights. This prompted Antonio Bermúdez, the director of Pemex, to state that it "would have been easier to change the colors of the Mexican flag than to change the country's laws relating to petroleum" (cited in Manke 1979, 85).

Financial restraints, mostly caused by the government's insistence that oil prices remain low, led Pemex in 1955 to enter into a 20-year contract to export "excess" production to the Texas Eastern Transmission Corporation. Later, Pemex also used this contract as collateral to gain large credits from US and French investors, which were then used to develop petrochemical and refining plants.

A new petroleum regulatory law, passed in November 1958, reaffirmed government control over the exploitation of Mexico's oil resources. The law extended coverage to include public control over refining, transportation, and marketing in Pemex's downstream domestic operations. Private participation was permissible only if Pemex deemed it to be in the public interest.

The discovery of major offshore oil reserves in 1976, notably in the Bay of Campeche, transformed Pemex into a world-scale producer and exporter. From a production level of under 1 million barrels per day and exports of 0.2 million barrels in 1977, oil production peaked in 1982 at 2.7 million barrels per day, of which 1.5 million barrels were exported at a value of $15.6 billion.

Oil revenues fueled an investment boom in the energy sector. Several projects initiated in the late 1970s allowed limited foreign participation on a project basis in areas where Mexican expertise was lacking; however, Pemex retained overall control. These projects included the development of the Bay of Campeche fields, the construction of a controversial 48-inch pipeline to carry natural gas from Tabasco to the Texas border, and the development of the petrochemical industry. These projects forced Pemex to purchase large quantities of drilling equipment, production machinery, pipeline steel, valves, turbines, bits, and compressors from multinational oilfield equipment firms, and contributed to a massive buildup of foreign debt.

The debt crisis in 1982, coupled with tumbling oil prices, put a severe crimp on Mexican investment in the energy sector. The 1984–88 energy program focused on conservation; although Mexico was not an OPEC member, Mexico's pricing policy followed the OPEC lead; and efforts were made to integrate the oil and petrochemical industries. Production plateaued at 2.5 million barrels per day, and exports gradually fell from 1.5 million to 1.3 million barrels per day as domestic demand began to increase.

Pemex: Current Activities

Pemex currently divides its oil production activities among three regional divisions based in Ciudad Carmen, Poza Rica, and Villahermosa. The first two divisions control the greater part of production and reserves.

Ciudad Carmen provides the base for offshore operations in the Bay of Campeche, where 1.75 million barrels of oil a day—some 70 percent of Mexico's total oil output—are produced from 10 fields. Pemex has stated that it will invest about $880 million in the Cantarell Secondary Recovery Project in the Bay of Campeche to ensure maximum recovery from the Campeche wells.[3]

---

3. Embassy of the United States in Mexico, cable to the US Department of State, 17 July 1990, 6.

A second division is based in Poza Rica, in the state of Veracruz, covering the northern onshore region. The Chicontepec field near Poza Rica is the second largest after the Campeche Maritime area. However, output from some 200 producing wells is low—between 50 and 100 barrels a day versus over 10,000 barrels a day from some offshore wells—because of high clay and water content in the strata.

Annual capital spending by Pemex on oil exploration and drilling fell from about $6 billion in 1982 to about $1 billion in 1990. Pemex drilled 70 exploratory wells in 1982, compared with only 42 in 1989; over the same period the number of new development wells plunged from 288 to 75. Production has been slowed by aging refineries, inadequate maintenance, deficient transportation infrastructure, and inefficient management and labor.

The National Energy Modernization Plan, put forward by the Ministry of Energy, Mines, and Parastatal Industry (Secretaría de Energía, Minas, e Industria Paraestatal, or SEMIP) as part of the 1989–94 National Development Plan, attempts to redress these problems (Mexico, SEMIP 1990). Its objectives are laudable: to guarantee sufficient energy supply for the internal market, which is projected to grow by 31 percent to 36 percent between 1988 and 1994; to increase foreign reserves and fiscal revenues; to enhance environmental protection; and to reorganize and decentralize the energy sector.

The energy plan sets out five strategies to achieve its broader goals: increase productivity, use energy more efficiently, create financing mechanisms for the expansion of supply (setting prices according to world levels and increasing private participation), diversify Mexico's energy sources, and build a stronger presence in international markets.

To meet its objectives, however, the Salinas administration will have to turn around Pemex's well-earned reputation for inefficiency and low productivity. Venezuela, for example, produces the same amount of oil as Mexico with one-fourth the work force. Pemex has slashed its labor force and cut costs by 17 percent, or $1 billion per year, since 1988 (*Financial Times*, 31 May 1991, 25; *Journal of Commerce*, 21 July 1991, 1A). Nonetheless, its dominant role in the Mexican economy has made Pemex relatively immune to the stronger reformist medicine of the Salinas administration.[4]

Without substantial foreign investment and relaxation of the Pemex monopoly, Mexican oil resources are likely to be developed at an exceedingly slow pace. Loss of potential revenue from oil would mean a lost opportunity to earn

---

4. In 1990 Pemex earned revenues of $19 billion, representing 9 percent of Mexico's GDP. Pemex's export earnings of $10 billion in 1990 accounted for 37 percent of total Mexican merchandise exports (about 90 percent of this revenue came from crude petroleum sales). Moreover, taxes paid by Pemex represent the government's largest single source of revenue (Banco de México, *The Mexican Economy*, 1991).

foreign exchange that could play a major role in Mexico's economic development. Increased oil revenues would lighten the burden of Mexico's foreign debt service, and consequently facilitate current efforts to tap world capital markets for investment funds. A compromise should be found between economic realities and political rhetoric so that Mexico can attract the vital foreign investment and proprietary technology held by the major oil companies.

Developing Mexican Energy Resources

Mexico has vast reserves of oil and natural gas, but inadequate investment during the 1980s coupled with inefficient management has made it difficult to expand output. According to official estimates, as of January 1991, Mexican reserves of crude oil, condensate, and natural gas were equivalent to 65.5 billion barrels of crude oil—the eighth-largest reserves in the world.[5] However, independent analysis by a former senior Pemex official suggests that the reserves may actually be only about half of official estimates (*Journal of Commerce*, 11 December 1991, 6B; *Petroleum Intelligence Weekly*, 16 December 1991, 5). Even a ballpark estimate of that magnitude indicates that Mexico must intensify its exploration and drilling efforts to augment declining reserves and to accommodate increased domestic demand. To do so, Pemex will have to turn increasingly to foreign sources for financing and oil field technology.

Over the next five years, Pemex plans to invest $20 billion in production and refineries.[6] Pemex Director General Francisco Rojas estimates that 60 percent of the funds ($12 billion) will come from operations and that foreign bond flotations will provide $8 billion, of which a part ($2.5 billion) will be securitized by future oil sales. Testing the financial waters after an absence of eight years from the international capital market, Pemex floated a $150 million three-year bond issue in October 1990. In 1991 Pemex offerings included $125 million in three-year bonds in February and $150 million in seven-year bonds in September, plus a flotation of 100 million ecus in July.[7]

---

5. Recent oil finds in the Bay of Campeche and the state of Chiapas will, it is claimed, increase Mexico's reserves to as high as 92 billion barrels. However, exploration and exploitation of these finds will require increased participation by foreign companies, since the fields seem to be located at depths below 16,500 feet, the current limit of Pemex technology (*Journal of Commerce*, 17 June 1991, 6B).

6. This discussion draws on *Financial Times*, 31 May 1991, 25; 13 June 1991, 27; *Journal of Commerce*, 17 June 1991, 6B; 25 June 1991, 6B; *Wall Street Journal*, 28 November 1990, A24.

7. Although Pemex issues have been well received, they yield a substantial premium (several hundred basis points) over US Treasury notes of comparable maturity. Pemex's ecu-denominated bonds are among the highest yielding in that currency (see *Financial Times*, 31 May 1991, 25; 2 July 1991, 25; 13 September 1991, 21).

Pemex also expects the US Eximbank to provide $5.6 billion over the next five years to US companies that enter into service-and-supply contracts with Pemex. Through September 1991, Eximbank had approved $1.16 billion in loan guarantees to promote the export of US drilling and oil field services to Mexico (*Journal of Commerce*, 17 June 1991, 6B; 23 September 1991, 13B). In addition, the Export-Import Bank of Japan will lend about $0.4 billion for development of new unleaded gasoline refining capacity.

However, Mexico faces strong competition for foreign funds and technology from other countries that are also expanding their energy production. Many of those countries are reducing their barriers to foreign participation in the energy sector and providing other incentives to attract the major oil companies. For example, Venezuela, which plans to expand its oil production capacity by 40 percent by 1996, has proposed tax rate cuts from 82 percent to 35 percent for joint ventures with the state oil company (*The Economist*, 13 July 1991, 67–68; *Wall Street Journal*, 2 October 1991, A1). Peru has reformed its laws, ending the state monopoly power and allowing foreign participation for the first time (*Wall Street Journal*, 12 September 1991, A12). Argentina plans to privatize its state oil monopoly and gas distribution company. In addition, the newly independent states of the former Soviet Union are actively encouraging foreign investors to help them exploit their massive reserves. If Mexico is to achieve its ambitious investment goals in the energy sector, it will need to compete with the increasingly attractive terms—including some form of operating control—offered by other countries.

While its rivals have opened their doors wide to invite foreign oil companies, Pemex has kept the front door shut but left the back door slightly ajar. In 1991 Pemex contracted with a US company, Triton, to drill an exploratory well in the Bay of Campeche; Pemex then assumed ownership of the well after the drilling was completed.[8] The gains in efficiency were pronounced: Triton drilled a 5,210–meter well twice as fast as past Pemex operators, for half the cost (*Journal of Commerce*, 7 November 1991, 5A). Overall, however, the basic terms offered by Pemex for foreign participation in the production process remain less attractive to the major oil companies than those provided by other countries.[9]

---

8. Pemex reportedly paid Triton $20 million and allowed the company to use its own equipment and technology instead of subcontracting and working under the direction of Pemex. The contract was the first under a 1989 law that frees Pemex from the traditional requirement to use Mexican labor (*New York Times*, 25 September 1991, D1; *Journal of Commerce*, 17 June 1991, 6B; 7 November 1991, 5A).

9. One example of the chilly conditions: Pemex does not allow "package service contracts," in which foreign oil companies bid to supply a combination of oil field services such as seismic testing, exploration, and development, even though this approach is more attractive to many firms than unbundling their expertise.

On the marketing side, Pemex has been more willing to participate in creative investment schemes with foreign firms. A recent joint venture between Mexican private investors and Repsol, a Spanish petroleum firm, is one such example. The new firm—40 percent owned by Repsol, 60 percent owned by Mexican investors—will distribute petroleum products in Mexico and elsewhere in Latin America. Among other uses, the new investment will upgrade refinery operations at Tula, Salina Cruz, and Cadereyta, three of the most modern plants in Mexico. These plants should soon produce a combined output of 900,000 barrels of refined product per day.[10] Three older refineries at Minatitlán, Salamanca, and Madero will also be upgraded to improve the quality of existing production.

Pemex also plans to spend heavily for environmental purposes over the next four years. Important goals include increasing the production and use of unleaded gasoline in Mexico and replacing the large Azacapotzalco refinery that was closed on 18 March 1991 to alleviate air pollution in Mexico City. Smaller refineries at Poza Rica and Reynosa have also been shut down for environmental and safety reasons. The Azacapotzalco plant had been processing 105,000 barrels per day, or about 4 percent of domestic production, but was responsible for 15 percent of the country's industrial air pollution. As a result of its closing, imports of gasoline from the United States have soared (*Financial Times*, 13 June 1991, 27; *Journal of Commerce*, 17 June 1991, 6B). A replacement plant, which would process 300,000 barrels of oil per day, is being planned; construction costs are estimated at between $3 billion and $5 billion.

Petrochemicals

Mexico's petrochemical industry is the 15th-largest in the world and accounted for 3 percent of world production and 2.5 percent of Mexican GDP in 1989 (see tables 10.2 and 10.3 for a breakdown and illustration of Mexico's petrochemical classification system). In 1988 the industry employed 95,000 people and produced $5 billion worth of goods (see US General Accounting Office 1991a, 14).

Basic Petrochemicals

Basic petrochemicals are those that result from the first chemical or physical transformation of crude petroleum or natural gas. The 30 November 1958 Petro-

---

10. Other foreign investments are also under consideration. The Italian state energy company, Ente Nazionale Idrocarburi (ENI), is assessing a joint project with Pemex in which it would invest $350 million in a 500,000 metric-ton MTBE (methyl tertiary butyl ether) petrochemical plant to increase Pemex's gasoline production (*U.S.-Mexico Free Trade Reporter*, 22 July 1991, 2).

Table 10.2 Mexican classification of petrochemicals

Basic petrochemicals

Ammonia
Benzene
Butadiene
Carbon black
Dodecylbenzene
Ethane
Ethylene
Heptane
Hexane
Methanol

Methyl tertiary butyl ether
n-Paraffins
ortho-Xylene
para-Xylene
Pentane
Propylene
Propylene tetramer
Tert amyl methyl ether
Toluene
Xylenes

Secondary petrochemicals

2-ethyl hexanol
Acetaldehyde[a]
Acetic acid
Acetic anhydride
Acetylene
Acetone
Acetone cyanohydrin
Acetonitrile[a]
Acrelein
Acrylonitrile[a]
Acrylonitrile styrene
Acrylonitrile-butadiene-styrene
alpha-Olefins[a]
Ammonium nitrate
Ammonium phosphate
Ammonium sulfate
Aniline
Butyraldehyde
Caprolactam
Chlorobenzenes
Chloromethanes
Chloroprene
Cumene[a]
Cyanohydric acid
Cyclohexane[a]
Cyclohexanone

Ethylene oxide[a]
Ethylene-propylene copolymer
Ethylene-propylene elastomers
Formaldehyde
High-density polyethylene[a]
Internal olefins[a]
Isobutanol
Isobutyraldehyde
Isoprene
Isopropanol[a]
Low-density polyethylene[a]
Linear low-density polyethylene
Maleic anhydride
Methyl methacrylate
Methylamines
N-Butanol
Nitrobenzene
Nitrotoluene
Oxo-alcohols
Paraformaldehyde
Pentaerythritol
Phenol
Phthalic anhydride
Polybutadiene
Polypropylene
Propylene oxide

Table 10.2 Mexican classification of petrochemicals (continued)

Secondary petrochemicals (continued)

Dichloroethane[a]	Styrene[a]
Dimethyl terephthalate	Styrene-butadiene oil
Ethanolamine	Terephthalic acid
Ethyl chloride	Urea
Ethylamines	Vinyl acetate monomer
Ethylbenzene[a]	Vinyl chloride[a]

a. Reclassified from basic to secondary in 1989.

Source: Chemical Week, 30 August 1989, 25, as reproduced in US International Trade Commission, *Review of Trade and Investment Liberalization Measures by Mexico and Prospects for Future United States–Mexico Relations* (USITC Publication 2275), April 1990, E-2. Reprinted with permission of the publisher.

Table 10.3 Illustration of the Mexican petrochemical classification system

Raw material (ownership reserved to Pemex)	Basic (ownership reserved to Pemex)	Secondary (100 percent private Mexican; 40 percent foreign ownership)	Finished product (unrestricted ownership)
Natural gas liquids	Ethylene	Ethylene oxide	Antifreeze Polyester
Natural gas liquids	Propylene	Polypropylene	Molded plastics Automobile parts
Crude oil	Benzene	Ethyl benzene Styrene	Polystyrene (styrofoam) Synthetic rubber

Source: US General Accounting Office, *U.S.–Mexico Energy: The U.S Reaction to Recent Reforms in Mexico's Petrochemical Industry*, May 1991, appendix I, 12.

chemical Law grants Pemex the exclusive right to manufacture basic petrochemicals. As a result of product reclassifications in 1986 and 1989, however, only 20 basic petrochemicals are still reserved exclusively for Pemex.[11] US officials con-

---

11. The 1986 Petroleum Development Plan reclassified 36 products, including carbon tetrachloride, polypropylene, and vinyl acetate, from the basic petrochemical list to the secondary and tertiary categories. In 1989, SEMIP reclassified another 15 basic petrochemicals as secondary, including vinyl chloride, styrene, and ethylbenzene, leaving a total of 20 basic petrochemicals (including one new product, tert amyl methyl ether, an octane enhancer for gasoline).

tend that Mexico could still retain control over the raw materials needed for petrochemicals if the list of basic petrochemicals were reduced to only 10 items (US General Accounting Office 1991a, 5).

Secondary Petrochemicals

Secondary petrochemicals are derived from basic petrochemicals or are manufactured from feedstocks obtained from crude petroleum and natural gas. Mexico permits private investment in the manufacturing and distribution of secondary petrochemicals, but foreign investors are limited to a 40 percent equity share. However, foreign investors can take up to a 100 percent equity position if they enter into a special trust arrangement with a Mexican credit institution. The trust disburses the profits from the venture to the foreign investor, while direct control of the company remains with the trustee (US General Accounting Office 1991a, 4).

Producers must obtain a license from the Petrochemical Commission of SEMIP to produce certain secondary petrochemicals; however, applications are automatically approved if the Petrochemical Commission does not act within 45 business days. In the 1986 and 1989 reforms, the number of secondary petrochemicals subject to licensing control was reduced from 800 to 66.

Tertiary Petrochemicals

Tertiary petrochemicals are those derived from secondary petrochemicals and include all petrochemicals except those in the basic and secondary categories. Under the 1973 Law on Foreign Investment, foreign participation in the production of tertiary petrochemicals was limited to 49 percent of equity. However, as a result of recent reforms that allow 100 percent foreign ownership in tertiary petrochemicals, about 748 petrochemicals have been newly classified or reclassified as tertiary products, thereby allowing unrestricted foreign participation in production.

Investment in petrochemicals dropped by about two-thirds with the onset of the debt crisis of 1982 (see table 10.4), leading to a sharp increase in imports.[12] However, reforms under the 1986 Development Plan and the 1989 petrochemical

---

12. The US General Accounting Office (1991a, 3) estimates that, between 1980 and 1988, Mexico spent about $5.5 billion to import basic petrochemicals. See also Bucay (1991, 125).

Table 10.4 Mexico: investment in the petrochemical industry, 1980–87[a] (millions of 1980 dollars)[a]

Year	Basic	Secondary	Total
1980	780.3	613.8	1,394.1
1981	529.7	948.9	1,478.6
1982	318.2	37.7	355.9
1983	386.6	8.9	395.5
1984	279.7	113.3	393.0
1985	149.0	187.2	336.2
1986	149.1	0.5	149.6
1987	219.5	43.7	263.2

negl. = negligible.

a. Based on the 1980 exchange rate of 22.95 pesos to the dollar.

Source: US General Accounting Office, *US–Mexico Energy: The U.S. Reaction to Recent Reforms in Mexico's Petrochemical Industry*, May 1991, figure 1.

reclassification have served to attract more foreign investment.[13] In addition, Pemex has contracted technical assistance and licensed processes from foreign suppliers (for which foreign investors often receive payment in kind or reduced rent on facilities) and has established joint ventures with leading multinational producers (Verut 1988, 5–6).

Nevertheless, wholly foreign-owned plants are still not allowed to produce basic petrochemicals, and foreign investors are still prevented from establishing vertically integrated facilities. These restrictions are an important obstacle to a competitive Mexican petrochemical industry. Moreover, without increased investment in this sector, growing domestic demand in Mexico will have to be met through sharply higher imports.[14]

13. For example, in 1988 the Mexican Petroleum Commission approved about 50 investment permits totaling $250 million; in October 1989 the Commission approved four private investment projects in secondary petrochemicals totaling $520 million. A side effect of the reclassification is that it served to shift the burden of imports into the secondary petrochemicals category (Embassy of the United States in Mexico, cable to the US Department of State, 17 July 1990).

14. Per capita demand today is only 180 kilograms versus about 1,000 kilograms in the United States, but Mexican demand will grow rapidly with development (Bucay 1991, 122).

Energy Trade in North America

Energy accounts for a substantial share of North American trade, even though it is encumbered by both border restrictions and domestic regulatory barriers.[15]

Crude Oil

Pemex exported 51 percent of its crude oil production, valued at $8.9 billion, in 1990. The value of Pemex exports peaked in 1982, when exports of crude oil equaled $15.6 billion; as a percentage of production, exports peaked in 1983 at 58 percent (table 10.5). Since then exports have dropped from 1.5 million barrels per day in 1983 to 1.3 million barrels per day in 1990. Crude oil represents 89.2 percent of total petroleum products exports, while refined oil products and petrochemicals represent about 8.1 percent and 2.7 percent, respectively. The United States is Mexico's primary export market for crude oil, accounting for 56.2 percent of the total in 1990; Spain was the second-largest market with 16.7 percent, followed by Japan with 11.4 percent, France with 4.4 percent, and Israel with 2.3 percent.[16]

To date, Mexico has supplied about 42 percent of the US Strategic Petroleum Reserve (SPR). However, the contract for 50,000 barrels per day has not been renewed because the SPR now needs to buy lighter and sweeter (lower-sulfur) grades of crude than those produced in Mexico.

Energy trade between Mexico and Canada is minimal, consisting of a small amount of Mexican crude petroleum, which reaches Canada by tanker. Canadian imports of Mexican crude have never been greater than 3 percent of Mexico's total crude exports and have steadily declined from a high of 48,000 barrels per day in 1982 to about 10,000 barrels per day in 1989 (Székely 1989).

US duties on crude petroleum and refined petroleum products are minimal: 0.5 percent and 1.1 percent, respectively. The elimination of these duties under a NAFTA will have little effect on US energy trade with Mexico. The United States is by statute prohibited from exporting crude petroleum to Mexico or elsewhere (even if there were no prohibition, Mexican refineries are already operating at capacity; US International Trade Commission 1991a, 4–30). However, as a

---

15. This section draws on Banco de México, *The Mexican Economy*, 1990 and 1991; Embassy of the United States in Mexico, cable to the US Department of State, 17 July 1990; US International Trade Commission (1991a, 4–29 to 4–30); Verut (1988, 1–6).

16. In 1990 Mexico was the fifth-largest supplier of crude oil and products to the United States, providing about 9 percent of total US imports. Canada is the third-largest supplier, providing 12 percent of the US total (Banco de México, *The Mexican Economy*, 1991; US Department of Energy, *Petroleum Supply Monthly*, February 1991, 61).

Table 10.5 Mexico: crude oil and natural gas production and exports, 1981–90

| Year | Total production (thousands of barrels per day) | Crude oil | | | Natural gas | |
| | | Exports | | | | |
		Thousands of barrels per day	Millions of dollars	As percentage of production	Exports (millions of dollars)	Exports as a percentage of production
1981	2,312	1,098	13,305	48	526	7
1982	2,746	1,492	15,622	54	476	6
1983	2,665	1,537	14,821	58	354	5
1984	2,685	1,525	14,968	57	232	6
1985	2,630	1,438	13,267	55	293	n.a.
1986	2,428	1,290	5,582	53	167	n.a.
1987	2,541	1,345	7,876	53	117	n.a.
1988	2,507	1,307	5,855	52	136	n.a.
1989	2,513	1,278	7,291	51	170	n.a.
1990[a]	2,548	1,295	8,920	51	n.a.	n.a.

n.a. = not available.

a. Estimated.

Source: Banco de México, *The Mexican Economy*, 1991; US Department of Commerce, *Mexican Petroleum Industry*, 17 July 1990.

Year	US imports from:		Average price[a]	US exports to:		Average price[a]
	Canada	Mexico		Canada	Mexico	
1980	796,507	102,410	4.28	113	3,886	4.70
1981	762,107	105,013	4.88	106	3,337	5.90
1982	783,407	94,794	5.03	162	1,705	5.81
1983	711,923	75,361	4.78	136	1,646	5.10
1984	755,368	51,502	4.08	127	1,786	4.92
1985	926,056	0	3.21	178	2,207	4.77
1986	748,780	0	2.43	9,203	1,896	2.81
1987	992,532	0	1.95	3,297	2,125	3.07
1988	1,276,322	0	1.84	19,738	2,327	2.74
1989	1,339,357	0	1.82	38,443	17,004	2.52
1990	1,448,065	0	1.94	17,359	15,659	3.10

a. In dollars per thousand cubic feet.

Source: US Department of Energy, Energy Information Agency, *Annual Report for Importers and Exporters of Natural Gas*, various issues.

result of the Canada–US FTA, Canada is eligible to receive US exports of crude petroleum—the only exception to the restriction. For symmetry, similar waivers should be extended to Mexico under a NAFTA.

Natural Gas

Mexico is the sixth-largest producer of natural gas in the world. As a percentage of Mexico's total energy production, however, natural gas has diminished in importance from 33 percent in 1970 to 19 percent in 1988 (table 10.1). In 1982 Mexico produced 4.3 billion cubic feet of natural gas per day; by 1989 the figure had fallen to 3.6 billion cubic feet. The explanation is again the Pemex monopoly and the lack of financial resources for exploration and development. For example, the number of new gas wells drilled in Mexico decreased from 56 in 1982 to 6 in 1989.

Mexico switched from being a net exporter to a net importer of natural gas during the 1980s (tables 10.5 and 10.6). The United States supplies almost 90 percent of Mexican natural gas imports; most of the supplies are used by the border cities of Juárez, Mexicali, and Tijuana (US International Trade Commission 1991a, 4–30). In an attempt to curb pollution in Mexico City, imports of "cleaner" gas from Texas increased sixfold in the first half of 1991 (*Journal of Commerce*, 26 July 1991, 10B). According to Robles Segura, Pemex deputy director for petrochemicals and gas, Pemex plans to increase imports of natural gas to 240 million cubic feet a day in 1991.[17]

Electricity

The United States is a net importer of electricity from both Canada and Mexico. As table 10.7 shows, most of North American trade in electricity takes place between the United States and Canada. Most of the electricity imported to the United States originates in Canadian facilities powered by large hydroelectric plants. The United States and Canada have a long-term supply arrangement, under which Hydro Quebec has agreed to expand its hydrogeneration capacity and deliver the increased output of these facilities to New England through a new dedicated intertie.

New England, New York, and California—regions that have high-cost fossil-fuel generating capacity—are the main US importing regions of Canadian electricity. US demand for Canadian electricity exports grew steadily in the 1980s and peaked in 1987 at 50 billion kilowatt-hours (valued at $1 billion). Since the FTA went into effect, however, US imports have fallen sharply while US exports to Canada have almost tripled.[18]

US electricity trade with Mexico has increased significantly with the signing in 1987 of a 220-megawatt firm power purchase agreement between the Comisión Federal de Electricidad (CFE) and local US utilities in California. Since 1987, US electricity imports from Mexico have averaged about 2 billion kilowatt-hours annually, accounting for almost 2 percent of Mexico's gross generating capacity. US imports totaled $87 million in 1990. In contrast, US exports to Mexico grew sharply in 1989–90 to an average of about 600 million kilowatt-hours but still are equivalent to only 3 percent of US shipments to Canada (table 10.7).

The NAFTA negotiations could promote greater liberalization of trade in electricity, yielding three specific benefits: from an engineering point of view, greater integrity and reliability of the system;[19] from an economic point of view, cheaper

---

17. In addition, Pemex is supporting a plan to build a 3.5-mile natural gas pipeline from Valero's existing pipeline near Penitas, Texas, across the border to connect with a Pemex pipeline. The connecting pipeline would have a capacity of 400 million cubic feet of gas per day (*Journal of Commerce*, 16 August 1991, 8B).

18. Such sharp shifts in trade patterns are not unusual given the impact of weather changes on electricity trade. In 1990, for example, US electricity trade with Canada was almost in balance (around $435 million in trade each way) because the weather in Canada was exceptionally dry that year, causing hydroelectric output to fall.

19. Despite growing Mexican exports to the United States since 1984, grids differ between Mexico and Texas, and the Mexican and the Arizona and New Mexico electrical supply systems are not synchronized (US Trade Representative 1991, 171).

Table 10.7 United States: trade in electric power, 1981–90 (millions of kilowatt-hours)

Year	Exports to Canada	Imports from Canada	Net imports from Canada	Exports to Mexico	Imports from Mexico	Net imports from Mexico	Net US imports from North America
1981	2,455	35,456	33,091	330	44	−286	32,805
1982	3,523	32,845	29,322	14	8	−6	29,316
1983	3,321	38,579	35,258	16	88	72	35,330
1984	2,479	42,034	39,555	79	185	106	39,661
1985	4,813	45,655	40,842	152	241	88	40,931[a]
1986	4,689	39,215	34,526	126	1,168	1,042	35,897
1987	5,750	50,176	44,426	130	2,042	1,912	46,338
1988	6,888	36,840	29,952	179	1,996	1,817	31,770
1989	14,514	24,176	9,662	621	1,934	1,313	10,976
1990	19,936	20,555	619	590	1,951	1,361	1,980

a. Excludes 5 million kilowatt-hours transferred by Ontario and Quebec through New York and returned to Canada.

Source: US Department of Energy, Energy Information Agency.

Table 10.8 Mexico: exports of basic petrochemicals, 1980–90

Year	Exports (tons)	Annual change (percentages)	Exports (millions of dollars)	Annual change (percentages)	Exports as a percentage of production
1980	755,200	0.7	125	16.3	10.4
1981	812,457	4.6	154	22.6	8.9
1982	872,920	7.4	140	−8.6	8.2
1983	805,998	−7.7	124	−11.7	7.2
1984	576,145	−28.5	128	3.7	5.1
1985	339,452	−41.1	76	−40.7	2.7
1986	190,655	−43.8	30	−60.3	1.5
1987	194,641	2.1	31	2.4	1.4
1988	517,458	165.9	74	138.0	3.3
1989	450,398	−13.0	110	50.0	2.8
1990[a]	895,044	98.7	269	143.3	5.1

a. Preliminary.

Source: Pemex, *Memoria de Labores,* 1990.

energy for the consumer; and from an environmental point of view, greater reliance on a relatively clean source of energy and deferred construction of new power plants in both the United States and Mexico.[20]

The main impediment to freer trade in electricity in North America arises from the patchwork of regulations and conflicting interests of states in the United States and provinces in Canada. Neither the United States nor Canada regulates electric power imports and interconnections at the federal level. Exports, however, are regulated at the federal level by the Economic Regulatory Administration (an agency of the Department of Energy) in the United States and by the National Energy Board in Canada. In Mexico, the CFE regulates all international electricity trade and interconnections. Although the Canada–US FTA eliminated some of the barriers to electricity trade, it left the regulatory patchwork intact.

Petrochemicals

Mexico's trade in petrochemicals was in deficit throughout the 1980s; in contrast, the United States had a petrochemicals trade surplus of about $6 billion in 1988. Mexican exports of basic petrochemicals fell from a high of $154 million in 1981 to $30 million in 1986 (table 10.8). This decline reflected both inadequate

---

20. However, in the United States, increased electricity trade raises specific environmental concerns as well (see US Trade Representative 1991).

investment[21] and problems relating to subsidized feedstocks under the US countervailing duty law, which were substantially mitigated by the 1985 bilateral accord (see chapter 1). The 1986 and 1989 reforms have begun to reverse this trend, and in 1990 exports of basic petrochemicals reached $269 million (table 10.8). Meanwhile, Mexican imports of basic petrochemicals fell from $632 million to $273 million between 1982 and 1989, and imports of secondary petrochemicals rose from $219 million to $769 million (Embassy of the United States in Mexico, cable to the US Department of State, 17 July 1990).

Oil Field Equipment and Services

Mexico purchases about $1 billion per year in petroleum equipment and services from the United States. US producers of oil and gas field equipment have traditionally been the primary foreign supplier for Pemex, representing about 70 percent of imports in 1988 (Verut 1988, 4). With Pemex's current focus on exploration and development, purchases from foreign suppliers—especially technologically sophisticated equipment from the United States—should continue to grow, particularly given the abundant export financing offered by the US Eximbank.

Energy Provisions of the Canada–US FTA

The Canada–US FTA energy provisions resolved many contentious issues that once plagued the bilateral relationship.[22] The FTA energy provisions cover trade in petroleum, natural gas, coal, electricity, and uranium and other nuclear fuels. The FTA contains broad-based commitments to limit government interference in energy trade except in extraordinary circumstances. The FTA prohibits minimum export price requirements as well as export taxes, unless the tax is also levied on sales for the domestic market. The prohibition on export taxes and minimum export price requirements effectively limits the tools often used to implement government-enforced price discrimination in favor of domestic energy users. Hence, US–Canada energy trade will generally be based on commercial considerations, with prices set by market forces.

---

21. Inadequate investment in basic petrochemicals had a domino effect in secondary petrochemicals, and both were affected by insufficient investment in the oil fields, which caused a drop in the output of natural gas, the predominant feedstock for most of the petrochemical industry.

22. This section draws on Plourde (1990), Schott (1988), and US Department of Commerce (1989a, 23–25).

Narrowly defined exceptions to the prohibition on trade restrictions are limited to situations involving national security. In addition, either country may restrict exports for three specific "economic" reasons: to alleviate supply shortages, to maintain a domestic price stabilization program, or to prevent exhaustion of a finite energy resource. However, the export restriction must meet the conditions of FTA Article 904(A), the so-called proportional access clause, which limits the scope of the economic restriction: it should not reduce the proportion of total supply historically available to the other country (based on the most recent 36-month period for which data are available); it should not disrupt the normal channels of supply or mix of energy products; and it should not impose a higher price on exports than for comparable domestic sales. Further, the FTA provides for consultation in the event that one country undertakes energy regulatory actions that the other country deems discriminatory or otherwise inconsistent with the FTA provisions.

Annexes to the Canada–US FTA list regulatory changes that conform existing laws to the FTA provisions. One change allows the United States to export a maximum of 50,000 barrels per day of Alaskan crude oil to Canada, previously restricted under Section 7(d) of the Export Administration Act, provided the oil is transported to Canada from somewhere in the lower 48 states. This provision, designed to protect US maritime jobs by foreclosing the sale of Alaskan oil by pipeline to Canada, could also serve as a precedent for the US–Mexico talks.

In another annex, Canada agreed to eliminate its electricity export price test, used at times to regulate power exports. When applied, the test required that the Canadian export price not be significantly less than the equivalent price of alternative energy forms available to the importer. Other Canadian export tests—price tests and surplus tests—must be administered in a manner consistent with the FTA. In addition, the FTA addressed the problem caused by the denial to British Columbia Hydro of access to the Northwest Intertie by the Bonneville Power Administration. In FTA Annex 905.2, British Columbia Hydro is given "treatment no less favorable than the most favorable treatment afforded to utilities located outside the Pacific Northwest."

Both countries acknowledge their obligations under the International Energy Program (IEP) of the International Energy Agency (IEA). The FTA specifies that, in the event of an inconsistency between the FTA and the IEP, the provisions of the IEP will prevail. Although Mexico is not an IEA member, it could take advantage of its prospective accession to the Organization for Economic Cooperation and Development to join the IEA as well. In that case, the precedent of IEP provisions could be incorporated in the NAFTA provisions.

The FTA allows both parties to maintain and enhance their incentives for oil and gas exploration and development (e.g., depletion allowances in the US tax code). Public incentives are not restricted by specific limits; however, the freedom to provide incentives does not preclude the potential imposition of countervailing duties by the FTA partner country.

The FTA grandfathers Canadian ownership restrictions in the energy sector.[23] The failure to negotiate significant changes in Canadian investment policy in the energy sector raised concerns about the role foreign capital will play in the long-term development of Canadian energy supplies (see Verleger 1988, 117–19). Nationalistic sentiment in Canada was largely responsible for this outcome. To date, however, Canadian policies have not significantly deterred activities by US oil companies in the Canadian market; indeed, Amoco bought Dome Petroleum soon after the entry into force of the FTA (following the required screening process).[24]

In 1991 Canada opened 18.8 million acres in the northwest corner of Canada near the Alaskan border for oil exploration (*Wall Street Journal*, 31 May 1991, A9). The region, which includes portions of the Mackenzie River delta and the Beaufort Sea, has considerable oil and gas reserves. However, huge exploration costs effectively foreclose development by Canadian companies. In fact, two major oil companies decided to reduce their northern activities because of uneconomic exploration costs.[25] Nevertheless, this opening of Canadian territory for exploration, together with Mexico's recent discovery of vast oil reserves in deep waters, could push the liberalization process.

To summarize, the Canada–US FTA reduces the scope for government intervention in energy trade but permits considerable government guidance of investment decisions. The aim is to create more market-oriented energy policies, in the interests of both efficiency and energy security. The outcome of the Canada–US FTA may well foreshadow the NAFTA energy negotiations, especially given Mexican constitutional restrictions on foreign participation in the energy sector. If the FTA becomes the precedent, Mexican policy toward energy trade, characterized as it is by heavy government involvement, would have to be significantly altered to achieve a comparable degree of market orientation. However, Mexican invest-

---

23. Prior to the FTA, foreigners were prohibited from directly acquiring financially healthy Canadian-owned oil and gas firms with over $5 million in assets. The acquisition of smaller or unhealthy firms was subject to a review of the buyer's planned future activities in Canada. Under the FTA, the takeover of Canadian oil and gas firms is still subject to review. However, foreign-owned firms will be allowed to participate in oil- and gas-related activities on the same terms as Canadian-owned firms except in the frontier region, where 50 percent Canadian ownership is required to obtain a production license.

24. The Amoco takeover saved Dome from bankruptcy. Because of the capital needs of other Canadian energy companies, the Canadian government is now considering reforms of its investment restrictions (*Financial Times*, 20 November 1991, 8).

25. The Canadian division of Amoco and Gulf Canadian Resources Ltd. will give up their rights to 1 million acres and 600,000 acres, respectively. Exploration in Canada's Beaufort Sea costs on average C$60 million per well, compared with C$500,000 for the average onshore well.

ment restrictions might be able to be tailored to fit within the loose framework of FTA obligations.

Recommendations

The NAFTA chapter on energy should focus more on investment than on trade and should promote the liberalization of foreign investment restrictions in Mexico and Canada. Both countries place a high political premium on domestic control and, in the Mexican case, state control of energy resources. The resulting limitations on foreign investment serve to inhibit development, with consequences for both Mexican and Canadian economic growth and for producer and consumer interests in the United States. US oil companies are likely to oppose the NAFTA accord unless the issue of foreign participation is satisfactorily addressed, either in the NAFTA text or in side agreements.[26]

A strict reading of the 1917 Constitution has become a rallying point for elements of Mexican society that are broadly opposed to NAFTA talks. The United States should sidestep this ideological trap by promoting a results-oriented strategy rather than a rules-oriented approach.[27]

The United States should recognize that the new atmosphere created by the NAFTA will, in the long run, relax Mexican and Canadian anxieties over sovereignty, just as that atmosphere will help the United States overcome its long-standing phobia against universal banking or effective labor adjustment programs. Just as the text of the NAFTA will neither repeal the McFadden Act nor beef up the Jobs Training Partnership Act, it should not be expected to amend the Mexican Constitution. Instead, increased oil production in Mexico and trilateral energy trade should be the goal. In turn this will require operational reforms within Pemex to increase efficiency and productivity and to promote greater foreign participation in exploration and development of energy resources.

One way of finessing the obstacles would be for Mexico to develop a strategy for doubling oil production to 5 million barrels a day by the year 2005. Mexico would decide on the means of reaching its target, and in the course of marketing its surplus on world markets it could allow for quasi-equity participation by foreign oil companies. Of its own accord, Mexico could introduce a competitive

---

26. The US Industry Sector Advisory Committee on Energy has argued that the Mexican government could enter into "contractual arrangements" consistent with the Mexican Constitution, which would allow US firms to participate in Mexican oil and gas exploration and development (*Inside U.S. Trade*, 6 December 1991, 1).

27. The political dimensions of the issue are well understood by US Trade Representative Carla A. Hills: "I would not use a FTA to change a country's constitution" (*Inside U.S. Trade*, 24 May 1991, 1).

spirit into its energy industry by dividing Pemex into three companies, corresponding to the divisions already established: Ciudad Carmen, Poza Rica, and Villahermosa. These new companies could issue minority shares to private investors, with initial restrictions on foreign ownership (precedents exist in the banking sector: see chapter 15).

Liberalization of the energy sector could provide dramatic gains both to the Mexican economy and to US consumers.[28] Philip K. Verleger, Jr., has calculated that, between 1991 and 2010, Mexico could increase its GNP by 2 percent to 5 percent annually, generating a cumulative gain of $140 billion to $300 billion in 1989 dollars, as a result of opening the sector to private investment and increasing Mexican production to 5 million barrels per day by the year 2005. Furthermore, government revenue could increase by a cumulative total of $100 billion to $300 billion over the same period.

Increased Mexican production would benefit the United States and other consuming countries through lower prices. The US Department of Energy baseline projections suggest that, between 1991 and 2010, oil prices will rise 4.2 percent per year in constant US dollars. If, however, Mexico production were to rise to 5 million barrels per day between 1995 and 2005, the increase in world prices could be moderated to 3.8 percent per year. The difference of 0.4 percent per year in oil costs would result in global savings of $600 billion over the period.[29]

Another possible approach would be to allow foreign companies to operate in Mexico on a contractual basis. This approach would not threaten the Mexican ownership of oil reserves, and the Mexican government could increase its earnings through taxation (following the British and Norwegian model).

Canada's recent opening of a large part of its northern territories to oil exploration could set a precedent for introducing new technology into the Mexican oil industry. Following the Canadian precedent, the new Mexican petroleum companies could permit quasi-equity participation by foreign firms in realms where high technology is required. An obvious starting place is offshore production at depths beyond Pemex's technological capacity. Likewise, through progressive reclassification of basic and secondary petrochemicals, foreign companies could be permitted to provide the technology and investment required to revitalize the Mexican petrochemical industry.

---

28. This section draws on analysis by Philip K. Verleger, Jr., at the Institute for International Economics on the potential gains of opening the Mexican oil sector to private investment. Verleger used the Oil Market Simulation Model of the US Department of Energy.

29. This figure represents reduced transfers from consumers to OPEC and other oil exporters and reflects the very low price elasticity of crude oil demand. Future benefits are discounted at a real interest rate of 3 percent.

11

Automobiles

The automotive industry is Mexico's second-biggest foreign-exchange earner behind energy products, and automotive products are the largest component of bilateral trade between the United States and Mexico and between Canada and Mexico.[1] Some of the most contentious trade issues in the NAFTA talks will center around automobiles.

Mexican automotive production is already partly integrated with US and Canadian production. As a result of Big Three investment in Mexico, a *de facto* hexagonal trading regime has been created. Four of the six trade flows are largely unhindered: US–Canada trade in both directions is essentially free, and Mexican exports of assembled automobiles and parts enter duty-free or at low rates into the United States (under HTS 9802.00.80 and the Generalized System of Preferences, GSP). Mexican auto parts usually enter Canada duty-free under the Auto Pact terms; in fact engines are now the most important single good traded between Canada and Mexico (Hart 1990, 70, 118). But US and Canadian exports to Mexico are still severely restricted. Automobile manufacturers face tariff and nontariff hurdles in shipping assembled automobiles to Mexico, and Mexico's local content rules act as a stiff barrier to imports of US and Canadian auto parts.

Mexico's automotive sector is undergoing massive reconstruction on the heels of five years of cumulative growth in exports to the United States of 142 percent (from 1985 to 1989) and in anticipation of continued growth spurred by North American integration. As a result, the five major automobile companies operating in Mexico—General Motors, Ford, Chrysler, Nissan, and Volkswagen—are injecting substantial new investments into their Mexican assembly and auto parts plants (see the appendix to this chapter for details).[2]

---

1. This chapter draws on Automotive Parts Manufacturers' Association (1990), Womack (1990), and US International Trade Commission (1990b and c, 1991a). Valuable comments on this chapter were provided by Jack Eby and A. L. Halliday.

2. According to the *Financial Times*, the Mexican export boom in automobiles and parts is slowing down mainly because of the US recession. However, demand in the Mexican domestic market continues to grow: "The big five car companies cannot even match customer demand" (*Financial Times*, 25 October 1991, 7). The *Journal of Commerce* (24 September 1991, 1A) predicts that "Mexico's domestic market is the best North American bet for increased sales over the mid-term, at least."

During the 1980s, Mexican automotive production was buffeted by the same forces that rocked the economy. Vehicle production plummeted from 600,000 vehicles in 1982 to about 350,000 during the mid-decade recession, then recovered to 547,000 vehicles in 1990.[3] Throughout the decade, trade and production were strictly regulated. The local vehicle market was regarded as the preserve of Mexican producers, capacity was allocated among those producers, and exports were forced by government decree.

The 1989 Automotive Decree introduced a new policy of *apertura* (opening). This decree modestly liberalized Mexican trade rules, but the Mexico automobile market remains highly restricted by US and Canadian standards. With further NAFTA reforms, we think Mexico will be assembling at least 1.0 million vehicles per year within five years. This compares with 1988 figures of 11.2 million vehicles assembled in the United States and 1.9 million vehicles in Canada (Motor Vehicle Manufacturers Association of the United States, *World Motor Vehicle Data*, 1990, 8). The experience of Spain after its accession to the European Community suggests that two-way US–Mexico trade in automotive goods could easily double or triple in the first five years of a NAFTA, growing from $8.3 billion in 1989 to perhaps $20 billion by 1995.

The three most distortive Mexican nontariff barriers (NTBs) are export performance requirements established under the 1989 decree, local content rules that discourage the importation of US and Canadian parts, and the partial ban on imports of used cars. The most distortive Canadian NTBs are the production-to-sales ratio test and Canadian value-added safeguards applied under the Auto Pact (R. Wonnacott 1991, table 1).

Between 1981 and 1985 the United States limited automobile imports from Japan by means of a "voluntary" restraint agreement (VRA). President Ronald Reagan discontinued the VRA in 1985, but at that point Japan, concerned about congressional and industry reaction, adopted its own voluntary export restraint (VER), limiting its vehicle exports to the United States to 2.3 million units annually. Since 1985 the VER has occasionally restrained imports of some models, but usually it has not been binding (US International Trade Commission 1989b, 3-18 to 3-19). For example, in 1990 Japan shipped only 1.7 million vehicles to the United States (*Wall Street Journal*, 14 January 1991, B1).

Currently the worst US nontariff barrier in the automotive sector is the complicated "two-fleet" provision (*Financial Times*, 12 March 1991, 3). The Energy Policy and Conservation Act of 1975 requires assemblers producing for the US

---

3. US International Trade Commission (1991a, 4–19). The 1990 figure is based on research by Ford Mexico (Ford Mexico data differ both from the commission's figures and from the data in table 11.5). During the first quarter of 1991, the Mexican automobile industry grew by 35 percent over the first quarter of 1990. Growth in truck production was 50 percent (*El Nacional*, 8 June 1991, 25).

market to meet two corporate average fuel economy (CAFE) standards, one for their domestically produced vehicles and a second for their imported vehicles.[4] The political purpose of the two-fleet rule was to ensure that the Big Three would continue to manufacture small, fuel-efficient automobiles in the United States and Canada, and hence continue to hire US and Canadian auto workers. The two-fleet rule was put in place to slow efforts by the Big Three to source small automobiles from abroad. In turn, the firms have found ways around the rule.

If the vehicle contains over 75 percent US or Canadian value added it is classified as domestic; if the figure is under 75 percent it is considered an import under CAFE definitions. The rule of origin under CAFE thus differs from that under the Auto Pact, and some firms play this difference to their advantage. For example, Ford's Crown Victoria and Mercury Grand Marquis models, produced in Canada, contain just enough imported content to qualify for import status, thereby not jeopardizing the overall performance of Ford's domestic fleet. Likewise, Ford's Hermosillo plant in Mexico produces fuel-efficient Escorts with less than 25 percent value added in Mexico, so they are considered domestic under CAFE provisions. The two-fleet rule prompts bizarre sourcing decisions for auto parts: "Around 400 US workers lost their jobs when Ford Motor Co. switched to foreign suppliers for a dozen or so parts for the low fuel mileage Crown Victoria to be able to call it an import and average it with the fuel-stingy Festiva, which Ford buys from the Korean auto maker Kia Motors Corp" (*Wall Street Journal*, 11 November 1991, 1A).

Meanwhile a soft variant of managed trade is emerging in auto parts. The bilateral US–Japan trade deficit in auto parts reached $9.8 billion in 1990, provoking considerable congressional criticism.[5] In an attempt to blunt protectionist pressures, Nissan and Toyota "volunteered" in late 1991 to buy $3.3 billion a year in American-made auto parts by 1994.[6] Nonetheless, the automobile trade issue received prominent attention during President Bush's January 1992 visit to Japan. With leading executives from the US automotive industry at his side, President Bush received commitments from Japanese producers to more than

---

4. Currently (early 1992) the established fuel economy average is 27.5 miles per gallon. Both domestic vehicles and imports must meet this standard to avoid paying substantial fines on each vehicle sold.

5. In 1990 Japan imported approximately $0.8 billion in auto parts from the United States, while the United States imported about $10.6 billion parts from Japan (*Journal of Commerce*, 15 November 1991, 1).

6. *Journal of Commerce*, 15 November 1991, 1. As the "voluntary" plan evolves, a portion of this sourcing could come from Canada and Mexico—in fact, this is one of our recommendations later in this chapter.

double their purchases of US–made automobiles and parts, to reach $19 billion by 1994[7] (*Wall Street Journal,* 20 January 1992, A1).

Tariff barriers to automotive trade are important but less significant than the NTBS. US tariffs on imports of cars, trucks, and auto parts from Mexico are 2.5 percent, 25 percent, and 3.1 percent, respectively;[8] Mexican tariffs on automobiles and auto parts are 20 percent and 13.2 percent, respectively;[9] meanwhile the Canadian duty on all automobiles and parts is 9.2 percent.

These tariffs are reduced by preferential arrangements affecting North American trade. Roughly half of US auto parts imports from Mexico enter at an average rate of 3.1 percent, while the rest enter at preferential rates under the GSP system or under HTS 9802.00.60 and 9802.00.80 (old TSUS items 806.70 and 807.00; US International Trade Commission 1991a, 4-19). About 95 percent of US–Canada automobile and original parts trade is tariff-free under the Auto Pact. Moreover, Canada waives its tariff on parts imports from third countries (e.g., Mexico), if the imports are destined for firms that qualify under the Pact (the major firms that qualify are the Big Three and CAMI, the General Motors–Suzuki joint venture). Canada also waives its import duties for other firms that meet special Canadian production tests (these include Honda, Toyota, and Hyundai), although this waiver is scheduled to be phased out by 1996. Mexico allows maquiladora firms to sell automobiles they assemble on the Mexican market at the tariff levied on components, rather than at the higher tariff applied to finished vehicles.

A NAFTA would confront many Mexican auto parts plants—which historically have served a protected domestic market—with new competition. For example, if there were no local content requirements, Ford could ship US–made car radios to its Mexican assembly plant, causing the Mexican radio firm Clarion to lose a big part of its market. Mexican assembly plants, on the other hand, can generally withstand the pressures of free trade. One notable example is Ford's Hermosillo plant, which has achieved world-class levels of quality and efficiency (see below).

---

7. In 1990 Japanese transplants operating in the United States purchased $7 billion worth of US auto parts; this figure is targeted to rise to $15 billion by 1994. Meanwhile imports of US–manufactured auto parts by Japan are targeted to rise from $2 billion in 1990 to $4 billion by 1994.

8. The 25 percent tariff on trucks is the so-called "chicken war" tariff. This tariff on light trucks and vans was introduced in the early 1960s in a dispute with Germany over the import of American chickens. It has remained at 25 percent even as other American motor vehicle tariffs have been cut from about 10 percent to 2.5 percent over the past two decades. The figure of 3.1 percent for the average US auto parts tariff refers to items that do not get the advantage of GSP or HTS 9802.00.60 or 9802.00.80 benefits.

9. Tariff rates are from US International Trade Commission (1991, 4-18, 4-19) and Chrysler Corp. et al. (1991, 5). The International Trade Commission quotes a Mexican tariff of 15 percent on passenger cars, but the Big Three cite a figure of 20 percent.

North American Trade in Automobiles and Auto Parts

Automotive trade between the United States and Canada is large: in 1989, two-way trade amounted to $45.5 billion, consisting of Canadian exports of $27.7 billion and US exports of $17.8 billion (Lenz 1992, table 5.78.4). Similarly, automobiles and parts comprise the largest single component of US–Mexican nonoil trade, even though the absolute levels are much smaller than the US–Canada flows. In 1989, US imports from Mexico of automobiles and parts were valued at $4.9 billion, while US exports to Mexico were valued at $3.4 billion (see table 11.1).

Mexican exports of automobiles increased from 4 percent of domestic production in 1980 to 34 percent in 1988 (table 11.2). The number of automobiles exported increased from 18,000 in 1980 to 173,000 in 1988. Much of this export growth was force-fed by a succession of Mexican decrees, but it also reflected improved quality and productivity in new Mexican assembly plants and a sharply devalued peso.

Initially, most Mexican automobile exports went to countries in Central and South America where local production was nonexistent and standards and styles were roughly similar. As the Mexican industry continued to improve, exports to North America and Europe increased. Mexican automobile exports to the United States have increased dramatically, from practically no vehicles in 1981 to almost 150,000 in 1988, and now account for 3 percent of total US automotive imports (see table 11.2; percentage figure from US International Trade Commission 1990c, 2-13). US imports of trucks from Mexico likewise increased, reaching 9,782 in 1989, or 1 percent of total US truck imports (Motor Vehicle Manufacturers Association, *Facts and Figures,* 1990). It is worth noting that several Mexican assembly plants are located far from the US–Mexico border. In contrast, the auto parts industry is clumped at the border and in Mexico City.

Mexican auto parts trade, almost all of which is with the United States, has also grown dramatically. US auto parts imports from Mexico grew from $2.1 billion in 1985 to $3.6 billion in 1989 and now represent 12 percent of total US auto parts imports (US International Trade Commission 1990c, 2-13). US exports of auto parts to Mexico likewise grew by 79 percent, from $1.9 billion to $3.4 billion, over the same period (US International Trade Commission 1990c, 2-13). Most of the recent growth can be attributed to original-equipment parts manufactured by the Big Three and sold to their assembly operations in both directions across the border.

Mexico has traditionally run a deficit in auto parts trade (for example, about $400 million in 1982). However, in 1987 Mexico registered a parts surplus for the first time, and in 1988 the surplus reached $250 million, according to the Automotive Parts Manufacturers' Association (APMA 1990, 40). The surplus

Table 11.1 United States and Mexico: trade in automobiles and parts, 1986 and 1989

| | US imports from Mexico | | | US exports to Mexico | | |
| | | As a percentage of: | | | As a percentage of: | |
Year	Billions of dollars	Total US manufactured imports from Mexico	Total US auto and parts imports	Billions of dollars	Total US manufactured exports to Mexico	Total US auto and parts exports
1986	2.7	25.7	4.0	1.7	16.8	9.0
1989	4.9	25.0	6.3	3.4	16.5	12.3

Sources: US Department of Commerce data sheets: *US Foreign Trade Highlights 1989*; US International Trade Commission data sheets; *Review of Investment Liberalization Measures by Mexico and Prospects for Future United States–Mexico Relations* (USITC Publication 2326), October 1990.

Table 11.2 Mexico: motor vehicle exports, 1980-88

	Total exports		Exports to United States	
Year	Units	As a percentage of total production	Units	As a percentage of total exports
1980	18,245	4	negl.	negl.
1981	14,428	2	3	negl.
1982	15,819	3	623	4
1983	22,456	8	203	1
1984	33,635	9	13,448	40
1985	58,423	13	47,197	81
1986	72,429	21	60,466	84
1987	163,073	41	140,641	86
1988	173,147	34	148,017	86

negl. = negligible. ·

Source: Automotive Parts Manufacturers' Association, *The Mexican Auto Industry: A Competitor for the 1990's* (Toronto: Automotive Parts Manufacturers' Association, September 1990), 35.

reflects not only Mexican production skills but also local content requirements that limit imports of US, Canadian, and third-country auto parts.

Mexican Policy Toward the Automotive Industry

From 1962 to 1977, the Mexican government advocated a policy of import substitution. After 1977 the policy focus gradually shifted toward rationalizing the industry and encouraging export-led growth. The new direction was capped by the 1989 decree. Even after this policy reorientation, however, the Mexican automotive industry remains much more regulated and protected than the US and Canadian industries.

The 1962 Decree

Under the 1962 Automotive Decree, the Secretariat of Commerce and Industrial Development (Secretaría de Comercio y Fomento Industrial, or SECOFI) was mandated to prohibit the import of engines for automobiles and trucks, thereby encouraging the manufacture of major mechanical components and the establishment of automobile assembly operations. The decree sought to increase the degree of Mexican value added in the manufacture of motor vehicles to 60 percent from a previous average of 20 percent. However, because the domestic market was so small—only 100,000 vehicles—many plants experienced problems of scale and often did not meet local value-added requirements. Rather than shut down such operations and face the inevitable loss of jobs, the Mexican government decided to use price controls, production quotas, import permits, and corporate taxes to gain compliance with the 1962 decree. The end result was that the decree failed to generate competitive auto parts and vehicle manufacturing plants and instead fostered inefficient operations.

The 1972 Decree

In a continuing effort to develop a vehicle manufacturing infrastructure, the 1972 decree mandated that, by 1974, vehicle manufacturers use 40 percent of their foreign-exchange earnings to buy auto parts, other goods, and services from Mexican suppliers. At the same time, automotive assemblers were given greater freedom to export automotive products. Like the 1962 decree, the 1972 decree did not promote a self-sustaining Mexican vehicle infrastructure.

The 1977 Decree

The 1977 decree shifted attention from an import substitution approach toward a trade-balancing approach. Strict restrictions were imposed on any foreign investment that was not designed to promote exports. To meet the new trade-balancing requirements, the six multinational assemblers then operating in Mexico—General Motors, Ford, Chrysler, Volkswagen, Renault (whose Mexican facilities were acquired by Chrysler in 1987), and Nissan—all invested in engine manufacturing plants, primarily for export, along the US–Mexican border.

The US recession in the early 1980s, coupled with pressure from Japanese producers, sent US manufacturers searching out alternative low-cost production sites for their new, more fuel-efficient vehicles. US producers were not, however, attracted to Mexico at that time because the overvalued peso and the inflated economy had left Mexican labor less competitive than Korean or Brazilian labor. It took several years and policy twists for Mexico's potential advantage to be realized.

The 1983 Decree

The 1983 decree, also known as the Rationalization of the Car Industry Decree, took a new, pro-efficiency tack. It set three requirements:

■ To encourage higher production volumes per model, each assembler was restricted in the number of its production lines[10] for the domestic market—

---

10. As defined in the decree, a "line" consists of automotive units that have the same front end platform, basic body, and drive train.

three distinct lines were allowed in 1984, two in 1985, and one in 1986 and 1987; this was intended to create economies of scale and bring down prices in order to stimulate the slumping Mexican market.

■ Assemblers were permitted to produce another line for export, but production had to meet a sliding scale of local content requirements (for example, if 80 percent of the production was exported, the local content requirement was 30 percent; if only 50 percent of production was exported, the local content requirement rose to 56 percent).

■ Automakers were required to earn enough foreign exchange to cover their imports and other foreign costs. Indirectly, this provision acted as an export incentive: Mexico's major producers soon recognized that they could achieve substantial cost savings by producing enough automobiles to qualify for lower local content requirements and shipping them to the United States, thereby meeting the foreign-exchange requirements.

Vehicle manufacturers responded favorably to the combination of the 1983 decree and the extremely rapid depreciation of the Mexican peso.[11] Since 1983 Mexico has registered a surplus in its automotive trade balance. From 1981 through 1986 the balance improved by $3 billion, from a deficit of about $2 billion to a surplus of about $1 billion.

The 1989 Decree

The 1989 decree, which took effect on 1 November 1990, further liberalized the conditions governing foreign automobile producers.[12] The decree has three key provisions:[13]

---

11. In 1980 the exchange rate was 22.95 pesos to the dollar; by 1983 the rate was 150.29 to the dollar, and in 1989 it was 2,474.80 to the dollar (US Federal Reserve statistics). More important, between 1980–82 and 1990 the peso depreciated in real terms by about 31 percent (Morgan Guaranty Trust Co., *World Financial Markets*, 1991, issue 1, 19).

12. There were actually two 1989 decrees: the Decree for the Development and Modernization of the Automotive Industry regulates the automobile and auto parts industry; the Decree for the Development and Modernization of the Transportation Vehicles Manufacturing Industry covers heavy-duty trucks and buses. According to the Motor and Equipment Manufacturers Association (MEMA, Bates 1990), although the decrees have been characterized as trade-liberalizing and deregulatory, it is necessary to monitor the implementation process to determine the extent of actual liberalization and deregulation. The association points out that the Mexican government has maintained important regulatory controls and trade restrictions.

13. This summary draws heavily on APMA (1990, 97–98) and on comments by several automotive industry experts who attended the study group meeting at the Institute for International Economics on 25 July 1991.

- The total number of vehicles each manufacturer imports into Mexico may not exceed 15 percent of the total number of vehicles sold in the domestic market during the 1991 and 1992 model years. In the 1993 and 1994 model years, this figure rises to 20 percent. Restrictions regarding the number of lines and models that automakers may produce were dropped.

- Overall, each vehicle manufacturer must maintain a positive trade balance to be eligible for these imports. For every dollar of imports of new cars into Mexico, the manufacturer must export $2.50 for the 1991 model year, $2.00 for the 1992 and 1993 model years, and $1.75 for the 1994 model year. This provision ensures that growth in the Mexican market will be matched by Mexican production and that a trade surplus will be maintained by manufacturers that plan to take advantage of the growth in the Mexican market. The provision has a stronger flavor than the Canadian production-to-sales requirement under the Auto Pact: it only gives credit to vehicles exported from Mexico, whereas the Auto Pact credits Canadian vehicle manufacturers with all production, including automobiles sold on the Canadian market (APMA 1990, 97).

- There is a local content requirement for vehicles sold on the domestic market. At least 36 percent of the value added must stem from purchases from "Mexican parts manufacturers" (which must be at least 60 percent Mexican-owned) and "Mexican suppliers" (which may be majority foreign-owned but not by the assembly firm in question; Chrysler Corp. et al. 1991, 6). Further, the Mexican auto parts firms must maintain their own 30 percent level of local content.[14] Unlike the 1983 decree, the 1989 decree does not contain a sliding scale trade-off between the local content rule and the export-sales ratio.

To round out the policy environment created in the wake of the 1989 decree, two other policies deserve mention: Mexican limits on used car imports, and Mexican sales taxes. In October 1990, the Mexican government published a new version of its ban on imports of used cars, trucks, and buses (US Department of Commerce, unclassified communication from the Embassy of the United States in Mexico, 20 November 1991). The new version allows most used motor vehicles to be imported into the northern border zone. Although the imported vehicles are not supposed to be driven elsewhere in the country, it seems doubtful that intra-Mexican trade in used vehicles can be effectively prohibited.

Although not traditionally regarded as a trade policy instrument, Mexican automotive sales taxes are noteworthy because they are so high. Mexico imposes

---

14. An auto parts company is defined in the 1989 decree as a firm for which annual invoices to the automotive industry account for over 60 percent of total sales (the 1983 decree had set this figure at 50 percent; US International Trade Commission 1990b, 4-11).

both a 15 percent value-added tax on automobiles and special excise taxes that differ according to the size of the car (Sandoval 1990). All told, vehicle taxes in Mexico range from 21 percent on a compact car to 49 percent on a luxury car. (For comparison, state sales taxes on automobiles in the United States range from 4 percent to 8 percent.) Not surprisingly, automobile producers take the position that high Mexican sales taxes have retarded the growth of the automotive industry in Mexico (Chrysler Corp. et al. 1991, 13).

Truck and Bus Decree

Mexican officials correctly perceive that buses and heavy trucks are vital to the country's entire transportation system for goods and people, and therefore rules governing their manufacture and trade require fast liberalization (APMA 1990, 99; US International Trade Commission 1990b, 4-11). Hence, when the Truck and Bus Decree took effect on 1 January 1990, manufacturers were given free rein to decide which heavy vehicles they would make. Unlike the trade surplus required by the automobile decree, heavy equipment manufacturers must simply balance their exports and imports dollar for dollar. During established transition periods, 40 percent of the domestic value added must be accounted for by parts produced by the domestic industry, and assemblers must maintain the one-for-one trade balance in order to qualify for imports.

The transition period for buses is the 1990 calendar year; tractor trailers must adjust during 1990–92, and heavy trucks by 1993. When these periods expire, the local value-added requirement will be dropped, and foreign producers not currently in the market may qualify for imports (APMA 1990, 99). As of this writing, the major manufacturers of heavy equipment are Kenworth, Diesel Nacional (DINA, which uses Navistar technology), and FAMSA (which uses Daimler-Benz technology; Mexico, SECOFI 1990). In a few years' time, these established producers will face stiff competition from large US truck and bus manufacturers, especially General Motors.

Preview of an Integrated North American Market

Before turning to the negotiating details, it is worth speculating about the shape of a future integrated North American market, free of all trade barriers. Broadly speaking, in this scenario Mexico will become an increasingly attractive location for North American automobile and parts production. The reason is that Mexican productivity will rapidly converge toward US and Canadian levels, while Mexican wage rates converge at a much slower rate.

Mexican efficiency will rapidly improve with new equipment, reduced labor turnover, work force training in statistical process control, and other shop floor measures. In addition, reduction of model proliferation at Mexican automobile plants will boost productivity levels. The existing plants often produce as many as four or five different models, compared with one or two in most modern plants. For example, Chrysler's Toluca plant and Ford's Cuautitlán plant each produce five models; Volkswagen's Puebla plant produces four models.[15]

In contrast, Ford's Hermosillo plant, which produces only two models (the Ford Escort and the Mercury Tracer), is a harbinger of future efficiency. The Hermosillo plant has outperformed not only other North American and European plants in terms of quality (as measured by the number of defects per 100 vehicles directly traceable to the assembly plant), but also Japanese plants both in Japan and North America. Moreover, the Hermosillo plant can keep up in productivity terms (hours to produce one vehicle) with the average North American plant and is fairly near the levels achieved by Japanese plants in Asia and North America.[16]

Against a backdrop of rapidly rising efficiency levels, Mexican wages will rise more slowly, perhaps by 4 percent a year in real terms. Including fringe benefits, compensation for Mexican production workers in the automotive industry is currently about $4 per hour. In the United States (according to Ford Motor Co.) the comparable figure is about $30 per hour. Since the production payroll accounts for about 26 percent of value added by motor vehicle firms (*Statistical Abstract of the United States*. 1990, table 1296), it is evident that potentially large cost savings can be realized by relocating production in Mexico. In fact, industry estimates indicate that, even with current labor efficiency conditions, the Big Three US automakers can increase their profit margins by 4 percent to 10 percent of sales by producing in Mexico. This gain can only grow as Mexican efficiency improves (US International Trade Commission 1991a, 4-22).

---

15. Hunter et al. (1991) constructed a numerical model that stresses differences in the "style" of trade liberalization. According to their model, if free trade among Canada, Mexico, and the United States only applies to automobile producers (as in the Canada–US FTA), the producers will price-discriminate across borders. In particular, they will charge high prices for new vehicles sold in Mexico. As an indirect result, Mexican output per firm would increase only modestly from 71,000 cars to 85,000 cars. But if the free trade is extended *both* to producers and to consumers, Mexican firms would be forced to rationalize and cut costs. Mexican output per firm would then jump to 181,000 cars. See also US International Trade Commission (1991, 4-20 to 4-21). Automakers stoutly deny that they price-discriminate now or that they would discriminate in the future, no matter what the "style" of liberalization. They contend that any existing price differences are the result of tariff rates and the stiff Mexican value-added and excise taxes. In any event, the outcome of larger car production per plant, and lower costs per car, will be accelerated by the NAFTA.

16. These comparisons are cited in a recent analysis by the International Motor Vehicle Program at the Massachusetts Institute of Technology, cited in APMA (1990, 30).

For several decades to come, Mexican wage costs per unit of output should be low enough to overcome the disadvantages of inadequate urban infrastructure (high transportation costs, poor telecommunications, etc.). Over the medium term, therefore, the pull of automobile and parts production toward Mexico is likely to be very strong. At the same time, the high Mexico income elasticity of demand for automobiles, trucks, and buses will ensure future large-scale imports of parts and built-up equipment from the United States and Canada as Mexican incomes rise.

A comparison with Spain's experience following its accession to the European Community in 1986 is appropriate. In 1985 Spain exported $1.9 billion worth of automobiles and parts to the European Community and imported $2.9 billion from the Community. In 1990, Spain exported $9.4 billion worth of automobiles and parts to its fellow EC members and imported $9.3 billion worth from them (European Community, *European Statistics*, various issues). Although the appreciation of the ecu during this period (from $0.76 to $1.27) somewhat exaggerates this dramatic expansion when stated in dollar terms, the comparison suggests that two-way US–Mexico automotive trade could double or triple during the five years after the NAFTA enters into force.

Taking into account Mexico's competitive strength and the prospective rapid growth of two-way trade, the industrial profile of an integrated North American market might have four major features in the late 1990s.[17] The first is a change in the product composition of the countries' output: Mexican assembly plants are likely to concentrate on the production of less expensive cars and light trucks, in part representing a shift in the location of this production from Asia. Specialization along these lines will depend on liberalization of the two-fleet CAFE rules, as recommended below.[18] Meanwhile, US and Canadian assembly plants will concentrate on larger cars and heavy trucks. With the phased-out repeal of its ban on used vehicles, Mexico will become a large importer of second-hand cars, trucks, and buses.

Second, Mexico will add to its strength as a producer of auto parts. Parts firms that are affiliated with the assembly companies they supply will set up operations to build power trains and other major components. In addition, Mexico will become a major auto parts supplier to US and Canadian assembly plants, largely through firms affiliated with the assembly companies. The United States has traditionally imported large volumes of auto parts from Canada and Japan: $10.8 billion and $11.6 billion, respectively, in 1989 (APMA 1990, 40). In the 1990s,

---

17. This section draws on Womack (1990, 36, 42–45).

18. The Economic Strategy Institute advocates rules of origin and other measures that would enhance this shift (Prestowitz and Cohen 1991). Protective rules of origin could, however, be subject to a GATT complaint and in any event would invite emulation by Europe and Asia in their own regional groupings.

Table 11.3 Membership in the United Auto Workers, 1980–90
(thousands of workers)

Year	Total membership[a]	Total employment in the US motor vehicles and equipment industries
1980	1,357	789
1981	1,275	789
1982	1,151	699
1983	1,057	754
1984	1,124	862
1985	1,161	884
1986	1,106	872
1987	1,103	867
1988	944	857
1989	922	860
1990	868	809

a. Includes currently working and nonworking members.

Sources: United Auto Workers; US Bureau of Labor Statistics.

after the NAFTA comes into force, Mexico will become a major competitor to both Canada and Japan for the US auto parts business.

Third, an integrated North American market will preserve more US and Canadian jobs on balance than would a continuation of the present trade regime, both because the Big Three will be more competitive with Japanese and Korean producers, and because Asian and European producers will relocate part of their production to North America.[19]

Fourth, the United States and Canada will continue to see a long-term decline in the number of unionized jobs in the motor vehicle industry. Reflecting broader social trends and the rise of nonunionized transplant automobile firms, membership in the United Auto Workers (UAW) decreased by about 36 percent between 1980 and 1990, even though total employment in the motor vehicle and equipment industries actually increased slightly (see table 11.3).[20] The NAFTA represents a further milestone along the path toward a less unionized labor force. Union plants will face greater competitive pressure from nonunion plants, both north and south of the border. Correspondingly, the UAW will probably experience a

---

19. As mentioned earlier, in response to political pressures, large amounts of Japanese auto parts sourcing will soon be shifted to North America. In addition, with the NAFTA, auto parts manufacturing costs should drop in North America relative to Asia.

20. The Canadian Auto Workers union (CAW), now independent from the UAW, has experienced a similar decline in membership. However, the CAW is busy recruiting new members in other industries.

further membership decline in the 1990s. In order to survive, the union will need to emphasize its role in upgrading auto workers' skills and ensuring the flexibility of the work force, and to downplay its historic mission of enhancing compensation and seeking job security for its members.

The Auto Pact and the Canada–US FTA

The starting point for the NAFTA negotiations relating to automobile trade is the Canada–US Auto Pact (see P. Wonnacott 1988). The Auto Pact negotiations began in 1964 to resolve an escalating dispute over Canadian export subsidies. They resulted in a sectoral free trade agreement that came into force in January 1965. The immediate outcome was that the Big Three automakers were relieved of burdensome tariffs, whether their production was located in the United States or Canada or elsewhere.

However, the Auto Pact did more than create a tariff-free region for automotive trade. It also specifically protected production in Canada. Canadian goals were served by a production-to-sales ratio test and a Canadian value-added test: producers given favored treatment under the Auto Pact either had to maintain the preagreement ratio between the number of cars they assembled in Canada and the number they sold in Canada or ensure that the ratio was at least 0.75 (if that was higher than the preagreement ratio); the favored companies also had to increase their Canadian value added by at least 60 percent of their growth in sales.[21]

The reward for firms that met these tests was duty-free entry of automobiles and auto parts into Canada. In fact, the favored firms could even import vehicles and parts duty free from third countries. The Canadian operations of the Big Three significantly benefit from this feature of the Pact. Their imports from non–US sources now total about C$3 billion annually; by avoiding the Canadian MFN tariff of 9.2 percent, the US firms save nearly C$300 million annually (P. Wonnacott 1988, 104).

The United States was never enamored of the Canadian production safeguards and continued to argue over the years that they should be viewed as temporary measures and phased out. The issue flared when Canada extended parallel

---

21. The value-added test was agreed to in an exchange of letters between the Big Three and the Canadian government; the production-to-sales ratio test was included in the text of the Auto Pact itself. The value-added test has been more than met by the operations of the Big Three in Canada since the early 1980s.

benefits, in the form of a production-based duty remission waiver, to Asian automobile companies.[22]

The United States viewed the Canadian parallel benefit package as a production subsidy, since there was no requirement that the imported parts and vehicles enjoying the benefit of a duty waiver had to be embodied in the products actually exported to the United States. (Had such a requirement been in effect, the duty waiver would have been regarded as a normal duty drawback program, permitted under the GATT Code on Subsidies and Countervailing Measures). The Big Three were concerned that Japan could export vehicles and parts into Canada duty-free, take advantage of the profitable Canadian market, and at the same time sell automobiles into the US market, all in direct competition with their own models.

To address these issues, five important changes were made to the Auto Pact in the Canada–US FTA:

- The Auto Pact itself was limited to current participants, thereby freezing out potential Japanese producers.[23]

- For non–Auto Pact producers, the practice of receiving duty drawback on imported components upon reexport of the assembled product will be phased out for all trade between the United States and Canada, not just trade in automobiles.[24] This change will ensure that third-country components ordinarily pay some duty—whether at Canadian or US rates—when they enter the free trade area. But auto parts imported into Canada from any source by qualified Auto Pact companies will still pay no duty. In other words, Japanese automobile producers (outside the Auto Pact) will lose their duty drawback on imported components, but US producers (members of the Auto Pact) will still enjoy drawback benefits.

---

22. The parallel benefit concept was inaugurated in the 1970s, when Volkswagen obtained duty remission benefits based on its exports, even though there was no physical connection between the components imported by Volkswagen and the products it exported. Taking advantage of the parallel benefits, the first Japanese automobile company to set up manufacturing operations in Canada was Honda (June 1984). It was followed by Toyota (January 1986) and Suzuki (October 1986). Suzuki later formed a Canadian joint venture (CAMI) with General Motors. Still later the Korean automobile firm Hyundai also obtained parallel benefits.

23. Nearly 200 firms are registered under the Auto Pact, but the most important are the Big Three and CAMI. Japanese firms could have joined the Auto Pact prior to 1988, but they chose not to do so because they did not wish to meet the Canadian production-to-sales ratio test.

24. "Same-condition drawback" will still be permitted: for example, an item imported into Canada from Japan and exported to the United States in the same condition will pay no duty to Canada.

- As of January 1989, Canadian duty remissions based on exports were abolished for US–Canada trade, and they will be entirely phased out by January 1998; duty remissions based on the alternative production test will end by January 1996.[25]

- The North American content requirement was set at 50 percent. This is usually characterized as a tougher test for assemblers than the one previously applied in the Auto Pact, because it is calculated on the basis of the "direct cost of manufacturing," also known as "factory cost," which includes only labor, materials, and direct processing and excludes advertising and overhead.[26]

- As a result of the general elimination of US–Canada tariffs by 1998 under the FTA, the implicit sanctions for noncompliance with the Auto Pact will lose their punch for imports into Canada from the United States; but they will retain their impact for imports into Canada from offshore sources.

These changes answered many of the concerns expressed over the Auto Pact, but they did not completely resolve the question of the "right" amount of local content, nor did they address the "roll-up" issue. The local content issue divides players more sharply along industry lines than along national lines (P. Wonnacott 1988, 108). Most auto parts manufacturers represented by the US–based MEMA and the Canada-based APMA have pressed for a higher local content requirement. A MEMA report (1991, 7) points out that, because of the way local content is calculated under the FTA, on a typical $10,000 automobile only $2,778 of the parts need be produced in the United States or Canada to meet the test of 50 percent factory cost.[27] Thus, a car can enjoy FTA benefits even though its power train (engine and transmission) are totally imported. The MEMA and the APMA propose that the local content requirement be increased to 75 percent; the UAW proposes 80 percent.[28]

---

25. The alternative production test applies to Honda, Hyundai, CAMI, and Toyota. Under the alternative test as now applied, no duty waiver is permitted on production sold in the US market, but duty is waived for eligible automobiles sold in the Canadian market.

26. Jon R. Johnson (1991) from the law firm of Goodman & Goodman, Toronto, argues that it is not accurate to characterize the FTA test as tougher because of other differences between it and the Auto Pact test.

27. See chapter 8 for the problems of defining local content, as illustrated by the Honda case.

28. *Journal of Commerce*, 24 September 1991, 3A. The APMA has also suggested a 50 percent Canadian content rule, in addition to the 75 percent North American content rule, for automobiles sold in Canada. This idea is likely to go nowhere (*Globe and Mail*, 12 October 1991, B3; *Inside U.S. Trade*, 18 October 1991, 1). Canada's Motor Vehicle Manufacturers' Association (MVMA) has not offered specific recommendations for NAFTA's local content rule but insists that the current 50 percent rule be kept for Auto Pact firms. The MVMA agrees that so-called tier 1 firms should be given preferential treatment (see the recommendations discussed later). The MVMA's members are Chrysler Canada Ltd.; Ford Motor Company of

In contrast, the Asian automobile firms with transplant operations in Canada—Honda, Hyundai, and Toyota—would find it costly to meet a local content test higher than 50 percent; correspondingly they oppose any change. The Big Three also oppose any change as applied to them, but they favor a 60 percent to 70 percent content rule for the transplants. In this debate, the United States has so far sided with the parts producers, asking for a higher content requirement across the board, while Canada has favored the status quo of 50 percent.

The second unresolved FTA issue is the "roll-up" issue. Under the Canada–US FTA, origin is treated under an all-or-nothing rule. This means that 100 percent origin is attributed to the country of majority content. Thus, for example, a part shipped from the United States to Canada containing $49 worth of third-country content and $51 worth of US content is regarded as of US origin and will enter Canada duty-free. If the part is combined in Canada with another third-country component worth $80 and then reenters the United States, all $180 will be regarded as Canadian origin and therefore eligible for FTA benefits, even though only $51 is of US or Canadian origin (APMA 1990, 111). In the NAFTA negotiations, the Big Three want new rules against roll-up practices, to ensure that Asian transplants include a predominant share of North American content in their automobiles before they can benefit from unhindered access to the integrated North American market.

Recommendations

Several thorny issues must be addressed in the NAFTA negotiations on the automotive industry. It is useful to deal with them one by one: local content requirements and import quotas on new vehicles, the importation of used vehicles, export performance requirements, rules of origin, CAFE rules, and tariff barriers. We propose far-reaching policy reforms, but we also propose a special safeguards regime for the automotive sector.

The central theme in our reform package is transparency. The public should be able to understand the trade barriers that exist without having to spend hours digesting the sort of technical exposition contained in this chapter. North American automobile trade is now burdened with so many nontariff barriers that it is exceedingly hard for the public, or for that matter even senior trade officials, to discern their net impact on consumers versus producers, on assembly firms versus parts firms, and on the Big Three versus the transplants.

Canada Ltd.; General Motors of Canada Ltd.; Mack Canada Inc.; Navistar International Corporation Canada; Paccar of Canada Ltd.; Volvo Canada Ltd.; and Western Star Trucks Inc. (*Inside U.S. Trade*, 18 October 1991, 1).

Nor is it easy to discern which barriers exert a binding effect and which do not. For example, the present FTA rules of origin permit cars with little US and Canadian content to be considered North American (the roll-up problem); the CAFE rules have not prevented imports of small cars by the Big Three; Mexican limits on used vehicle imports are probably evaded on a large scale; and Mexican export performance requirements may work more as an access barrier to the profitable Mexican automobile market than as a spur to Mexican exports. Our strong policy recommendation is to eliminate this clutter and instead rely on transparent measures to implement public policy goals.

At the same time we take the pragmatic view that the immediate elimination of all impediments to North American automobile trade is not possible; instead transition periods will be necessary. Further, we think that the established North American producers, whose investment was subject to onerous performance criteria, should enjoy a headstart over newcomers. But the undergrowth of opaque nontariff barriers should be cleared away as quickly as possible.

Local Content Requirements and Import Quotas

Unlike its North American partners, the United States has not explicitly adopted its own local content requirements; moreover, since 1985 the United States has allowed voluntary restraints on Japanese automobile imports to fade into the shadow of a nonbinding quota. However, the focus of US trade policy in the automotive sector has now shifted to auto parts, and the makings of a "voluntary" purchase regime, to be applied to Japanese transplants, can be discerned. Meanwhile, Mexico presently and Canada potentially require minimum degrees of local content in the output of their automotive sectors.

The 1989 Mexican Automotive Decree requires that a large fraction of auto parts be sourced in Mexico if the automobiles produced therefrom are to be sold in Mexico. In addition, in 1992 Mexico limited new car imports to 15 percent of the market and restricted used car imports through a partly porous ban. The US–Canada Auto Pact contains a production-to-sales ratio test that requires each firm favored under the pact to ensure that its Canadian production (with a 60 percent incremental value-added requirement) is proportional to its sales in Canada.[29] Canada, which also has a used car import ban, is phasing out that ban by 1994.

---

29. The 60 percent Canadian value-added figure has been exceeded for many years and thus is not binding. The production-to-sales ratio test is not binding for the Big Three, which assemble more automobiles in Canada than they sell there; the parallel production tests are probably binding on the Japanese transplants operating in Canada (R. Wonnacott 1988).

The Big Three, which collectively account for the majority of vehicles produced in Canada and Mexico, have come to accept the Canadian production safeguards, and they welcome Canadian and Mexican import limitations on used cars. But the Big Three propose to use the NAFTA talks to reform the Mexican local content requirements—and much else in Mexican automobile industry policy—on a two-tier basis (Chrysler Corp. et al. 1991).

According to the Big Three plan, producers would be divided into two groups: those that had established assembly operations in Mexico as of January 1991 (tier 1, which would include Chrysler, Ford, General Motors, Nissan, and Volkswagen), and those that had not (tier 2, including Toyota, Honda, Hyundai, Mercedes-Benz, and Fiat, among others). The broad idea behind the two-tier approach is to accord accelerated benefits to tier 1 firms and delayed benefits to tier 2 firms, on the rationale that the former have paid their dues by meeting past Mexican performance requirements—often at considerable expense in terms of extra investment and training costs. Although past profits in the Mexican market have been good, the tier 1 firms argue that they need continuing high profits to amortize the extra expense entailed by Mexican performance requirements.[30] A supplementary argument, to which the Big Three only quietly refer, is that Asian producers should not be allowed to sweep in behind the NAFTA negotiations and convert Mexico into an "export platform." Needless to say, the concept of a two-tier approach sets off alarms in both Mexico and Japan.[31]

Applying the two-tier idea to the issue of local content requirements, the Big Three recommend an immediate reduction in the requirement imposed on tier 1 firms, from 36 percent to 25 percent, followed by a gradual phaseout over 15 years. For tier 2 firms they recommend keeping the local content at 36 percent for five years and then phasing it out over the following 10 years.

The Big Three, together with Volkswagen and Nissan, have indeed incurred substantial extra costs in building the Mexican automobile industry because of the succession of Mexican automobile decrees. Their profits through 1991 may not yet have amortized those extra costs. But the Mexican local content rules, just like their Canadian counterparts in an earlier period, clearly work against US parts firms and US jobs, requiring as they do minimum levels of Mexican

---

30. In this spirit, the National Association of Manufacturers recommends that provisions be established so that "companies that invested in Mexico under its traditional restrictive policies should get the NAFTA benefits sooner than potential new investors, particularly if they are not from North America" (*Inside U.S. Trade*, 18 October 1991, 13).

31. According to the President of the Mexican Foreign Trade Board, José Santos Gutierrez Luken, tier 1 firms "should receive no preferential treatment under the NAFTA" (*Inside U.S. Trade*, 1 November 1991, 5). The Japanese Ministry of International Trade and Industry does not like the idea either: its position is that preferential treatment in regional blocs "could yield an appeal at the GATT or other international trade fora by those who are forced to remain outside" (*Inside U.S. Trade*, 8 November 1991, 8).

production. We see little merit in requiring the Big Three to purchase Mexican parts rather than Canadian or US parts, nor do we see the benefit of forcing Toyota, for example, to follow the same pattern of distortion. Moreover, so long as Mexico is enjoying a surplus in parts trade, with every prospect of continued export growth, there is even less reason for continued hothouse treatment in the form of local content rules.[32]

The same objections apply to the made-in-Canada tests. The Canadian automotive industry ran a trade surplus of nearly $10 billion with the United States in 1989. The argument for local content "safeguards" in US–Canada trade has long been an anachronism.

To start, we recommend that both the Canadian and the Mexican local content tests be phased out on a straight-line schedule over 10 years. Thus, the Mexican value-added requirement would decline by 3.6 percentage points a year, and its Canadian counterpart would drop by 6.0 percentage points per year.

Next, we recommend that the Mexican quota that limits 1992 imports of new automobiles to 15 percent of the market should be replaced by a one-for-one production-to-sales ratio test, patterned after the Canadian example. This new test would give the established Mexican assembly firms (the tier 1 producers) the head start they seek, since their production facilities are already in place. New producers, such as Toyota, Honda, and Fiat, would have to build Mexican assembly plants before they could acquire a share of the lucrative Mexican market.

Third, and most important, we strongly recommend that the production-to-sales ratio test in both Canada and Mexico be phased out according to a schedule to be determined in the negotiations. For example, it could be phased out in straight-line fashion over 10 years: from a 1:1 ratio in 1993, to a 0.9:1 ratio in 1994, to a 0.8:1 ratio in 1995, and so forth. Unless there is an agreed phaseout, the new production-to-sales ratio test is likely to prove just as durable in the NAFTA as the Canadian test has proved in the Auto Pact, lasting far beyond any reasonable transition period and deterring new investment in US assembly plants.

Finally, although we are not enthusiastic about an auto parts "voluntary" purchase arrangement negotiated for the Japanese transplants, we think there is room for close surveillance of parts purchasing practices—especially in Japan itself. In any event, commitments by Japanese transplant firms to purchase local auto parts should be satisfied by sourcing from anywhere in North America, not just from the US auto parts industry.

---

32. We readily acknowledge that the hothouse rules mainly protect the Mexican-owned auto parts firms, whereas it is the affiliates of foreign-owned assembly plants that account for most of the industry's export growth. Hence we propose a phaseout of the Mexican local content requirement rather than its instant abolition.

Used Car Imports

At the moment, Mexico, like Canada, limits the import of used cars, although the Mexican restrictions are harder to enforce because used vehicle imports are permitted for the US border area. While the Canadian ban will be phased out by 1994, automakers want the partial Mexican ban to continue (Chrysler Corp. et al. 1991, 10; *El Nacional,* 8 June 1991, 25). In our view, a permanent ban on used car trade has no more justification between Los Angeles and Mexico City than between Los Angeles and Denver. We recommend a five-year phaseout of the Mexican partial ban on imports of used cars.

Export Performance Requirements

Mexico's export performance test is quite explicit. Under the 1989 decree, Mexico requires automakers to achieve $2.50 in automobile exports for every $1.00 of automobile imports in the 1991 model year. That figure is scheduled to drop to $2.00 in the 1992 and 1993 model years. For tier 1 firms, the Big Three recommend sticking with the reduction to $2.00 for 1992, followed by a phaseout over 15 years. For tier 2 firms, the Big Three recommend keeping the ratio at its current $2.50 level for the first five years of the NAFTA accord and then phasing it out over 10 years.

Since the tier 2 producers will be slow to build up their Mexican exports, the schedule proposed by the Big Three would delay their entry into the profitable Mexican market. In other words, Toyotas and Hondas made in the United States would be slow to find their way to Mexico. At a later stage, the $2.50 requirement would prompt the Asian entrants to step up their exports of Mexican-assembled automobiles to the United States and Canada.

In our view, whether export performance requirements work to slow the entry of Asian firms into the Mexican domestic market, or serve to propel exports to the United States and Canada, they are bad policy. In the first instance, the test (if binding) will retard competition in Mexico, keeping the price of automobiles to the Mexican consumer higher than need be and limiting US and Canadian exports; in the second instance, the test (if still binding) will work as an indirect subsidy on exports to the United States and Canada.

Our proposed production-to-sales ratio test undercuts the main rationale for continued Mexican export performance requirements. The ratio test ensures a certain level of Mexican production, and it allows automakers flexibility as to the types of vehicles produced: assembly firms in Mexico can satisfy the ratio test through exporting as well as through sales to the local market. Accordingly, we recommend the fast phaseout of the Mexican export performance requirement for all firms, say at the rate of $0.50 per year over five years, starting at $2.00 in 1992, dropping to $1.50 in 1993, and so forth.

Rules of Origin

The Big Three recommend that tier 1 firms be subject to a 50 percent North American "factory cost" standard to qualify for NAFTA benefits, and that tier 2 firms be subject to a 60 percent or 70 percent standard for the Mexican component of their production.[33] The auto parts manufacturers (MEMA and APMA) and the UAW recommend a 75 percent standard or higher for all firms, both as a way of encouraging North American sourcing of "essential" parts (i.e., power trains) and as a way of protecting US jobs.[34]

In our view, opaque rules of origin should be used neither to discriminate against Asian firms nor to encourage the production of "essential" auto parts in North America. Thus, we recommend keeping the existing 50 percent local content rule. However, if concessions must be made, we prefer a 60 percent rule to a 70 percent rule, and the rule should be the same for all firms. We also recommend the introduction of a new "overlay" test to prevent roll-up abuses by the large automakers (see chapter 8).

CAFE Rules

CAFE standards have arguably made American cars more economical to drive.[35] But the two-fleet rule is not essential to the basic CAFE concept. Instead, masquerading under the environmental banner, the two-fleet provision has discouraged (but not prevented) the Big Three from importing small cars.[36]

---

33. The Big Three also recommend that these percentages should be based on company-wide averages as opposed to the current model-by-model approach. A company-wide average would permit the companies to combine their established US and Canadian production models, which have high local content, with their newer models which have relatively high import content (*Financial Times*, 25 October 1991, 6). Canada's MVMA supports a rule of origin based on company averaging (*Inside U.S. Trade*, 18 October 1991, 1).

34. In early January 1992 Canada requested the formation of a bilateral panel to settle a dispute with the United States over rules of origin. Under the Canada–US FTA, the panel's recommendations will not be binding (*Journal of Commerce*, 17 January 1992, 3A).

35. The fuel economy of the average new car sold in the United States is now 28 miles per gallon, up from 14 miles in 1975 (*Washington Post*, 9 June 1991, H1). The recent introduction by Honda of a family-size car that achieves 48 miles per gallon in the city will put pressure on Congress to raise the CAFE figure (*New York Times*, 20 September 1991, D1).

36. US automakers have imported many small automobiles (for example, the Korean-built Ford Festiva and the Japanese-built Geo Metro from Japan) and sold them as part of their "foreign" fleets (*Washington Post*, 9 June 1991, H6).

A first-best policy would be to eliminate the CAFE requirement and replace it with a high gasoline tax—say, $1.00 or more per gallon.[37] But this solution raises major political questions that go beyond either the scope of this study, or the context of NAFTA talks.

Assuming the CAFE requirement remains in place, the two-fleet rule should be transformed into a one-fleet rule. The jobs rationale for the two-fleet rule is already being eroded, as the Big Three import more small cars as part of their "foreign" fleet. The sourcing games inspired by the two-fleet rule should be ended by including all the automobiles of each manufacturer in a single fleet.

If the two-fleet concept survives the NAFTA talks, its erosion should be hastened by allowing Mexican- and Canadian-assembled vehicles to enter the United States with either a "domestic" or a "foreign" classification, at the option of the producer. This option, replacing the present classification based on shares of value added, will allow maximum flexibility for Mexico and Canada to specialize in the classes of vehicles that they can produce most competitively. Both US producers and Mexico will benefit, and the resultant dilution of the two-fleet rule will lead more quickly to its demise.

Tariff Rates

Current tariff rates on North American automobile and parts trade, described above, are a patchwork affair. Under the NAFTA, the United States, Mexico, and Canada will necessarily commit themselves to eliminate tariffs on all goods, including vehicles and parts. The key question is not the ultimate goal, but the pace at which tariff-free trade is achieved.

For tier 1 firms, the Big Three recommend the immediate elimination of Mexican motor vehicle and parts tariffs. For tier 2 firms, they recommend the retention of the tariffs for five years and then a phaseout over 10 years. We oppose the two-track approach, both because it is bad policy for North America, and because it is an outright affront to the national treatment and MFN principles of the GATT. The idea that established producers in an FTA would enjoy zero tariffs, whereas new producers would pay higher tariffs, represents a radical departure from the norms of the world trading system. Even if this discrimination could be sanctioned by a GATT waiver, it would set a bad precedent for Asia and Europe. Instead we propose that all tariffs on North American trade be eliminated imme-

---

37. See, for example, Giberson (1991). Another alternative, a tax credit for automobile owners who trade in their gas-guzzlers for new, more fuel-efficient cars, was being considered by the administration in late 1991 "as an environmental and energy conservation measure" (*Wall Street Journal*, 23 December 1991, A2).

diately. Zero tariffs in this key sector will send a dramatic signal to the industry and to the public that the NAFTA is open for business.

We have a final recommendation on tariffs. At the end of 10 years, the partners should negotiate a common external tariff (CET) specifically for the automotive sector. The CET would eliminate automobile and parts transshipments inspired by North American tariff differentials. The CET might be a weighted average of MFN rates applied by the three countries in the year 2000; at present tariff rates that might work out to close to 4 percent. Under this plan there would be duty-free trade for all automobiles and parts made in North America, while all automobiles and parts arriving from Asia, Europe, and elsewhere would face the CET.

Safeguards

Automobile and parts producers, like other firms, would have recourse to the normal escape clause measures sanctioned by GATT Article 19 and implemented by national bodies (e.g., the Canadian Import Tribunal and the US International Trade Commission). However, because of the possibly far-reaching consequences of eliminating NTBS to automobile and parts trade, we propose an additional special test for relief available to this sector.[38]

Under our proposal, if any partner should experience a substantial adverse surge in its North American trade balance in automobiles and parts over base-year levels, the surge alone would be grounds for safeguard relief. The base-year levels could start with the average for 1988 to 1991 and then be updated with a three-year lag. A "substantial adverse surge" might be defined as 20 percent per year or faster growth in a country's North American automotive trade deficit (or decline in its North American surplus) sustained over a period of three years or longer. The request for relief could be initiated only by the authorities in the affected country, not by the firms themselves.

The preferred relief in surge cases would take the form of accelerated liberalization by the partner enjoying the corresponding favorable surge. Only if accelerated liberalization was not feasible (e.g., because the partner's market was already totally liberalized) would other forms of relief come into play. Any relief that involved a slowdown of liberalization should end once the sectoral trade balance test was no longer met.

---

38. Similar special relief would be available to other sensitive sectors broadly defined, such as steel (see chapter 12), textiles and apparel (see chapter 13), and agriculture (see chapter 14).

Appendix: Motor Vehicle and Parts Manufacturers in Mexico

Tables 11.4 through 11.6 give a statistical profile of the Mexican automotive industry. This appendix sketches the history of the various motor vehicle and parts firms operating in Mexico.

Chrysler

Chrysler Corp. has been a major producer in the Mexican automotive industry since the 1930s. In 1989, Chrysler de México sold about 93,000 units in the Mexican market and exported 62,000 vehicles to the United States (91 percent of its total exports).[39]

Chrysler has three manufacturing sites in Mexico. Lago Alberto, at the city of Anahuac, near Chihuahua about 200 miles from the US–Mexican border, employs 4,500 people and also serves as the Chrysler de México headquarters. Different models of light trucks are produced and assembled for the US or Mexican markets at Lago Alberto. The Toluca plant, west of Mexico City and about 500 miles from the border, employs 5,400 people and is comprised of five operations: a vehicle assembly plant, two components plants, an engine manufacturing plant, and a standard transmissions plant. The Toluca plant assembles about 100,000 units a year. The Chrysler plant in Saltillo, about 150 miles from the border, builds engines for the Mexican market and for export to the United States.

Chrysler has invested heavily in Mexico, averaging about $100 million a year since 1985. Chrysler purchased Renault's North American operations in 1987 and is now interested in buying Diesel Nacional, S.A. (DINA), Mexico's state-owned heavy truck manufacturer, which produced 4,613 units in 1989. Chrysler de México is willing to strengthen ties with Canadian manufacturers by buying parts directly from Canadian plants; supporting joint ventures, especially involving technical assistance agreements; and encouraging the import of Canadian subassemblies and components into Mexico for further manufacturing (APMA 1990, 49). Of all the automobile producers, Chrysler has the most to gain, in relation to its overall operations, from a NAFTA.

Nissan

In 1989 Nissan sold 96,000 vehicles in the Mexican market, but the company plans to expand production and overtake Chrysler as Mexico's top automobile

---

39. The figure for the total units sold is based on Ford Mexico research.

Table 11.4 Mexico: characteristics of maquiladoras in the automobile industry, 1984–88

	All maquiladoras			Maquiladoras in the automobile industry		
	1984	1986	1988	1984	1986	1988
Value added (millions of dollars)	1,120	1,290	1,570	195	304	487
Employment	202,100	268,400	361,800	29,378	49,048	77,502
Number of plants	722	987	1,450	51	78	129

Source: Automotive Parts Manufacturers' Association, *The Mexican Auto Industry: A Competitor for the 1990's* (Toronto: Automotive Parts Manufacturers' Association, September 1990), 102.

Table 11.5 Mexico: vehicle production and exports by manufacturer, 1988–89

Manufacturer	Total production (units)		Exports as a percentage of production		Exports to the US as a percentage of total exports	
	1988	1989	1988	1989	1988	1989
Chrysler	130,468	161,446	39	42	93	91
Ford	128,753	126,271	52	31	98	100
General Motors	84,056	112,786	43	36	100	100
Nissan	101,140	120,880	19	21	0	0
Volkswagen	59,134	108,374	1	20	9	92
Total	506,915	641,132	34	30	86	83

Source: Automotive Parts Manufacturers Association, *The Mexican Auto Industry: A Competitor for the 1990's* (Toronto: Automotive Parts Manufacturers' Association, September 1990), 27, 37.

assembler.[40] Nissan's long-term strategy is to supply Central and South America from its Mexican-based operations and to expand exports to the United States. Nissan employs approximately 7,600 people and trains many of its personnel in statistical process control and problem-solving and advanced production techniques. Nissan already has three plants at Cuernavaca, about 500 miles from the border, producing passenger automobiles, light trucks and buses, and various components, including the "J" engine (both 1,600-cc and 1,800-cc models), engine blocks, cylinder heads, steering box assemblies, and flywheels. In addition, Nissan's Mexican operations supply the Smyrna, Tennessee, assembly plant with about 6,000 of its 1.5-liter engines a month, and the firm has introduced a new 2.4-liter engine for export to Japan to be used in commercial vehicles. Nissan also owns and operates a foundry at Lerma, about 650 miles south of the border.

Nissan now plans to build an assembly plant at Aguascalientes, 400 miles from the border, with a capacity of 200,000 vehicles a year by 1994 or 1995. The plant, which will cost about $1 billion, will concentrate on producing a new Stanza-class passenger car beginning in 1993. Some 80 percent of the units will be exported to the US and Canadian markets, and the remaining 20 percent will be sold on the domestic market. Nissan is adamantly opposed to a 70 percent

---

40. "Most of the growth has been in the compact and subcompact segments. Nissan with its Tsuru (22 percent of the market) has had one of the highest growth rates. Chrysler has concentrated on luxury cars and has lost market-share accordingly" (*Financial Times*, 25 October 1991, VII).

Table 11.6 Mexico: investment and exports of foreign automobile manufacturers

Manufacturer	Investment	Exports (units)
Chrysler	$100 million annually on average since 1985	62,000 in 1989
Nissan	$1 billion cumulative	160,000 annually by 1994–95
Volkswagen	$1 billion cumulative	100,000
Ford		
Hermosillo plant	$500 million in 1984	170,000 in 1991
	$300 million in 1990	
Chihuahua plant	$700 million in 1991	500,000 engines by 1995
General Motors	$100 million annually on average since 1985	100,000 to 200,000 by early 1990s

Source: Automobile Parts Manufacturers' Association, *The Mexican Auto Industry: A Competitor for the 1990's* (Toronto: Automotive Parts Manufacturers' Association, September 1990); *Journal of Commerce*, 14 February 1991, 4A; *Financial Times*, 22 January 1991, 8; *Wall Street Journal*, January 1991, A6.

North American rule of origin and has stated that this requirement would jeopardize its investment plans.

Volkswagen

Volkswagen sold 86,000 vehicles in the Mexican market in 1989. It also exported 20,000 vehicles to the United States, up from only 7 vehicles in 1987. Its main plant, located 500 miles south of the border at Puebla, can now produce more than 100,000 copies of the original VW Beetle a year; a major ($1 billion) investment program is under way, and capacity will be boosted to 300,000 units a year by 1993. With its best-selling Beetle (22 percent of the market), Volkswagen has enjoyed one of the highest growth rates among automakers in Mexico (*Financial Times*, 25 October 1991, VII). The expanded Puebla plant will produce subcompact Golf and Jetta models exclusively for the United States and Canadian markets and will also become a major supplier of engines to Europe.

Volkswagen already has 2 percent of the US market, but with a NAFTA and the transfer of many overseas operations from Germany to Mexico, car exports to the United States and Canada are expected to reach over 100,000 per year (*Journal of Commerce*, 14 February 1991, 4A; 12 July 1991, 3A). However, among all the producers, Volkswagen could be most adversely affected by stricter pollution requirements, and it would be severely disadvantaged by a stricter North American rule of origin.

Ford

Ford's operations in Mexico include both final assembly and automotive components. Ford Mexico has been producing for export since 1987, and its exports now go to the United States and Canada. Total motor vehicle exports were 51,000 units in 1987, and 66,000 units in 1988, declining to 40,000 units in 1989.[41] In 1984, Ford pledged $500 million to its Hermosillo plant, located 160 miles from the border, to build Mercury Tracers for the 1987 model year. Initially, the Hermosillo plant was to produce 130,000 Tracers annually from parts supplied by Mazda (Japan), but it has only met about half the original production target.[42] Nevertheless, Ford Mexico has maintained its competitive advantage. A

---

41. Ford's total production of cars and trucks in Mexico declined from 128,700 units in 1988 to 126,300 units in 1989. Meanwhile Ford's production of cars for the Mexican market increased from 32,400 to 47,600 units (APMA 1990, 27). The Hermosillo plant was temporarily closed in 1989 for a changeover to a new model.

42. Because all Tracer production was exported, Ford did not have to meet the usual Mexican local content requirements. And because the assembly occurred in Mexico, US quotas on Japanese finished units did not apply.

further $300 million in new investment in the plant enabled Ford to start producing 165,000 units annually of the CT20, the successor to the Tracer, starting in the autumn of 1990. Export production at Hermosillo in 1991 was expected to consist of 170,000 Mercury Tracers and Ford Escorts.

In January 1991 Ford announced a $700 million investment plan to expand and upgrade its engine plant in Chihuahua (230 miles from El Paso, Texas). The plant, which opened in 1983, currently produces 270,000 engines a year, but production will increase to 500,000 engines a year by 1995. Most of these engines are destined for the United States and Canada. In mid–1993, production of a new multivalve, four-cylinder engine will begin. Employment at the plant will increase by 22 percent to 1,100 workers (*Wall Street Journal,* 15 January 1991, A6; *Financial Times,* 22 January 1991, 8). Ford is spending another $350 million to upgrade its export plant at Hermosillo (*Financial Times,* 25 October 1991, VII).

General Motors

In 1989, GM's two main plants at Ramos Arizpe, near Saltillo 150 miles from the border, produced 50,000 passenger cars and 30,000 commercial vehicles (including pickups). In 1989, GM sold 73,000 vehicles in the Mexican market and exported 40,000 vehicles, the majority of which were Chevrolet Celebrities. By the early 1990s, GM expects to produce 100,000 to 200,000 Chevrolet Celebrities for export to the United States.

GM's headquarters and a truck assembly plant are located in Mexico City, some 475 miles from the border. Two assembly plants, one building engines and the other a metal foundry producing automotive castings, are located further south in Toluca. In the last several years, GM has invested an average of $100 million annually in its Mexican operations.

GM is the largest private employer in Mexico, employing over 41,000 workers (APMA 1990, 72). Maquiladora parts plants, located close to the border, are the dominant part of the GM Mexico story. GM operates more than 30 maquiladora plants, which employ over 30,000 people and make GM the largest parts manufacturer in Mexico by far.

Honda

As of this writing Honda produces only motorcycles in Guadalajara, 500 miles south of the border. Honda is considering investing in automobile assembly facilities.

Mercedes-Benz

By 1993, Mercedes will start assembling "kit" cars in Mexico (starting at about 300 per year). Mercedes officials have no current plans for selling to the United States; instead, the Mexican plant is designed to gain access to the local market and to serve as an export base for the rest of Latin America (*Journal of Commerce*, 18 July 1991, 5A). Over the next 5 years, Mercedes will also invest more than $146 million to increase its truck production from 700 to 1,500 per year, and to produce 1,500 buses (*El Nacional*, 7 August 1991, 27).

Auto Parts Manufacturers

About 500 auto parts firms operate in Mexico, concentrated in Mexico City and near the US border. (This geographic pattern contrasts sharply with that of assembly operations, which are found in central as well as northern Mexico.) Parts production expanded by an annual rate of 19 percent between 1986 and 1989, reaching an estimated total of $7.0 billion. The industry employs about 165,000 people and can be divided into three groups:

- well-established Mexican-owned suppliers that traditionally made parts for the domestic market and in some cases have not met international standards of quality and efficiency;

- maquiladora plants, mostly US–owned, which are located in Mexico to take advantage of low-cost labor and ship their production to the United States under favorable tariff treatment (see table 11.4; in 1989, the United States provided about 73 percent of total foreign investment in Mexico's auto parts industry—other major investors were the United Kingdom, Germany, and Japan; US International Trade Commission 1991a, 4-20);

- new firms formed through joint ventures and technical assistance agreements with Canadian and US parts companies; these firms are poised to compete with the Canadian and US parts firms for sales to Canadian and US assembly operations.

Long protected by tariffs and local content requirements, the Mexican parts industry grew up as a hothouse sector. But the industry has now moved beyond its sheltered status. Mexican quality standards, especially in the maquiladoras and among newer suppliers, are improving. The range of manufactured parts products is expanding well beyond the scope of purely labor-intensive, low-value-added production (APMA 1990, 84). Mexico's role as an exporter of parts to the United States and Canada could continue to grow at a rapid rate, within the NAFTA policy framework. But in the NAFTA talks Mexico is likely to pay a price for continued rapid expansion of its parts industry, namely, an end to Mexican local content requirements.

12

Steel

During the 1980s both the US and the Mexican integrated steel industries were radically transformed. In the United States, old integrated mills in the Ohio Valley and elsewhere were closed, industry production was cut from 154 million to 117 million metric tons, new capital outlays totaled $20.6 billion, and the labor force was slashed from 399,000 to 164,000 workers, as the industry underwent a significant consolidation.[1] During the 1980s several Japanese and other foreign steel firms entered the US industry with $4 billion of new investment, mainly via joint ventures with US steel firms (some 30 joint ventures in all; *Business Week*, 1 July 1991, 27–28).

Despite the substantial new capital expenditure, the infusion of Japanese management and technology, and overdue cutbacks in capacity and employment, the US steel industry again faces hard times. With a weakening economy, the spot price for a ton of hot rolled steel dropped from about $345 in early 1990 to $280 in late 1991. During the first half of 1991, US steel firms recorded losses of about $1 billion.[2] Nevertheless, the rationalizations of the past decade have paid off: the US industry is far more competitive and its losses are far smaller than in the bleak days of the mid–1980s.

Rationalization of a different kind has occurred meanwhile in Mexico. The parastatal Fundidora de Monterrey S.A. (FMSA) was shut down in May 1986, cutting Mexican capacity by over 1 million metric tons. Industry employment was reduced from 65,000 to 57,000 between 1980 and 1988. In 1988 the World Bank provided a $400 million loan to restructure and modernize the Mexican steel industry. With the addition of new facilities at the SICARTSA II plant (Siderúr-

---

1. The most notable merger involved Jones & Laughlin Steel and Republic Steel (the third- and the fifth-largest US steel producers), which became LTV Steel (the second-largest producer) in June 1984. For a current overview of the industry, see US International Trade Commission (1991c).

2. *New York Times*, 12 August 1991, D1. Losses continued in the third quarter of 1991: Bethlehem Steel, for example, reported a $61 million loss, and Armco reported a $27 million loss (*Wall Street Journal*, 31 October 1991, A8).

Joanna M. van Rooij helped draft this chapter. Robert Crandall gave helpful suggestions.

gica Lázaro Cárdenas las Truchas S.A.), total Mexican capacity increased from 9.6 million metric tons in 1987 to 11.6 million metric tons in 1989.

In 1989 capacity utilization reached 84 percent in the US integrated mills and 67 percent in the Mexican mills, compared with average capacity utilization rates of 76 percent and 62 percent, respectively, between 1985 and 1989. Shedding their image as hopeless laggards in the world market, both countries accomplished substantial export growth. Between 1985 and 1989, US steel exports increased by 47 percent to $3.0 billion, while Mexican exports increased by 43 percent to $0.7 billion (US International Trade Commission 1991a, table 4-1).

The 1980s marked the advent of the mini-mill in both countries. These mills, which typically process scrap metal in electric furnaces, accounted for 29 percent of US steel production and about 17 percent of Mexican production in 1990. Traditional mini-mill products are nonflat items such as wire rod, concrete reinforcing bars, and bars and shapes. US mini-mills have now expanded to include low-quality flat-rolled production, while Mexican mini-mills have extended their product range to include pipes and tubes. Mini-mills are more labor intensive than integrated steel mills, usually pay lower hourly wage rates, are located closer to markets, and, in their product markets, can generally outcompete the integrated mills.

In both countries, wages in the integrated steel mills are higher than the average manufacturing wage. Wages in the US integrated mills are about $25 per hour, compared with a manufacturing average wage of $10.50; the comparable figures for Mexico are about $3.00 and $2.30 an hour (US International Trade Commission 1991a, table 4-36). Productivity in the US integrated steel mills is far greater than in their Mexican counterparts: 3.2 man-hours per ton versus 9.6 (US International Trade Commission, *Monthly Report on the Status of the Steel Industry*, November 1990, vi). Further, US steel output is concentrated in the higher grades, which command substantially higher prices per ton.

The Mexican steel industry is spread out geographically. In the northeast, the AHMSA plant (Altos Hornos de Monclova S.A.) is located near the city of Monclova, and the HYLSA plant (Hojalata y Lámina S.A.) is situated near Monterrey. In the east, TAMSA (Tubos de Acero de México S.A.) is located in Veracruz, close to the oil field of Poza Rica, its principal market, and conveniently placed to import steel ingots for the production of seamless steel pipe. In the southeast, SICARTSA is located near the port of Lázaro Cárdenas on the Pacific; SICARTSA II at Lázaro Cárdenas was built primarily to export slab and plate.

The Mexican integrated steel industry buys practically all its raw material (iron ore, coking coal, and flux) from domestic sources.[3] However, in 1989 Mexico

---

3. In 1989, Mexico imported 0.7 million metric tons of iron ore. Occasionally SICARTSA imports small quantities of coking coal or pellets.

imported 0.3 million metric tons of scrap (half of it from the United States) for use in its mini-mills.

Mexican iron ore is produced in five open pit mines that operate as captives of the integrated mills. These mines yield low-grade ore, and some of them are nearing exhaustion. The northern mines are La Perla in Chihuahua state and Hércules in Coahuila. The southern mines, located near the Pacific coast, are Las Truchas in Michoacán, Peña Colorada in Colima, and El Encino in Jalisco. The SIDERMEX firm owns 100 percent of the Las Truchas and Hércules mines and 55 percent of Peña Colorada. The remaining 45 percent of Peña Colorada is owned by HYLSA (28.5 percent) and TAMSA (16.5 percent). HYLSA owns 100 percent of the El Encino mine.

Mexico has coal-mining operations only in the northeastern state of Coahuila. Unlike its mediocre iron ore reserves, Mexico's coal reserves are of relatively high grade and abundant. SIDERMEX is the main producer of coking coal, operating about nine mines in the state of Coahuila. Another coal-bearing region with promising potential is Tezoatlán-Mixtepec in the state of Oaxaca. SIDERMEX is interested in this region because it is only 120 miles from the SICARTSA mills at Lázaro Cárdenas, whereas the Coahuila coal region is about 1,000 miles away.

The Development of the Mexican Steel Industry

Modern steel production in Mexico began in the 1940s and grew slowly through the 1950s. Aided by import substitution policies, the annual growth of crude steel production averaged 10.2 percent in the 1960s and 7.5 percent in the 1970s. Growth continued at a slower rate in the 1980s: from 1980 to 1990, Mexican crude steel production increased from 7.1 million to 8.7 million metric tons, and finished steel production grew from 5.9 million to 6.2 million metric tons. In 1990 Mexico ranked 14th among world steel producers and accounted for 1.1 percent of world production.[4]

Since 1983, in overall terms, Mexican steel exports and imports have been approximately matched (table 12.1). However, within product groups, Mexico generally imported high-quality flat products such as cold rolled steel and tin plate, as well as alloy steel required by the automobile and parts industries; Mexico exported nonflat products such as concrete reinforcing bars and seamless and welded tubes.

---

4. By comparison, US and Canadian crude steel production in 1990 was 88.9 million and 12.1 million metric tons, respectively, out of a total world production of 770.2 million metric tons. The major world producers in 1990 were the Soviet Union (20 percent), the European Community (18 percent), Japan (14 percent), and the United States (12 percent).

Table 12.1 Mexico: steel production, consumption, and trade, 1980–89 (thousands of metric tons)

	1980	1981	1982	1983	1984	1985	1986	1987	1988	1989
Production										
Crude steel	7,156	7,663	7,056	6,978	7,560	7,399	7,225	7,642	7,779	7,850
Finished steel[a]	5,930	6,209	5,515	5,418	5,873	5,907	5,575	5,897	6,002	6,057
Consumption										
Crude steel	10,317	11,369	8,181	6,296	7,331	7,693	6,608	6,485	6,969	7,256[b]
Finished steel	8,343	9,234	6,711	5,311	6,172	6,446	5,503	5,461	5,885	6,150[b]
Exports	67	42	293	1,004	894	433	1,081	1,332	1,247	1,118
To US	67	41	113	651	797	272	431	487	471	440
Imports	3,597	3,836	1,639	823	1,161	1,362	1,119	877	1,585	1,558
From US	1,241	823	295	114	138	152	142	197	344	473

a. Data for finished steel production for 1987 through 1989 are based on the ratio of crude steel production to production for 1986.

b. Estimates.

Sources: International Iron and Steel Institute, Committee on Statistics, *Steel Statistical Yearbook 1990*, (Brussels: International Iron and Steel Institute, 1990), tables 2, 10, and 12; *Steel Statistics for Developing Countries*, 1989; American Iron and Steel Institute, "Written Statement of the American Iron and Steel Institute for the Record of the United States International Trade Commission Investigation No. 332–297, 'Likely Impact of a Free Trade Agreement with Mexico on the United States,'" 26 November 1990.

Before privatization, the Mexican steel industry was dominated by the state-owned SIDERMEX, which was established to manage four large integrated steel mills—AHMSA, SICARTSA I and II, and FMSA—plus about 87 steel-related subsidiaries. Through liquidation, consolidation, or sale, the number of subsidiaries was cut back to about 20 units. FMSA was closed down in May 1986; together the three remaining integrated mills under SIDERMEX accounted for about 56 percent of total Mexican steel production in 1990 (table 12.2).

The private sector operates two large integrated steel mills: HYLSA, a subsidiary of Grupo Alfa, and TAMSA. Together these mills account for 28 percent of Mexican steel production (table 12.2).[5] TAMSA is the only Mexican producer of seamless pipes (primarily used for oil exploration), and its main customer is the Mexican state oil company, Pemex. In 1989 mini-mills—nine privately owned and one government-owned—accounted for the remaining 17 percent of steel production.

In March 1990 SIDERMEX was offered for sale as part of the Salinas administration's privatization drive. There were few takers, reflecting hard times in the steel industry worldwide, resistance from Mexican unions toward shedding excess labor in the plants, and SIDERMEX's debt burden.

In an effort to make SIDERMEX more attractive to domestic and foreign investors, the Mexican government assumed all the firm's debt[6] and split SIDERMEX into three separate units: AHMSA, SICARTSA, and SIBALTSA (*Financial Times*, 6 November 1991, 24). In addition, the government rewrote existing labor contracts and introduced environmental regulations.[7]

In November 1991 the Mexican government finally succeeded in selling off the state steel firms, raising a total of $340 million in cash (*Wall Street Journal*, 25 November 1991, A9). AHMSA, with an annual capacity of 3.8 million tons of liquid steel and flat products (*Journal of Commerce*, 25 October 1991, 5A; *Financial Times*, 6 November 1991, 24), was sold to Grupo Acerero del Norte for $270 per ton of capacity (including new investment to refurbish the AHMSA facilities).

---

5. In 1988, HYLSA and TAMSA had installed capacity of 1.9 million and 0.9 million tons, respectively.

6. In late 1990 estimates of SIDERMEX debt ranged from $1.5 billion to $3.0 billion (*Financial Times*, 11 September 1990. 8). Assumption of this debt by the Mexican government was inspired by the realization that the plant was worth far less than its debt burden. Throughout the 1980s, SIDERMEX received regular public subsidies of $75 million to $100 million per year, plus extraordinary subsidies in the form of debt assumption and equity infusion (World Bank 1988).

7. The new labor contracts entailed massive layoffs, which the unions accepted under the threat of plant closure. The work force of the three mills was scheduled to fall from 25,000 in 1990 to 12,000 in 1991. To improve environmental safety, the government shut down the Siemens Martin open hearth furnaces, costing AHMSA a fifth of its total production (*Financial Times*, 6 November 1991, 24).

Table 12.2 Mexico: steel production by company, 1980–90[a] (thousands of metric tons)

Company	1980	1981	1982	1983	1984	1985	1986	1987	1988	1989	1990
Integrated mills	5,977	6,456	5,947	5,806	6,334	6,109	6,129	6,423	6,464	6,479	7,235
State-owned	4,038	4,289	3,985	3,777	4,354	4,159	4,314	4,276	4,214	4,199	4,847
AHMSA	2,272	2,424	2,279	2,227	2,468	2,603	2,868	3,086	3,083	2,862	3,178
FMSA	974	961	837	537	858	943	254	NA[b]	NA	NA	NA
SICARTSA	792	904	869	1,013	1,028	613	1,192	1,190	1,131	1,337	1,669
Privately owned	1,939	2,167	1,962	2,029	1,980	1,950	1,815	2,147	2,250	2,280	2,388
HYLSA	1,562	1,775	1,579	1,643	1,637	1,671	1,582	1,662	1,710	1,812	1,874
TAMSA	377	392	383	386	343	279	233	485	540	468	514
Nonintegrated mills[c]	1,179	1,207	1,109	1,172	1,226	1,290	1,096	1,219	1,315	1,372	1,447
Total	7,156	7,663	7,056	6,978	7,560	7,399	7,225	7,642	7,779	7,851	8,682

NA = not applicable.

a. Figures for 1990 are estimated by apportioning total crude steel production for 1990 among firms according to their 1989 share of steel production.

b. FMSA ceased operations in 1986.

c. Principally mini-mills (approximately 10 firms).

Sources: US International Trade Commission, Monthly Report on the Status of the Steel Industry (USITC Publication 2332), November 1990, table a, iii; The WEFA Group.

Grupo Acerero paid $145 million in cash, took over the company's debt of $350 million, and promised to invest another $535 million in the plant.

An 80 percent stake in SICARTSA, which has total annual capacity of about 2 million tons, was sold to Grupo Villacero for $170 million in cash (or about $110 per ton), leaving the government with 20 percent control. Given proper management, the SICARTSA plant, located near the deep-water port of Lázaro Cárdenas, could provide a springboard for exports to the United States (US International Trade Commission 1990b, 3-13).

The third steel plant, SIBALTSA, with an annual capacity of 2.5 million tons, was sold to Grupo Caribbean Ispat for $100 per ton. Despite the fact that SIBALTSA is considered one of the most modern steel plants in the world, part of the plant was never finished. The plant is reported to be operating at one-third of capacity (*Financial Times*, 6 November 1991, 24). Ispat bid $25 million in cash, committed itself to invest $50 million in modernization, and assumed $195 million in debt (*Wall Street Journal*, 25 November 1991, A9).

Expressed on a per-ton-of-capacity basis, the purchase prices for SICARTSA and SIBALTSA appear to have been substantially below the going price to acquire existing integrated steel capacity in the United States (about $250 to $300 per ton; according to Robert Crandall in a presentation at the Center for Strategic and International Studies, 27 June 1991). Needless to say, the low purchase prices paid by the new owners for SIDERMEX come nowhere near covering its historical costs. Nevertheless, low capital and labor costs should give the new Mexican companies a competitive edge in the US market. However, when the time comes to expand SICARTSA and SIBALTSA, if the capital costs per ton of expansion are anywhere near current US construction costs (estimated by Crandall at $1,400 per ton),[8] their exports will have difficulty competing with US integrated steel mills that still have spare capacity.

Foreign Participation in the Mexican Steel Industry

There are no restrictions on foreign investment in the Mexican steel industry: under regulations enacted in May 1989, foreign firms may now own 100 percent of iron and steel producers. Yet there is no US investment in the Mexican steel industry. In fact, in 1986 Armco divested its interests both in Armco Mexicana S.A., a sheet steel and welding company, and Aceros Nacional S.A., a mini-mill wire product plant.

---

8. The last integrated steel mill constructed in the United States was erected in 1962, so cost estimates of a newly constructed mill in 1992 are necessarily speculative. However, the construction cost of the unfinished SIBALTSA plant was about $800 per ton, and the new owner, Ispat, has committed itself to additional capital outlays of at least $20 per ton.

Other foreign firms have invested in Mexico but maintain a minority stake. Productora Mexicana de Tubería, a pipe and tube plant, is a joint venture of NAFINSA, SIDERMEX, and a number of Japanese firms. TAMSA operates a pipe and tube mill with the backing of Italian and Argentinian financiers. Precitibe S.A. de C.V. is a carbon steel pipe and tube plant owned 49 percent by Transmesa from Spain and 51 percent by the domestic firm Industrias Nacobre S.A. de C.V. Recently, Thyssens (Germany) and Acerinox (Spain) acquired partial ownership in Mexico's only stainless steel producer, Mexinox, which exported $45 million worth of product to the United States in 1990.[9] Extensive foreign participation creates the possibility that Mexican steel will be more competitive in the American market. It would be logical, for example, for Grupo Villacero to team up with an Asian or a European firm to export a large share of SICARTSA output to the United States.[10]

Trilateral Steel Trade

In 1990 total US exports of steel products amounted to $2.8 billion, of which $0.5 billion consisted of exports to Mexico (US Department of Commerce). As shown in table 12.3, in 1990 major US exports to Mexico were cold rolled sheet and strip (27 percent by weight); angles, shapes, sections, and rails and rail products (15 percent), and plate (13 percent). Although steel is not a major US export, US performance in the Mexican market is respectable: exports to Mexico accounted for 18 percent of total US steel exports;[11] in contrast, shipments to Mexico accounted for only 7 percent of total US merchandise exports.

On balance, total US steel trade showed a $5.6 billion deficit in 1990; however, the United States ran a $0.3 billion steel trade surplus with Mexico. This figure, coupled with the resource constraints on the Mexican steel industry, goes far to explain the qualified support for the NAFTA shown by the US steel industry.[12]

---

9. In 1989 US imports of stainless products were temporarily halted when the US Department of Commerce found that Mexico had overshipped its allotment of stainless steel under the voluntary restraint arrangement (US International Trade Commission 1991c).

10. SICARTSA already has a history of foreign involvement. New facilities at SICARTSA II were constructed with financial and technical assistance from Japan and the United Kingdom. British Steel Corp. is SIDERMEX's largest foreign creditor from the steel industry.

11. Moreover, in 1990 US steel exports to Mexico increased by 25 percent over 1989, while steel exports to all markets decreased by 1 percent (US International Trade Commission 1991c).

12. In a written statement sent to the US Trade Representative, dated 26 August 1991, the American Iron and Steel Institute strongly supported a NAFTA, conditioned on the absence of change in US countervailing and antidumping duty law, the elimination of duty drawback, open government procurement by Mexico, and other specific conditions.

Table 12.3 Mexico: steel trade with the United States, by product, 1980–90 (thousands of metric tons)

	Total US imports		Imports from Mexico		Total US exports		Exports to Mexico	
	1980	1990	1980	1990	1980	1990	1980	1990
Total steel mill products	15,495	15,575	67	585	4,101	3,903	1,241	591
Semifinished steel[a]	155	2,144	0	214	912	474	377	15
Flat-rolled								
Hot rolled sheet strip	1,523[b]	2,157	0	8	252	687	113	68
Cold rolled sheet strip	1,524	1,985	0	31	171	432	11	160
Plate[c]	2,437	1,947	0	39	1,094	575	247	78
Other sheet and strip[d]	1,432	1,740	0	99	212	397	36	61
Bar and rod[e]	860	980	3	12	431	400	186	45
Angles, shapes, sections, and rails and rail products[f]	2,243	951	19	24	288	347	121	88
Wire and wire products[g]	1,544	1,263	5	30	267	160	43	44
Pipe and tube[h]	3,777	2,355	40	128	470	427	107	30
Tool steel	0	53	0	0	3	4	0	2

a. Ingots, blooms, billet, and slabs.

b. Includes 15,328 tons of hot and cold rolled strip.

c. Cut lengths and in coils, plates, black plate, tin plate and tin free.

d. Galvanized hot dipped and electrolytic, all other metallic coated and electrical.

e. Hot rolled, shapes under three feet, concrete reinforcing, cold finished and hollow drill steel.

f. Structural shapes (three feet and over), steel piling, rails and track acessories, and wheels and axles.

g. Drawn wire, baling wire, galvanized wire fencing, wire nails, barbed wire, and wire rods.

h. Standard pipe, oil country pipe, line pipe, mechanical tubing, pressure tubing, stainless pipe and tubing, nonclassified pipe and tubing, structural pipe and tubing, and pipe for piling.

Sources: American Iron and Steel Institute, 1990 Annual Statistical Report, tables 17 and 22; "Written Statement of the American Iron and Steel Institute for the Record of the United States International Trade Commission Investigation No. 332–297, 'Likely Impact of a Free Trade Agreement with Mexico on the United States,'" 26 November 1990.

In general, the United States exports high-quality steel products to Mexico and imports lower-quality steel products. The average value per metric ton of exports to Mexico was $782 in 1990; the corresponding figure for imports from Mexico was $486 (table 12.4). The export potential for US firms selling to Mexico depends on the growth of upscale markets in capital goods and consumer durables (especially automobiles and appliances). Significant US export gains can also be expected in nontubular products for construction and oil industry use.[13]

In 1990 the major Mexican steel exports to the United States were semifinished steel (37 percent), pipe and tube (22 percent), and other sheet and strip (17 percent; table 12.3). The export potential of the integrated Mexican steel industry is bound up with two issues: foreign participation, to add product, processing, and marketing strength to the Mexican industry; and greater reliance on imports of raw materials, especially high-grade iron ore (e.g., from Brazil or Australia) and, to a lesser extent, coking coal.

The export potential of the Mexican mini-mills depends on access to cheap electric power, vigorous entrepreneurial skills, and an ever-expanding range of mini-mill products. The NAFTA talks should provide a commitment to link the electric power grids of the southwestern United States and northern Mexico, thereby augmenting the power supplies of Tijuana, Juárez, and other northern cities (see chapter 10). Existing Mexican mini-mills will show entrepreneurial vigor once they are in private hands, and US mini-mill firms will probably open new plants in Tijuana, Mexicali, Juárez, and Nuevo Laredo. The immediate growth of Mexican mini-mill exports will probably be concentrated in commercial-grade semifinished steel products, such as steel slabs and wire rod, but within a decade the product range could be much larger.

A computable general equilibrium model constructed by Trela and Whalley (1991) suggests that, over a long period of time, the Mexican steel industry might make huge inroads into the US market. According to Trela and Whalley, over a time horizon of 40 years, US steel imports from Mexico could increase by over 3,000 percent, while US steel imports from Canada might drop by 35 percent. Applying this model to 1990 data, the implication is that US production would fall by 9.5 percent, from 88.9 million to 80.5 million metric tons, while Mexican production would grow by 87 percent, from 8.9 million to 16.2 million metric tons. Canadian production would decrease slightly, by 0.2 million metric tons (Trela and Whalley 1991, table 6).

---

13. In 1984 the Mexican construction industry accounted for 44 percent of domestic steel shipments, the automotive industry for 12 percent, industrial goods and packaging for 10 percent, appliances for 9 percent, agriculture for 4 percent, railways and shipbuilding for 3 percent, and all others for 8 percent. This breakdown indicates that some of the biggest markets are concentrated in areas where US producers have a good chance as steel suppliers (World Bank 1988).

Table 12.4 United States: steel mill product imports from Canada and Mexico, 1990[a]

	Canada		Percent of total US imports		Mexico		Percent of total US imports	
	Quantity	Value	Quantity	Value	Quantity	Value	Quantity	Value
Carbon and certain alloy								
Semifinished	189	51	8	10	228	51	10	9
Plate	271	97	47	18	43	14	8	1
Sheet and strip	807	358	12	11	130	76	2	2
Bars and light shapes	339	147	33	31	13	4	1	1
Wire rod	345	123	36	36	30	8	3	2
Wire	161	97	39	31	3	2	1	1
Steel wire products	98	83	15	13	34	27	5	4
Structural shapes and units	279	153	27	32	37	21	4	4
Rails and related products	200	47	57	35	negl.	negl.	negl.	negl.
Pipe and tube	400	243	16	17	140	73	6	5
Stainless steel								
Semifinished	26	38	43	47	negl.	1	1	1
Plate	negl.	negl.	1	1	0	0	0	0
Sheet and strip	2	6	2	2	22	42	15	14
Bars and shapes	5	14	12	12	negl.	negl.	negl.	negl.
Wire rod	negl.	negl.	1	1	0	0	0	0
Wire	2	11	13	16	0	0	0	0
Pipe and tube	6	29	12	16	1	2	1	1
Alloy tool steel	6	10	negl.	negl.	8	2	17	1
Total	3,137	1,508	19	17	689	323	5	47

a. Including certain fabricated steel products. Quantities are in millions of metric tons, values in millions of dollars.

Source: US International Trade Commission, Quarterly Report on the Status of the Steel Industry, (USITC Publication 2364), March 1991.

Almost anything can happen over a period of 40 years. In the next ten years or so, it is unlikely that Mexico will dramatically enlarge its integrated steel mill capacity. There is a vast excess of steel capacity in the world today, and new integrated plants cannot compete with existing facilities.[14]

However, there is some incentive for Mexican integrated steel production to expand on the basis of wage differentials, using existing capacity. As noted above, wages in the integrated steel industry are substantially lower in Mexico than in the United States: about $3 per hour compared with $25 per hour. To produce one ton of steel takes about 3.2 man-hours in the US integrated steel industry and about 9.6 man-hours in Mexico (figures are based on the presentation by Crandall cited above, 1991). With steel selling in early 1992 at $400 to $800 per ton, depending on the type and grade, a labor cost difference of $51 per ton (calculated as 3.2 hours times $25 per hour for the United States, less 9.6 hours times $3 per hour for Mexico) is moderately attractive. In the short run, therefore, Mexican integrated mills might boost production by 2 million tons for export markets—provided that existing capacity can be operated efficiently. At the same time, there is substantial scope for US mills to sell high-grade products into Mexico.

Historical support for these conclusions can be drawn from the Portuguese and Spanish experience after the accession of these countries to the European Community.[15] In 1985 Portugal exported $193 million worth of steel and products to the Community and imported $85 million. By 1990 Portugal had increased its exports eightfold, to $833 million, while Portuguese imports had increased threefold to reach $224 million. In 1985 Spain exported $1.2 billion worth of steel to the Community and imported $0.7 billion. By 1990 exports had surged to $3.1 billion while imports reached $2.2 billion. The European experience suggests that the steel trade within a NAFTA could at least double and perhaps triple from present levels.

Once existing Mexican capacity is put back into production, future integrated mill expansion will depend on two factors: the pace of absorption of idle capacity around the world (a process that could take five years), and relative construction costs. If Mexico can achieve the construction costs of Korea ($700 to $900 per ton; the construction costs experienced by SIDERMEX were above this range), and

---

14. Assuming that new capacity can be built for only $1,000 per ton, and that interest and depreciation charges are 15 percent per year, the extra cost of steel produced from a new plant would be about $150 per ton, compared with steel produced from a fully depreciated idle plant.

15. Data from the European Community, *European Statistics*, various issues. The dollar figures for the expansion of Spanish and Portuguese trade with the European Community are overstated because of exchange rate fluctuations. Between 1985 and 1990, the ecu appreciated from $0.76 to $1.27.

if US and Canadian construction costs prove to be 50 percent higher, then Mexico might dramatically increase exports from its integrated mills along the lines of the Trela-Whalley model. Otherwise Mexico will have no commanding advantage over the US and Canadian integrated steel industries; instead, trilateral trade of integrated mill products will likely settle into niches of specialization.

In the meantime, growth of Mexican mini-mill exports is practically assured. Labor costs in US mini-mills are about $20 per hour, compared with about $3 per hour in Mexico. US mini-mills require about 1.5 man-hours to produce a ton of steel; the current Mexican figure is not known, but even if it is 4 hours (a narrower differential than for the integrated plants), Mexican labor costs would be only half the US figure. With easy entry and low capital costs in the mini-mill sector, Mexican exports of mini-mill products to nearby markets in the southwestern United States should reach 500,000 tons within five years.

US Restrictions on Bilateral Steel Trade

US–Mexico steel trade is restricted by tariff and nontariff barriers on both sides of the border. US tariffs on steel imports range from 0.5 percent to 11.6 percent ad valorem, while Mexican tariffs range from 10 percent to 15 percent. In addition, "voluntary" restraint agreements (VRAS) initiated by the United States limit Mexican steel exports; some states in the United States also limit steel imports through their procurement policies. As of this writing, however, the most important constraint on US steel imports is the VRA system.

On 18 September 1984, President Ronald Reagan determined that, although the steel industry was being injured by imports, taking escape clause action on behalf of the steel industry would not be in the national economic interest.[16] Instead, the President directed the US Trade Representative to negotiate VRAS with countries whose steel exports to the United States had increased significantly. The United States eventually negotiated VRAS with Australia, Austria, Brazil, Czechoslovakia, the European Community, Finland, East Germany, Hungary, Japan, Korea, Mexico, China, Poland, Romania, South Africa, Trinidad and Tobago, Venezuela, and Yugoslavia.

Under the first VRA, which applied from September 1984 to September 1989, Mexico agreed to limit its exports to 0.49 percent of US steel consumption. Steel products (for example, automobile components) processed in Mexico's maquiladora plants using imports of US steel were excluded from the restrictions. In exchange, antidumping and countervailing duty cases filed against Mexican

---

16. The legal authority for this determination was Section 202(b)(1) of the Trade Act of 1974.

steel producers by the United Steelworkers of America and the Bethlehem Steel Corp. were terminated.

On 25 July 1989 President George Bush announced a Steel Trade Liberalization Program that extended the VRA system until 31 March 1992. Under the renewal agreement, Mexico's quotas increased to 0.95 percent of US consumption from October 1989 to December 1990, and to 1.1 percent through March 1992; in addition, there is a special tonnage limitation on semifinished steel imports (table 12.5). In return, Mexico committed itself to limit subsidies and other trade-distorting practices in steel. The volume of US steel imports from Mexico rose from 398,000 to 585,000 metric tons from 1989 to 1990, an increase of 47 percent; the value of those shipments, however, rose only from $231 million to $284 million, or by 23 percent.

In the initial period of the Steel Trade Liberalization Program (October 1989 to December 1990) Mexico filled only about 65 percent of its export quota. Mexico did not fill its quota for bars, semifinished products, and structural steel. However, Mexico exceeded its export ceiling for wire and wire products, other wire products, and oil country tubular goods.[17]

Not all US provisions relating to Mexican steel trade are restrictive. Some steel imports ($2.1 million in 1990) enter under the Generalized System of Preferences. Far more important, US steel imports from Mexico are partly governed by the duty relief provisions under Harmonized Tariff Schedule (HTS) subheadings 9802.00.60 and 9802.00.80 (previously TSUS 806.30 and 807.00).[18] Articles of metal that have been manufactured in the United States, exported for processing or assembling, and then returned to the United States for further processing are subject to duty only on the value of the foreign processing or assembling activity. These duty relief provisions are a harbinger of arrangements under a NAFTA accord, which should eventually eliminate all tariff and nontariff barriers on trilateral steel trade.

In 1989 total US imports of iron and steel products under subheading HTS 9802.00.60 were $118 million. US imports from Mexico under these provisions

---

17. In 1987, steel wire products such as steel fence products, steel wire fabric, and welded wire mesh for concrete reinforcement were added to the list of steel products covered by the VRA. In 1989 preferential treatment under the Generalized System of Preferences was withdrawn for wire and wire mesh.

18. See chapter 5 on maquiladoras. Subheading 9802.00.60 includes iron and steel mill products; copper wrought; aluminum wrought; nickel wrought; lead wrought; tantalum wrought; titanium wrought; tungsten wrought and unwrought; hinges, fittings, and mountings; interchangeable tools for hand tools or machine tools; and other products. Subheading 9802.00.80 includes metallic containers; locks and padlocks; hand tools; structures of base metal; nonelectric heating and cooking apparatus other than cast iron stoves; miscellaneous metal products and articles; and all other articles (US International Trade Commission 1991b, A-4).

were $63 million (of which 72 percent represented raw US iron and steel and thus was duty-free). HTS 9802.00.60 imports accounted for 25 percent of US iron and steel imports from Mexico in 1989. The big items under 9802.00.60 were imports of sheets and strip ($54 million) and pipe and tube ($7 million).[19]

Mexican Restrictions on Bilateral Steel Trade

Historically, the Mexican steel industry has been protected by quantitative restrictions, high tariffs, high official reference prices for calculating customs duties, domestic content requirements, and preferential public procurement. During the 1960s and 1970s, quantitative restrictions covered about 60 percent to 65 percent of steel imports. With the debt crisis of 1982, restrictions were extended to 100 percent of steel imports. The restrictions were reduced in 1985 to 39 percent of steel imports and were totally eliminated in 1987.

Until the mid–1980s, Mexican tariffs on steel imports ranged up to 50 percent ad valorem; moreover, duties were assessed on the basis of artificially high official reference prices, thereby increasing the degree of protection. The overall Mexican policy of exceptionally high tariff protection was reversed in the late 1980s. In 1986 Mexico joined the GATT and lowered its maximum tariffs on steel imports from 50 percent to 20 percent. In December 1987 all steel tariffs were lowered to a maximum of 15 percent, and current steel tariffs now range from 10 percent to 15 percent. Official reference prices were phased out by the end of 1990.

In 1990 Mexico joined the Steel Committee of the Organization for Economic Cooperation and Development, a group that seeks to reduce barriers on steel trade. This step foreshadows Mexican membership in the OECD itself, a development that could come in 1993, following ratification of the NAFTA accord. In the Uruguay Round, Mexico supports the US position on steel trade liberalization coupled with an end to government subsidies.

Nonetheless, free trade has not yet made its way to the Mexican steel sector. Local content requirements play an important role in the automotive industry, a major user of steel products. Some 36 percent of automotive value added must be comprised of components produced by Mexican automobile parts firms, which in turn are also subject to a 36 percent domestic content rule. Pemex buys nearly all its steel pipe from TAMSA, and other state enterprises probably favor domestic steel. Indirectly, these various rules and practices translate into a protected market for Mexican steel.

---

19. In addition, in 1989, when the United States imported $412 million worth of mineral and metal products under subheading 9802.00.80, US imports from Mexico were $218 million and accounted for 53 percent of duty relief imports under subheading 9802.00.80 (of this amount, locks and padlocks accounted for $99 million).

Table 12.5 Mexican steel products subject to VRAS[a]

	First period: October 1989 to December 1990		Second period: January 1991 to March 1992	
	Import penetration (percentage of US consumption)	Export ceiling[b] (metric tons)	Import penetration[c] (percentage of US consumption)	Export ceiling[d] (metric tons)
Semifinished steel	0.24	259,195	0.27	271,127
Carbon and certain alloy rolled[e]	0.28	118,415	0.33	127,694
Hot rolled sheet and strip	0.23	43,514	0.27	47,706
Cold rolled sheet and strip	0.19	31,439	0.22	32,194
Plate	0.70	43,953	0.81	47,345
Stainless flat rolled	0.88	11,942	1.02	13,439
Coated flat rolled	0.67	130,992	0.77	133,749
Bar and rod	0.99	211,058	1.15	236,771
Carbon cold finished bar	0.53	7,065	0.62	7,866
Carbon wire rod	2.17	128,464	2.51	144,545
Stainless bar and rod	0.03	72	0.03	69
Angles, shapes, sections and rails and rail products	0.72	70,351	0.83	75,478
Wire and wire products	3.00	62,940	3.47	66,581
Wire rope	2.54	4,978	2.94	5,954
Wire strand	—[f]	2,000	—[f]	2,317
Panels and mesh	0.86	17,639	1.00	18,800
Other wire	1.82	37,328	2.10	39,480

Pipe and tube	2.55	184,416	2.95	232,534
Oil country tubular goods	2.00	31,820	2.60	55,705
Line pipe	3.64	63,591	4.17	86,006
Standard pipe	4.21	90,431	4.83	97,868
Tool steel	0.31	322	0.36	338

a. Including certain fabricated steel products.

b. Tonnage estimate as based on May 1990 forecast of apparent consumption.

c. Import penetration figures are based on a February 1991 forecast of 1991 US apparent consumption.

d. Unadjusted final period ceilings.

e. "Certain alloy" refers to alloy steel other than stainless or tool steel.

f. Export ceilings are fixed tonnages for the entire period.

Sources: US International Trade Commission, *Review of Trade and Investment Liberalization Measures by Mexico and Prospects for Future United States–Mexican Relations*, (USITC Publication 2326), October 1990; *Quarterly Report on the State of the Steel Industry* (USITC Publication 2364), March 1991, F-9.

Recommendations

It should be possible to eliminate tariffs on North American steel trade by 1998 and to abolish nontariff barriers on an even faster timetable.[20] The most important step toward liberalization of US–Mexico steel trade could be decided before the free trade negotiations reach a conclusion. In March 1992, President Bush must decide whether to extend once again or to phase out the VRA system on steel. If the VRA system is abolished on schedule, trade liberalization in North America can proceed in tandem with global liberalization. On the other hand, if the VRA system is extended for another year or two, NAFTA liberalization could come first.

One thing is relatively certain. As the VRA system is phased out, the US steel industry will bring antidumping and countervailing duty cases against individual foreign suppliers, including Mexican firms.[21] In response, Mexican steel companies will bring their own antidumping cases against US steel shipments.[22]

To reduce the scope of conflict, the NAFTA countries should agree to zero subsidies on steel, either in the context of a GATT steel agreement or in a separate NAFTA chapter. At the same time, they should agree that subsidies and dumping margins of less than 2.5 percent in North American trade are *de minimis* and will not be subject to countervailing or antidumping duties. Finally, and this is quite important, the new owners of the SIDERMEX plants should not be subject to countervailing or antidumping duties on account of subsidies and debt relief received by the state company *prior* to privatization.[23] Instead, the new owners should start with a clean state. Otherwise, US–Mexico steel trade will be burdened by unfair-trade litigation for years to come.

Rather than look to the unfair-trade laws to address the problem of injurious commerce in steel, a special safeguard mechanism should be put in place to

---

20. For the recommendations of the American Iron and Steel Institute (AISI), see the AISI's letter to the US Trade Representative dated 26 August 1991. A leading Mexican objective, in direct conflict with the AISI recommendations, is to reform the US unfair-trade laws (see *Inside U.S. Trade,* 12 July 1991, 1).

21. On 24 September 1991, 10 US steel and pipe makers filed unfair-trade cases against imports from Mexico, Korea, Brazil, Romania, Taiwan, and Venezuela. Mexico was accused of dumping margins between 29.6 percent and 91.2 percent (*Inside U.S Trade,* 27 September 1991, 6). The cited margins reflect public subsidies and debt forgiveness extended to the component operations of SIDERMEX when they were still state-owned.

22. Mexican wire rod producers recently filed a blanket antidumping complaint against all US rod producers, even though some do not ship to Mexico. This complaint was interpreted as a retaliatory action for the dumping complaint against Mexico filed by 10 US producers of standard pipe (*Metal Bulletin,* 10 October 1991).

23. The idea that prior subsidies and debt relief should be disregarded appears to be the position adopted by the US Commerce Department in two previous cases, involving lime from Mexico (1989) and cold rolled flat products from Sweden (1991). However, it should be codified in the NAFTA accord.

address the possibility of a "substantial adverse surge" in each partner's steel trade balance with the other NAFTA countries.[24] Our proposed transitional safeguard would not be triggered if *both* imports and exports grow dramatically—as we can expect from the Spanish experience. Only lopsided trade growth would trigger the special remedy. Moreover, the special safeguard would expire once full liberalization was achieved.

In deciding unfair-trade cases, Mexico should make its administrative procedures more transparent and consistent with US and Canadian norms. The first step is Mexican accession to the GATT Code on Subsidies and Countervailing Measures and adoption of antidumping procedures fully consistent with the GATT antidumping code (see chapter 2). Thereafter, Mexican accession to the dispute settlement procedures of Articles 18 and 19 of the Canada–US FTA will provide a mechanism for reviewing antidumping and countervailing duty determinations of all three parties to ensure their procedural and substantive fairness.

One other aspect of liberalization will need to be addressed in the NAFTA talks. Preferential state, provincial, and parastatal procurement methods should be abolished, and Mexican domestic content rules should correspondingly be scrapped.[25] In August 1991 the US governors signaled their support to expand the GATT procurement code and to drop buy-American and buy-local provisions if Europe and Japan do likewise (*Journal of Commerce*, 22 August 1991, 1A). With this signal from the governors, the United States, Canada, and Mexico can certainly agree to open up all forms of public and parastatal steel procurement.

---

24. A "substantial adverse surge" could be defined as an annual growth in the North American trade deficit for any NAFTA partner over some base-period level at a rate greater than 20 percent per year (or a decline in its base-period trade surplus at a rate greater than 20 percent). The base-period level could be initially calculated as a three-year average trade balance and subsequently updated with a three-year lag. We propose similar safeguard mechanisms, triggered by "substantial adverse surges" in trade balances, for other sensitive sectors: automobiles (chapter 11), textiles (chapter 13), and agriculture (chapter 14).

25. John Griffin from the Washington-based American Institute for International Steel has argued that buy-domestic laws retard the sale of imported steel to the US construction industry (*Journal of Commerce*, 16 October 1991, 9A).

13

Textiles and Apparel

The prospective liberalization of textiles and apparel trade within North America has provoked intense opposition in the United States, both from organized labor and from a solid core of textile and apparel manufacturers, even though Mexico currently accounts for only 2 percent of total US imports of textiles and apparel. The US textile and apparel industry has a long history of protection from developing-country goods (see Cline 1990). US and Canadian producers fear that lower trade barriers will prompt the industry to relocate on a grand scale to take advantage of low Mexican labor costs, and thus convert Mexico into an export platform for huge shipments to the United States and Canada.

The US textile and apparel industries do not, however, speak with a single voice on these matters. A number of firms claim that increased imports are inevitable as the US and Canadian industries adjust to the realities of world competition. They predict that production will gradually shift to other low-wage countries—in East Asia, South Asia, or the Caribbean—if North American trade is not liberalized. Textile producers such as Du Pont and apparel makers such as Warnaco argue that a NAFTA will enable US makers of clothing and other textile products to achieve the same economies as their Asian-based rivals, who prosper by taking advantage of differences in wage rates and skill levels in neighboring countries (*Washington Post*, 12 May 1991, H8).

Furthermore, US textile and apparel trade with Mexico is not a one-way street, as it is with many Asian producers. In 1990 Mexico accounted for 15 percent of US apparel exports and 14.2 percent of US textile exports (tables 13.1 and 13.2). Although much of that is reexported back to the United States after additional processing in maquiladora plants, the United States now runs a small textile and apparel trade surplus with Mexico.

Canadian textile and apparel producers are likely to pay close attention to the NAFTA agreement because of the importance to Canada of the United States as a market and as a supplier.[1] The US market accounts for 60 percent and 81 percent

---

1. The Canada–US FTA is estimated to have generated more than $126 million in additional Mexican exports of apparel, while diverting $36 million in Mexican textiles exports (Mexico,

---

Rosa M. Moreira and Martin Cohen helped draft this chapter.

Table 13.1 United States: trade in textiles and apparel, 1978–89[a]
(millions of dollars)

Year	Textiles		Apparel	
	Imports	Exports	Imports	Exports
1978	2,400	2,225	6,108	677
1979	2,399	3,189	6,291	931
1980	2,676	3,632	6,849	1,202
1981	3,250	3,619	8,008	1,232
1982	3,000	2,784	8,703	953
1983	3,460	2,368	10,292	818
1984	4,874	2,382	14,513	807
1985	5,274	2,366	16,056	755
1986	6,151	2,570	18,554	900
1987	6,918	2,900	21,960	1,132
1988	6,748	3,651	22,877	1,575
1989	6,417	3,897	26,026	2,087
1990	6,800	3,700	24,740	2,240

a. Values are for Standard International Trade Classifications 65 (textiles) and 84 (apparel). Imports are stated on a c.i.f. basis, exports on an f.a.s. basis. Import volumes are in millions of square-yard equivalents.

Source: William R. Cline, *The Future of World Trade in Textiles and Apparel rev. ed.* (Washington: Institute for International Economics, 1990), table 12.1; US Department of Commerce, *U.S. Industrial Outlook*, 1991.

of total Canadian exports of textiles and apparel, respectively, but together these shipments amount to only $0.6 billion, or less than 1 percent of total Canadian exports. Canadian imports are more substantial, totaling almost $5 billion in 1989. The United States accounted for 48 percent of Canadian textile imports, but only 8 percent of Canadian apparel imports (GATT, *International Trade 89–90*, tables A6 and A7). With the advantage of a semi-integrated US–Mexican apparel industry, the United States could become a far more competitive apparel supplier to Canada.

Structure of the US and Mexican Industries

United States

The US textile and apparel industry consists of 29,000 plants spread throughout every state of the union. In terms of total shipments, both textiles and apparel

Economic Adviser to the Minister of Industry and Trade, 1990). See also US International Trade Commission (1991a, 4-40).

Table 13.2 United States: textiles and apparel trade with Mexico, 1985–90 (millions of dollars)

Year	Total trade^a			Textiles			Apparel		
	Imports	Exports	Balance	Imports	Exports	Balance	Imports	Exports	Balance
1985	289	180	−109	52	110	58	237	70	−167
1986	362	250	−112	92	180	88	270	70	−200
1987	501	426	−75	135	252	117	366	174	−192
1988	566	596	30	128	358	230	438	238	−200
1989	653	700	47	149	404	255	504	296	−208
1990	688	862	174	174	526	352	514	336	−178

a. Trade in products of textile mills and apparel made from textiles. Excluded are raw cotton, unspun wool, and man-made fiber that have not been processed into yarns with twists. Also excluded is apparel made from plastic, fur, or leather.

Sources: American Textile Manufacturers Institute, "The Problems with the US-Mexican Free Trade Agreement" (Washington: American Textile Manufactures Institute, 1990); US Department of Commerce, Office of Textiles and Apparel, Export Market Report, December 1990; Major Shipper Report 1990, 1991; Textiline, various years.

are large industries: in 1990 the US textile industry shipped $64.7 billion of goods and the US apparel industry $63.3 billion (table 13.3). The textile industry enjoyed a 19 percent increase in its shipments from 1985 to 1990, but the apparel industry, facing greater import competition, experienced only a 4 percent increase during the same period (*U.S. Industrial Outlook,* 1991).

Combined, the two industries employ 9 percent of the US manufacturing work force. Largely as a result of automation, but also as a consequence of rising imports, textile and apparel employment declined throughout the 1980s. Between 1980 and 1990, employment in the textile industry dropped from 848,000 to 550,000 production workers (*U.S. Industrial Outlook,* 1991; Hufbauer et al. 1986, 132). Apparel employment decreased from 1.3 million production workers in 1980 to 824,000 in 1990. These numbers go far to explain the strident opposition of textile and apparel unions to further trade liberalization of any kind.

Within manufacturing, textile and apparel jobs are at the lower end of the wage scale. Apparel workers earned an average of $6.85 per hour in 1990, while textile workers averaged $8.30 per hour (table 13.3). These figures are well below the average wage for all US manufacturing workers of $10.47 per hour (US Department of Commerce, Office of Textiles and Apparel 1990), but compare more favorably with the average wage in services trade ($6.31 per hour in 1988). For many textile and apparel workers, living in isolated towns and possessing few skills, alternative employment at $7.00 per hour is simply not available.

New York, Pennsylvania, and California have the greatest concentrations of US apparel workers, many of whom are minority and women employees working in large metropolitan areas. In contrast, US textile workers are chiefly located in the Carolinas and Georgia. About two-thirds of the 6,000 textile mills in the United States are located in nonmetropolitan areas, and the mill is often the principal employer in its community. Both industries thus face difficult labor adjustment problems: apparel because many of its workers are unskilled, and textiles because many of its workers reside far from alternative employment centers.[2]

Textiles and apparel represent an important and growing part of US merchandise trade (table 13.1). In 1990 the United States exported $3.7 billion worth of textile goods and imported $6.8 billion. The US trade balance in textiles shifted from a small surplus in 1980 to a trade deficit of $3.1 billion in 1990. The US trade deficit in apparel goods is, of course, much larger, reaching $22.5 billion

---

2. Nevertheless, a North Carolina study of 3,650 laid-off textile and apparel employees found that their unemployment experience paralleled that of other manufacturing employees. Some 92 percent of the sample found jobs; their average length of unemployment was 2.4 quarters, and their average wage in their new positions was 9 percent higher (Field and Graham 1991).

in 1990. Between 1980 and 1990, US imports of apparel jumped from $6.8 billion to $24.7 billion, while US apparel exports only increased from $1.2 billion to $2.2 billion.

Mexico

Until the recent economic reforms, Mexican production of textiles and apparel was highly protected and inefficient, and geared mostly to the domestic market. Trade reforms have spurred a sharp increase in imports and a subsequent restructuring of the Mexican industry.[3]

In 1989 the Mexican textiles and apparel industry employed 758,000 workers (US International Trade Commission 1991a, table 4-1). Three-quarters of the jobs were in the apparel sector, but only 5 percent were in maquiladora plants. However, the maquiladoras have been the most dynamic sector of the industry. The production of textiles and apparel in the maquiladoras grew by an annual average of 17 percent between 1985 and 1989, while output growth in nonmaquiladora firms was more or less flat (US International Trade Commission 1991a, table 4-1). Maquiladora plants now account for 15 percent of total Mexican textile and apparel production. Almost 90 percent of Mexican exports of textiles and apparel to the United States originate in the maquiladora sector (see chapter 5).

The United States has a competitive advantage over Mexico in most textiles. The domestic Mexican textile industry suffers from low-quality inputs, outdated technology, and capacity underutilization. As a result, production costs run 25 percent to 150 percent higher than in the United States, despite much lower Mexican wages (US International Trade Commission 1991a, table 4-39). Fabric finishing and dyeing, the weakest links in the Mexican textile value-added chain, limit the production of quality fabrics that could be exported or incorporated into apparel exports. However, the Mexican yarn-spinning and fabric-weaving sectors are competitive in a few products such as acrylic yarns and cotton sheeting. Both areas have improved rapidly in the last ten years.

Overall, the Mexican apparel industry is considerably stronger than the textile industry. Cutting and sewing operations in Mexico have a cost advantage over US producers of 30 percent to 50 percent, largely because of low Mexican wages (Botella et al. 1991, 206). In 1988 the average hourly compensation for textiles and apparel workers in Mexican maquiladoras was $0.76 (US Department of Labor, Bureau of Labor Statistics, Office of Productivity and Technology, data

---

3. Investment reforms have also influenced the restructuring of the Mexican industry; a notable example is the Wal-Mart and Cifra joint venture, linking the largest retailers in the United States and Mexico. The new venture plans to open wholesale stores throughout Mexico (*Financial Times*, 10 July 1991, 20).

Table 13.3 United States: textiles and apparel employment, production, and trade, 1990

	Textiles	Apparel
Total employment (thousands)	650	1,024
Production workers (thousands)	550	824
Average hourly earnings (dollars)	8.30	6.85
Product shipments (billions of dollars)	64.7	63.3
Trade (billions of dollars)		
Imports	6.8	24.7
Exports	3.7	2.2
Balance	−3.1	−22.5

Source: US Department of Commerce, *U.S. Industrial Outlook*, 1991.

sheets). Mexican wages in the textile and apparel industries are about on par with a number of Asian countries that export substantial amounts of apparel to the United States, for example, the Philippines, Thailand, Indonesia, and Sri Lanka.

In the past, the limited supply of locally produced quality fabrics and the lack of marketing expertise held back Mexican export growth. But import liberalization by both Mexico and the United States sparked a sharp growth in Mexican apparel exports, with the value of shipments to the United States more than doubling from 1985 to 1990 (table 13.2).

Trade Barriers

A liberal NAFTA accord on textiles and apparel would find ample precedent in recent US–Mexico trade policy. Since 1985, Mexico and the United States have significantly liberalized the tariff and nontariff barriers (NTBS) that restrict bilateral trade. Mexico has slashed its NTBS, especially its restrictive import licensing requirements, and has sharply cut its tariffs, which currently range from 12 percent to 18 percent for textiles and 20 percent for apparel (US International Trade Commission 1991a, table 4-38).

The overall regime of US protection for the textile and apparel industry has changed little in recent years (Cline 1990). The US average trade-weighted duty on imports from all countries is about 11.5 percent on textiles and 22 percent on apparel. Total US protection, taking into account the restrictive effect of quotas, is estimated at about 28 percent on a tariff-equivalent basis for textiles and about 56 percent for apparel (Cline 1990, 163–64). However, the restrictions have been noticeably relaxed for Mexico and the Caribbean countries (discussed below). Because of tariff preferences granted to exports from maquiladora plants, the average trade-weighted duty on US imports from Mexico is about 6 percent (US International Trade Commission 1991a, table 4-38), and, as detailed below, the quota regime applied to Mexico is noticeably less restrictive than that applied to most developing countries.

In 1989, 90 percent of US imports of textiles and apparel from Mexico benefited from duty relief provisions under subheading 9802.00.80 of the Harmonized Tariff System (HTS; previously TSUS 807.00).[4] Under these provisions, duty is only charged on the foreign value added when goods are assembled abroad from US components. (In 1989 only 30 percent of the total value of US imports of textiles and apparel items from Mexico represented value added in Mexico; see table 13.5). Mexican exports made from foreign fabrics cut in Mexico are subject to US tariffs on the total value of the imported good.

These tariff preferences work as a strong incentive for two-way trade. Between 1986 and 1989, global US imports of textiles, apparel, and footwear under HTS 9802.00.80 almost doubled, from $1.43 billion to $2.76 billion, for a rate of growth roughly three times that for total US imports of these goods (table 13.4).[5] Mexico is a major user of HTS 9802.00.80: Mexican textile and apparel imports comprised 24 percent of total US imports for consumption of textiles and apparel in 1989 under HTS 9802.00.80 (table 13.5).

In addition to tariff barriers, Mexican textile and apparel exports to the United States have long been subject to quotas established under the Multi-Fiber Arrangement (MFA).[6] However, in 1988 the United States concluded bilateral accords with Mexico that significantly liberalized quotas on Mexican textiles and apparel, especially on garments assembled with US components.

Pursuant to the 1987 Framework Understanding between Mexico and the United States, the two countries negotiated a four-year agreement on textiles and apparel trade in February 1988. The agreement created a "special regime" for most apparel and selected made-up textiles from Mexico that enter the United States under HTS 9802.00.80. Under the special regime, new quotas were created for articles assembled with US–made and US–cut fabric. Applying the established

---

4. HTS 9802.00.80 prescribes tariff treatment for eligible imported goods that contain US–made components. Textiles, apparel, and footwear are the main items subject to this provision.

5. Apparel accounted for 80 percent of combined apparel-textile-footwear imports under HTS 9802.00.80, textiles accounted for 2 percent, and footwear accounted for the remaining 18 percent.

6. The MFA is an exception to the GATT ban on quantitative restraints in that it permits country-specific import restrictions on textiles and apparel of cotton, other vegetable fibers, wool, man-made fibers, and silk blends. Under US law, MFA products are not eligible for duty-free treatment under the Generalized System of Preferences.

Table 13.4 United States: imports of textiles, apparel, and footwear, 1985–89 (millions of dollars except where noted)

Year	Total imports	HTS 9802.00.80 imports	Duty-free component		Tariff rate on HTS 9802.00.80 imports	
			Value	As a percentage of total	Nominal	Effective
1986	29,976	1,434	906	63	19.9	7.3
1987	34,778	1,841	1,065	58	19.8	8.3
1988	36,595	2,382	1,312	55	19.2	8.6
1989	39,635	2,757	1,511	55	15.2	6.9

Source: US International Trade Commission, *Production Sharing: US Imports under Harmonized Tariff Schedule Subheadings 9802.00.80 and 9802.00.60, 1986–1989* (USITC Publication 2353), March 1991, 6-1.

Table 13.5 United States: imports under HTS 9802.00.80, by commodity group, 1989 (millions of dollars)

Commodity	From Mexico			Total imports		
	Total value	Duty-free value	Dutiable value	Total value	Duty-free value	Dutiable value
Textiles and apparel						
Women's, girls', and infants' shirts and blouses	44	25	18	185	106	78
Women's, girls', and infants' coats and jackets	10	7	3	74	42	33
Women's, girls', and infants' trousers, slacks	73	47	26	275	160	116
Men's and boys' shirts	20	14	6	210	125	83
Men's and boys' coats and jackets	20	14	7	80	49	30
Men's and boys' trousers, slacks, and shorts	160	113	47	501	341	160
Body-supporting garments	41	31	10	260	171	83
Gloves	9	8	1	34	20	14
Footwear	82	62	20	500	90	409
All other articles	194	138	56	643	406	237
Total	655	460	195	2,756	1,510	1,245

Source: US International Trade Commission, US Imports under Harmonized Tariff Schedule Subheadings 9802.00.80 and 9802.00, 1986–1989 (USITC Publication 2365), March 1991, B48—B50.

principle of HTS 9802.00.80, US textiles and apparel imports from Mexico that are made of fabrics formed and cut in the United States (special regime HTS 9802.00.80.10), or made from foreign-origin fabrics cut in the United States (normal regime HTS 9802.00.80.60), are charged duty only on the value added in Mexico. However, the new allotments for these items increased the overall Mexican quotas by 50 percent to 90 percent (Trela and Whalley 1991, 5).

In February 1990, pursuant to the 1989 Consultative Understanding Regarding Trade and Investment Facilitation Talks, the special regime was expanded: the United States eliminated quotas on 52 items and increased quotas by an average of 25 percent on the remainder. Flexibility provisions were also added to allow for fashion trends (*International Trade Reporter*, 21 February 1990, 256–57).

The special regime applies only to exports from Mexico of products assembled from US–formed and US–cut fabrics (special regime HTS 9802.00.80.10). Each category enumerated in the special regime is subject to specific limits (SLs) or designated consultation levels (DCLs).[7] The remaining Mexican exports, consisting of assembled products that incorporate foreign fabric cut in the United States (normal regime HTS 9802.00.80.60), and products made with foreign fabric not cut in the United States, are subject to the normal MFA quotas. Although the basic Mexican MFA quotas are renegotiated about every four years, the additional Mexican quotas under the special regime regularly increase by 6 percent per year.

The special regime was designed to spur US exports of textiles and garment parts to Mexico for assembly and subsequent reexport to the United States as finished garments. It succeeded. Since the special regime went into effect, exports of US textiles to Mexico have increased by 47 percent and exports of apparel by 41 percent (table 13.2).

Prior to the special regime, the average Mexican quota utilization rates under MFA limits were 35 percent in the 1981–83 period, and 51.5 percent in the 1985–89 period (Erzan and Yeats 1991). Since the special regime and Mexico's own trade reforms came into effect, Mexico has occasionally approached its quota limits, but fewer than a fifth of imports from Mexico faced binding restrictions during the period 1985–89.[8] The US Commerce Department frequently accommodates increased Mexican exports by augmenting the DCLs under the special regime—as it did with the quota for cotton trousers and coveralls in 1990.

---

7. More than 50 percent of Mexican textile and apparel exports, based on 1989 trade volumes, entered the United States under SLs or DCLS (see the estimates, presented in US International Trade Commission 1991a, table 4-39). Within each SL there is a cross-referenced sublimit for products not made from US–formed and US–cut fabrics (these products enter under the normal MFA quotas).

8. However, some of the binding restrictions have been important. In 1989, for example, Mexican quotas were binding in acrylic spun yarn, cotton sheeting fabric, underwear, trousers and slacks, and shirts and blouses (US International Trade Commission 1991a, 4-39).

US–Mexico Bilateral Trade

Spurred both by the special regime and by Mexican trade reforms, US textile and apparel trade with Mexico has grown rapidly in recent years. Between 1985 and 1990, bilateral trade (exports plus imports) increased threefold from $469 million to $1,550 million (table 13.2). US exports to Mexico grew from $180 million to $862 million; Mexican exports to the United States increased from $289 million to $688 million. The overall US trade balance with Mexico in textiles and apparel thus shifted from a deficit of $109 million to a surplus of $174 million. The shift was mainly due to a sharp increase in US textile exports, which generated a bilateral surplus of $352 million in 1990. The US deficit in apparel trade remained in the range of $167 million to $200 million during this period.

In the textile and apparel complex, Mexico is extremely dependent on the US market. Mexico ships 91 percent of its total exports of apparel and textile goods to the United States, and 64 percent of Mexican imports come from the United States (US International Trade Commission 1991a, table 4-1). Canada is Mexico's second-largest export market, accounting in 1988 for 5 percent of Mexican exports (Botella et al. 1991, 193).

Competition from the Caribbean Basin

Although much of the congressional fast-track debate focused on the threat to US firms from maquiladora plants in Mexico, both US and Mexican firms face growing competition in the apparel sector from Caribbean producers. Caribbean producers benefit from the same tariff benefits as Mexican maquiladoras under HTS 9802.00.80, and they enjoy even better special quota preferences under the Caribbean Basin Initiative (CBI).

In 1986 the United States established a "Special Access Program" (also referred to as 807A) for apparel exports from CBI countries arriving under HTS 9802.00.80. Like the subsequent special regime for Mexico, the CBI program was designed both to increase production in the Caribbean and to expand exports of US fabric and garment parts. The link is the requirement that the apparel be made from US–formed and US–cut fabric. Largely as a result of the Special Access Program, most of the CBI countries more than doubled their exports of apparel to the United States under HTS 9802.00.80 between 1986 and 1989 (table 13.6). Exports of the Dominican Republic, Costa Rica, Haiti, and Jamaica, which represent the vast majority of the trade, totaled $793 million in the latter year.

The Special Access Program established guaranteed access levels (GALS) that are separate and usually higher than the levels set by MFA quotas; it also established DCLs applicable to products that are not assembled solely from US–made

Table 13.6 United States: textiles, apparel, and footwear duty-free component of US imports under HTS 9802.00.80, 1986 and 1989 (millions of dollars)

Country	1986	1989
Mexico	363	460
Dominican Republic	190	390
Costa Rica	84	172
Haiti	78	116
Jamaica	49	115
Colombia	26	57
Honduras	20	50
Guatemala	9	42
El Salvador	6	21
Philippines	17	15
All others	64	73
Total	906	1,511

Source: US International Trade Commission, *Production Sharing: US Imports under Harmonized Tariff Schedule Subheadings 8902.00.80 and 9802.00.60, 1986–1989* (USITC Publication 2365), March 1991, 6-1.

and US–cut fabric.[9] GALs may be increased on request by the exporting country; barring a finding of "market disruption," increases are virtually automatic.[10]

The average effective US tariff rate on apparel imports entering under GALS from Caribbean Basin countries in 1988 was 4.9 percent (compared with 8.6 percent for imports from Mexico in that year); and some 75 percent of the total value of these goods consisted of US–made components (versus 55 percent for Mexican exports).

The CBI countries have abundant low-cost labor, and their proximity to the US market provides an advantage over East Asian firms in terms of greater control over production and shorter delivery times. The Caribbean countries also

9. Under the traditional interpretation of HTS 9802.00.80, the fabric need only be cut (as opposed to produced) in the United States in order for the imported article to be exempt from duty on the value of the fabric (US International Trade Commission 1989c, 6-5). Hence, the HTS 9802.00.80 tariff regime encompasses a wider range of products than the GAL system.

10. The term "market disruption" refers to the weak injury test that has long been used to limit textile and apparel imports under the MFA.

attract US and other foreign firms through various incentives such as tax breaks and free trade zones. Of the four leading Caribbean suppliers, the Dominican Republic and Haiti offer the largest pools of labor and the lowest hourly wage rates: $0.55 and $0.58, respectively (US International Trade Commission (1989c, 6-4). The use of Caribbean-assembled textile and apparel products results in cost savings of between 15 percent and 30 percent compared with products from Hong Kong: Caribbean garment assembly costs are thus about 75 percent of Hong Kong costs and about 33 percent of US costs.

The CBI countries (and Mexico) have indirectly benefited from sharply reduced quota growth rates applied to Hong Kong, Korea, and Taiwan (now about 1 percent annually). Stricter limits on textile and apparel imports from the Asian "Four Tigers" have encouraged firms to shift production elsewhere, including the Caribbean Basin.

However, the Caribbean nations are now worried about the liberalization of textiles and apparel under the NAFTA. The Caribbean nations derive about 25 percent of their export income from textiles and apparel (about $2 billion annually), and the United States accounts for 90 percent to 95 percent of this trade (*Journal of Commerce,* 22 November 1991, 3A). The Caribbean nations rightly fear that granting Mexico equal access to the US market under the NAFTA will erode their own preferential arrangements (*Financial Times,* 26 November 1991, 6). A similar fear has prompted the Caribbean (and Central American) nations to seek a go-slow approach toward phasing out the MFA system and bringing textile trade into the normal structure of GATT discipline.[11]

Recommendations

The textiles and apparel sector is one of the few areas where a NAFTA could cause significant trade diversion, if the NAFTA reforms are not matched by a multilateral commitment to phase out the MFA. In the short run, the Caribbean Basin countries would be adversely affected, as the Mexican regime became more favorable than their own. In the long run, free trade with Mexico could prompt the United

---

11. For example, the Jamaican Ambassador to the GATT urged the Uruguay Round textiles negotiating group to accord special and differential treatment to small textile suppliers. Special treatment could take the form of faster growth rates, an increase in base-level quotas, a higher share of liberalized trade than other countries, and a 15- to 20-year transition period. Fearing the domination of China in the textiles and apparel industries following a 10-year phaseout of the MFA, the Caribbean nations also recommended that the transitional arrangement be extended only to current GATT signatories, which would exclude China (*Journal of Commerce,* 13 November 1991, 4A; *Inside U.S. Trade,* 29 November 1991, 5–6).

States and Canada to take a less liberal view toward other developing countries, and thus undercut support for the gradual elimination of MFA quotas.[12]

In late 1991 various textile and apparel industry groups offered their own recommendations for the NAFTA. The United States 'Apparel Industry Council (USAIC)[13] recommended that, in order to qualify for NAFTA preferential access, apparel products should be assembled in a NAFTA country from US, Canadian, or Mexican cut and formed fabric. In addition, USAIC recommended extension of any NAFTA benefits to the CBI countries, the immediate removal of tariffs and quotas on 807A imports,[14] a six-year tariff phaseout period for non–807A imports to match the Canada–US FTA phaseout period, duty-free entry of 20 million square meters of non–NAFTA textiles under a tariff rate quota system, and the adoption of a safeguard mechanism for a period of 10 years based on Article 3 of the MFA (the market disruption clause).

In many respects, the recommendations offered by the American Textile Manufacturers Institute (ATMI) and the American Apparel Manufacturers Association (AAMA) parallel the USAIC recommendations. But the ATMI and the AAMA initially called for even stricter rules of origin: NAFTA treatment should be given only to textile products made of North American content "down to the cotton ball." Their recommendations would also deny NAFTA benefits to CBI countries and set a special sublimit of 2 million square meters on duty-free entry of wool fabrics from each non–NAFTA country. The ATMI and the AMA later modified their position, seeking a "yarn forward" rule that would allow importation of non–North American fibers.

In some ways our proposals are similar to those made by the industry groups. We would apply the upwardly flexible approach used in the Caribbean GAL quota regime to the Mexican special regime. Special regime quotas would be adjusted upward, upon request, unless a showing of "market disruption" could be made. Meanwhile tariffs would be phased out. Over a 10-year transition period, quotas would become redundant and tariffs on intraregional trade would be eliminated. We would not extend NAFTA tariff benefits to the CBI until the CBI countries join the NAFTA. However, unlike USAIC, ATMI, and AAMA, we oppose the introduction

---

12. Even in the early stage of freer imports from Mexico and the Caribbean, there is active political opposition against dismantling the MFA. In late 1991, 150 members of the US House of Representatives urged President Bush to reject the 10-year phaseout period of the MFA proposed by GATT Director General Arthur Dunkel, on the grounds that 1.4 million US jobs would be lost and two-thirds of US production displaced. The letter calls for a minimum phaseout period of 15 years (*Inside U.S. Trade*, 29 November 1991, 5–6).

13. USAIC is a group of 29 apparel firms with assembly plants overseas (*Inside U.S. Trade*, 18 October 1991, 7).

14. The elimination of quotas for non–807A imports would be conditioned on the elimination both of duty drawback and in-bond processing of textiles from non–NAFTA countries.

of stricter rules of origin—either a "down to the cotton ball" standard or a "cut *and* formed" standard (as opposed to the present "cut *or* formed" standard).

During the transition period, however, any partner country should be able to seek temporary safeguard measures in the event of a "substantial adverse surge" in its North American trade balance in textiles and apparel taken as a group.[15] The preferred safeguard would be accelerated liberalization by the partner country with a rapidly growing trade balance; only if accelerated liberalization is not feasible would protective measures be considered. The North American trade balances test ensures that each partner's export as well as import growth with the other two partners is considered before special transition safeguards can be invoked. At the end of the transition period, all quotas and tariffs on North American textile and apparel trade would be scrapped, and normal (i.e., GATT) safeguards procedures would be applied in the event of injurious trade.

The rule of origin will become critical as North American trade in textiles and apparel is liberalized. Under the Canada–US FTA, a special provision determines whether products qualify for preferential treatment: apparel must be either made from fabric woven in the United States or undergo a "second transformation," to qualify for preferential entry into the US market. Rather than devise new and complicated tests, the same rules of origin should be applied to North American textile and apparel trade—unless and until a North American firm can establish a case of abuse (see chapter 8).

Gradual elimination of quotas and duties under the NAFTA would spur bilateral US–Mexico trade in textiles and apparel. US export growth would continue to be associated with unfinished goods that are processed and subsequently reexported to the United States. In addition, the United States would ship larger quantities of up-market apparel to Mexican consumers (US International Trade Commission 1991a, table 4-38). Mexican export growth would be concentrated in made-up garments.

The KPMG Peat Marwick model suggests that, with free trade, Mexican exports might increase by $460 million, while US exports would only grow by $40 million (see table 3.6 of this study). Similar results have been calculated using other models. For example, Sam Laird has estimated that, if only tariffs are

---

15. A "substantial adverse surge" could be defined as an annual growth in the North American trade deficit for any NAFTA partner over its base-period level at a rate greater than, say, 20 percent per year (or a decline in its trade surplus at a rate greater than 20 percent). The base-period level could be calculated starting with the 1988–91 three-year average trade balance figures, which would be subsequently updated with a three-year lag. Similar safeguards tests, involving "substantial adverse surges" in trade balances, are proposed for other sensitive sectors: automobiles (chapter 11), steel (chapter 12), and agriculture (chapter 14). Note that a "substantial adverse surge" test is reminiscent of the "market disruption" test in the MFA, but with an important difference: the "excessive surge" refers to trilateral trade *balances* in a *group* of products, not merely import growth in a single product.

eliminated, US imports of apparel from Mexico will increase by 53 percent; if free trade is achieved through the Uruguay Round and the NAFTA, imports of clothing from Mexico should more than double.[16]

In our view, these various econometric estimates dramatically understate the potential trade gains. Using the history of Spain's accession to the European Community as our guide, we would not be surprised if Mexican exports of textiles and apparel reach $3 billion to $5 billion in 10 years—an export gain of $2 billion to $4 billion. In the five years between 1985 and 1990, after the enlargement of the European Community to include Spain and Portugal, Spanish and Portuguese exports of textiles and apparel to the Community soared from $1.7 billion to $5.0 billion.[17] Over a 10-year period, Mexico can achieve even larger gains in the US and Canadian markets. At the same time, the United States will sell more fabric and clothing to Mexico. Again, between 1985 and 1990, Spanish and Portuguese textile and apparel imports from the Community grew from $0.6 billion to $4.0 billion. A similar leap in US exports to Mexico can be anticipated. All told, by the end of the 1990s, the United States could easily run a textile and apparel trade deficit of $1 billion to $2 billion annually with Mexico. But far more important than possible growth in the sectoral trade deficit will be the enormous and beneficial surge in two-way commerce.

Mexico's advantages under a NAFTA would be reduced if the MFA were phased out over the next 10 years, as currently proposed in the Uruguay Round negotiations.[18] However, Mexico (and the CBI countries) would still maintain their competitive advantage based on proximity to the United States, the special tariff preferences of HTS 9802.00.80, and the NAFTA itself, as North American tariffs are eliminated.

---

16. Laird (1990). Laird's estimates are based on 1983 data adjusted to 1989 levels.

17. Data from European Community, *European Statistics*, various issues. The dollar figures for the expansion of Spanish and Portuguese trade with the European Community are overstated because of exchange rate fluctuations: between 1985 and 1990 the ecu appreciated from $0.76 to $1.27.

18. The phaseout currently proposed by GATT Director General Arthur Dunkel, in the December 1991 Draft Final Act of the Uruguay Round, would immediately enlarge all quotas by 12 percent upon reaching a deal, followed by another 17 percent enlargement after three years, 18 percent after seven years, and the elimination of the remaining quotas after 10 years.

14

Agriculture

Agriculture is a highly protected activity in all three countries participating in the NAFTA negotiations. Liberalization holds the promise of significant trade gains in specific agricultural sectors for each country but will also create large adjustment problems, particularly in Mexico where farming is the mainstay of 26 percent of the working population (compared with 3 percent in the United States and 5 percent in Canada; see table 6.1 of this study).

US and Canadian agricultural interests stand counterpoised to those of Mexico. The United States and Canada are two of the world's largest and most efficient grain exporters, whereas Mexico is a competitive exporter of horticultural products. A NAFTA will expose the highly protected and labor-intensive Mexican field crop sector, together with the protected US and Canadian horticultural sectors, to tough new competition.

Finally, in dealing with agriculture, the NAFTA negotiators will need to revisit issues discussed in the Canada–US FTA, which eliminated agricultural tariffs and removed some nontariff barriers but left the major farm policies in both countries untouched. In addition to the US and Canadian differences with Mexico, the NAFTA will have to deal with unresolved US–Canadian agricultural disputes such as Canadian "crow's nest" subsidies.[1]

Agricultural trade among the prospective NAFTA partners has grown rather slowly. Since 1980, US–Mexican two-way agricultural trade has increased by an average of only 4 percent annually, from $3.5 billion to $5.2 billion, compared with an average annual growth rate of 8 percent for all merchandise trade. Between 1980 and 1990, US exports to Mexico (mostly field crops) first dropped to $1.1 billion in 1986, but thereafter bounced back to 1980 levels ($2.5 billion)

---

1. These are freight rate subsidies to Canadian exporters of barley, wheat, and oats. The 1984 Western Grain Transportation Act (WGTA) expanded the coverage of transportation subsidies to include other commodities such as alfalfa pellets, millfeeds, and oilseed meals. The FTA eliminated the WGTA subsidies, but only for agricultural products shipped to the United States through western Canadian ports.

Joanna M. van Rooij helped draft this chapter. Dale E. Hathaway of Hathaway International, Inc., gave valuable comments.

by 1990; Mexican exports to the United States (mostly horticultural products)[2] more than doubled from $1.1 billion to $2.6 billion (US General Accounting Office 1991d, table 3.1; US Department of Commerce, *U.S. Foreign Trade Highlights*, 1990).

Since 1980, Canadian-Mexican two-way agricultural trade has also increased by an average 4 percent annually, from $150 million to $220 million, versus 9 percent annually for all merchandise trade. Between 1980 and 1989, Canadian agricultural exports to Mexico increased from $80 million to $130 million, while Mexican agricultural exports to Canada grew from $70 million to $90 million. From 1987 to 1989, on average, Canadian agricultural exports accounted for 28 percent of total Canadian exports to Mexico. Major Canadian agricultural exports to Mexico are oilseeds (47 percent of the total), dairy products (23 percent), and grains (14 percent). From 1987 to 1989, on average, agricultural imports accounted for 8 percent of total Canadian imports from Mexico. Major Canadian agricultural imports from Mexico were vegetables (33 percent of the total), plantation crops (28 percent), and fruits and nuts (27 percent; North-South Institute 1990).

In 1990, the average US tariff on Mexican agricultural imports was 4 percent, while the average Mexican tariff on US products was 11 percent. Nontariff barriers are far more significant. The United States imposes quantitative restraints on meat and dairy products, sugar and products containing sugar, peanuts, and cotton; in addition the United States indirectly regulates trade in fruits and vegetables through marketing orders and health and sanitary requirements. Mexico imposes licensing requirements on imports of grains and oilseeds, and health and sanitary requirements on live animals and animal products (US International Trade Commission 1991a, table 4-1).

Successive Mexican presidents have pursued two national goals: self-sufficiency in staple food production and preservation of farm income levels through income assistance to peasant farmers.[3] To those ends, Mexican agricultural policy has relied heavily on price supports for basic food, oilseeds, and feed grains and on input subsidies to promote domestic production (Rosson and Angel 1991, 4). Conasupo (Compañia Nacional de Subsistencias Populares) is the national agency charged with administering the price support program and acting as the primary

---

2. The horticulture industry includes all fruits and vegetables, fresh-cut flowers, live plants and other foliage, nuts, and certain spices. Although technically a horticultural product, coffee is classified separately.

3. For example, in mid–1980 President José López Portillo established the Mexican Food System (Sistema Alimentario Mexicano) to promote rain-fed field crops (practically synonymous with peasant agriculture), and to attain self-sufficiency in the production of corn and beans by 1982. In 1982 the program was abandoned, even though the goals had not been met.

importer of grains and oilseeds. To enforce the price support system, which establishes higher domestic prices than world prices, Mexico requires import licenses for many grain and oilseed products.[4] The Secretary of Commerce and Industrial Development (Secretaría de Comercio y Fomento Industrial, or SECOFI) authorizes imports through Conasupo only after the domestic crop has been purchased.

Since the 1960s Mexico has been a net food importer, for two reasons. First, population growth outstripped production. From the 1960s through the 1970s, the average annual agricultural growth rate dropped to 2.7 percent, while the average annual population growth increased to 3.2 percent.[5] Second, Mexico's import substitution policies led to more diversified but less efficient production.

From 1980 to 1990, Mexican production of grains increased only modestly, from 17.6 million to 20.4 million metric tons, while consumption increased from 22.4 million to 27.0 million metric tons.[6] In 1990 some 5.8 million metric tons of grain were imported to fill the deficit, with the United States accounting for the bulk of the imports (table 14.1).

The Structure of US, Canadian, and Mexican Agriculture

The small family farm is rapidly becoming part of the nostalgic past in American and Canadian agriculture, but it is very much alive in Mexico. Today the US and Canadian industry is dominated by large-scale farms and giant food processing firms, while the Mexican industry is dominated by myriad small-scale farms and food processors (for example, in Mexico City alone there are at least 100,000 tortilla manufacturers; US International Trade Commission 1991a, 4-10). In general, US and Canadian farms are far more productive than their Mexican counterparts: in 1989, for example, US farm employment was about half of Mexican farm employment, but US sales were more than five times Mexican sales.[7]

---

4. For example, for the fall-winter crop of 1987–88, the guaranteed price was 1.73 times the estimated average Mexican production cost for corn, 2.0 times the average cost for wheat, and 1.8 times the average cost for sorghum. Mexican production costs are usually above US levels for field crops (Hall and Livas-Hernández 1990, table I8).

5. In contrast, in the 1950s and early 1960s, Mexican agricultural production grew at an average annual rate of 4.5 percent, while the Mexican population grew at an average annual rate of only 2.9 percent (Contreras 1987).

6. The US Department of Agriculture classifies corn, barley, oats, and sorghum as feed grains (or coarse grains). However, in Mexico corn is the primary staple of human consumption.

7. In 1990, US sales of agricultural products were $110 billion (2 percent of GDP), compared with Mexican shipments of $21 billion (9 percent of GDP).

Table 14.1 Mexico: production, consumption, and trade in grains, 1980–90 (thousands of metric tons)

	1980	1981	1982	1983	1984	1985	1986	1987	1988	1989	1990
Total production	17,600	20,330	14,730	17,300	19,011	19,603	19,731	18,590	17,221	18,450	20,355
Food grains	2,910	3,440	4,540	3,490	4,491	4,898	4,851	4,080	3,466	4,370	4,100
Wheat	2,650	3,050	4,200	3,200	4,200	4,400	4,500	3,700	3,200	4,000	3,900
Feed grains	14,690	16,890	10,190	13,810	14,520	14,705	14,880	14,510	13,755	14,080	16,255
Corn[a]	10,400	12,500	7,000	9,300	9,900	10,500	10,000	9,900	10,100	9,750	12,000
Sorghum	3,800	4,000	2,800	4,000	4,100	3,700	4,300	4,000	3,110	3,750	3,700
Total consumption	22,435	25,080	23,328	22,945	23,616	23,360	24,405	23,459	24,002	24,988	27,010
Food grains	3,870	4,279	4,483	4,510	4,775	5,076	5,445	4,740	4,643	4,632	4,815
Wheat	3,500	4,000	4,093	4,100	4,350	4,640	5,000	4,300	4,213	4,192	4,375
Feed grains	18,565	20,801	18,845	18,435	18,841	18,284	18,960	18,719	19,359	20,356	22,195
Corn[a]	12,800	13,518	12,300	11,600	11,800	11,986	13,250	13,275	13,429	14,000	15,000
Sorghum	5,200	6,758	6,100	6,300	6,425	5,702	5,110	4,828	5,300	5,625	6,500
Total imports	8,499	2,581	7,282	6,545	4,943	2,514	4,683	4,794	6,847	8,560	5,830
Food grains	1,375	955	50	672	694	115	463	752	1,345	390	700
Wheat	1,235	938	50	566	491	92	463	752	1,156	260	500
Feed grains	7,124	1,626	7,232	5,873	4,249	2,399	4,220	4,042	5,502	8,170	5,130
Corn	3,833	571	4,003	2,459	1,684	1,736	3,400	3,150	3,120	5,000	2,500
Sorghum	3,193	945	3,227	3,329	2,481	627	810	850	2,277	3,025	2,500

Total imports from US	7,582	1,979	7,267	5,470	3,793	2,127	4,114	4,283	3,512	7,239	7,436
Food grains	1,181	747	35	negl.	27	5	123	318	1,152	983	898
Wheat	1,173	717	35	negl.	27	4	122	317	963	401	372
Feed grains	6,401	1,232	7,232	5,470	3,766	2,122	3,991	3,965	2,360	6,256	6,538
Corn[a]	3,700	571	4,003	2,459	1,593	1,640	3,200	3,130	negl.	3,844	3,468
Sorghum	2,647	544	3,227	3,011	2,170	466	790	832	2,256	2,268	2,899
Total exports	10	5	10	2	5	6	3	52	231	202	n.a
Food grains	10	5	10	2	5	6	3	52	231	200	n.a
Wheat	10	5	10	2	5	6	3	52	231	100	n.a
Feed grains	negl.	negl.	negl.	negl.	negl.	negl.	negl.	negl.	negl.	2	n.a
Corn[a]	negl.	negl.	negl.	negl.	negl.	negl.	negl.	negl.	negl.	negl.	n.a
Sorghum	negl.	negl.	negl.	negl.	negl.	negl.	negl.	negl.	negl.	negl.	n.a

n.a. = not available.

negl. = negligible.

a. On a worldwide basis, the US Department of Agriculture classifies corn as a feed grain. However, in Mexico, corn is a principal food grain.

Source: US Department of Agriculture, Economic Research Service, data sheets.

The Mexican farm sector is composed of *pequeños propietarios* (private farmers), *comunidades* (village-based organizations), and *ejidos* (small collective farms, which primarily produce corn, rice, or beans). The latter two forms of organization were established by the first Agrarian Reform Act of 1915, which also gave the government authority to expropriate and redistribute agricultural land, and are protected by Article 27 of the Constitution of 1917. They benefit from various input subsidies as well as price support schemes.[8] Today, 54 percent of Mexican territory belongs to *ejidos* and other semicollective farms, and two-thirds of the arable land is held in parcels of less than five acres.[9] The small size of plots and the resulting inefficiency of Mexican agriculture reflect the continuing division of land holdings since the Mexican revolution. In fact, although one-third of Mexico's population lives in rural areas, it produces only one-tenth of the country's GDP.[10]

President Salinas has embarked on a program of dramatic reform in the Mexican farm sector.[11] As a first step, the government allowed cooperative farmers to form joint ventures with private companies. As of November 1991, the Mexican Secretary of Agriculture had approved 37 projects, signed letters of intent on 15 others, and had another 86 projects under consideration.[12] Those projects served as experiments for the second and bolder step of agriculture reform.

That step was taken in late 1991, when the Salinas government proposed a constitutional amendment that would alter the foundations of collective land

---

8. For example, the Mexican Trust for Shared Risk provides production benefits that include a 25 percent reduction in the price of improved and native seed, a 30 percent reduction in the price of fertilizers, a reduction of interest rates to 12 percent for short-term loans, and a reduction in crop insurance premiums to 3 percent (Johnston et al. 1987, 322).

9. Small private land holdings are often rented out or farmed in larger parcels. This trend would be greatly accelerated by the agrarian reforms proposed by President Salinas, discussed below.

10. *New York Times,* 29 November 1991, A4. A study by the agriculture center, INIFAP, stated that only about 40 percent of agriculture land, and 25 percent to 30 percent of corn farms, are able to produce over 2.2 tons of corn per hectare (*Financial Times,* 25 October 1991, VI).

11. This discussion draws on *Journal of Commerce,* 7 November 1991, 8A.

12. Despite the relatively small amount of investment involved in those projects, the political repercussions are considerable. After Pepsico acquired the Mexican cookie maker Gamesa, the company established a $12 million joint venture with cooperative farmers and small farmers to grow beans, wheat, and corn in the state of Nuevo León. Other examples are the provision of $10 million by Trasgo, a Mexican poultry processor working with the Japanese company C. Itoh, for *ejido* farmers to raise chickens in Durango and Coahuila; and the provision of $20 million by the Mexican milk company Leche, working with the Canadian firm Ault Foods, for *ejidos* involved in the production of milk and fruit in Veracruz and Oaxaca.

tenure. The Mexican constitution enshrines the Agrarian Reform Act of 1915 and prohibits *ejido* lands from being rented or sold. The proposed amendment would end these prohibitions and allow farmers on the *ejidos* to rent out their land, to become landowners by purchasing their land, and to form joint ventures with private firms (*Financial Times*, 8 November 1991, 9). In addition, land would no longer be guaranteed to every Mexican, the size of farms would no longer be restricted to 100 irrigated acres, and 100 percent foreign ownership would be permitted. If the reforms are carried out, Mexican agriculture will be transformed within a generation; as a by-product, US investment in Mexican agriculture and food processing could redouble several times during the next decade.

To be sure, foreign direct investment is already permitted in Mexican agriculture, but prior approval by the Mexican Investment Commission is required for a foreign party to hold a majority interest in a Mexican farm or food processing firm. In 1988, cumulative US investment in the Mexican agricultural sector was approximately $20 million—very small compared with total US investment in Mexico of $19.1 billion in 1990.[13] US investment in the Mexican horticulture processing industry was considerably larger ($466 million in 1989); of the 73 food processing plants in Mexico, 12 are owned by or affiliated with US firms. Still, these numbers allow great scope for growth.

US Exports to Mexico

Mexico has ranked among the top eight markets for US agricultural goods since 1980 and took 6 percent of US agricultural exports in 1990. (Japan with 20 percent and the European Community with 17 percent remain the top US export markets.) In 1990 US agricultural exports totaled $40 billion, of which $2.5 billion went to Mexico. For comparison, Canada bought $4.7 billion worth of US agricultural products (US Department of Commerce, *U.S. Foreign Trade Highlights*, 1990, table 18).

The principal US agricultural exports to Mexico are feed grains, oilseeds, and meat and dairy products. In 1990, US exports of field crops to Mexico totaled $1.3 billion, representing 50 percent of total US agricultural exports to Mexico. Major field crop exports were grains and feeds ($1.0 billion) and oilseeds and oil products ($0.3 billion; table 14.2). In 1990, US exports of live animals and animal products were $0.8 billion, accounting for 26 percent of US agricultural exports to Mexico. About 42 percent of US agricultural exports to Mexico benefit

---

13. Foreign direct investment statistics for agriculture cover only primary agricultural activities, and therefore exclude indirectly related activities such as food processing.

Table 14.2 United States: agricultural trade with Mexico, 1980 and 1990 (millions of dollars)

	1980		1990	
	US exports	US imports	US exports	US imports
Animals and animal products	277	99	662	466
Animals, live	18	89	82	420
Meats and meat products	39	1	227	n.a.
Poultry and poultry products	23	0	73	n.a.
Dairy products	48	1	60	15
Fats, oils, and greases	65	0	87	1
Other	84	8	133	30
Grains and feeds	1,222	10	960	28
Feed grains and products	1,042	5	776	17
Corn	678	0	401	0
Grain sorghums	319	0	328	n.a.
Other feed grains and products	45	5	47	17
Other	180	5	184	11
Fruits, fruit juices, and nuts	20	125	64	388
Fresh and frozen fruits	9	102	31	216
Prepared or preserved fruits	3	16	14	28
Fruit juices	1	7	2	101
Nuts	7	0	17	43
Vegetables	239	347	190	1,074
Fresh and frozen vegetables	7	303	22	899
Prepared and preserved vegetables	226	44	111	103

Table 14.2 United States: agricultural trade with Mexico, 1980 and 1990 (continued)

	1980		1990	
	US exports	US imports	US exports	US imports
Dried beans	220	0	102	9
Other vegetables	6	0	57	72
Oilseeds and products	502	27	325	44
Soybeans	259	n.a.	201	n.a.
Other oilseeds and products	243	n.a.	124	n.a.
Sugar and coffee	n.a.	358	163	358
Sugar and related products	n.a.	21	117	21
Coffee	n.a.	311	2	338
Other agricultural products	208	93	189	253
Total agricultural products	2,468	1,059	2,553	2,611

n.a. = not available.

Source: US Department of Agriculture.

from the General Sales Manager (GSM) export credit guarantee program, a subsidy scheme managed by the US Department of Agriculture.[14]

Mexican Exports to the United States

In 1990 Mexican agricultural exports to the United States were $2.6 billion, accounting for about 96 percent of total Mexican agricultural exports, and 9

---

14. Under the GSM program, loans are guaranteed for periods of 6 months to 10 years. The total annual amount of GSM credit guarantees for agricultural exports to Mexico spiraled from $38 million in 1982 to $1.1 billion in 1989. Private loans would not have been available in such amounts because of Mexico's low credit rating. Hence, the GSM program can be viewed as the subsidized absorption of risk. See US General Accounting Office (1991d, 24–25).

percent of total Mexican exports to the United States. Approximately $200 million in Mexican agricultural exports benefited from zero tariff rates under the US Generalized System of Preferences; these products included tequila ($35 million), cucumbers ($22 million), and pecans ($13 million). The largest categories of Mexican agricultural exports to the United States are horticultural products, coffee, and live animals (table 14.2).

In 1990 Mexican horticultural exports to the United States were $1.5 billion, accounting for 56 percent of Mexican agricultural exports. Principal commodities in this group are fresh and frozen vegetables (61 percent) and fresh and frozen fruits (15 percent). Tomatoes, peppers, and cucumbers are important vegetable items; among fruit exports, melons account for about half the total.

In addition, Mexican coffee exports to the United States in 1990 were $0.3 billion, some 13 percent of Mexican agricultural exports to the United States. In 1990 Mexico was the fourth-largest coffee producer in the world, and the United States was the largest consumer. Total Mexican production was 4 million bags (one bag is approximately 150 pounds). Total US consumption was 21 million bags, of which 3.4 million were imported from Mexico. The United States and Mexico are both members of the International Coffee Organization (ICO), a producer-consumer group that tries to establish minimum prices and maximum export quotas for coffee. A NAFTA will call into question the continued participation of both countries in the ICO.

Mexican exports of meat and dairy products to the United States (primarily cattle) were $0.4 billion in 1990, accounting for 16 percent of Mexican agricultural exports to the United States. Mexico previously imposed a 5 percent ad valorem duty on exports of feeder cattle to ensure adequate domestic supply, but this tax was lowered to 1.67 percent in September 1991. Mexican cattle exports to the United States are partly determined by weather conditions in Mexico's northern region: extreme drought forces Mexican ranchers to slaughter cattle for export to the United States.

Mexican Barriers to Trade

Since its accession to the GATT in 1986, Mexico has substantially reduced its tariff and nontariff barriers to trade. Nonetheless, numerous tariffs, licensing requirements, and sanitary requirements continue to act as barriers to US agricultural exports.

Mexico continues to impose high duties on processed foods and specialty crops such as temperate fruits, nuts, and alcoholic beverages at the maximum rate of 20 percent. US vegetable exports to Mexico routinely face import tariffs that average 16 percent (*Journal of Commerce*, 2 October 1991, 5A). Mexican tariffs on packaged beef are about 20 percent.[15] Bulk commodities such as wheat, corn, sorghum, and soybean oil are exempt from duties, but these zero tariffs are a misleading indicator of the extent of Mexican protection. Mexico does impose a duty on rice imports (*Journal of Commerce*, 3 September 1991, 3A).

Mexico maintains an agricultural price support program for basic foods, oil-seeds, and feed grains. Since it usually maintains domestic prices above world prices, Mexico requires import licenses for many grain and oilseed products; in fact, trade in these products is essentially monopolized by Conasupo.

The US Department of Agriculture has estimated that, from 1982 to 1987, the panoply of Mexican agricultural programs conveyed on average a 56 percent subsidy on domestic grain and oilseed crops, in producer subsidy-equivalent (PSE) terms. The most highly subsidized crops are those in which the United States is highly competitive: corn (with a PSE of 66 percent), sorghum (56 percent), soybeans (50 percent), and wheat (20 percent). The effect of the various measures is to tax Mexican agricultural consumers by a weighted average of about 35 percent by comparison with world prices.[16]

Licensing requirements are the major Mexican border impediment to imports. In 1983 all Mexican agricultural imports were covered by prior licensing require-ments; in 1985, 317 agricultural commodities still required prior import licenses. Although unilateral reform reduced that number to 57 by 1990, over 50 percent of US agricultural exports to Mexico were still subject to import controls. Major US agricultural exports affected by the requirements are wheat (20 percent of US agricultural exports to Mexico), corn (16 percent), barley (11 percent), poultry products (3 percent), and dairy products (2 percent). The basic Mexican rationale for these protective measures is that, without them, vast numbers of peasants would leave the rural areas, descend on the Mexican cities, stream across the border, and cause social unrest both in Mexico and in the United States.[17]

Mexico maintains strict phytosanitary standards, which at times have restrained imports of US agricultural products. For example, during the Mexican

---

15. The Mexican tariff on live animals for slaughter is lower, at 10 percent. Moreover, imports by the parastatal Industrial de Abasto are not subject to import duties (see *Journal of Commerce*, 4 October 1991, 1A).

16. US International Trade Commission (1991a, 4-12). The 35 percent figure is expressed in terms of the consumer subsidy-equivalent.

17. Santiago Levy and Sweder van Wijnbergen (1991a) estimated that, without liberaliza-tion of corn, the cumulative rural-to-urban migration over a period of 10 years would equal 1.2 million workers, whereas a scenario of complete liberalization would entail a migration of 1.8 million workers. Much of the additional migration would occur during the first year of liberalization. If liberalization is instead stretched over five years, the model forecasts slower migration in the first year, although total migration after 10 years would be the same.

domestic soybean harvest, the authorities temporarily closed the border to soybean meal imports, allegedly to inspect for aflatoxin, mycotoxins, and pesticide residues (US General Accounting Office 1990, 16). Lengthy processing procedures for various certificates likewise inhibit agricultural exports to Mexico.

Finally, Mexico has severe "natural" trade barriers. In particular, the volume of agricultural trade has outgrown the capacity of Mexico's transportation network. The rail system is congested, there are few storage facilities, roads are in disrepair, and port facilities are inadequate. (For example, the Union Pacific Railroad found that the average turnaround time for railcars going from Mexico to the United States is 20 days, while that for railcars going from the United States to Mexico is 40 days.)

Bottlenecks and bureaucracy cause excessive delays at border crossing points. Between 1987 and 1990, commercial northbound truck traffic increased by 42 percent and railcar traffic by 29 percent. Southbound traffic probably rose by similar percentages. In response to the resulting extreme congestion at the border, some 14 border infrastructure projects are under development or expansion, and another 8 to 10 have been proposed (*Journal of Commerce*, 8 July 1991, 1A). For 1990 the US Congress allocated $357 million for border infrastructure development. During the early to mid–1990s an estimated $1 billion will be invested by public and private sources in US highway and inspection facility infrastructures, including new bridges at many of the 51 existing crossings. On the Mexican side, for example, the McAllen-Hidalgo-Reynosa bridge is being financed by toll-backed US municipal bonds ($16 million) and Mexican private banks and investors ($20 million; *Journal of Commerce*, 8 July 1991, 1A). With this program under way, border bottlenecks will be eliminated long before Mexico's internal transportation system reaches an adequate level of service.

US Barriers to Trade

Mexican agricultural exports to the United States are limited both by US tariffs and by nontariff barriers such as quantitative restrictions, marketing orders, and health and sanitary requirements.[18] Transport bottlenecks limit Mexican agricultural exports as well as imports.

On average, US tariffs are relatively low (4 percent) and cover only about 25 percent of US agricultural imports from Mexico. Most Mexican exports of horticultural products are subject to a cents-per-kilogram charge under the Harmonized Tariff Schedules; in 1988 these specific duties corresponded to ad

---

18. Some nontariff barriers are less orthodox: in February 1990, for example, the US Court of International Trade ruled that Mexican broccoli exporters should label their products with the country of origin (*Journal of Commerce*, 20 June 1991, 1A).

valorem equivalents ranging from 0.5 percent to 37.6 percent of product value. For example, US tariffs on cucumbers, which range from 3.3 cents to 4.9 cents per kilogram, translate into an ad valorem equivalent of 9.4 percent to 37.6 percent (US General Accounting Office 1990, table I.1).

The highest US tariffs are imposed on a seasonal basis to coincide with the marketing period of domestic US fruits and vegetables. For example, the US tariff on tomatoes is 4.6 cents per kilogram from 1 March through 14 July and from 1 September through 4 November; for the remainder of the year the tariff drops to 3.3 cents per kilogram (US General Accounting Office 1990, table I.1).

The United States maintains marketing orders for various agricultural products under the authority of section 80 of the Agricultural Marketing Agreement Act of 1937. Marketing orders are agreements among domestic producers of a given commodity to provide collective solutions for marketing and distribution problems. The orders, which apply to both domestic and imported products, regulate the size, grade, maturity, and quality of products sold in the US market. Major Mexican exports covered by marketing orders are tomatoes ($371 million) and onions ($67 million). Mexican exporters are generally able to meet the standards set under the marketing orders, but they may face problems when marketing orders are changed or new commodities are added.[19] However, the Food Agriculture Conservation and Trade Act of 1990 provides some safeguard against abuse by requiring the US Trade Representative to examine within 60 days whether changes in marketing orders would be inconsistent with US obligations under the GATT.[20]

The United States also uses quotas to limit the import of certain agricultural commodities, most importantly meat and sugar. The Meat Import Act of 1979, buttressed by voluntary restraint agreements under the US Agricultural Act of 1956, frequently limits Mexican exports of fresh, chilled, or frozen meat to the United States.[21] Although the act has triggered the imposition of US import quotas only once (in 1976), Mexico has agreed to voluntary export restraints in 1982, 1984, 1987, and 1988. In the future, the Meat Import Act could discourage Mexican development of feedlot operations.

---

19. Commodities subject to marketing orders include avocados, dates, filberts, grapefruit, Irish potatoes, limes, olives, onions, oranges, prunes, raisins, table grapes, tomatoes, and walnuts. Commodities not subject to a marketing order but covered by the 1937 act include cucumbers, eggplants, green peppers, and mangoes. In addition, legislation is pending to add kiwi fruit, nectarines, papayas, peaches, pears, and plums.

20. In 1991 the Florida grapefruit growers tried to change the marketing order for grapefruits. The USTR did not approve the proposal, and the growers were unable to implement the proposed changes.

21. Australia (the source of 50 percent of US meat imports) and New Zealand (the source of 30 percent) are the main targets of US meat quotas and voluntary export restraints.

Sugar imports are limited by the Agriculture and Food Act of 1981, which established country-by-country quotas for sugar exports to the United States. Mexico is entitled to the minimum quota allocation, namely, 0.3 percent of the total quota. For the quota year starting in October 1990, Mexican sugar exports were restricted to a mere 8,030 metric tons. By April 1991 Mexico had filled its sugar export quota. Mexico exports sugar to the United States mainly to preserve its existing quota rights. Mexican sugar exports to the United States for refining and subsequent reimport by Mexico are small and are not subject to the sugar quota. In 1990 total Mexican sugar exports to the United States were 250,000 metric tons. US sugar exports to Mexico were 160,000 metric tons, nearly all of which were reexports.

US sanitary requirements, phytosanitary standards, animal health standards, and consumer safety standards also block some Mexican agricultural exports. In 1990, 1,830 shipments of Mexican food worth $24.5 million were detained for food safety reasons at the US border (*Journal of Commerce*, 27 September 1991, 1A and 12A). Most Mexican horticulture exports, such as oranges, grapefruit, and tangerines, undergo a treatment to kill the Mediterranean and Mexican fruit flies, but the treatment also damages the exterior of the products, thus reducing their market value. Fruit exports from Sonora have been exempt since the US Animal and Plant Health Inspection Service (APHIS) declared Sonora free of fruit flies in 1988.

Since 1954 the United States has prohibited the import of Mexican avocados, supposedly because of seed weevil infestation.[22] Once the seed weevil problem has been resolved, Mexico could become the premier world exporter of avocados. Mexico produces about 900 million pounds of avocados annually (roughly 50 percent of world production) and could easily satisfy worldwide demand, in the process wiping out traditional avocado growers not only in California but also in Israel and South Africa (*Wall Street Journal*, 5 February 1991, A23).

From 1982 to January 1989, Mexican exports of meat and meat products to the United States were prohibited because of animal health and sanitary standards. These actions were taken primarily to guard against bovine tuberculosis, brucellosis, and fever tick. By the end of 1990, six Mexican plants were authorized by the US Department of Agriculture to export packaged beef to the United States. The United States still prohibits Mexican swine exports as a precaution against hog cholera, Mexican poultry exports because of the "exotic New-Castle" disease, and Mexican sheep and goat exports because of scrapies (US General Accounting Office 1990, 16).

---

22. The United States, with the exception of California, allows transshipment of avocados to other destinations. Europe has no restrictions on Mexican avocado imports.

The United States also restricts some Mexican agricultural exports deemed unsafe for human health and safety.[23] These cases often involve products containing residues of certain chemicals, banned pesticides such as DDT, or higher than acceptable standards of pesticide. For example, in 1985 the US Environmental Protection Agency banned the use of ethylene dibromide because of its adverse effect on US dockworkers. The result was to effectively eliminate Mexican mango exports to the United States. Later the United States approved Mexican mango exports subjected to an alternative treatment that, if not done carefully, adversely affects ripening.

The Spanish–EC Example

The example of Spanish accession to the European Community illustrates the possible impact of a NAFTA on Mexican agricultural trade with its northern neighbors. In 1985 Spain exported $40 million in horticultural products to the Community and imported $1,160 million. In 1990 Spain exported $490 million in horticultural products and imported $3,190 million. Two-way Spanish–EC horticulture trade thus tripled in five years, from $1,200 million to $3,680 million, and became more balanced in the process.[24]

Trade expansion in field crops was equally impressive. In 1985 Spain exported $40 million in field crops to the Community and imported under $10 million. Spanish field crop exports increased to $240 million in 1990, while imports surged to $210 million. In other words, two-way field crop trade grew from about $40 million to about $450 million, an approximately 11-fold expansion. The Spanish experience suggests that agriculture trade under a NAFTA will significantly expand and that the expansion will not be one-sided.[25]

---

23. See chapter 7 for a discussion of environmental issues related to liberalization of the agricultural sector under the NAFTA.

24. The data are derived from European Community, *European Statistics*, various issues. The growth of EC–Spanish trade when expressed in dollars is somewhat overstated because the ecu appreciated from $0.76 to $1.27 over the period.

25. Using a computable general equilibrium model, Antonio Yúnez-Naude (1991) has estimated the effects of a NAFTA on agricultural trade. According to his model, elimination of agricultural tariffs through a NAFTA would produce a 38 percent increase in Mexican fruit and vegetable exports to Canada and the United States, while Mexican imports of field crops would grow by about 25 percent. The model also estimated a 18 percent increase in Mexican imports of livestock. These estimates are substantially lower than the Spanish–EC experience would suggest.

Recommendations

The Canada–US FTA achieved little in agriculture, largely because the agricultural sectors of the two countries were basically similar. The underlying circumstances are different with Mexico. Trade within the North American region has a more complementary character, with Mexico exporting primarily fruits and vegetables and the United States and Canada exporting mostly grains, oilseeds, and livestock.

There was another reason why agriculture was barely addressed in the FTA. Both Canada and the United States thought that more would be gained, in terms of worldwide agricultural reform, by addressing the hard issues in the Uruguay Round. The United States and Canada could not generate domestic support for agricultural reform as long as potential free riders, particularly the European Community, continued to subsidize their exports.

If the Uruguay Round breaks down, or if it makes little progress in agriculture, the question would then arise whether the NAFTA should seek to build a distortion-free system of agriculture solely for North America. Our view is that the United States, Canada, and Mexico all rely too much on world markets to make dramatic reform of their agricultural subsidy and support systems solely for the North American market a viable alternative. We think that existing systems of agricultural protection will endure for years unless they can be politically neutralized by the lure of free world markets. If progress on a world scale proves unattainable, we think that agriculture reform within the NAFTA will at best be a slow, crop-by-crop and year-by-year proposition, and that a sweeping embrace of market-oriented agriculture cannot be expected in the NAFTA accord alone.

Although the potential economic gains of North American agricultural liberalization are substantial, political opposition to reform is entrenched, and the prospective losers are sure to put up a stiff fight. After the 1993 congressional redistricting, Florida, Texas, and California—the largest horticultural states—will gain 14 seats in the House of Representatives while most Midwestern states—growers of field crops—will lose members. Similarly, the Institutional Revolutionary Party (Partido Revolucionario Institucional, or PRI) in Mexico depends heavily on the agricultural vote of the *ejidos* and *communidades,* the principal producers of Mexican field crops.

These cautions are not voiced as an argument for abandoning all hope for agricultural reform within the NAFTA. Rather, they are made to underscore the point that liberalized agricultural trade is likely to result in a significant migration of Mexican peasants to urban areas and a downsizing of US and Canadian fruit and vegetable production. To make the adjustment burden politically acceptable, the NAFTA should link Mexican agricultural reforms in field crops to US and

Canadian reforms in horticulture, and it should ensure that agricultural liberalization lags industrial liberalization by about five years.[26]

As a further safeguard, Canadian, Mexican, and US farmers would have recourse to the normal unfair-trade and escape clause measures sanctioned by GATT Articles VI and XIX, respectively, as implemented by national bodies. Under the Canada–US FTA, producers can, moreover, appeal to a tariff snapback provision when agricultural products are sold below prevailing market prices. In three out of nine cases, Canadian producers of perishable fruits and vegetable have successfully invoked the snapback provision to curb US imports into the Canadian market.[27]

We think that liberalization of agricultural trade in North America, as in Europe, will greatly boost two-way flows. But no analyst can guarantee that large areas within each country's agricultural sector would not be decimated under a regime of free trade. Because of the unpredictable consequences of eliminating barriers, we propose an additional avenue for relief. Under our proposal, when a trading partner experiences a substantial adverse surge in its North American trade balance for a group of agricultural products over the base-period level, the surge alone would be grounds for safeguard relief. For this purpose, horticultural products would form one agricultural group, and field crops a second. A "substantial adverse surge" might be defined as a growth in the sectoral trade deficit (or a decline in the sectoral trade surplus) by more than 20 percent per year by comparison with its base-period level. The base-period level, in turn, might be initially defined as the 1988–91 three-year average and subsequently updated with a three-year lag.

Sectoral surge relief under our proposal could only be invoked by the authorities of the affected country. If this special safeguard were invoked by Mexico, relief would most likely be sought in field crops; the United States and Canada, on the other hand, would most likely seek relief for their horticultural producers. The first line of relief would entail accelerated liberalization by the advantaged country of its remaining sectoral barriers; only after free imports are permitted by the advantaged country could the disadvantaged country propose to limit

---

26. Levy and Wijnbergen (1991b) present a strong case for delayed implementation of agricultural reform.

27. In order to invoke snapback relief, the provision requires a monitoring of import prices and two working days' notice to the offending country. Since the prior tariffs were often less than the corresponding price drop, Canada has since proposed that a tariff surcharge be allowed in addition to the tariff snapback. Following a surge of imports of West Coast asparagus into the Canadian market, for instance, Canada applied the snapback provision by imposing a 3 percent tariff, but since prices had decreased from 85 cents to 30 cents (a price fall of 65 percent), the snapback provided rather little relief (*Journal of Commerce*, 7 October 1991, 5A).

sectoral imports.[28] The special safeguard provision would expire once North America agricultural trade has been liberalized.

Bearing in mind this careful staging of trade reforms, and the special safeguards, the five principal product groups that could be affected by the NAFTA (with or without a successful Uruguay Round) are horticulture, field crops, livestock, coffee, and sugar. These are analyzed in detail below.

Horticulture

The US horticultural industry consists of produce farmers, with annual production of $20 billion in crops, and food processors, with annual production of $40 billion worth of canned and frozen goods. Most fresh fruit and vegetables are grown and processed in the warm-weather states of California, Florida, and Texas. Other states produce temperate-climate horticultural crops such as apples, pears, berries, other noncitrus fruits, potatoes, and greenhouse products. The horticultural industry in Mexico is concentrated in the northwestern states of Sonora and Sinaloa and specializes in high-value crops such as citrus and tropical fruits, tomatoes, asparagus, broccoli, and cauliflower.

Horticultural exports account for 56 percent of total Mexican agricultural exports to the United States. The extent to which Mexican horticulture competes with US domestic production largely depends on the product range and harvesting times. Table 14.3 summarizes harvesting times and marketing periods for the principal Mexican fresh horticultural exports to the United States. The winter vegetable season is divided into three cycles: fall (November-December), winter (January-March), and spring (April-June). California and Texas primarily produce in the fall and early spring seasons; only Florida and Sinaloa produce over the entire winter season (Mares 1987, 178–79).

In other words, on the US side of the border, weather conditions are best in Florida, and even there conditions are less favorable than in Culiacán, the chief producing region in Sinaloa (on the Gulf of California). Florida suffers occasional freezes while Culiacán has never recorded a freeze.

Production costs are the other major factor in competition between the US horticultural states and Sinaloa. Low wages are a cost advantage to Mexican producers, while sophisticated production and marketing techniques are a cost advantage to US producers. But modern horticulture technology will increasingly find its way to Mexico, especially as US growers and food processors, encouraged by relaxation of Mexican investment restrictions, expand their operations south

---

28. We propose parallel special safeguards for other sensitive sectors, namely, automobiles (chapter 11), steel (chapter 12), and textiles and apparel (chapter 13).

Table 14.3 Mexico and United States: fresh horticulture harvesting and marketing seasons

Product	Mexican exports to US, 1989 (millions of dollars)	Mexican harvesting season	Competing US harvest	
			State	Season[a]
Tomatoes	222	November-May	Florida	November-May
Cucumbers	85	December-March	Florida	December and March
Bell peppers	62	November-April	Florida	November-April
			Texas	November
Onions	58	November-June	California	May-June
			Texas	April-May
			New York	January-March
			Idaho	September-February
Cantaloupes	53	November-June	California	June-July
			Texas	May-July
Mangoes and guavas	37	April-August	Florida	May-September
Squash	36	November-June	Florida	November-May
Grapes	32	April-June	California	June
Watermelons	21	January-May	Florida	May
Melons	19			
Asparagus	14	January-March	California	March
Strawberries	14	March-May	California	April-May
Total listed items	652			
Total fresh horticulture	791			

a. Indicates only the overlapping season for US states, not the total harvesting season for states.

Source: US General Accounting Office, *U.S.-Mexico Trade: Extent to Which Mexican Horticulture Exports Complement U.S. Production,* March 1991, table 1.1 and figures 1.1 to 1.13.

of the border. The NAFTA thus foreshadows an extremely competitive Mexican horticulture industry, one that will make major inroads in the US market.[29] For example, the Florida tomato industry estimates that its production costs are 25 percent higher than those of its Mexican competitors, as a result of US health, safety, and labor regulations. The Florida industry projects a $125 million loss in domestic sales, amounting to 20 percent of annual production, if the NAFTA resembles the Canada–US FTA (*Journal of Commerce*, 2 October 1991, 5A).

There are two main barriers to this outcome: phytosanitary standards and tariffs. The United States and Mexico are already on their way toward adopting streamlined health and safety inspection standards. According to the US Animal and Plant Health Inspection Service, Mexican horticultural exports are generally free of significant plant health problems (US General Accounting Office 1990, 15). The US–Mexican working group, composed of representatives of the agricultural departments of the two countries, has made substantial progress on the remaining problems. In 1990 the United States declared Mexican citrus products free of citrus canker and agreed to evaluate whether certain areas of Mexico are free of seed weevil (avocados) and fruit fly infestation. In 1991 Mexico was declared free of screwworm infestation. The concept of pest-free zones, now applied to fruit crops from Sonora, could be extended to other Mexican states. The Canada–US FTA details a program for consultation on phytosanitary regulations in an annex to Article 708. The program could be extended to include Mexico.

With fast progress on phytosanitary issues, the United States and Mexico can move toward a gradual phaseout of tariffs and marketing order restrictions. Given US political sensitivities, our suggestion is to eliminate horticultural tariffs over a period of 15 years, tying the phaseout to Mexican liberalization of corn imports (discussed below).

Field Crops

The US field crop sector is composed of two farm product groups (grain and oilseeds) and three processing industries (fats and oils, milled grain, and animal

---

29. Luis Téllez Kuenkler, Undersecretary in the Mexican Ministry of Agriculture and Water Resources, points out the obstacles to a rapid increase in Mexican production: small private land holdings and inefficient transportation, storage, and distribution systems. Téllez contends that an "overnight flood of Mexican oranges and tomatoes feared by US producers, is unfeasible and unjustified." He predicts that Mexican horticultural production will not increase by more than 40 percent within 5 years after a NAFTA (*Journal of Commerce*, 17 September 1991, 7A). We think the Téllez projections (partly offered to allay US producers) are much too conservative, unless the United States maintains its protective barriers. Mexico currently devotes only about 1 million of its 23 million hectares of arable land to fruit and vegetable production. The land devoted to horticulture could thus increase dramatically without encroaching on traditional field crops.

feed). In 1990 US grain production totaled 312 million metric tons. In contrast, Mexican grain production was only 22 million metric tons because of the poor quality and ineffective cultivation of Mexico's arable farmland.

Liberalization of US–Mexico field crop trade is under way. The parastatal Conasupo plays an important role in the Mexican field crop sector as the primary importer and distributor of basic foodstuffs such as grains, oilseeds, and certain fats and oils. Recently, in the spirit of privatization, Conasupo divested some of its marketing, milling, and oilseed processing plants to private Mexican firms and surrendered its role as exclusive importer of sorghum and soybeans (US International Trade Commission 1991a, 4-12).

Wheat may be the place to start in the NAFTA. In May 1991 Canada removed its import licensing requirements on wheat from the United States as part of the Canada–US FTA. Canadian and US subsidies on wheat average about 31 percent and 27 percent of production value, respectively; Mexican subsidies average about 20 percent of production value. Reforms in the Uruguay Round should reduce the value of domestic subsidies and cause subsidy rates among the three NAFTA countries to converge.[30] Under those conditions, the NAFTA negotiators could then aim to remove all other tariff and nontariff barriers to wheat trade over five years.

The major remaining impediments to free trilateral grain trade revolve around Mexican nontariff import restrictions on corn, the basic staple in the Mexican diet and the mainstay of Mexican agriculture.[31] Because of the attendant social difficulties, Mexico should be allowed to stretch out its liberalization program over a period of 15 years, with the pace tied both to the US and Canadian elimination of trade barriers on Mexican horticultural exports, and to the end of direct and indirect subsidies to US corn growers.[32]

---

30. US imports of Canadian durum wheat increased from zero in 1985 to a projected 12 million to 13 million bushels in 1991. Rep. Byron L. Dorgan (D-ND) contends that Canadian rail transportation subsidies are responsible for the jump. This episode suggests that wheat subsidy issues will have to be ironed out in the GATT or the NAFTA as a precursor to free trade (*Inside U.S. Trade*, 26 July 1991, 1).

31. Corn is grown by 2.3 million Mexican farmers who currently receive about $200 per metric ton—about double the world price (*Wall Street Journal*, 27 December 1991, A5). On average, Mexico produces one ton of corn per hectare, compared with seven to eight tons per hectare in the United States (*Journal of Commerce*, 3 September 1991, 3A).

32. If progress in the GATT does not compel the United States to phase out its corn subsidies, Mexico could impose a negotiated countervailing duty on corn imports equal to the PSE of remaining US subsidies. According to Mexican Commerce Minister Jaime Serra Puche, "if the subsidy systems of the United States and Canada remain in place, this must necessarily be associated with a similar protection scheme for Mexican producers" (*Journal of Commerce*, 3 September 1991, 3A).

Livestock

As the Mexican standard of living rises, Mexican demand for meat products will increase dramatically, leading to substantial US exports.[33] But Mexican tariffs will need to be slashed from their current level of 20 percent on packaged beef and 10 percent on animals to zero in five years. Moreover, the Mexican government will need to update its procedure for issuing health and safety documents so that they no longer act as a nontariff barrier (*Journal of Commerce,* 4 October 1991, 1A).

The two main US nontariff barriers affecting livestock and meat trade are health and safety inspection and US quotas under the Meat Import Act of 1979. As part of the Canada–US FTA, border inspection arrangements for livestock and meat trade were streamlined at the 17 inspection stations. Before the FTA, the US Department of Agriculture stopped every truck crossing the border. In February 1991 Canada and the United States informally agreed to allow meat already inspected at home to move across the border without reinspection. However, spot checks are permitted, and once a lot has been rejected the next 15 loads from the plant where it originated must be checked.[34] In turn, Agriculture Canada proposed in June 1991 to subject US meat imports to reinspection because the United States conducts more spot checks than Canada (*Journal of Commerce,* 24 June 1991, 4A). As a practical result, a good deal of US–Canada meat trade is once again being conducted in pre–FTA fashion, but over time the more efficient inspection systems already designed will come into full force.

Similar snags over health and safety standards arise in US–Mexico trade. However, steps have already been taken to facilitate trade. For example, by the end of 1990 the United States had approved six Mexican packing plants for export to the United States, and Mexican exports of live cattle are now permitted after inspection in Mexico by the USDA Veterinary Service. Mexico already exports about 1 million feeder cattle to the United States annually (*Journal of Commerce,* 4 October 1991, 1A). The NAFTA should encourage this trade with additional facilities for inland and border inspection (*New York Times,* 31 May 1991, A31).

Mexico should remove its import licensing requirements for poultry products in exchange for US approval of Mexican poultry exports from disease-free zones. Some progress has already been made in this direction: in 1990 the United States allowed limited imports of Mexican lambs, because lambs under a certain age do not carry or transmit scrapies.

---

33. Mexican beef consumption is about 26 pounds per person, compared with 70 pounds per person in the United States (*Journal of Commerce,* 4 October 1991, 1A).

34. This system apparently results in about 1 out of every 15 trucks being inspected. Instances of unsanitary meat imports from Canada have been widely publicized (*New York Times,* 31 May 1991, A31).

Mexican beef imports are currently subject to the 1979 US Meat Import Act. The quota has never in fact inhibited beef trade, mainly because it has been Mexican policy to limit beef exports through an export tax. Assuming that the same rules are applied to Mexican trade that have already been worked out in the Canada–US FTA, Mexico would be exempt from US Meat Import Act quotas, and Mexico would abandon its tax on beef exports (at least for North American shipments).

Coffee

Commodity cartels are historically antithetical to US economic doctrine, raising the question of whether the United States and Mexico would abandon the ICO in the context of a NAFTA accord. In our view, the United States, the world's largest consumer of coffee, and Mexico, the world's fourth-largest producer, should withdraw their participation. In addition, Mexico should eliminate its domestic price support program for coffee and concurrently allow coffee imports.

Recent events point to such an outcome. In the mid–1980s, the United States supported an international coffee accord, strictly as a political gesture to stabilize the Latin American economies. With the continued move toward market systems throughout Latin America and a greater degree of Latin political stability, there is less reason to play ICO politics. In 1989 the ICO could not agree on country quotas and minimum prices.[35] The quota system broke down, and Mexican coffee exports to the United States almost doubled in volume (from 106,000 metric tons in 1988 to 201,000 metric tons in 1989), although lower prices resulted in only a small increase in export revenues, from $300 million to $340 million (US Department of Agriculture, *Foreign Agricultural Trade of the United States*, January-February 1990, 1991). Mexico, Brazil, and Colombia now have approximately equal shares of the US market (about $300 million to $400 million each).

In late 1991, the ICO Council extended the accord for another year and established a working group to design a new coffee agreement by October 1993 (*Journal of Commerce*, 3 October 1991, 9A). However, without Brazilian and US

---

35. A sketch of the negotiating history is of interest. Colombia, which earns about 30 percent of its foreign exchange from coffee, urged the United States to support the revival of the ICO on the grounds that higher coffee prices would help fight the war against drugs. The United States agreed to negotiate if the quota scheme was changed to allow greater Central America participation. Brazil refused to take part in the agreement if its quota was lowered to 28 percent, claiming that, under free trade conditions, its share of the market would be above 30 percent. Hence the breakdown.

commitment to a new agreement, the prospects for its renewal are dim.[36] In addition, if Mexico is granted unrestricted access to the US market under the NAFTA, the value of an agreement to other coffee-exporting countries would be reduced, and the ICO might enter the annals of economic history. In late 1991, however, Colombia and Brazil were discussing the formation of a "Latin America coffee axis" with the intention of boosting prices. Their aim was to work out a common plan involving their own 40 percent of world production plus the Central American crop (*Financial Times*, 9 August 1991, 26).

Sugar

Although the Mexican sugar industry ranks among the world's largest, Mexico is a net sugar importer. Mexico has one of the highest per capita sugar consumption rates in the world, about 85 pounds per year, largely as a result of high levels of soft drink consumption. In 1990, Mexican production of sugar was 3.1 million metric tons, imports were about 1.1 million tons, and consumption was 4.0 million metric tons.[37] By comparison, in 1990 US production of sugar was about 5.7 million metric tons, imports were 1.9 million metric tons, and consumption was about 8.0 million metric tons.

The Mexican sugar industry was long dominated by the parastatal Azucar S.A., which owned and managed 75 percent of Mexican sugar mills and was the sole distributor and importer of sugar. As part of its broader privatization effort, the Mexican government sold all but three of its sugar mills and eliminated Azucar's marketing monopoly.

Mexico still controls wholesale and retail sugar prices, however. In November 1990 the government set the price for cane delivered to the mill at a figure that works out to 11.2 cents per pound of contained sugar. In December 1990 the Mexican government set the wholesale price at 18.7 cents per pound for raw sugar delivered from the mills (thereby allowing a processing margin of about 7.5 cents per pound).[38] By comparison, the world raw sugar price is about 10

---

36. After the price collapse of 1991, only Brazil still holds substantial stocks of coffee (17 million bags of 60 kilograms each). Colombia has already sold a substantial amount of its stocks to compensate for lower prices (*Journal of Commerce*, 6 August 1991, 6A; 3 October 1991, 9A).

37. *Financial Times*, 5 July 1991, 26. Inventory changes account for the residual between production plus imports on the one hand, and consumption on the other. In 1991, Mexican sugar production will be about 3.6 million metric tons, and consumption will be about 4.3 million metric tons.

38. The Mexican government also sets the wholesale price for refined sugar at 23.2 cents a pound and the retail price at 27 cents a pound, thereby allowing a very small retail markup (Buzzanell 1991, 24–27).

cents per pound, and the US raw sugar price is about 22 cents per pound. Mexico imposes a variable levy to ensure that the landed cost of imports is equal to the official reference price of 14.5 cents per pound for raw sugar. Not coincidentally, the average cost of production at the Mexican sugar mills is also estimated at 14.5 cents per pound (Buzzanell 1991; some of the mills are burdened by huge overstaffing, but this should be corrected by privatization). Hence, in principle, importers and domestic mills are allowed the same markup for delivering sugar to the wholesale market.

Mexican sugar cannot compete with output from Australia, Brazil, Cuba, or the Dominican Republic, but it could be competitive within continental North America, if North American sugar trade is liberalized internally while barriers to the world market remain in place. US sugar growers receive about 15 cents per pound for sugar contained in beets or cane, whereas Mexican growers receive only 11.2 cents. Moreover, with appropriate economic incentives, Mexican cane producers might increase the sugar content of their cane by 10 percent to 20 percent. (The present cane price system does not differentiate on the basis of cane quality, a fact that has discouraged the cultivation of high-sugar-bearing cane.) Thus, Mexican cane growers are well positioned to compete in a protected North American market.

In the 1960s and 1970s, annual Mexican sugar exports averaged 0.5 million and 0.3 million metric tons, respectively (nearly all to the United States). With the stimulus of higher US price levels, Mexican cane producers could probably fill local demands and once again send 0.5 million metric tons annually to the United States. With NAFTA liberalization, but without other reforms in the US sugar program, Mexican exports would substantially reduce US sugar imports from third countries (which reached 1.9 million metric tons in 1990).

The key policy issue is whether the North America free trade area is going to wed itself to a long-term, high-cost policy of sugar self-sufficiency. We think this would be a major mistake, and the ensuing trade diversion would certainly anger third-country suppliers of sugar. Our suggestion is that the NAFTA negotiators avoid this restrictive outcome by deferring liberalization of sugar quotas in the region until a liberal global sugar bargain has been struck in the Uruguay Round.

15

The Mexican Financial System

The financial system plays a critical role in marshaling and guiding the disposition of a country's resources, well beyond what the financial sector's share of national income would suggest.[1] In addition to its role in assembling and allocating domestic finance, a well-functioning financial system is critical for attracting capital from abroad. Continued rationalization of the Mexican financial system, spurred by competition from foreign financial firms, should thus be a key goal of the free trade talks.

In its structure and regulation the Mexican system parallels the US system. The Mexican system is divided into credit institutions (mainly banks), brokerage houses and the securities markets, and other nonbanking financial institutions (mainly insurance firms). These institutions are monitored and regulated by many agencies: the Secretariat of Finance and Public Credit (Secretaría de Hacienda y Crédito Público, SHCP), the Banco de México (the central bank), and three commissions—the National Banking Commission, the National Insurance and Bonding Commission, and the National Securities Commission—which are charged with the inspection and surveillance of banks, insurance firms, brokerage houses, and securities markets (Solís Soberón and Trigueros 1991, 99, 122, 150).

The SHCP is responsible for the overall coordination of the banks, security institutions, other financial institutions, and supervisory agencies. It authorizes the creation of insurance firms, provident societies, credit unions, brokerage houses, and securities markets. It controls the operations of the Banco de México and the three national commissions (Solís Soberón and Trigueros 1991, 111, 136, 161).

By law, the Banco de México is authorized to set commercial bank interest rates, commission rates, and loan and deposit maturity terms, and to supervise

---

1. In 1989 the Mexican financial system accounted for 3.3 percent of GDP; by comparison, the US financial system accounted for 5.3 percent of GDP.

Magnus Lambsdorff and Diana E. Clark helped draft this chapter. Sander Bieber of Covington and Burling provided useful comments. This chapter draws on Banco de México (1991), US International Trade Commission (1990b and c, 1991a), and Solís Soberón and Trigueros (1991).

credit decisions. The Banco de México also controls dealings in gold, silver, and foreign exchange; it buys and sells various public debt obligations for the federal government, and it advises insurance firms and brokerage houses as to the interpretation and implementation of financial statutes (Solís Soberón and Trigueros 1991, 111, 136, 161).

Commercial Banks

Structure

The Mexican banking sector is made up of commercial banks, development banks, and development trust funds.[2] The private commercial banks were nationalized by President José López Portillo in 1982, when the entire Mexican financial system was overwhelmed by an inability to service $60 billion of external debt. Subsequent consolidation in the industry reduced the number of banks from about 64 to 20. Of the survivors, 18 were government controlled; 6 of these operate on a national basis, 7 on a multiregional basis, and 5 on a regional basis (table 15.1). The remaining two, Banco Obrero and Citibank, are private-sector banks.

Banco Nacional de México (Banamex) is Mexico's largest commercial bank, with total assets of about $29 billion in 1991. Following Banamex in size are Bancomer, with total assets of about $25 billion, and Banca Serfin, with total assets of about $19 billion (table 15.1). These three banks account for some 70 percent of the total market capitalization of the Mexican banking sector, which reached $7 billion in mid–1991.[3]

The commercial banks can issue various credit instruments similar to those issued by the US banking system. Since 1988 they have been permitted to sell bankers' acceptances to the public at interest rates related to those in the money market.[4] At the same time the banks were authorized to issue "bank bonds for housing" at interest rates freely determined by themselves. These new deposit

---

2. The latter two provide financing for agriculture, industrial development, export promotion, and public works. Nacional Financiera is the largest state development bank and Fideicomisos Instituidos en Relación con la Agricultura (FIRA) the largest development trust fund. In 1990 total deposits with development banks were $3.4 billion, and total credit outstanding with development trusts was $3.7 billion (including $2.5 billion at FIRA).

3. In 1990 Banamex had a market capitalization of $1.7 billion, Bancomer $1.4 billion, and Banca Serfin $0.7 billion (*Wall Street Journal*, 24 June 1991, A8).

4. Bankers' acceptances are in effect commercial paper issued by an industrial firm and guaranteed (for a fee) by a bank. By the end of 1988, bankers' acceptances accounted for 60 percent of all bank deposits in Mexico (Skiles 1991, 18).

forms were created to stem the flow of savings out of the formal banking system. In 1989 limits on other kinds of bank deposits were also lifted, and savings in the formal banking system rose from 22 percent of GDP in 1988 to 40 percent in 1990 (Skiles 1991, 12–13).

The Mexican financial infrastructure is limited by comparison with those of the United States and Canada. In 1988 there was only one bank branch for every 186,000 persons, compared with one branch for every 3,800 persons in the United States, and one for every 3,600 persons in Canada. In 1988 Mexicans held 0.4 bank account per person (35 million accounts total), compared with 1.5 accounts per person in Canada (38 million accounts total; Canadian Bankers Association 1991, 7).

The only foreign bank that operates a banking subsidiary in Mexico is Citibank. (When the Mexican private-sector banks were nationalized in 1982, Citibank was allowed to continue operating.) In 1990 Citibank's five branches in Mexico City accounted for 6 percent of total Mexican bank assets, but less than 1 percent of bank employment. Citibank is the main custodian for foreign investors who hold shares in the Mexican stock market, with 60 percent of the total shares held (Canadian Bankers Association 1991, appendix 2). Besides Citibank, 138 foreign banks have 110 representative offices in Mexico. The Canadian presence in Mexico is limited to the four representative offices of the Bank of Montreal, the Bank of Nova Scotia, the Royal Bank of Canada, and the Canadian Imperial Bank of Commerce.

Banking Reforms

Beginning in the mid–1970s, Mexico embarked on a process of financial reform. At that time the existing regime of functionally specialized banking was transformed into a system of universal commercial banks. However, the distinction between investment banking and commercial banking was maintained until 1990, and bank ownership of industrial, commercial, and nonfinancial services companies is still restricted.

Deposit rates continued to be regulated during the period of rampant inflation in the 1980s. Rates paid to depositors were far below the rate of inflation, spurring the creation of an informal money market and the rapid growth of brokerage firms as an alternative center of financial power. Meanwhile, savings in the nationalized domestic banking system fell from 30 percent of GDP in 1981 to 22 percent in 1985 (Skiles 1991, 7).

Disintermediation was facilitated by skillful Mexican brokerage houses. Unable to accept deposits from the public, the brokerage firms instead developed an active money market that allowed the Mexican public to cope with inflation by earning high yields on government bills (CETES). Today the money market is well

Table 15.1 Employment and financial profile of selected Mexican banks, 1989 and 1991
(millions of dollars except where noted)

Bank	1989[a]							1991[b]	
	No. of employees	Assets	Net worth	Net income	Assets per employee	Return on assets (percentages)	Return on net worth (percentages)	Assets	Net income
National									
Banco Nacional de México (Banamex)	29,482	18,406	1,143	164	0.6	0.9	14.3	29,437	409.5
Bancomer	35,492	15,929	1,181	246	0.4	1.5	20.8	25,393	298.1
Banca Serfin	20,436	8,459	398	97	0.4	1.1	24.4	18,710	76.9
Multibanco Comermex	12,209	3,400	196	56	0.3	1.6	28.6	7,339	58.9
Banco Internacional	12,936	3,054	154	40	0.2	1.3	26.0	7,791	18.8
Banco Mexicano Somex	7,247	1,739	130	2.3	0.2	1.5	17.7	4,361	−5.2
Multiregional									
Banca Cremi	5,081	943	60	12	0.2	1.3	20.0	2,537	15.3
Banca Confia	3,635	814	56	16	0.2	2.0	28.6	2,354	27.8
Multibanco Mercantil de México	3,490	765	48	14	0.2	1.8	29.2	3,541	19.1
Banco Del Atlántico	7,409	1,381	65	n.a.	n.a.	n.a.	n.a.	3,121	10.9
BCH	4,457	594	n.a.	n.a.	n.a.	n.a.	n.a.	3,067	12.8
Banpaís	n.a.	n.a.	n.a.	n.a.	n.a.	n.a.	n.a.	1,241	6.4
Bancreser	n.a.	n.a.	n.a.	n.a.	n.a.	n.a.	n.a.	3,093	2.6

Regional								
Banco del Centro	2,767	736	69	24	0.3	3.3	34.8	984	23.0
Banco de Oriente	779	156	20	7	0.2	4.5	35.0	501	4.5
Mercantil del Norte	n.a.	784	98	n.a.	n.a.	n.a.	n.a.	1,715	51.9
Promex	n.a.	705	70	n.a.	n.a.	n.a.	n.a.	1,374	31.9
Banoro	n.a.	327	89	n.a.	n.a.	n.a.	n.a.	1,041	42.1

n.a. = not available.

a. Employment, assets, and net worth data are as of the end of the year.

b. Assets are as of the end of August.

Sources: Bolsa Mexicana de Valores, *Company Handbook*, 1990; *The Banker*, October 1988, 125; *Development Business*, "Mexico's Banks up for Sale," no. 309, 31 December 1990, 1 and 3. Data for 1991 are from *Financial Times*, 25 October 1991, IV.

developed, with a wide variety of financial products such as TESOBONOS, PAGAFES, and AJUSTABONOS, as well as CETES (these instruments are described further below).

The authorities eventually took steps to stem the flow of savings out of the formal banking system. Regulations on deposit rates, loan rates, and credit allocation were slowly removed and finally abandoned in 1989. Today Mexican banks are empowered to allocate their funds freely and to set their own interest rates (US International Trade Commission 1990, 2-19 to 2-21). But they are still required to maintain a liquidity reserve equal to 30 percent of liabilities with the Banco de México.[5] In addition, restrictions remain on cross-ownership between industrial, commercial, and services companies. In general, a commercial bank's investment in related firms cannot exceed 5 percent of its own deposits. Further, as a general rule, a bank cannot hold more than 5 percent of the equity market capitalization of an issuing industrial or commercial company.[6]

The bank nationalization of 1982 was partly reversed in 1987, when President Miguel de la Madrid sold up to 34 percent of the nationalized banks to private Mexican investors. The banking law was entirely reformed in July 1990, when the Mexican Congress passed the Credit Institutions Act aimed at complete privatization of the commercial banks.

The system of bank privatization brought about by the 1990 reforms was designed to ensure that control of the banking system would remain solidly in Mexican hands. Majority stakes of 51 percent are auctioned as "A" shares to the state development banks, the development trust funds, the Bank Fund for Savings Protection, and financial holding companies. The remaining shares are auctioned as "B" shares. "B" shares may be purchased by "A" shareholders, by institutional investors, by Mexican companies (with an exclusion clause for foreigners), and by investment funds. "C" shares may also be issued by the "A" and "B" shareholders but are limited to 30 percent of the total; they may be purchased by "A" and "B" shareholders, by Mexican companies (without an exclusion clause for foreigners), and by foreign investors.[7] As a general rule,

---

5. Unlike US bank reserves held at the Federal Reserve, Mexican bank reserves held at the Banco de México can take the form of interest-bearing public debt instruments such as CETES. Banks may also hold their reserves in the form of special deposits at the Banco de México. However, the interest rate on these deposits is 30 percent lower than the interest rate on CETES. As a result, the vast majority of banks hold their reserves in the form of CETES.

6. Solís Soberón and Trigueros (1991, 99). These restrictions parallel the Glass-Steagall Act limitations in the United States. Basically, the Mexican government is trying to avoid the close association between banks and industrial groups that once existed. However, as in the United States, the Mexican authorities are relaxing the barriers to cross-ownership between banks and other financial institutions.

7. After the 1987 reform, the capital of each state-owned bank was constituted as follows: 66 percent "A" Bank Equity Certificates (Caps) and 34 percent "B" Bank Equity Certificates (Caps). In the privatization, "A" Caps, representing 51 percent of bank capital are

individual investors and single companies are not permitted to hold more than 5 percent of any bank, but this limit will not apply to the controlling companies of Mexican financial groups.[8]

To date the Mexican government has raised $7 billion from the sale of nine banks. On average the banks have been sold for close to three times their book value (*Journal of Commerce*, 7 November 1991, 5A). Most state banks were sold to brokerage firms headed by former bankers who left the banking industry after it was nationalized in 1982. For example, the Mexican brokerage house Probursa bought Multibanco Mercantil for $203 million. A Mexican holding company that includes the brokerage house Mexival acquired Banpaís for $182 million. A group of investors led by Multivalores, another Mexican brokerage firm, bought Banca Cremi for $249 million (*Wall Street Journal*, 24 June 1991, A8; 25 June 1991, A18).

In late August 1991 the Mexican government sold 50.7 percent of Banamex to a group of 800 investors led by Roberto Hernández, president of the brokerage firm Acciones y Valores de México (Accival) for $2.3 billion. Having acquired a 17 percent stake in 1987, Accival now holds 68 percent of Banamex. In addition, the group of investors is allowed to buy any of the 20 percent of the shares initially offered to, but not taken by, the regional directors of Banamex. The group also obtained a two-year option to buy the remaining government holding of 19.7 percent. After establishing a banking holding company, Hernández plans to offer 19 percent of the holding company to foreign investors (*New York Times*, 27 August 1991, D1).

By the end of October 1991 the Mexican government had sold its 51 percent holding in Bancomer to Valores Monterrey and expected to sell 25 percent more to a regional group (*Wall Street Journal*, 29 October 1991, A19). In January 1992 a 51 percent stake in Banca Serfin was auctioned for $940 million to an investor group centered around the industrialist Adrián Sada González and the brokerage firm Operadoras de Bolsa (*Wall Street Journal*, 27 January 1992, A6). The next banks to be auctioned will be Somex and Multibanco Comermex. By the end of 1992 the government expects to have sold all 18 banks and to have raised more than $10 billion (*New York Times*, 1 November 1991, D3; *Journal of Commerce*, 7 November 1991, 5A).

In theory, "C" shares provide an avenue for foreign commercial banks to participate in the Mexican financial system. "C" shares were made slightly more attractive in the 1990 reforms, which accorded them voting rights. As a practical

---

exchanged for Series "A" shares. An additional 15 percent of "A" Caps are exchanged for nonvoting "B" shares, and all "B" Caps are exchanged for nonvoting "B" shares. The issue of "C" shares will be decided by the "A" and "B" shareholders, with permission from the SHCP.

8. In special cases, the SHCP may raise this figure to 10 percent. Institutional investors may hold up to 15 percent of any financial institution.

matter, however, few American, European, Canadian, or Japanese banks are interested in taking a small minority stake in a Mexican bank. Moreover, foreign bank subsidiaries operating in Mexico may only offer offshore banking services; they are not allowed to offer services to Mexican residents.

As a result of these continuing restrictions, US interest in the Mexican banking sector has been sluggish. The one exception is Citibank with its privileged, but limited, grandfather position. In October 1990 Citibank was authorized to pay interest on deposit accounts and to lower its reserves from 90 percent to 30 percent of its deposits. In addition, Citibank received permission to open a sixth branch in Monterrey. Canadian and European banks have shown some interest in reentering the Mexican market; Banque Nationale de Paris, for example, has expressed interest in acquiring Somex (Conger 1991, 124).

The one area where foreign banks have made inroads is the Mexican charge card market. Previously, the Mexican authorities restricted the use of charge cards to purchases made in Mexico, for fear of capital flight. In 1988 the ban was lifted, and the usage of charge cards increased dramatically. The two largest Mexican debit card issuers are Banamex and Bancomer with 2 million cards each. American Express is the largest US card issuer with 300,000 cards, followed by Citibank with 100,000 cards. In 1991 Banamex became the first Mexican bank to certify its automatic teller machines for the CIRRUS and Mastercard ABM networks (Canadian Bankers Association 1991, 7–8). However, with only 9 million debit and credit cards outstanding (an average of two cards per card-carrying person), the Mexican market still remains underdeveloped: in Canada and the United States the average is seven cards per card-carrying person (Canadian Bankers Association 1991, 8). An important negotiating issue for the NAFTA relating to credit cards is access to the bank clearing system. So far the Mexican authorities, unlike their US and Canadian counterparts, have excluded nonbanks such as American Express from direct access to the clearing system. As a result, the nonbank credit card issuers incur an interest rate penalty.

Until foreign banking restrictions are relaxed, the domestic Mexican banking industry will remain largely insulated from foreign competition. Compared with US and Canadian banks, Mexican banks show a high net income as a percentage of assets, despite their labor-intensive operations (table 15.2). In 1989 the national Mexican banks recorded an average return on assets of 1.3 percent, versus 0.2 percent for US banks and 0.4 percent for Canadian banks, even though bank assets per employee amounted to only $0.4 million, compared with about $2.2 million in the United States and Canada (these figures are unweighted averages for the banks listed in tables 15.1 and 15.2). Aggressive cost cutting by newly privatized Mexican banks could dramatically improve their performance.

Even though US banks are well positioned to enter the Mexican market, they could face strong European and Japanese competition, especially in wholesale banking activities. Table 15.3 compares the intermediation spreads, profits, and

Table 15.2 Employment and financial profile of selected US and Canadian banks, 1989[a]
(millions of dollars except where noted)

Bank	Employees	Assets	Net income	Assets per employee	Return on of assets (percentages)
United States					
Citicorp	92,000	230,643	498	2.5	0.2
BankAmerica Corp.	54,779	98,764	1,103	1.8	1.1
Chase Manhattan Corp.	41,610	107,369	−665	2.6	−0.6
Chemical Banking Corp.	29,139	71,513	−482	2.5	−0.7
Bank of New York	14,883	48,857	51	3.3	0.1
Homefed Corp.	4,591	17,680	116	3.9	0.7
Southeast Banking Corp.	7,665	16,230	1	2.1	0.0
Citizens & Southern Corp.	30,000	22,580	238	0.8	1.1
Suntrust Banks	19,397	31,040	337	1.6	1.1
Canada					
Royal Bank of Canada	47,989	97,657	444	2.0	0.5
Imperial Bank of Commerce	36,466	85,353	378	2.3	0.4
Bank of Nova Scotia	29,618	68,990	186	2.3	0.3
Bank of Montreal	33,666	67,218	43	2.0	0.1
Toronto-Dominion Bank	23,881	53,717	583	2.2	1.1

a. Employment and asset data are as of the end of the year.

Sources: Bolsa Mexicana de Valores, *Company Handbook*, 1990; *Euromoney*, June 1990, 86; September 1990, 182; *Fortune*, 30 July 1990, 324.

Table 15.3 Intermediation spreads, profits, and operating costs of commercial banks, selected countries
(percentages of average assets)

Country	Interest margin[a]	Gross margin[b]	Operating costs
France	2.72	3.18	2.12
Germany	2.35	2.95	1.85
Japan	1.27	1.58	1.02
Spain	4.07	4.86	3.26
United Kingdom	3.06	4.92	3.32
United States	3.34	4.76	3.18
Average	2.80	3.71	2.46
Mexico	2.75	10.20	8.82

a. Interest received minus interest paid.

b. Difference between all costs of funding and all income generated by lending activities.

Source: Marilyn E. Skiles, "Stabilization and Financial Sector Reform in Mexico," *Federal Reserve Bank of New York Research Paper* 9125, August 1991, table 7. Adapted with permission.

operating costs for commercial banks. On average, the US gross margin was 4.8 percent of assets, compared with 3.0 percent for German banks and 1.6 percent for Japanese banks. Similarly, US operating costs were 3.2 percent of assets, versus 1.9 percent for German banks and 1.0 percent for Japanese banks (Skiles 1991, table 7). By these measures, US banks are "high-cost" operations compared with their major foreign competitors.

Insurance Firms

Structure

There are 43 insurance firms in Mexico; 38 of these are equity companies (two of which are reinsurance firms), 2 are mutual companies, and 3 are state-owned institutions. To a large extent, Mexican insurance firms act as intermediaries rather than financial powerhouses: they do business with the public through independent agents, and they reinsure many of their policies.[9] In 1989 life

---

9. Solís Soberón and Trigueros (1991, 145). Thirty years ago, independent agents likewise dominated the retail end of the US insurance industry. In some lines such as automobile, life, and health they have been largely supplanted by direct sales and group policies.

insurance premiums amounted to $0.7 billion (34 percent of total insurance premiums), automobile insurance premiums amounted to $0.6 billion (28 percent), and fire, maritime, transport, and other insurance amounted to $0.8 billion in premiums (38 percent).[10]

The insurance industry is relatively small in Mexico. Premiums expressed as a fraction of GDP are 1.0 percent in Mexico, 2.2 percent in Chile, 3.3 percent in Spain, 5.4 percent in Canada, and 9.1 percent in the United States. The leading Mexican insurance firms are not particularly large. At the end of 1989 the stock market capitalization of all Mexican insurance companies was only $2.3 billion.[11] However, some of these companies earned attractive returns on assets (table 15.4). Mexican insurance firms appear weak in certain lines: insuring large risks, insuring professional risks, and managing pension plans (Solís Soberón and Trigueros 1991, 155). In part their product weakness reflects low spending on R&D, little internal training, and weak data processing (Solís Soberón and Trigueros 1991, 147). In addition, Mexican insurance firms rely heavily on the reinsurance market, which concentrates on standard life and casualty policies.

Mexican firms show higher net incomes as a percentage of assets and lower assets-per-employee ratios than do US firms. As in the banking sector, these figures reflect good profitability in a sheltered market, but also low efficiency (table 15.4).

Insurance Reforms

Until December 1989 the Mexican insurance industry was tightly regulated. Premium rates and reserves were fixed, the range of permitted investments was restricted, and market entry was limited (Solís Soberón and Trigueros 1991, 150). There was some deregulation in 1990; the surviving regulations largely deal with minimum reserves, maximum shareholder positions, and entry into the industry. Acquisition of 10 percent or more of a Mexican insurance firm requires permission from the SHCP (Solís Soberón and Trigueros 1990b, 21).

---

10. Closely related to the insurance industry is the bonding sector. In November 1989 the outstanding face value of bond guarantees written by 14 bonding companies amounted to $7.2 billion. This service yielded revenues of $54 million. According to Solís Soberón and Trigueros (1990b), only seven firms offer insurance in agriculture. Until January 1990 there was a public insurance firm that provided agricultural insurance at subsidized rates.

11. Solís Soberón and Trigueros (1990b, 8). Peso figures are converted using end–1989 data from International Monetary Fund, *International Financial Statistics*, June 1991.

Table 15.4 Employment and financial profile of selected US and Mexican insurers, 1989
(millions of dollars except where noted)

Company	Employees	Assets	Net income	Assets per employee	Return on assets (percentages)
United States[a]					
Prudential of America	69,551	129,118	644	1.9	0.5
Metropolitan Life	46,000	98,740	494	2.1	0.5
Equitable Life Assurance	23,000	52,512	193	2.3	0.4
Aetna Life	17,377	52,023	341	3.0	0.7
Mutual of New York	4,453	17,181	154	3.9	0.9
New England Mutual Life	6,235	16,667	26	2.7	0.2
General American Life	7,840	5,551	13	0.7	0.2
Mexico					
Valores de Monterrey	3,040	465	28	0.2	6.1
Seguros América	2,600	463	1	0.2	0.3
Seguros de México	2,471	447	29	0.2	6.5
Seguros Monterrey	2,321	351	6	0.2	1.7
Seguros La Comercial	1,624	221	2	0.1	0.7
Seguros Tepeyac	649	73	<1	0.1	n.a.

n.a. = not available.

a. US life insurance companies only.

Source: Fortune, 4 June 1990; Bolsa Mexicana de Valores, *Company Handbook,* 1990.

Foreign companies are currently permitted to hold a minority participation of up to 49 percent in Mexican insurance and bonding institutions.[12]

The National Insurance and Bonding Commission supervises the insurance and bonding industry. Many activities are exclusively reserved for national firms, including:

- insurance of a person who is situated in Mexican territory at the moment of signing the contract;

- insurance of imported or exported goods if a Mexican resident is liable for the risk;

- insurance of a motor vehicle with Mexican license plates or owned by a Mexican resident;

- credit insurance if the insured is subject to Mexican legislation; and

- insurance of civil liability or damages caused by events that take place in Mexico.

Mexican companies can, however, enter into reinsurance contracts with foreign firms.

Despite the restrictions, if the insurance in question is not available from a national firm, the person seeking coverage can be authorized to buy it from a foreign firm (Solís Soberón and Trigueros 1990b, 21).

The premiums paid by business firms for certain types of insurance policies are tax deductible, but only if the insurance is purchased from a Mexican firm. This works as an additional form of protection from foreign competition.[13]

Limited deregulation of the Mexican insurance industry in December 1989 (the reforms were published on 3 January 1990) triggered a minor invasion by foreign investors. Twelve of the 25 largest insurance firms in the world now have offices in Mexico and provide reinsurance and consultant services (Solís Soberón and Trigueros 1991, 152). In 1990 alone, American International Group, Connecticut General, and Cigna (United States), Allianz (Germany), Mapfre (Spain), Commercial Union Assurance (United Kingdom), and Assicurazioni Generali (Italy) bought stakes in Mexican insurance firms (*Institutional Investor*, March

---

12. There is no restriction on foreign participation in the reinsurance industry, provided at least 50 percent of the reinsurance business is placed within Mexico. Foreign governments and other official entities are excluded from buying the stock of Mexican insurance and bonding companies.

13. Solís Soberón and Trigueros (1990b, 22). Examples are contributions to pension funds and health insurance plans.

1991, 129). Despite investment restrictions, five Mexican insurance firms already have foreign participation (Solís Soberón and Trigueros 1991, 152).

Brokerage Houses and Securities Markets

Brokerage Houses

Mexican brokerage firms have existed for decades, but their operations were long controlled by the commercial banks. As part of the 1982 bank nationalization, the Mexican government sold off the banks' brokerage operations. Often they were acquired by energetic ex-bankers, who then made substantial inroads into the turf of the nationalized banks. The brokerage houses built a flourishing money market business in highly inflationary circumstances, at a time when banks could only offer low-interest deposits that practically guaranteed losses to deposit holders. From 1985 to 1990, brokerage firms experienced real asset growth of about 774 percent (Eggerstedt 1991). Their encroachment into the banking industry's territory was tolerated and even welcomed by the Mexican government because it provided a way to finance the burgeoning public deficit by issuing huge amounts of CETES.

Some 25 brokerage houses provide investment services for Mexico's financial system (Solís Soberón and Trigueros 1991, 130). The leading brokerage firm in 1989, in terms of assets, was Grupo Bursátil Mexicano (GBM) with total assets of about $1.5 billion. Operadoras de Bolsa and Inverméxico followed with about $1 billion each (Bolsa Mexicana de Valores, *Company Handbook,* 1990).[14] The brokerage houses focus on four areas of operation (listed here by percentage of total revenues): acting as securities agents and trading in the secondary market (41 percent), brokering (16 percent), mutual fund administration (15 percent), and investment banking (3 percent).

The large Mexican brokerage firms, with their pool of banking talent, will almost certainly come to serve as controlling companies of financial groups. The pattern for this was set in 1987, when President de la Madrid sold off 34 percent of the banking sector, and brokerage firms bought large stakes. The brokerage house Acciones y Valores (Accival), for example, bought 17 percent of Banamex, 9 percent of Bancomer, 12 percent of Banca Serfin, and 20 percent of Comermex. In August 1991, Accival gained control of Banamex, the largest commercial

---

14. Although the brokerage industry is characterized by a rather low degree of concentration, certain firms dominate some products: in 1990, equity shares were dominated by Accival; CETES (Treasury bills) were dominated by Operadora, Inverlat, and GBM; investment trusts were dominated by Accibur (Solís Soberón and Trigueros 1990c, 10).

bank. As noted above, an investor group organized around Operadores de Bolsa acquired a 51 percent stake in Banca Serfin in early 1992. Probursa, Mexival, and Multivalores are also involved in acquiring regional banks.

The concept of financial groups was formalized in 1990 when conglomerates were authorized by the federal government to acquire majority stakes in a broad variety of financial services activities. The financial services firms eligible for control include general warehouses, stockbrokers, foreign-exchange brokers, factoring companies, insurance and bond companies, and managers of investment companies. This approach follows the world trend of closer ties among banks, insurance firms, brokerages, and other financial activities. Among the members of a Mexican "financial services group," at least three must belong to different financial industries, and only one firm in each industry may join the group.[15] Once a bank and a brokerage firm establish such a holding company, it must hold a majority stake in each of its subsidiaries. The group members may use the same or similar trade names to identify themselves to the public.

Mexican brokerage firms have been authorized to invest abroad (through overseas subsidiaries) only since July 1989. To date, at least 5 of the 25 brokerage houses are registered to do business in the United States, and others do business abroad through their links with foreign securities firms.[16]

Foreign investment in Mexican brokerage houses is still restricted. It can be authorized by the SHCP, but total foreign investment in a brokerage firm may not exceed 30 percent, nor may any individual foreign holder hold more than 10 percent (Solís Soberón and Trigueros 1991, 123).

As measured by employment and net worth, Mexican brokerage houses are much smaller than their US counterparts. However, their profitability figures are similar, as shown by their net return on equity (table 15.5).

Securities Markets

The Stock Market Act of 1975 laid the cornerstone for the creation of the modern Mexican securities market. In 1978 the first CETES (short-term publicly traded bills) were issued by the Mexican government, both to finance public expenditure and to create an instrument for open-market operations. During the 1980s various new financial instruments were created. Triggered by liberalization, total

---

15. For this purpose, investment funds and insurance companies that operate in different market segments are regarded as belonging to different industries.

16. The Mexican brokerage firms registered in the United States include Probursa, Inverlat, Finamex, Operadora, and Abaco. Accival maintains a representative office in Denver. The owners of Multivalores also own InverWorld, a Cayman Islands company that owns a Delaware company that, in turn, owns a US brokerage dealer.

Table 15.5 Employment and financial profile of selected US and Mexican security brokerage firms, December 1989 (millions of dollars except where noted)

	Employees	Net worth[a]	Net income	Return on net worth[b] (percentages)
United States				
Salomon Brothers	8,900	2,865	470	16.4
Merrill Lynch	41,000	3,151	−213	−6.8
Morgan Stanley Group	6,700	2,021	443	21.9
Bear Stearns	5,994	1,066	172	16.2
Paine Webber Group	12,900	1,001	52	5.2
Charles Schwab	2,838	172	19	11.0
Mexico				
Grupo Bursátil Mexicano	208	80	10	12.0
Operadora de Bolsa	1,546	88	9	9.8
Inverméxico	410	60	8	13.3
Valores Finamex	376	44	9	19.5
Acciones y Valores de México	328	102	38	37.3
Interacciones Casa de Bolsa	177	32	4	11.6
Casa de Bolsa Inverlat	1,020	149	38	25.5
CBI Casa de Bolsa	348	51	16	31.4
Multivalores	n.a.	34	8	24.4
Afin Casa de Bolsa	177	12	1	10.8
Inversora Bursátil	146	195	16	8.2
Estrategia	224	19	3	15.3
Probursa	1,168	59	13	22.0
Casa de Bolsa Prime	225	25	3	10.4
Casa de Bolsa Arka	239	28	−2	−6.4
Vector Casa de Bolsa	273	22	3	13.6
Mexival	191	7	<1	n.a.

n.a. = not available.

a. For the United States, stockholders' equity. For Mexico, total assets minus the sum of total current liabilities, total long-term liabilities, and deferred income.

b. For the United States, net profits as a percentage of stockholders equity. For Mexico, total current assets divided by total current liabilities.

Sources: Bolsa Mexicana de Valores, *Company Handbook,* 1990; *Fortune,* 4 June 1990, 316–17.

Table 15.6 Profile of emerging stock markets, 1989

	Number of listed companies	Market capitalization (billions of dollars)	Average market capitalization per company (millions of dollars)	Market capitalization as a percentage of GNP
Latin America				
Argentina	174	3	17	5.6
Brazil	591	30	51	6.5
Chile	213	12	56	52.2
Colombia	80	2	25	5.4
Mexico	203	30	148	16.0
Venezuela	66	2	30	4.9
East Asia				
Korea	654	110	168	52.4
Philippines	151	10	66	22.7
Taiwan	188	120	638	78.4
South Asia				
India	2,453	33	13	12.6
Indonesia	92	7	76	7.9
Malaysia	263	46	175	127.8
Pakistan	463	3	6	7.7
Thailand	191	34	178	49.3

Sources: International Finance Corporation, *Quarterly Review of Emerging Stock Markets, Second Quarter 1990*, August 1990, 3; World Bank, *World Debt Tables 1990–91;* Central Bank of China, *Financial Statistics, Taiwan District*, January 1991. International Finance Corporation and World Bank data adapted with permission.

market capitalization increased in real terms by a factor of 28 between 1982 and 1991, rising from $2 billion to $56 billion (*Latin Finance*, June 1991, 32).

In recent years the Mexican stock market (Bolsa de Valores) has ranked among the most attractive in Latin America. Market capitalization relative to GNP in 1989 was comparatively high by Latin American standards, but still low compared with successful countries in East and South Asia (table 15.6). As the third-best emerging stock market in 1991, the Bolsa increased by 99 percent in dollar terms between January and December 1991.[17] The booming Mexican stock market, a tangible result of the anticipated NAFTA, has no doubt persuaded many Mexican capitalists that free trade is not a bad idea after all.

---

17. *Financial Times*, 18 December 1991, 36. By January 1992 the Mexican share price index, expressed in US dollars with a 1988 value of 100, had reached 1,028 (*Barron's*, 27 January 1992, 60).

The Mexican securities market deals in both public- and private-sector instruments. In 1989 the stock exchange's trading volume reached $413 billion, of which $399 billion (97 percent) represented trading in fixed-income securities, mainly public debt instruments. Equity shares accounted for only $14 billion (3 percent) of total trading. However, the trading volume in equity shares should spur as Mexican firms take advantage of the buoyant market. Most recently, Grupo Carso and Empaques Ponderosa announced international offerings, led by Salomon Brothers, of $250 million and $65 million, respectively. Televisa, the Mexican television and publishing group, is expected to follow suit with a $500 million equity issue, led by Goldman Sachs (*Financial Times*, 4 September 1991, 24). In all, about 19 Mexican companies are lined up to offer new stock to the public (*Financial Times*, 7 August 1991, 30).

Trading volume in public-sector instruments is dominated by short-term ($364 billion) and fixed-rate long-term ($19 billion) instruments. CETES (28- to 91-day bills) are sold at a discount in weekly auctions. TESOBONOS (three- to six-month bills) are indexed to the US dollar. BONOS (with maturities of 364, 532, or 725 days) are fixed-coupon bonds. In addition, there are various instruments with different maturity terms payable in pesos but linked to external indicators such as the US dollar (PAGAFES), the dollar-based oil price (PETROBONOS), or the National Consumer Price Index (AJUSTABONOS). Private-sector debt instruments, such as bankers' acceptances (guaranteed by commercial banks) and commercial paper (issued by industrial firms without a bank guarantee), are also traded on the exchange. In early 1990 the Mexican rating firm Calificadora de Valores (CAVAL) started operations, thereby adding credibility to commercial paper issued in the Mexican money market.

After the 1982 financial crisis, debt placements in the international bond market dried up for Mexico and other Latin American countries. This situation started to change in 1988, and the Banco Nacional de Comercio Exterior de México was able to raise $100 million through a private placement in the Eurobond market in June 1989. In February 1991 the Mexican government floated its first bond in a decade, for DM300 million (Comisión Económica para América Latina y el Caribe 1991, 13). In September 1991 the state oil monopoly Pemex launched a $150 million, seven-year bond issue, only one year after it had successfully floated a three-year, $150 million issue (*Financial Times*, 13 September 1991, 21). In addition, in October 1991 Nacional Financiera launched a $150 million 10-year bond issue, arranged by Chase Investment Bank.[18] Many other issues are in the wings (see *Financial Times*, 25 October 1991, IV).

---

18. This issue was characterized by "a maturity longer than any Latin American debt issued since the debt crisis of 1982" (*Financial Times*, 24 October 1991, 24).

Regulation

The Comisión Nacional de Valores (CNV), an agency responsible to the SHCP, is charged with monitoring the exchange houses,[19] approving public offerings of securities (including mutual funds),[20] inspecting transactions of brokerage firms and ensuring their solvency, and conciliating and arbitrating conflicts.

The CNV has negotiated a memorandum of understanding with its US counterpart, the Securities and Exchange Commission (SEC). This agreement is similar to those signed between the United States and Canada. The major objective is to provide mutual cooperation and information sharing in the enforcement of securities laws. The memorandum also provides a framework for extensive technical assistance by the SEC to the CNV.

Together with its normal regulatory functions, the CNV is responsible for limiting foreign participation in the equity market.[21] Stocks are classified according to their availability for acquisition by foreigners. Series "B" nonvoting shares can be purchased by foreigners without restriction, while series "A" shares can only be purchased by Mexican nationals and by so-called neutral trust funds.[22] In addition, at least 10 Mexican companies have issued American Depository Receipts (ADRs), corresponding to nonvoting or limited-voting shares. The ADRs trade on US markets, while the underlying Mexican shares are held in the custody of INDEVAL, the authorized depository institution (for additional information on Mexican ADRs see chapter 4).

An important international financial development has been the growth of closed-end "country" funds that specialize in shares issued in an individual developing country.[23] The pioneer in this area was the Mexico Fund, which holds a portfolio of representative Mexican shares and trades on the New York Stock Exchange. By the middle of 1991, the market value of the Mexico Fund

---

19. An automated monitoring system is in place to monitor daily operations and detect violations of rules. Some 19 watch list parameters (e.g., simultaneous movements of prices and large amounts of stocks) have been identified.

20. For example, mutual funds are limited in terms of their asset concentration by industry and their holdings of companies belonging to the same group.

21. This section draws on Bolsa Mexicana de Valores and Instituto Mexicano del Mercado de Capitales (1990).

22. The list of "A" and "B" shares can be found in Bolsa Mexicana de Valores, *Company Handbook*, 1990, 30-31.

23. Unlike the more familiar open-end mutual funds, closed-end mutual funds issue a fixed number of shares, which then trade on the stock exchanges, with the result that their selling price can differ from the net asset value of the underlying portfolio.

was $463 million. The total market value of country funds that specialize or have significant holdings in Mexican shares was about $700 million in mid–1990.[24]

Recommendations

Despite the reforms instituted in recent years, the Mexican financial system remains far less developed and more protected than its counterparts in the United States and Canada. Canadian and US financial firms continue to face discrimination in Mexico, while Mexicans enjoy unrestricted freedom to invest, borrow funds, and establish financial institutions outside Mexico. This imbalance needs to be righted, both to increase the efficiency of the Mexican financial sector and to establish the right of establishment and national treatment for foreign financial firms doing business in Mexico.[25]

Two issues need to be addressed regarding the liberalization of the Mexican financial sector: the pace of reform (rapid liberalization versus gradualism) and the sequencing of expanded foreign access to ownership stakes in individual companies and evolving Mexican financial groups, on the one hand, and increased foreign ability to enter into head-to-head competition in the product markets, on the other.

Rapid liberalization would quickly bring the benefits of a highly competitive financial system, but it runs into three practical difficulties. First, it would hasten the default of thinly capitalized and weakly managed local insurance companies and multiregional banks. Second, it could overwhelm the vital, but still small, Mexican securities firms. Third, and this refers mainly to the banking system, it would strike at the heart of Mexican "financial sovereignty." The sovereignty problem is not unique to Mexico. As a practical matter, Canada's five large banks are off limits to foreign control, and even the United States is only slowly moving toward political and regulatory acceptance of controlling foreign stakes in large US banks.[26]

---

24. The three Mexican investment funds traded on the New York Stock Exchange are the Mexico Equity and Income Fund, the Emerging Mexico Fund, and the Latin American Income Fund. Total foreign investment in Mexican equities, including direct shareholdings, ADRs, closed-end funds, and neutral trust holdings, was estimated at about $9.6 billion in mid–1991 (Shearson Lehman Brothers 1991).

25. Unequal access was less of a problem in the Canada–US FTA because of the substantial prior direct investment of US and Canadian banks and insurance companies in each other's market.

26. The foreign-owned share of US banking assets (including US subsidiaries acquired in the 1980s) rose from 16.1 percent in 1985 to 21.2 percent in 1990 (Graham and Krugman 1991, 29). During the course of this rise, a few cases have occurred where foreign-controlled banks were plagued by scandal. The most notable of these was First American Bankshares, which was found in 1991 to be secretly controlled by the Bank of Credit and Commerce International (BCCI) of Luxembourg (see *Wall Street Journal*, 13 June 1991, 1).

These considerations argue for a pragmatic approach. In the banking sector, foreign banks should immediately be allowed to acquire voting minority shares of up to 49 percent in Mexican institutions and to offer wholesale banking services; after five years they should be allowed to acquire controlling stakes.[27] Moreover, by the late 1990s, qualified US banks in border cities such as San Diego and El Paso should be allowed to expand their networks into Mexico, and qualified Mexican banks should be extended similar access to the United States. Some Mexican banks have already acquired US banks in the border region to tap into the US Hispanic market. For example, Banamex owns California Commerce Bank (San Jose), and Bancomer owns Grossmont Bank (La Mesa, California). Further acquisitions should be conditioned on the ability of US banks to branch into Tijuana, Mexicali, and Juárez.[28]

Unlike in the Canada–US FTA, where preferential treatment was accorded to financial firms of the partner countries, Mexican banking reforms should be extended on a nondiscriminatory basis to all foreigners. This step will add resources to the Mexican financial sector, and it will enable Mexico to participate in the financial services accord currently under negotiation in the Uruguay Round of the GATT. In addition, Mexico should open its financial clearing system to foreign credit card issuers.

In the insurance sector, easily the weakest of the three major Mexican financial sectors, the need for foreign capital and expertise is greater. The resources and technical skills of foreign companies far exceed the levels of the Mexican industry. The solution is association on a large scale between Mexican and foreign firms. Here, the NAFTA ought to open the market to majority foreign ownership of existing Mexican companies and, perhaps five years later, to free competition via newly minted subsidiaries.

The brokerage industry, the strongest segment of the Mexican financial sector, remains small compared with its US and Canadian counterparts. In 1990 the market capitalization of the Mexican brokerage firms was less than 1 percent that of US and Canadian firms. Mexican brokerage houses traditionally focus on money market operations, unlike US and Canadian brokerage houses, which deal on a large scale in stock brokerage and mutual fund management. With

27. The Bankers' Association for Foreign Trade (BAFT) task force has recommended that Canada and Mexico permit US banks to engage in all activities that those countries grant to their own commercial banks (BAFT Update, January 1992, 1).

28. Several Mexican banks are interested in acquiring other US banks in the border region. For example, Banamex applied to buy American National Bank (Houston), Bancomer targeted Executive National Bank (San Antonio), and Banca Serfin applied to buy Falcon National Bank (Laredo). Deputy Assistant Secretary of the US Treasury Barry Newman points out that US banks will not "overwhelm" Mexican banks because "they are too preoccupied with domestic problems" (*Journal of Commerce*, 6 November 1991, 2A).

immediate liberalization, US firms such as Merrill Lynch and Fidelity might overwhelm the Mexican brokerage houses.

The United States and Canada should strive for a gradual opening of the Mexican securities industry. For starters, trading in shares of foreign firms should be permitted on the Mexican stock exchange. At a later stage, foreign firms should be permitted to underwrite securities and to become members of the Bolsa. Within five years of the entry into force of the NAFTA they should be allowed to offer their full range of financial services to the Mexican public. In the meantime, the Mexican brokerage houses will have strengthened their own capabilities by underwriting debt and equity issues and by sponsoring mutual funds.

In the NAFTA negotiations, Canada aims to improve on the deal achieved for Canadian banks in the US–Canada trade pact. Canada has more liberal nation-wide banking laws than the United States: US banks are free to open a branch anywhere in Canada, but Canadian banks still face state-level obstacles to branch expansion in the United States.[29] In the context of sweeping bank reform legislation in the United States, including repeal of the Glass-Steagall and McFadden acts, this is a concession that the United States should make both to Canada and to Mexico.

---

29. *Wall Street Journal*, 10 June 1991, A5. Moreover, unlike the US Congress, which failed to enact bank reform legislation in late 1991, the Canadian Parliament will soon permit banks to offer additional financial services. Among the proposed changes: banks will be allowed to own insurance firms, trust companies will be given banking powers, and insurers will be able to sell products of other financial institutions and will have wider lending powers (*Financial Times*, 4 December 1991, 21).

IV

Summary and Conclusions

16

Summary and Conclusions

When the negotiations on a North American Free Trade Agreement or NAFTA were launched in June 1991, the trade ministers of the three participating countries predicted that the agreement could be concluded in short order, perhaps by the end of 1991 or soon thereafter.[1] Their bold pronouncements reflected a strong commitment to promote freer trade in the region and a belief that few major obstacles lay in the path. Our analysis basically confirms the optimism but not the timetable: the NAFTA negotiators have a lot of ground to cover before a satisfactory agreement can be wrapped up, and they will need to labor well into 1992.

As the previous chapters have amply demonstrated, the negotiation of a NAFTA is a complex task. The agenda covers a broader range of issues than does the Uruguay Round of multilateral trade negotiations in the General Agreement on Tariffs and Trade (GATT); the shape of the NAFTA provisions will be influenced significantly by the GATT negotiations; and the prospective ratification debate will provoke a reassessment of important domestic policies in all three countries, especially toward labor and the environment.

In the previous 15 chapters we have examined the shape, form, and content of the prospective NAFTA, its potential trade and employment effects, the environmental concerns associated with it, and the implications for key sectors of each national economy. Most of the chapters conclude with detailed recommendations concerning NAFTA rights and obligations and the reforms of national laws, regulations, and trade practices required to implement NAFTA commitments. This final chapter summarizes our main policy recommendations and their implications for each of the participating countries. We start with proposals regarding the preferred structure and coverage of the NAFTA. We then analyze the implications of a NAFTA for each country, including the complementary domestic policy reforms that need to be implemented in parallel with the agreement. We conclude with a discussion of how the NAFTA could affect trade relations with nonmember countries.

---

1. Indeed, *during* the congressional debate over fast-track authority for the negotiations, US Commerce Department officials stated that the NAFTA could be completed in 1991 and submitted to Congress for approval in early 1992 (see *Wall Street Journal*, 30 April 1991, A15).

Because the NAFTA will have a greater impact on US–Mexico trade relations than on US–Canada or Canada-Mexico ties, and because the Mexican story is not widely understood outside Mexico, our analysis focuses more on that country than on Canada. However, research under way in Canada is already filling in many of the details not covered by our study.

The NAFTA: Structure and Composition

We recommend that the negotiators follow seven basic principles in drafting the rights and obligations of countries under the NAFTA.

First, the NAFTA should be modeled on and augment the Canada–US Free Trade Agreement (FTA). Most barriers to trade and investment in goods and services should be phased out; where restrictions remain, the NAFTA should significantly enlarge the scope of competition from suppliers in the other NAFTA countries. In addition, the NAFTA should augment the member countries' rights and obligations regarding *inter alia* the protection of intellectual property, disciplines on subsidies, competition in transportation services, and enhanced environmental protection. In essence, the NAFTA should produce an improved, trilateral version of the Canada–US FTA.

Second, the NAFTA should be consistent with the GATT and should build on the results of the Uruguay Round, assuming that the GATT talks bear fruit before the conclusion of the North American negotiations. GATT agreements in the "new" areas of services, investment, and intellectual property should be extended in the NAFTA; the modest GATT results in subsidies and countervailing duties should be enhanced. The NAFTA needs to deepen the trade liberalization achieved in the Uruguay Round, especially in agriculture, textiles and apparel, and other sensitive sectors and industries. In short, the NAFTA should aim to be a GATT-plus accord, one that serves as a model for future trade pacts both regionally and multilaterally.

Third, all three countries should commit themselves to symmetrical obligations. Mexico should not be accorded special treatment because of its level of development, nor should the United States or Canada be allowed lengthy transition periods to eliminate protection for their uncompetitive industries. Except for agriculture, transition periods for phasing out protection and reservations for sensitive sectors should be limited to a maximum of 10 years: prolonging the liberalization process would only generate pressure to unravel the basic commitments that underpin the NAFTA.

Fourth, because of the adjustment demands likely to arise from NAFTA commitments, the member countries should be allowed to impose safeguard actions during the transition period. However, these measures should be more narrowly limited than are standard GATT safeguards: the adjustment will result more from intraindustry specialization than from the wholesale cross-border migration of industries. To a large degree, the adjustment burdens will be moderated by rapid two-way growth in intraindustry trade. A country should only impose safeguards when NAFTA reforms result in a "substantial adverse surge" in sectoral trade with its North American partners. Moreover, unlike the so-called escape clause in the GATT, the preferred remedy should be an acceleration of liberalization in the product sector in question by the country enjoying the corresponding export surge. If trade barriers need to be raised temporarily, the NAFTA should allow only a snapback to prior tariffs (or to the tariff equivalent of prior quantitative restraints).

Fifth, the NAFTA should incorporate the general rules of origin set forth in the Canada–US FTA and should keep sectoral and product-by-product exceptions to a bare minimum. In most cases, special rules will only serve special, protectionist interests.[2] The NAFTA will need to be flexible enough to address those cases where the FTA rules of origin are overly burdensome or invite abuse. To that end, the NAFTA should establish a trinational committee to review petitions for special rules of origin or changes in existing rules, and to put forward recommendations for revision of the rules when appropriate (subject to veto by any of the member governments).

Sixth, the NAFTA should go beyond the GATT and address the intersection of trade and environmental issues. In particular, environmental commitments should be backed up by mutual surveillance, and enforcement of existing national standards should be strengthened. In addition, an effort should be made to identify those cases in which differences in standards are causing trade to be diverted to the countries with the weaker standards, and three years after the NAFTA enters into force, negotiations should be undertaken to "harmonize up" those less-demanding standards to the higher common denominator. Only if such talks fail to reach agreement on higher NAFTA standards should trade measures be applied to protect product sectors meeting stricter environmental standards. Environmental standards should not be used as a cover for protectionism, and trade countermeasures against environmental dumping should be regarded as a last resort.

Finally, membership in the NAFTA should be open to all countries in the Western Hemisphere that agree to adhere to all its obligations.[3] The NAFTA should

---

2. In that regard, we reject the proposal advocated by the Economic Strategy Institute that the NAFTA rules of origin be tailored to displace Asian imports from North America (see chapter 8).

3. Our proposed limitation of the geographical scope of this provision is not an optimal arrangement. However, a more open-ended clause that would permit the accession of East Asian and other countries would be likely to generate a protectionist backlash in Congress and lead to a significant watering down of the liberalization achieved in the NAFTA.

include an accession clause, modeled on GATT procedures, that enables candidate countries to negotiate the terms of their accession protocols with the existing NAFTA members, but that also allows current members to invoke a nonapplication provision and deny extension of the pact to any country at the time of its accession.

Implications for Mexico, the United States, and Canada

The NAFTA will promote substantially greater trade and investment flows within North America. Mexico will enjoy the biggest relative gains—and will have to make the largest adjustments—but each partner will of necessity commit itself to important trade and domestic economic reforms. This section reviews the prospective gains and the policy reforms required of Mexico, the United States, and Canada.

Mexico

As the *demandeur* of the negotiations and the smallest and least developed of the three economies, Mexico stands to gain the most in relative terms from the NAFTA trade reforms. At the same time, however, Mexico must do the most to adapt its policies to fit the NAFTA mold.

For Mexico, a NAFTA will provide above all an insurance policy. The accord will ensure relatively open access to the US market (and promises to eliminate most existing barriers to boot); the accord will also reinforce the domestic economic reforms instituted since the mid–1980s that have already sparked the Mexican economy. The insurance policy has already paid generous dividends, even before completion of the NAFTA, in the form of a large increase in foreign direct investment in Mexico, greater foreign participation in the Bolsa, and a surge in equity values. Ratification of the NAFTA should reinforce these trends. But investors will still look first and foremost at the macroeconomic climate in Mexico. To continue on a path of 4 percent to 6 percent real annual growth, Mexico must maintain fiscal discipline, progressively reduce inflation, and ensure that the peso does not become significantly overvalued. Stable macroeconomic policies and the liberalization of barriers to foreign investment are essential to Mexico's objectives in joining the NAFTA.

Projections based on the historical model discussed in chapter 3 (the IIE model) suggest that Mexico will continue to run large trade and current account deficits, with or without a NAFTA; by 1995 Mexico's global trade deficit is projected to increase by $12 billion (expressed in 1989 dollars) beyond the level likely to be achieved in the absence of a NAFTA and associated Mexican policy reforms. This projection implies a total deficit in 1995 of about $18 billion. Much of the increased Mexican deficit will represent substantial additional purchases of US goods and nonfactor services.

Mexico is already ahead of the optimistic forecast of the IIE model: the 1991 current account deficit reached $12 billion and was amply financed by substantial inflows of portfolio and foreign direct investment. Investors have clearly given Mexican policies a vote of confidence. Large capital inflows have put upward pressure on the peso, prompting President Carlos Salinas de Gortari to reduce the annual crawling peg devaluation of the peso to 2 percent for 1992.

With completion of a NAFTA—*and other, complementary economic reforms*— Mexico should continue to attract sufficient new capital inflows to accommodate the increase in net imports projected by the IIE model through 1995. Accordingly, we would expect the peso to appreciate in real terms: our results indicate a real appreciation, from the currency's January 1990 level, of 29 percent over the level that would be reached without the additional capital inflows. Indeed, by the end of 1991 the peso, as measured by its real effective exchange rate, had already appreciated by 13 percent (Morgan Guaranty Trust Co., *World Financial Markets*, January 1991 and January 1992).[4]

The IIE model also suggests that more than 600,000 new Mexican jobs could be created by 1995 as a result of the NAFTA trade reforms. We believe that most of the deterioration in the Mexican trade balance will represent increased imports of intermediate products and capital goods; in turn, these products will alleviate supply constraints in the economy and supplement Mexican production. The additional imports will not, on the whole, decrease Mexican employment: displaced Mexican workers in import-competing sectors should continue to find new job opportunities generated by the investment-led growth of the Mexican economy. Moreover, the likely appreciation of the real peso over the period through 1995 should provide a gain in real Mexican wages of almost 9 percent.

For the most part, US and Canadian "demands" on Mexico in the NAFTA negotiations entail pushing on an open door. As a result of its recent economic reforms, Mexico has already adapted many of its trade and investment policies to meet the norms established in the Canada–US FTA. The additional reforms advocated in this study are consistent with Mexico's overall economic objectives and can be achieved in the context of a comprehensive trilateral accord. However, in the absence of a NAFTA the required capital inflows would probably not be forthcoming: Mexican growth projections—and projected US trade gains— would have to be scaled back accordingly.

---

4. To be sure, Mexican productivity growth in the export sector will have to outpace the real peso appreciation to avoid the appreciation having a dampening effect on Mexican exports.

In brief, Mexican concessions in the NAFTA should reinforce and extend the reforms already adopted unilaterally since 1985. Mexican tariffs on North American trade, already reduced to an average of about 10 percent, need to be phased out entirely (as should the remaining US and Canadian tariffs).[5] In the investment arena, Mexico's Law on Foreign Investment needs to be amended to broaden the scope of activities in which inward foreign direct investment receives automatic approval, to facilitate the use of trust mechanisms as detours around constitutional constraints in politically charged restricted sectors (especially energy and basic petrochemicals), and to phase out local content and export performance requirements in specific sectors (notably automobiles). These reforms should enable Mexico to accept obligations comparable to those in FTA chapter 16 on investment (including national treatment, right of commercial presence, and international standards on expropriation and compensation).

The NAFTA will also mean the beginning of the end of the maquiladora program. With the advent of free trade in North America, the *raison d'être* for most maquiladoras will soon fade away, since duty relief on US and Canadian components that make the round trip to Mexico and back will be subsumed in the larger elimination of North American tariffs. Maquiladoras should no longer be able to receive duty drawbacks on third-country components included in exports to the United States and Canada, and they should be free to sell their products within Mexico, upon payment of appropriate duties.[6] These reforms will effectively remove the distinctions between maquiladoras and other producers, and—along with comprehensive NAFTA rules of origin—should mitigate concerns that Japan, Germany, and other countries might use Mexico as an export platform into the US market.

Finally, Mexico needs to ensure greater transparency in the administration of its trade policies and practices. Specific actions are required: adherence to the GATT code on subsidies and countervailing measures and the code on government procurement, and revision of administrative procedures in antidumping cases to guarantee open hearings and written opinions. Indeed, administrative reforms are a prerequisite for Mexican participation in a trilateral dispute settlement

---

5. As in the FTA talks, the initial tariff offers in the NAFTA negotiations posed a three-stage phaseout schedule, with the most import-sensitive items to be liberalized last (over perhaps 10 to 20 years). When the pact is up and running, however, the FTA precedent suggests that the tariff cuts will be accelerated (see *Journal of Commerce*, 27 September 1991, 12A; 7 October 1991, 5A; 9 October 1991, 4A.

6. Even though these provisions could leave third-country maquiladoras worse off than before the NAFTA, they would not constitute increased barriers to the Mexican market for foreign firms (which would violate obligations under GATT Article XXIV) since they would merely entail the removal of trade preferences that would be inconsistent with the logic of a free trade area.

mechanism for countervailing and antidumping duty cases modeled on FTA chapter 19.

Mexico's biggest challenge in the NAFTA will be to implement trade reforms in the automotive, energy, and financial services sectors, which together account for the bulk of intraregional trade in goods and services. In the automotive sector, tariffs should be eliminated immediately (and a common external tariff for the North American region should be agreed within 10 years); Mexican local content and export performance requirements should be phased out in incremental steps over 10-year and 5-year periods, respectively; Mexican import quotas should be replaced by a Canadian-style production-to-sales ratio test, which in turn should be phased out within 10 years; and the Mexican ban on used car imports should be removed within five years. These steps will promote intraindustry trade and investment and enable Mexico to become a major player in the North American automotive market.

These proposals accommodate many of the concerns of the Big Three North American automakers, which have already invested heavily in the Mexican market despite onerous government requirements and would be disadvantaged if new investors were allowed unrestricted entry. However, the longer transition periods and higher domestic content requirements proposed by the Big Three are not needed and would give excessive protection to established producers.

In the energy sector, NAFTA provisions should encourage Mexico to expand production of petroleum and natural gas and to liberalize trade in natural gas and electricity. These steps need not entail a frontal attack on Mexico's constitutional ban on foreign control of energy resources, but they will challenge Mexican policymakers to devise policies that attract foreign companies to explore and develop petroleum reserves, and to construct new gas pipelines and electricity grids. In the process, the state energy monopoly, Pemex, should be restructured into three regional holding companies to inject some competition into the Mexican energy sector, and the new companies should be empowered to engage foreign firms on a contractual basis in exploration and development projects.

In the financial services sector, a NAFTA will bring new competition and resources to, and thereby accelerate the process of structural adjustment in, Mexico's banking, insurance, and securities industries. Mexico needs to reform its financial sector in any event, and the gains anticipated under a NAFTA will reward Mexico for doing so; but the reforms need to be phased in gradually to avoid the collapse of Mexico's weak local insurance companies and multiregional banks and its vital but small securities firms.

In the banking industry, the NAFTA should allow foreign banks to acquire voting shares up to 49 percent of the shares outstanding in Mexican banks right away, and controlling stakes after five years. In addition, foreign banks should be allowed to offer wholesale banking services in Mexico immediately and to establish branch offices in Mexico within five years. In the insurance industry, the need for foreign capital and expertise is greater, and farther-reaching reforms are therefore required. The NAFTA should open the insurance market to majority foreign ownership of existing Mexican companies and allow free competition via newly formed subsidiaries within five years. For the securities industry, foreign competition should be phased in three steps: foreign securities firms should first be permitted to acquire seats on the Mexican stock exchange, later to underwrite securities within Mexico, and finally, within five years, to offer a full array of financial services to the Mexican public.

United States

A NAFTA will contribute to the broad US goal of promoting economic growth, political stability, and progress toward greater democracy in Mexico. The NAFTA's provisions should complement and augment the extensive economic reforms already under way in Mexico and provide an insurance policy against any reversion to past protectionist and interventionist policies that impeded US trade with and investment in Mexico. A NAFTA will not, however, provide immediate relief to the problem of illegal immigration, which is likely to persist for many years until the Mexican economy moves several rungs up the development ladder.

A NAFTA will serve US interests in two ways. First, a stronger Mexican economy will be a better customer for US (and Canadian) goods; US bilateral trade with Mexico should expand, generating small but not trivial net income and employment gains (as discussed below). Second, economic growth should promote political pluralism in Mexico: although democratic traditions are neither strong nor deep in Mexico, they seem to be taking root.[7]

The aggregate economic effects of a NAFTA on the US economy will be small. But for the southwestern states, and particularly the border states of California, Arizona, New Mexico, and Texas, the NAFTA is seen as a boon to local prosperity. Several important cities in the region, including San Diego, Tucson, Albuquerque, El Paso, Dallas, Houston, and to a lesser extent Los Angeles, see their futures tied to the success of the talks.

From a broader perspective, the NAFTA will encourage economies of scale in production and promote intraindustry specialization. As a result, many US firms will benefit from lower costs and higher productivity, improving their ability to compete against foreign suppliers both in North America and in world markets.

---

7. President Salinas negotiated electoral reforms with the main opposition parties after the 1988 elections, and subsequent elections have become more competitive, especially at the federal level. The commitment to democratic reforms was underscored in August 1991 when Salinas coerced his party's candidates to resign from governorships in two states after allegations of electoral fraud prompted large popular demonstrations.

On the basis of the IIE historical model discussed in chapter 3, we believe the NAFTA, *in conjunction with continuing Mexican economic policy reforms,* will generate, by 1995, $16.7 billion in additional US exports and $7.7 billion in additional US imports annually, for a net gain of $9 billion in the bilateral US trade balance with Mexico by 1995 (figures expressed in 1989 dollars). These figures represent only small increments in overall US trade volumes, but substantial increases in bilateral US exports and imports (up 51 percent and 25 percent, respectively, over 1989 levels).

In part, US export gains will reflect both intraindustry specialization and increased Mexican spending on capital goods. These factors should lead, for example, to a sharp increase in US exports of assembled automobiles and parts (see chapter 11) and high-grade steel goods (see chapter 12), as well as industrial chemicals. In addition, US pharmaceutical producers should be able to expand trade with Mexico under the new Mexican intellectual property regime, and US farmers should gradually increase their share of the Mexican market for grains.

Net US export expansion should generate about 130,000 net additional US jobs. This represents an insignificant proportion of overall US employment; consequently, there should be no measurable impact on overall or even sectoral US real wage rates.

However, the employment impact of the NAFTA will vary by sector, by region, and by job type. Although the aggregate impact of a NAFTA on US employment will be positive, the total masks important shifts in employment between firms in the same industry, between different industries, and between different regions of the country. We believe that more than 100,000 US workers will be displaced over a 10-year transition period; many of these workers will find new jobs in growing export sectors, but the adjustment burden will fall more heavily on unskilled low-wage workers than on skilled, high-wage workers (see below).

The NAFTA itself should bring wide-ranging benefits for the United States in the "new" areas of the global trade agenda. In the intellectual property and investment areas, for example, new NAFTA provisions should lock in recent Mexican legislative reforms and yield three specific benefits: a resolution of the longstanding dispute with Canada over pharmaceutical patents (if not resolved sooner in the GATT talks); new protection for US investors and holders of intellectual property rights in Mexico; and establishment of a model for future pacts with other developing countries. In services, US firms should win new opportunities in the Mexican market; this is especially so with respect to financial services (and thus provides further justification for a revival of US efforts to reform its own financial services laws, the Glass-Steagall and McFadden acts in particular).

The main US concessions involve the elimination of trade barriers, mainly in import-sensitive sectors such as agriculture and textiles and apparel. The NAFTA is likely to go beyond the Uruguay Round in eradicating both tariffs and quotas in the textile and apparel industries. Although the specter of free trade is anathema to most US textile and apparel firms and workers, existing barriers against Mexico are already quite low because of special US tariff preferences and recent quota expansions; hence, further liberalization should not severely disrupt the US industry.

Agricultural reform, especially in fruits and vegetables, will be much harder. In that sector we recommend an extended phaseout of tariffs and other trade barriers as part of a grand bargain that opens up the Mexican grain market to US and Canadian suppliers in return for increased access to the US and Canadian markets for Mexican fruits and vegetables.

The giant automotive sector offers an opportunity for the United States to augment the trade benefits already derived from the US–Canada Auto Pact and the extensive system of maquiladora operations in Mexico. In this sector the United States should eliminate its tariffs (especially the high "chicken war" tariff on light trucks) and extend the automotive rules of origin in the Canada–US FTA to include Mexican parts and vehicles. In addition, the two-fleet rule for the application of corporate average fuel economy (CAFE) standards, if not eliminated, should be modified to allow cars produced in Canada or Mexico to qualify as either foreign or domestic at the option of the producer.

Again, we believe that rules of origin should be strict enough to preclude Japanese and German producers from using Mexico as an export platform to the US market, yet not so strict as to preempt competition and discourage the restructuring of the North American industry. The current 50 percent North American content requirement in the Canada–US FTA best meets this test. Moreover, if the three countries move toward the establishment of a common external tariff for automobiles, the controversy over origin rules should rapidly abate.

As a practical matter, the export platform problem is overstated since the difference between the zero tariff rate under a NAFTA and the US MFN tariff for assembled automobiles is small and likely to be reduced further in the Uruguay Round. However, the export platform argument serves to draw attention to two issues: the export of light trucks by Mexico (currently subject to a 25 percent US tariff) and the concern that, in the future, all Mexican (and Canadian) production could be exempt from quotas established pursuant to new US safeguard actions on automobiles.

In most other respects, US "concessions" will involve the extension to Mexico of rights comparable to those accorded to Canada under the FTA. Most important, this includes rights under the dispute settlement mechanism to consult on future changes in US trade remedy laws, to contest final rulings in US countervail and antidumping cases, and to be exempted from general safeguard actions that sideswipe regional trade (i.e., cases in which Mexican or Canadian exports to the US market are a small portion of total US imports).

Canada

Canada is the reluctant third party to the NAFTA negotiations. Its economic ties to Mexico are growing rapidly, but from a small base; Canada's economic interests remain overwhelmingly in the US market. The NAFTA provides Canada a fresh opportunity to resolve bilateral problems with the United States that were not adequately addressed in the FTA (and where in many instances Mexico shares Canadian concerns).

Like the United States, Canada can expect growth in its trade with Mexico under a NAFTA to be small in relation to its overall trade, but large compared with current bilateral trade flows. The IIE model suggests that as a result of the NAFTA, by 1995, Canadian imports from Mexico could grow by an additional $350 million (in 1989 dollars), and exports to Mexico by an extra $200 million (these figures represent increases of 24 percent and 38 percent, respectively, from 1989 levels). Much of the additional trade should result from Mexican assembly operations in automobiles and parts, and in textiles and apparel. Since about one-third of Canadian exports to the United States are in the automotive sector, NAFTA reforms could indirectly lead to significant pressure on the Canadian automobile and parts industries.

The most important gain that Canada can expect to realize from the NAFTA is an ability to influence the process of setting rules in specific sectors and issues, especially the rules of origin. Canada should also benefit from NAFTA reforms in the areas of financial services, government procurement, and subsidies and countervailing duties. The major Canadian banks, such as the Royal Bank of Canada and the Canadian Imperial Bank of Commerce, should gain access to new markets in both the United States and Mexico as a result of the NAFTA reforms and prospective US banking legislation. In addition, the giant Canadian property developers, such as Olympia & York, could eventually become players in Mexico.

Canada faces two main challenges in the NAFTA: it needs to commit itself to reform of the Auto Pact and to revise its patent procedures for pharmaceuticals. Following the Mexican precedent, the local content and production-to-sales tests in the Auto Pact designed to safeguard Canadian producers should be phased out over a 10-year period. However, as noted above, the existing FTA rule of origin (50 percent) for automobiles should be maintained, but it should be supplemented by a new test to prevent roll-up abuses (see chapter 8).

The negotiation of NAFTA provisions on intellectual property will put Canada under strong pressure to accept obligations regarding pharmaceutical patents comparable to those recently legislated by Mexico. The pharmaceutical issue is a hangover from the FTA, but one that may well be preempted by an agreement on trade-related intellectual property issues in the Uruguay Round.

The Domestic Agenda

The trilateral negotiations highlight the need for domestic policy reforms in each country. These reforms should be pursued whether a trade pact is concluded or not, but they will become even more necessary with the signing of a NAFTA. As the US congressional debate in the spring of 1991 demonstrated, reforms of labor and environmental policies need to complement the NAFTA provisions.

Regulatory standards in these areas are now surprisingly similar in the three countries. But Mexico's inadequate enforcement of its standards over the years has allowed abusive labor practices and severe pollution problems to persist and to become a stumbling block to the NAFTA negotiations. Mexico's labor and environmental policies are explored in chapters 5 through 7. Our recommendations suggest that the solutions lie in both enhanced enforcement of existing laws and regulations, and increased financial commitment to labor adjustment programs and investment in environmental infrastructure.

Labor Issues

The NAFTA itself is likely to contain few provisions relating to workers' rights or trade in labor services beyond the limited obligations relating to temporary access for business persons in the Canada–US FTA. It will not deal at all with immigration issues. Overall, however, the main concern of labor in the United States and Canada is the threat to jobs.

In the aggregate, the NAFTA will have little effect on the US labor market or on US wages. Nonetheless, the aggregate trends can mask significant employment shifts within and between industries; in particular, unskilled US and Canadian workers are likely to bear a disproportionate share of the labor adjustment burden.

US policy therefore needs to devise a better mechanism to ease the transition from old jobs to new jobs. Dislocated American workers should be provided effective job retraining and income maintenance programs, and private firms should be encouraged to expand apprenticeship and other training programs. All this will cost money: we believe that the United States should budget at least $900 million over the next five years to handle up to an additional 112,000 US workers who could be dislocated by NAFTA trade reforms.

For Mexico, the NAFTA should produce clear gains of more than 600,000 new jobs. Mexico's main labor challenge will be to provide better enforcement of its labor laws, meaningful trade union representation, and a progressive upgrading of labor standards through both NAFTA commitments and domestic policy reforms.

In the short run, Mexico's increasing prosperity is unlikely to mitigate the problem of illegal migration to the United States. The rapid growth in the number of young workers in the northern Mexican cities, coupled with continuing large wage disparities between the United States and Mexico, will continue to attract Mexican workers across the border. It will take decades for economic development to stem the flow of illegal immigrants to the United States. As a way station toward accepting this fact of economic life, the United States should maintain (but not dramatically strengthen) its current border control program and its sanctions against employers who hire illegal aliens, and allow Mexican economic growth to gradually assuage the migration problem. Meanwhile, the NAFTA should authorize trinational reports on labor conditions in the region—including migration issues—to help guide labor adjustment policies in each country.

Environment

The United States and Mexico both need to address concerns relating to sustainable development and environmental dumping. Degradation of air, water, and land resources has already put huge strains on the environmental infrastructure. Recent reforms of Mexican laws and policies align them with North American norms, but the residue of years of environmental neglect will be difficult to redress and will require substantial public and private resources for cleanup and prevention programs.

As detailed in chapter 7, both Mexico and the United States need to commit billions of dollars to ensure adequate water quality and sewage disposal. The funds will need to come from general budgetary resources; schemes to earmark taxes and tariffs to fund environmental programs are neither effective nor desirable. Proposals to raise money through countervailing duties on environmentally subsidized or dumped goods are particularly suspect, both because countervailing actions often would not be pursued, given the substantial degree of intrafirm trade, and because countervailing actions are a sure-fire way to generate international ill will.

Instead, both countries need to establish minimum physical targets for pollution abatement, tighten regulatory standards that promote private investment in pollution control technologies, and impose specific user fees based on the "polluter pays" principle.

When dealing with issues relating to environmental standards, NAFTA provisions should dispel concerns about environmental dumping (and its inverse, overly stringent standards acting as nontariff barriers). The goal of the NAFTA provisions should be, as stated above, to "harmonize up" national standards. NAFTA rules should allow countries to bar trade in goods that violate internationally agreed standards, if local products are treated in a similar fashion. Existing federal *and subfederal* standards should be accepted "as is." Each country should be allowed to set standards higher than international norms, but new or revised standards should be subject to consultation with the other NAFTA partners to ensure that they do not mask protectionist intent. In addition, trilateral reports should be issued annually on the enforcement of environmental standards in each country. NAFTA dispute settlement procedures should be available to challenge new standards that act as a disguised restriction on intraregional commerce, and, as a last resort, to pursue trade "compensation" if adequate steps are not taken to enforce environmental standards.

The NAFTA and the World Trading System

The three participants in the NAFTA talks conduct about 60 percent of their total trade with countries outside the region. Each of the three depends on the GATT system to safeguard access to foreign markets and to continue efforts at multilateral trade liberalization. As the economies of North America restructure and grow in response to the combined stimulus of domestic economic reforms and NAFTA commitments, and thus become more competitive in world markets, the GATT system will become even more important.

For the United States, export expansion depends importantly on a strong and effective multilateral trading system. For Canada and Mexico, GATT rules serve as an effective ally in trade relations with their oversized neighbor. The NAFTA will thus reinforce the strong ties of the three countries of North America to the world trading system.

If the accord follows the guidelines noted above, the NAFTA should complement the results of the Uruguay Round of multilateral trade negotiations, and should be consistent with the provisions of GATT Article XXIV, which sanctions free trade areas that have comprehensive trade coverage provided they do not raise new barriers to third-country trade.

The NAFTA should meet those tests even though some foreign suppliers may find it harder to compete because of reduced drawback subsidies and new origin rules. To ensure that those NAFTA provisions do not mask new protection, however, the three countries should invite regular in-depth GATT reviews of NAFTA operations through both Article XXIV consultations and reports of the Trade Policy Review Mechanism. This high standard of review would set a valuable precedent for greater GATT surveillance of other preferential trading areas, including the rapidly expanding European Economic Area.

The NAFTA negotiations hold particular importance for the other countries of Latin America. The negotiated outcome is likely to provide a model for the types of rights and obligations that the United States will expect to seek in trade pacts under the Enterprise for the Americas Initiative; indeed, as suggested above, the

NAFTA itself could even become the text to which those countries eventually adhere. Meanwhile, the NAFTA may lead to a modest diversion of trade toward Mexican suppliers and away from other Latin American suppliers in a few important industries and sectors (e.g., apparel and agriculture).

The trade effects of the NAFTA on third countries depend both on the extent of liberalization achieved in the NAFTA itself and on trade reforms negotiated in the Uruguay Round. Most GATT members will generally come out ahead whatever happens with the NAFTA, as long as the Uruguay Round produces substantial liberalization of US tariffs and quotas; indeed, the extent of liberalization of US agricultural and apparel quotas seems to be the most important determinant of whether the NAFTA will divert trade from third-country suppliers. Trade diversion is likely to be greatest if the NAFTA reforms proceed in the absence of a successful GATT round. In that event, the erosion of multilateral discipline will make it easier for protectionist forces within the United States to offset North American liberalization by maintaining quotas against third-country imports, and by invoking excessively strict rules of origin.

Potentially, the benefits of a NAFTA extend well beyond the trade among the three countries of North America. For its full potential to be realized, the NAFTA needs a successful GATT system, and vice versa.

References

Advisory Council on Adjustment. 1989. *Adjusting to Win: Report of the Advisory Council on Adjustment*. Ottawa: Advisory Council on Adjustment.

American Federation of Labor and Congress of Industrial Organizations (AFL–CIO). 1991. *Exploiting Both Sides: US–Mexico Free Trade*. Washington: AFL–CIO (February).

Anderson, Jean. 1989. "Resolving Trade Disputes Through Binational Panels and Extraordinary Challenges: Issues in Implementing Chapter 19 of the Canada–United States Free Trade Agreement." In Richard G. Dearden, Michael M. Hart, and Debra P. Steger, eds., *Living with Free Trade: Canada, the Free Trade Agreement and the GATT*, 11–17. Halifax: Institute for Research on Public Policy.

Automotive Parts Manufacturers' Association. 1990. *The Mexican Auto Industry: A Competitor for the 1990's*. Toronto: Automotive Parts Manufacturers' Association (September).

Barro, Robert J., and Xavier Sala-i-Martin. 1991. "Convergence Across States and Regions." Cambridge, MA: Harvard University (mimeographed, April).

Baucus, Max. 1991. "Protecting the Global Commons: The Nexus Between Trade and Environment Policy." Speech delivered at the Institute for International Economics, Washington (30 October).

Bean, Frank D., Barry Edmonston, and Jeffrey S. Passel. 1990. *Undocumented Migration to the United States: IRCA and the Experience of the 1980's*. Washington: Urban Institute Press.

Bello, Judith H., Alan F. Holmer, and Debra A. Kelly. 1991. "Midterm Report on Binational Dispute Settlement Under the United States–Canada Free-Trade Agreement." *The International Lawyer* 25, no. 2 (Summer 1991): 489–516.

Ben-David, Dan. 1991. "Equalizing Exchange: A Study of the Effects of Trade Liberalization." *NBER Working Papers* 3706. Cambridge, MA: National Bureau of Economic Research.

Bolsa Mexicana de Valores and Instituto Mexicano del Mercado de Capitales. 1990. *How to Invest in Mexico: A Guide to the Securities Market*. Mexico City: Bolsa Mexicana de Valores and Instituto Mexicano de Capitales (June).

Borjas, Georges, Richard Freeman, and Lawrence Katz. 1991. "On the Labor Market Effects of Immigration and Trade." *NBER Working Papers* 3761. Cambridge, MA: National Bureau of Economic Research.

Botella, Ovidio, Enrique Garcia, and José Giral B. 1991. "Textiles: the Mexican Perspective." In Sidney Weintraub, ed., *U.S.–Mexican Industrial Integration: The Road to Free Trade*, 193–220. Boulder, CO: Westview Press.

Brown, Drusilla K., Alan V. Deardorff, and Robert M. Stern. 1991. "A North American Free Trade Agreement: Analytical Issues and Computational Assessment." Medford, MA: Tufts University, and Ann Arbor: University of Michigan (mimeographed, 27–28 June).

Bucay, Benito F. 1991. "Petrochemicals: Mexican Perspective." In Sidney Weintraub, ed., *U.S.–Mexican Industrial Integration: The Road to Free Trade,* 119–36. Boulder, CO: Westview Press.

Buzzanell, Peter. 1991. "Mexico's Sugar Industry in Transition: Implications for Sweetener Trade with the United States." In Economic Research Division, *Sugar and Sweetener: Situation and Outlook Report,* 21–35. Washington: US Department of Agriculture (March).

Canada. Standing Senate Committee on Foreign Affairs of the Parliament of Canada. 1990. "Monitoring the Implementation of the Canada–United States Free Trade Agreement." Ottawa: Canadian Government Publishing Centre (March).

Canadian Bankers Association. 1991. "The Mexican Financial Services Market: The Canadian Perspective." Montreal: Canadian Bankers Association (March).

Carr, Graham. 1991. "Trade Liberalization and the Political Economy of Culture: An International Perspective on FTA." *Canadian-American Public Policy Papers* 6. Orono, ME: Canadian-American Center, University of Maine.

Charnovitz, Steve. 1991. "Exploring the Environmental Exceptions in GATT Article XX." *Journal of World Trade* 25, no. 5 (October): 37–55.

Chrispin, Barbara R. 1990. "Employment and Manpower Development in the Maquiladora Industry: Reaching Maturity." In Khosrow Fatemi, ed., *The Maquiladora Industry: Economic Solution or Problem?* 71–90. New York: Praeger.

Chrysler Corp., Ford Motor Company, and General Motors Corp. 1991. "Proposed Policy Positions for the Automotive Provisions of a North America Free Trade Agreement" (9 September).

Cline, William R. 1990. *The Future of World Trade in Textiles and Apparel,* rev. ed. Washington: Institute for International Economics.

Collins, Susan M., and Dani Rodrik. 1991. *Eastern Europe and the Soviet Union in the World Economy.* POLICY ANALYSES IN INTERNATIONAL ECONOMICS 32. Washington: Institute for International Economics.

Comisión Economica para América Latina y el Caribe (CEPAL), International Trade and Development Division. 1991. "El Regreso de Paises Latinoamericanos al Mercado Internacional de Capitales Privados: Una Nota Preliminar." Santiago, Chile: CEPAL (April).

Conger, Lucy. 1991. "The Banks Go on the Block." *Institutional Investor* 25 (March): 123–29.

Contreras, Celso Cartas. 1987. "The Agricultural Sector's Contributions to the Import-Substituting Industrialization Process in Mexico." In Bruce F. Johnston, Cassio Luiselli, Celso Cartas Contreras, and Roger R. Norton, eds., *U.S.–Mexico Relations: Agriculture and Rural Development*, 111–22. Stanford, CA: Stanford University Press.

Council on Scientific Affairs, American Medical Association. 1990. "A Permanent US–Mexico Border Environmental Health Commission." JAMA: Journal of the American Medical Association 263, no. 24 (27 June): 3319–21.

Diwan, Ishac, and Nemat Shafik. 1991. "Towards a North-South Deal on the Environment." Paper presented at a symposium on "International Trade and the Environment" sponsored by the World Bank, Washington (21–22 November).

Economic Council of Canada. 1988. *Managing Adjustment: Policies for Trade-Sensitive Industries*. Ottawa: Canadian Government Publishing Centre.

Eggerstedt, H. 1991. "Country Operations (Mexico)." Washington: World Bank (unpublished, March).

Embassy of Mexico in the United States. 1991. *Protecting the Environment: Mexico's Public Works Program for the Border Region*. Washington: Embassy of Mexico in the United States.

Erzan, Refik, and Alexander Yeats. 1991. "Prospects for United States–Latin America Free Trade Areas; Empirical Evidence from the South." Washington: World Bank, International Trade Division (30 May).

Fatemi, Khosrow, ed. 1990. *The Maquiladora Industry: Economic Solution or Problem?* New York: Praeger.

Feltham, Ivan R., Stuart A. Salen, Robert F. Mathieson, and Ronald Wonnacott. 1991. "Competition (Antitrust) and Antidumping Laws in the Context of the Canada–U.S. Free Trade Agreement." Committee on Canada–United States Relations of the Canadian Chamber of Commerce and the United States Chamber of Commerce.

Field, Alfred, and Edward M. Graham. 1991. "Job Relocation of Workers Losing Employment in the State of North Carolina Due to Mass Layoffs or Plant Closing: A Comparison of the Textile and Apparel Industries with Other Industries." Department of Economics, University of North Carolina (unpublished working paper, February).

Fix, Michael, ed. 1991. *Employer Sanctions' Implementation, Impact, and Reform*. Washington: Urban Institute Press.

Flamm, Kenneth. 1990. "Semiconductors." In Gary C. Hufbauer, ed., *Europe 1992: An American Perspective*, 273–76. Washington: Brookings Institution.

George, Edward Y. 1990. "What Does the Future Hold for the Maquiladora Industry?" In Khosrow Fatemi, ed., *The Maquiladora Industry: Economic Solution or Problem?* 219–33. New York: Praeger.

Gephardt, Richard A. 1991. "News from the House Majority Leader." Speech delivered at the Institute for International Economics, Washington (10 September).

Giberson, Michael. 1991. "CAFE: Policy Failure and Proposals for Reform." *Economic Perspective Fact Sheet* (14 October). Washington: Citizens for a Sound Economy Foundation.

Giermanski, Jim. 1991. "The Potential Effect of a North American Free-Trade Agreement on the United States Maquila Industry in Mexico." Laredo, TX: Laredo State University (March).

Giermanski, Jim, Kelly S. Kirkland, Eduardo Martinez, David M. Neipert, and Tom Tetzel. 1990. "U.S. Trucking in Mexico: A Free Trade Issue." Laredo, TX: Texas Center for Border Economic and Enterprise Development, Laredo State University (September).

Grant, Michael. 1991. "Canada's Business Links with Mexico's Maquiladora Industry." Ottawa: Conference Board of Canada (June).

Grant, Michael, Stelios Loizides, and Mahmood Iqbal. 1991. "The Implications of Mexico's Maquiladora Industry for the Canadian Economy." Ottawa: Conference Board of Canada (January).

Grayson, George W. 1988. *Oil and Mexican Foreign Policy*. Pittsburgh: University of Pittsburgh Press.

Greenwald, Joseph. 1990. "Negotiating Strategy." In Gary C. Hufbauer, ed., *Europe 1992: An American Perspective*, 345–88. Washington: Brookings Institution.

Grossman, Gene, and Alan Krueger. 1991. "Environmental Impacts of a North American Free Trade Agreement." Paper presented at a conference on "The US–Mexico Free Trade Agreement," sponsored by the Secretaría de Comercio y Fomento Industrial (3 October).

Hall, Kent D., and Carlos Livas-Hernandez. 1990. *Mexican Agriculture Databook*. TAMRC Information Report No. IR-3-90. College Station: Texas Agricultural Market Research Center (September).

Hart, Michael M. 1989. "The Future on the Table: The Continuing Agenda under the Canada–United States Free Trade Agreement." In Richard G. Dearden, Michael M. Hart, and Debra P. Steger, eds., *Living with Free Trade: Canada, the Free Trade Agreement and the GATT*, 67–131. Ottawa: Centre for Trade Policy and Law, and Halifax: Institute for Research on Public Policy.

Hart, Michael. 1990. *A North American Free Trade Agreement: The Strategic Implications for Canada*. Ottawa: Centre for Trade Policy and Law, and Halifax: Institute for Research on Public Policy.

Hayes, Douglas L. 1991. "The All-American Canal Lining Project: A Catalyst for Rational and Comprehensive Groundwater Management on the United States–Mexican Border?" *Transboundary Resources Report* 5, no. 1: 1–3.

Herzog, Lawrence A. 1991. "Transfrontier Ecological Planning: Some Lessons from Western European–United States–Mexico Border Region Comparisons." *Transboundary Resources Report* 5, no. 2 (Summer): 6–7.

Hinojosa-Ojeda, Raul, and Sherman Robinson. 1991. "Alternative Scenarios of U.S.–Mexico Integration: A Computable General Equilibrium Approach." *Working Papers* 609. Oakland: Department of Agricultural and Resource Economics, Division of Agriculture and Natural Resources, University of California. (April).

Horlick, Gary N., Geoffrey D. Oliver, and Debra P. Steger. 1988. "Dispute Resolution Mechanism." In Jeffrey J. Schott and Murray G. Smith, eds., *The Canada–United States Free Trade Agreement: The Global Impact,* 65–100. Washington: Institute for International Economics, and Halifax: Institute for Research on Public Policy.

Hufbauer, Gary Clyde. 1989. *The Free Trade Debate: Report of the Twentieth Century Fund Task Force on the Future of American Trade Policy.* New York: Priority Press.

Hufbauer, Gary C., ed. 1990. *Europe 1992: An American Perspective.* Washington: Brookings Institution.

Hufbauer, Gary C. 1992. *U.S. Taxation of International Income: Blueprint for Reform.* Washington: Institute for International Economics (forthcoming).

Hufbauer, Gary Clyde, and Jeffrey J. Schott. 1991. "Reaching for the Stars." *Latin Finance* (March): 52.

Hufbauer, Gary Clyde, Diane T. Berliner, and Kimberly Ann Elliott. 1986. *Trade Protection in the United States: 31 Case Studies.* Washington: Institute for International Economics.

Hunter, Linda, James Markusen, and Thomas Rutherford. 1991. "US–Mexico Free Trade and the Structure of the North American Auto Industry." San Diego State University, University of Colorado, and University of Western Ontario (preliminary, January).

Husband, David, Ron Hood, David Swimmer, Rosemary MacDonald, and Ash Ahmad. 1991. "The Opportunities and Challenges of North American Free Trade: A Canadian Perspective." *Working Papers* 7. Ottawa: Investment Canada (April).

Interindustry Economic Research Fund. 1990. "Industrial Effects of a Free Trade Agreement Between Mexico and the USA." Washington: US Department of Labor (September).

Johnson, Jon. 1991. "The Effects of the Canada–US Free Trade Agreement on the Auto Pact." Paper presented at a research workshop on "The Auto Industry: Responding to a Changing North American Trade Environment," sponsored by the Centre for Trade Policy and Law, Carleton University (3–4 October).

Johnston, Bruce F., Cassio Luiselli, Celso Cartas Contreras, and Roger D. Norton. 1987. *U.S.–Mexico Relations: Agriculture and Rural Development.* Stanford: Stanford University Press.

Kamp, Dick, and Mary Kelly. 1991. "Mexico–US Trade Negotiations and the Environment: Exploring the Issues." Naco, AZ: Border Ecology Project, and Austin: Texas Center for Policy Studies (January).

Kneese, Allen V. 1990. "Environmental Stress and Political Conflicts: Salinity in the Colorado River." *Transboundary Resources Report* 4, no. 2 (Summer): 1–2.

Kochan, Leslie. 1988. "The Maquiladoras and Toxics: The Hidden Costs of Production South of the Border" (publication no. 186). Washington: American Federation of Labor and Congress of Industrial Organizations (February).

KPMG Peat Marwick. 1991. "Analysis of Economic Effects of Free Trade Agreement Between the United States and Mexico." Washington: US Council of the Mexico–US Business Committee (March).

Laird, Sam. 1990. "US Trade Policy and Mexico: Simulations of Possible Trade Regime Changes." Washington: International Economics Division, World Bank (August).

Leamer, Edward E. 1991. "The Probable Effects of a US–Mexican Free Trade Agreement on US Wages and Manufacturing Output." Los Angeles: Anderson Graduate School of Management and Department of Economics, University of California, Los Angeles.

Lenz, Allen J. 1992. *Narrowing the U.S. Current Account Deficit: A Sectoral Assessment.* Washington: Institute for International Economics.

Levy, Santiago, and Sweder van Wijnbergen. 1991a. "Labor Markets, Migration and Welfare: Agriculture in the Mexico–US Free Trade Agreement." Boston: Boston University, and Washington: World Bank (June).

Levy, Santiago, and Sweder van Wijnbergen. 1991b. "Transition Problems in Economic Reform: Agriculture in the Mexico–US Free Trade Agreement." Washington: World Bank (preliminary draft, November).

Lipsey, Richard G. 1990. "Canada at the U.S.–Mexico Free Trade Dance: Wallflower or Partner?" *Commentary* (whole issue, August). Toronto: C. D. Howe Institute.

Lipsey, Richard G. 1991. "The Case for Trilateralism." In Steven Globerman, ed., *Continental Accord: North American Economic Integration,* 89–123. Vancouver: Fraser Institute.

Lipsey, Richard G., and Murray G. Smith. 1989. "The Canada–US Free Trade Agreement: Special Case or Wave of the Future?" In Jeffrey J. Schott, ed., *Free Trade Areas and U.S. Trade Policy,* 317–36. Washington: Institute for International Economics.

Low, Patrick. 1991. "Trade Measures and Environmental Quality: The Implications for Mexico's Exports." Washington: World Bank (preliminary draft, June).

Lucas, Robert, David Wheeler, and Hemamala Hettige. 1991. "Economic Development, Environmental Regulation, and the International Migration of Toxic Industrial Pollution: 1960–1988." Paper presented at a symposium on "International Trade and the Environment," sponsored by the World Bank, Washington (21–22 November).

Manke, Richard B. 1979. *Mexican Oil and Natural Gas: Political, Strategic and Economic Implications*. New York: Praeger.

Mares, David R. 1987. "The U.S.–Mexico Winter-Vegetable Trade: Climate, Economics, and Politics." In Bruce F. Johnston, Cassio Luiselli, Celso Cartas Contreras, and Roger R. Norton, eds., *U.S.–Mexico Relations: Agriculture and Rural Development*, 178–79. Stanford: Stanford University Press.

Maskus, Keith E. 1989. "The Economics of International Protection of Intellectual Property Rights: Background and Analysis." Report to the US Department of Labor, Bureau of International Labor Affairs (June).

McCleery, Robert, and Clark Reynolds. 1991. "A Study of the Impact of a US–Mexico Free Trade Agreement on Medium-Term Employment, Wages, and Production in the United States: Are New Labor Market Policies Needed?" Stanford: Americas Program, Stanford University.

Mexico. Economic Adviser to the Ministry of Trade and Industry. 1990. "Tariff Elimination Betweeen the United States and Canada." Mexico: Ministry of Trade and Industry.

Mexico. Ministry of Trade and Industry (SECOFI). 1990. *Profile and Prospects for the Mexican Automotive Industry*. Mexico City: SECOFI (September).

Mexico. Secretaría de Energia, Minas, e Industria Paraestatal (SEMIP). 1990. *Programa Nacional de Modernización Energética 1990–1994*. Mexico: SEMIP (January).

Mexico. Secretaría de Hacienda y Crédito Públicos (SHCP). 1991. *The Tax System in Mexico*. Mexico City: SHCP (April).

Morici, Peter. 1991. *Trade Talks With Mexico: A Time For Realism*. Washington: National Planning Association.

Motor and Equipment Manufacturers Association (MEMA). 1991a. "Discussion Paper: Rule of Origin for the US–Mexico-Canada Free Trade Agreement." Washington: MEMA (14 October).

Motor and Equipment Manufacturers Association (MEMA). 1991b. "Objectives and Proposed Policy Approaches of the US Motor Vehicle Parts and Equipment Manufaturing Industry for a North American Free Trade Agreement." Washington: MEMA (14 October).

National Wildlife Federation. 1990. "Environmental Concerns Related to a United States–Mexico-Canada Free Trade Agreement." Washington: National Wildlife Federation (November).

North-South Institute. 1990. "Canadian Participation in USA–Mexico-Canada Free Trade Discussions: Preliminary Agricultural Perspectives." Ottawa: North-South Institute (October).

Organization for Economic Cooperation and Development (OECD). 1990. *Foreign Direct Investment and Industrial Development in Mexico*. Paris: OECD.

Organization for Economic Cooperation and Development (OECD). 1990–91. OECD *Economic Surveys—Canada*. Paris: OECD.

Overseas Development Council and World Wildlife Fund. 1991. *Environmental Challenges to International Trade Policy*. Washington: Overseas Development Council and World Wildlife Fund.

Palmeter, David. 1989. "The FTA Rules of Origin: Boon or Boondoggle?" In Richard G. Dearden, Michael M. Hart, and Debra P. Steger, eds., *Living With Free Trade: Canada, the Free Trade Agreement and the* GATT, 41–48. Ottawa: Centre for Trade Policy and Law, and Halifax: Institute for Research on Public Policy.

Palmeter, David. 1991. "Supporting Dolphins and GATT." *Journal of Commerce* (1 October): 12A.

Papageorgiou, Demetris, Michael Michaely, and Armeane M. Choksi, eds. 1991. *Liberalizing Foreign Trade: Lessons of Experience in the Developing World* (7 vols.). Washington: World Bank.

Papametriou, Demetrious G., and Mark J. Miller, eds. 1983. *The Unavoidable Issue: U.S. Immigration Policy in the 1980s*. Philadelphia: Institute for the Study of Human Issues.

Plourde, André. 1990. "Canada's International Obligations in Energy and the Free-Trade Agreement with the United States," *Journal of World Trade* 24, no. 5 (October): 35–36.

Prestowitz, Clyde V., Jr., and Robert B. Cohen. 1991. *The New North American Order: A Win-Win Strategy for US–Mexican Trade*, Washington: Economic Strategy Institute and University Press of America.

Price Waterhouse. 1990. *Corporate Taxes: A Worldwide Summary*. New York: Price Waterhouse.

Ramirez de la O, Rogelio. 1991. "The Mexican Economy: Outlook, Restructuring, and the Investment Climate." Paper presented at a conference on "Trade and Investment Prospects with Mexico," San Diego (9–11 January).

Ronfeldt, David, Richard Nehring, and Arturo Gandara. 1980. "Mexico's Petroleum and US Policy: Implication for the 1980s." Washington: US Department of Energy (June).

Rosson, C. Parr, III, and Amy L. Angel. 1991. "The U.S.–Mexico Free Trade Agreement: General Economic Issues." TAMRC *International Market Research Report* IM-12-91. College Station: Texas A&M University (April).

Ryan, Leo. 1991. "Canadian Culture Under Siege?" *Journal of Commerce* (8 August): 4A.

Salinas-León, Roberto. 1991. "A Mexican View of North American Free Trade." *Foreign Policy Briefs* 9. Washington: Cato Institute (21 May).

Sandoval, Eduardo. 1990. "CMP Industry Sector Analysis: Automobile Spare Parts and Repair Equipment." Washington: US Department of Commerce (March).

Schoepfle, Gregory K. 1990a. "Implications for US Employment of the Recent Growth in Mexican Maquiladoras." Washington: US Department of Labor, Bureau of International Labor Affairs.

Schoepfle, Gregory K. 1990b. "US–Mexico Free Trade Agreement: The Maquilazation of Mexico?" Washington: US Department of Labor, Bureau of International Labor Affairs (April).

Schoepfle, Gregory, and José Pérez-López. 1990. "The Impact of Maquiladoras on United States National Employment and Employment in Selected Industrial Sectors." Washington: US Department of Labor (March).

Schott, Jeffrey J. 1988. *United States–Canada Free Trade: An Evaluation of the Agreement.* POLICY ANALYSES IN INTERNATIONAL ECONOMICS 24. Washington: Institute for International Economics (April).

Schott, Jeffrey J., ed. 1989a. *Free Trade Areas and U.S. Trade Policy.* Washington: Institute for International Economics.

Schott, Jeffrey J. 1989b. *More Free Trade Areas?* POLICY ANALYSES IN INTERNATIONAL ECONOMICS 27. Washington: Institute for International Economics (May).

Schott, Jeffrey J. 1991. "Trading Blocs and the World Trading System." *The World Economy* 14, no. 1 (March): 1–17.

Schott, Jeffrey J., and Murray G. Smith. 1988. "Services and Investment." In Jeffrey J. Schott and Murray G. Smith, eds., *The Canada–United States Free Trade Agreement: The Global Impact,* 137–50. Washington: Institute for International Economics.

Scott, Richard C., and Joel K. Worley. 1990. "The Use of Maquiladoras by Non-American Companies: The Case of Japanese Multinationals." In Khosrow Fatemi, ed., *The Maquiladora Industry: Economic Solution or Problem?* 159–70. New York: Praeger.

Shah, Anwar, and Joel Slemrod. 1991. "Do Taxes Matter for Foreign Direct Investment?" *World Bank Economic Review* 5, no. 3 (September): 473–91.

Shearson Lehman Brothers. 1991. "From Inside the Beltway to South of the Border." New York: Shearson Lehman Brothers (8 May).

Simms, Margareth. "The Effectiveness of Government Training Programs." Paper prepared for the US Department of Labor, Commission on Workforce Quality and Labor Market Efficiency.

Skiles, Marilyn E. 1991. "Stabilization and Financial Sector Reform in Mexico." *Research Papers* 9125. New York: Federal Reserve Bank of New York.

Smith, Deborah. 1991. "EC Beef Ban: Food Safety as a Non-Tariff Barrier." Research paper in the Georgetown University Master of Science in Foreign Service Program, Washington (April).

Solís Soberón, Fernando, and Ignacio Trigueros. 1990a. "Bancos." New York: United Nations.

Solís Soberón, Fernando, and Ignacio Trigueros. 1990b. "Las Compañías de Seguros." New York: United Nations.

Solís Soberón, Fernando, and Ignacio Trigueros. 1990c. "El Mercado de Valores." New York: United Nations.

Solís Soberón, Fernando, and Ignacio Trigueros. 1991. "Servicios Financieros." In *México: Una Economía de Servicios*, 89–163. New York: United Nations.

Summers, Robert, and Alan Heston. 1991. "The Penn World Table (Mark 5): An Expanded Set of International Comparisons, 1950–1988." *Quarterly Journal of Economics* 106, no. 425, issue 2 (May): 327–68.

Székely, Gabriel. 1989. "Dilemmas of Export Diversification in a Developing Economy: Mexican Oil in the 1980s." *World Development Report* 17, no. 11 (November): 1777–97.

Ten Kate, Adriaan. 1990. "The Mexican Trade Liberalization of 1985–1987: Lessons of Experience." Washington: World Bank.

Trela, Irene, and John Whalley. 1991. "Bilateral Trade Liberalization in Quota Restricted Items: U.S. and Mexico in Textiles and Steel." Paper presented at a conference on "Modelling North American Free Trade," Washington (27 June).

Trigueros, Ignacio. 1989. "A Free Trade Agreement Between Mexico and the United States?" In Jeffrey J. Schott, ed., *Free Trade Areas and U.S. Trade Policy*, 255–67. Washington: Institute for International Economics.

Uimonen, Peter, and John Whalley. 1991. "Trade and Environment." Washington: Institute for International Economics (preliminary draft, September).

US Congress. House. Committee on the Budget. 1991. "Budgetary Examination of Health of the Unemployment Insurance System," hearings (6 June and 8 July). 102nd Cong., 1st sess.

US Congress. House. Committee on Ways and Means, Subcommittee on Trade. 1990. "US–Mexico Economic Relations," hearings (28 June). 101st Cong., 2nd sess.

US Congress. House. Committee on Ways and Means, Subcommittee on Trade. 1991. "Trade Adjustment Assistance," hearings (1 August). 102nd Cong., 1st sess.

US Congress. Senate. Committee on Finance. 1991. "Proposed North American Free Trade Negotiations," hearings. 102nd Cong., 1st sess.

US Congress. Senate. Committee on Foreign Relations 1991. "Issues Relating to a Bilateral Free Trade Agreement with Mexico," hearings (14 and 22 March, 11 April). 102nd Cong., 1st sess.

US Congress. Senate. Committee on the Judiciary. Subcommittee on Patents, Copyrights and Trademarks. 1991. "Fast-Track: Intellectual Property," hearings (14 May). 102nd Cong., 1st sess.

US Council of the Mexico–US Business Committee. 1990. "Memorandum on Trade Issues." Washington: US Council of the Mexico–US Business Committee (9 November).

US Council of the Mexico–US Business Committee. 1991. "Statement on the Economic Impact of a Free Trade Agreement with Mexico." Washington: US Council of the Mexico–US Business Committee (3 May).

US Department of Commerce. 1988. "Summary of the US–Canada Free Trade Agreement." Washington: US Department of Commerce (February).

US Department of Commerce. 1989. "United States–Canada Free Trade Agreement: Guide to Exporting Procedures." Washington: US Department of Commerce (April).

US Department of Commerce. 1990. "Monitoring the Implementation of the Canada–United States Free Trade Agreement." Washington: US Department of Commerce (March).

US Department of Commerce, Office of Textiles and Apparel. 1990. "The MFA and the U.S Textile Program." Washington: US Department of Commerce (6 December).

US Department of Justice, Immigration and Naturalization Service. 1987. *1987 Statistical Yearbook of the Immigration and Naturalization Service.* Washington: US Department of Justice.

US Department of Labor. 1990. "Industrial Effects of a Free Trade Agreement Between Mexico and the USA." Washington: US Department of Labor (15 September).

US Department of Labor, Bureau of International Labor Affairs. 1990a. "Labor Standards in Export Assembly Operations in Mexico and the Caribbean." Washington: US Department of Labor.

US Department of Labor, Bureau of International Labor Affairs. 1990b. "Worker Rights in Export Processing Zones: Mexico." Washington: US Department of Labor (August).

US Environmental Protection Agency. 1990. "Environmental Investments: The Cost of a Clean Environment." Washington: US Environmental Protection Agency (December).

US Environmental Protection Agency. 1991. "Note to Correspondents." Washington: US Environmental Protection Agency (1 August).

US Environmental Protection Agency and Secretaría de Desarrollo Urban y Ecologia. 1991. "Integrated Environmental Plan for the Mexico–US Border Area." (1 August).

US General Accounting Office. 1987. *Dislocated Workers: Local Programs and Outcomes Under the Job Training Partnership Act* (GAO/HRD 87-41). Washington: US General Accounting Office.

US General Accounting Office. 1988. "Rule of Origin for the US–Canada Free Trade Area." Washington: US General Accounting Office (November).

US General Accounting Office. 1990. "U.S.–Mexico Trade: Trends and Impediments in Agricultural Trade." Washington: US General Accounting Office (January).

US General Accounting Office. 1991a. "U.S.–Mexico Energy: The U.S. Reaction to Recent Reforms in Mexico's Petrochemical Industry." Washington: US General Accounting Office (May).

US General Accounting Office. 1991b. "U.S.–Mexico Trade: Concerns About the Adequacy of Border Infrastructure." Washington: US General Accounting Office (May).

US General Accounting Office. 1991c. "U.S.–Mexico Trade: Extent to Which Mexican Horticultural Exports Complement U.S. Production." Washington: US General Accounting Office (March).

US General Accounting Office. 1991d. "U.S.–Mexico Trade: Impact of Liberalization in the Agricultural Sector." Washington: US General Accounting Office (March).

US General Accounting Office. 1991e. "U.S.–Mexico Trade: Information on Environmental Regulations and Enforcement." Washington: US General Accounting Office (May).

US General Accounting Office. 1991f. "US–Mexico Trade: Some US Wood Furniture Firms Relocated from Los Angeles Area to Mexico." Washington: US General Accounting Office (April).

US International Trade Commission. 1985. *The Impact of Rules of Origin on US Imports and Exports* (USITC Publication 1695). Washington: US International Trade Commission (April).

US International Trade Commission. 1986. *The Impact of Increased US–Mexico Trade on Southwest Border Development* (USITC Publication 1915). Washington: US International Trade Commission (November).

US International Trade Commission. 1987. *Standardization of Rules of Origin* (USITC Publication 1976). Washington: US International Trade Commission (May).

US International Trade Commission. 1988a. *Foreign Protection of Intellectual Property Rights and the Effect on US Trade and Industry* (USITC Publication 2065). Washington: US International Trade Commission (February).

US International Trade Commission. 1988b. *The Use and Economic Impact of TSUS Items 806.30 and 807.00* (USITC Publication 2053). Washington: US International Trade Commission (January).

US International Trade Commission. 1989a. *Foreign Investment Barriers.* (USITC Publication 2212). Washington: US Interantional Trade Commission (August).

US International Trade Commission. 1989b. *The Economic Impact of Significant US Import Restraints* (USITC Publication 2222). Washington: US International Trade Commission (October).

US International Trade Commission. 1989c. *Production Sharing: U.S. Imports Under Harmonized Tariff Schedule Subheadings 9802.00.60 and 9802.00.80, 1985–1988* (USITC Publication 2243). Washington: US International Trade Commission (December).

US International Trade Commission. 1990a. *The Effects of Greater Economic Integration Within the European Community on the United States: First Follow-up Report* (USITC Publication 2268). Washington: US International Trade Commission (March).

US International Trade Commission. 1990b. *Review of Trade and Investment Liberalization Measures by Mexico and Prospects for Future United States–Mexican Relations. Investigation No. 332-282, Phase I: Recent Trade and Investment Reforms Undertaken by Mexico and Implications for the United States* (USITC Publication 2275). Washington: US International Trade Commission (April).

US International Trade Commission. 1990c. *Review of Trade and Investment Liberalization Measures by Mexico and Prospects for Future United States–Mexican Relations. Investigation No. 332-282, Phase II: Summary of Views on Prospects for Future United States–Mexico Relations* (USITC Publication 2326). Washington: US International Trade Commission (October).

US International Trade Commission. 1991a. *The Likely Impact on the United States of a Free Trade Agreement with Mexico: Report to the Committee on Ways and Means of the United States House of Representatives and the Committee on Finance of the United States Senate on Investigation No. 332-297 Under Section 332 of the Tariff Act of 1930* (USITC Publication 2353). Washington: US International Trade Commission (February).

US International Trade Commission. 1991b. *Production Sharing: U.S. Imports Under Harmonized Tariff Schedule Subheadings 9802.00.60 and 9802.00.80, 1986–1989* (USITC Publication 2365). Washington: US International Trade Commission (March).

US International Trade Commission. 1991c. *Quarterly Report on the Status of the Steel Industry* (USITC Publication 2364). Washington: US International Trade Commission (March).

US Trade Representative. 1991. *Review of U.S.–Mexico Environmental Issues: Prepared by an Interagency Task Force Coordinated by the US Trade Representative.* Washington: US Trade Representative (October).

Vega, Gustavo. 1991. "A Mexican Perspective." In C. Michael Aho, Murray G. Smith, and Gustavo Vega, *The Canada-Mexico–US Trade Talks: Three Perspectives.* New York: Council on Foreign Relations.

Verleger, Philip K., Jr. 1988. "Implications of the Energy Provisions." In Jeffrey J. Schott and Murray G. Smith, eds., *The Canada–United States Free Trade Agreement: The Global Impact*, 117–36. Washington: Institute for International Economics.

Verut, Caroline. 1988. "The Mexican Market for Oil and Gas Field Equipment." Report prepared for United States Trade Center, US Department of Commerce, Mexico City (November).

Weintraub, Sidney. 1983. "Treating the Causes: Illegal Immigration and U.S. Foreign Policy." In Demetrious G. Papametriou and Mark J. Miller, eds. *The*

Unavoidable Issue: U.S. Immigration Policy in the 1980s, 185–214. Philadelphia: Institute for the Study of Human Issues.

Weintraub, Sidney. 1990a. *A Marriage of Convenience: Relations Between Mexico and the United States*. New York: Twentieth Century Fund.

Weintraub, Sidney. 1990b. "The Maquiladora Industry in Mexico: Its Transitional Role." *Working Papers* 39. Washington: Commission for the Study of International Migration and Cooperative Economic Development (June).

Weintraub, Sidney. 1990c. "The North American Free Trade Debate." *Washington Quarterly* (Autumn): 119–30.

White House. 1991. "Response of the Administration to Issues Raised in Connection with the Negotiation of a North American Free Trade Agreement." Washington: White House (1 May).

Wilson, Patricia A. 1990. "Maquiladoras and Local Linkages: Building Transaction Networks in Guadalajara." *Working Papers* 32. Washington: Commission for the Study of International Migration and Cooperative Economic Development (April).

Winter, Audrey, Robert D. Sloan, George A. Lehner, and Vanessa Ruiz. 1989. *Europe Without Frontiers: A Lawyer's Guide*. Washington: Bureau of National Affairs.

Womack, James P. 1990. "Seeking Mutual Gain: North American Responses to Mexican Liberalization of Its Motor Vehicle Industry." Cambridge, MA: International Motor Vehicle Program, Massachusetts Institute of Technology (15 May).

Womack, James P. 1991. "Americars." *Latin Finance* no. 25 (March): 45–48.

Wonnacott, Paul. 1987. *The United States and Canada: The Quest for Free Trade*. POLICY ANALYSES IN INTERNATIONAL ECONOMICS 16. Washington: Institute for International Economics (March).

Wonnacott, Paul. 1988. "The Auto Sector." In Jeffrey J. Schott and Murray G. Smith, eds., *The Canada–United States Free Trade Agreement*, 101–09. Washington: Institute for International Economics.

Wonnacott, Ronald J. 1990. "U.S. Hub-and-Spoke Bilaterals and the Multilateral Trading System." *Commentary* (whole issue, October). Toronto: C. D. Howe Institute.

Wonnacott, Ronald J. 1991a. "Reconstructing North American Free Trade Following Quebec Separation: What Can Be Assumed?" In Gordon Ritchie, Ronald J. Wonnacott, W. H. Furtan, R.S. Grey, Richard Lipsey, and Rodritue Tremblay, *Broken Links*, 20–44. Toronto: C. D. Howe Institute.

Wonnacott, Ronald J. 1991b. *The Economics of Overlapping Free Trade Areas and The Mexican Challenge*. Toronto: C. D. Howe Institute, and Washington: National Planning Association.

World Bank. 1988. *Staff Appraisal Report: Mexico Steel Sector Restructuring Project*. Washington: World Bank (8 February).

World Bank. 1989. *World Development Report 1989*. Washington: World Bank.

Yúnez-Naude, Antonio. 1991. "Hacia un Tratado de Libre Comercio Norteameri-
cano; Efectos en los Sectores Agropecuarios y Alimenticios de Mexico." Mexico City: El Colegio de México (September).

Zoellick, Robert B. 1991. "North American Free Trade Agreement; Extending
Fast-Track Negotiating Authority." *Dispatch* (11 April). Washington: US
Department of State, Bureau of Public Affairs.

Index

financial profile 307, 308, 311, 313
foreign competition 311
impact of NAFTA 339
1980s nationalization 305, 309
privatization 79, 80, 309, 310
recommendations 324, 335
reforms 306, 309–11
structure of industry 305, 306
Banking, US 312, 325
Barriers to trade. *See also* Nontariff
barriers; Tariffs; *specific barriers*
in agriculture 280, 288–93
in automobiles 210, 212, 226–27,
232–33
in steel 255–57, 260
in textiles and apparel 268, 269, 272
Baucus, Max 134, 152
Bermúdez, Antonio 188
Bilateral FTAS, as framework for NAFTA
33, 34
Blanco, Herminio 33, 180
Bolsa de Valores 320, 321, 325
Bonding industry 314
Border Environmental Plan 139, 140
Border Environmental Treaty 138
Border Industrialization Program 91
Boren, David L. 152
Bracero Program 91
Broadcasting 177
Brokerages 306, 310, 317–19. *See also*
Securities industry
Bush, George 3, 24, 28, 169, 211, 256,
260

CAMI 161, 162, 212, 224
Canada–US Trade Commission 37
Canada—US Free Trade Agreement
(FTA)
agriculture 279, 294, 300, 301
as model for NAFTA 3, 24, 34, 35,
206, 330–31
automobiles 224–26
banking 325
conformity with GATT 9
dispute settlement 37, 38
energy 32, 185, 204–06
FDI 71, 75, 90
financial services 37, 324
intellectual property 26, 173, 177,
179, 180
nontariff barriers 148
rules of origin 31, 155–58, 160, 166,
167, 277
safeguards 9, 295

services 27
steel 261
subsidies 29
tariffs 9
taxation 89
textiles and apparel 263, 277
Canadian Auto Workers 222
Capital flight 6, 72, 311
Cardenas, Lázaro 82, 187
Caribbean Basin Initiative 107, 159,
273–76
Certificates of Ordinary Participation
(CPOS) 81
Change-in-tariff-heading test, as rule of
origin 156–57, 164, 165, 167, 168
Chemicals 65
"Chicken war" tariff 212, 338
Chihuahua 239
Child labor 120
China, People's Republic of 275
Chrysler 71, 162, 209, 216, 220, 234
Cifra 81, 267
Citibank 306, 311
Ciudad Carmen 189
Ciudad Juárez 91, 125, 139, 141, 200,
252
Clean Air Act (US) 28, 141
Coffee 288, 301, 302
Colorado River 140
Comisión Nacional de Inversión
Extranjera (CNIE) 76–78, 83, 95
Comisión Nacional de Valores (CNV)
322
Commercial banks. *See* Banking
Common Agricultural Policy (EC) 7
Common external tariff 6, 233, 335,
338
Compañia Nacional de Subsistencias
Populares (Conasupo) 280, 289, 299
Compulsory licensing 26, 173, 175–76,
179–81
Computable general equilibrium (CGE)
models, projections 50, 51, 57–61,
109, 110, 252, 293
Comunidades 284, 294
Confederacíon de Trabajadores
Mexicanos (CTM) 125
Constitution of 1917 (Mexico) 75, 82,
90, 187, 207, 284
Consultation clause, for accession of
new members 40
Copyright 80, 176–80

Hazardous waste 135, 136, 139, 140
Health and safety standards 29, 123,
124, 141, 280, 290, 292, 293, 300.
See also Phytosanitary standards
Hermosillo 211, 212, 220, 238
Hills, Carla A. 31, 124, 169, 174, 180,
207
Historical model, projections 52–60,
332, 337. *See also* Computable general
equilibrium models; Econometric
models
Hojalata y Lámina (HYLSA) 244, 245,
247
Honda 161, 163, 169, 212, 226, 239
Horticulture 279–80, 288, 296–98
Hub-and-spoke system of FTAS 24, 33,
34, 39
Hybrid trilateral approach to NAFTA 34
Hyundai 161, 169, 212, 226

IBM 71
IIE model. See Historical model,
projections
Immigration, illegal 7, 11, 125–27, 129,
336, 341
Import licensing 12–14, 280, 281, 289,
300
Income convergence, implications for
Mexico 61, 62, 110
Income disparities, within NAFTA 7
Inflation in NAFTA countries 5
Infrastructure, inadequate, as barrier to
trade 290
Insurance industry 78, 313–17, 324,
336
Integration, economic, forms of 6–8
Intellectual property
and FDI 80
broadcasting 177
compulsory licensing 26, 173,
175–76, 179–81
copyright 80, 176–80
cultural industries and 180
dispute settlement 181
enforcement 178–81
impact of NAFTA 337
in Canada–US FTA 26, 173, 177, 179,
180
in GATT 26, 181
issues in NAFTA 26
past Mexican policy 173, 174
patents 175, 179–81
recent Mexican reforms 12, 16,
173–79, 181

recommendations 180
royalties 177
trademarks 176
trade secrets 178, 180
Inter-American Development Bank 137
International Boundary and Water
Commission (IBWC) 138, 140, 141
International Coffee Organization (ICO)
288, 301, 302
International Energy Agency (IEA) 205
Inverméxico 317
Investment, foreign direct. *See* Foreign
direct investment
Investment Canada 90

Japan 73, 84, 210–12, 222, 229, 285
Job Training Partnership Act (JTPA) 114,
115
Joint negotiations, for accession of new
members 40

Korea 84
KPMG Peat Marwick 52, 64
Kyoto Customs Convention 156, 164

La Paz Agreement 103, 138, 139
Labor. *See also* Employment; Wages
adjustment programs 113–16, 128,
340
child, in Mexico 120
impact of NAFTA on US 107–13, 127
maquiladoras and 102–03
mobility 7
recommendations 340
worker rights 119–21, 128
Laredo 85
Law on Foreign Investment (Mexico)
76, 96, 196
Law of Inventions and Trademarks
(Mexico) 80, 174–76, 178
Law on Credit Institutions (Mexico) 79
Livestock. *See* Meat and dairy products
Local content rules 210, 212, 215–18,
225, 227–29, 231, 257, 261, 334,
335, 339. *See also* Performance
requirements
Los Angeles 150

Macroeconomic effects of NAFTA 47,
49–52
Macroeconomic policies, Mexico 19, 20,
332. *See also* Balance of payments,
Mexico; Exchange rates

Managed trade 109, 211
Maquiladoras
  as export enclaves 97
  automobiles and parts 212, 235, 239
  cities with largest concentration 91,
    93
  criticisms of 101
  definition 91
  domestic sales 100, 101, 105
  employment 92, 94, 95, 120, 125
  environmental concerns 103, 139
  exports 92, 96
  FDI in 72, 83, 84, 96
  forms of ownership 95
  history 91
  impact of NAFTA on 334
  impact on US labor 101–03
  output 97, 100
  performance requirements 100, 101,
    105
  recommendations 103–05
  rules of origin and 97, 104
  sectoral distribution 95
  tariff preferences 92, 93, 96, 97, 104
  textiles and apparel 95, 102, 267
  wages 121, 122
Marine Mammal Protection Act (MMPA)
  143
Marketing orders 280, 291, 298
Meat and dairy products 280, 288, 291,
  292, 300, 301
Mercedes-Benz 240
Mercosur 39
Mexicali 125, 139, 200, 252
Mexican Patent and Trademark Office
  (MPTO) 175, 178
Mexicana de Aviación 80
Mexico City 77, 137–38, 200, 213, 239,
  281
Mexico Fund 322
Migration, rural to urban 289
Mini-mills 244, 247, 252, 255
Minimum wages 120
Mining 245
Monetary integration 8
Monetary policy. See Exchange rates;
  Macroeconomic policies
Monterrey 77, 244
Montreal Protocol 135
Motor vehicles. See Automobiles and
  parts
Mulroney, Brian 24
Multi-Fiber Arrangement (MFA) 83,
  269, 272, 275, 276, 278

Mutual funds 81, 82, 322

National Commission for Foreign
  Investment (CNIE) 76–78, 83, 95
National Insurance and Bonding
  Commission (Mexico) 316
National Wildlife Federation 131
Natural gas 186, 199–201, 335
Negotiating groups in NAFTA talks 25
Nissan 31, 71, 166, 209, 211, 216, 228,
  234, 236
Nonapplication provision 41
Nontariff barriers. See also specific barrier
  environmental standards as 146
  in agriculture 280, 289–90, 292
  in automobiles 210, 226–27, 233
  in Canada–US FTA 148
  in steel 260
  in textiles and apparel 268
Nuevo Laredo 84, 85, 139, 252

Objectives, national, in NAFTA
  negotiations 12–22
Oil. See Petroleum
Omnibus Trade and Competitiveness
  Act of 1988 107
Operadoras de Bolsa 317, 318
Organization for Economic Cooperation
  and Development (OECD) 36, 257

Partido Revolucionario Institucional
  (PRI) 125, 294
Patents 175, 179–81
Pemex
  and Mexican steel industry 257
  current activities 189–91
  demonopolization 208
  environmental efforts 135, 137, 193
  exports 190, 198
  history 187–89
  investment plans 191, 192, 201
  petrochemicals 195
  procurement 204
  recommendations 335
  reputation for inefficiency 185
  ventures with foreign firms 192, 193,
    197, 208
Performance requirements 100, 101,
  105, 210, 216–18, 227–28, 230, 334,
  335. See also Local content rules
Pesticides 135, 136, 146, 147, 175, 293
Petrochemicals 36, 78, 185–87,
  193–97, 199, 203–04, 208

Petroleum 185, 186, 190, 198, 199, 204. *See also* Energy; Pemex
Pharmaceuticals 173, 175, 179, 180, 337, 339
Photocopiers 164
Phytosanitary standards 289, 290, 292, 298. *See also* Health and safety standards
Policy recommendations
  agriculture 294–96, 298–303, 338
  automobiles 105, 226–30, 335, 338
  banking 324, 335
  energy 207, 208, 335
  environment 144–48, 150–53, 341
  financial services 323–25, 335, 339
  FDI 90
  intellectual property 180
  labor issues 340
  maquiladoras 103–05
  Pemex 335
  rules of origin 166–71, 338
  steel 260–61
  tariffs 334–35
  textiles and apparel 275–78
Polluter-pays principle 145, 146
Pollution 137, 141–42, 150, 151. *See also* Environment
Population of NAFTA countries 5
Portillo, José López 76, 280, 305
Portugal, as model for Mexico 254, 278
Poza Rica 190, 193
Preemption of national environmental standards 146–48
Price supports 280, 289, 301, 302
Privatization 12, 78–80, 247, 309–10
Production-to-sales ratio test 210, 223, 227, 229, 230, 335, 339
Program for Older Worker Adjustment (Canada) 118
Puebla 220, 238

Quantitative restrictions and quotas 256, 257, 268, 291. *See also* Nontariff barriers

Reagan, Ronald 210, 255
Reference prices 12, 13
Reilly, William K. 145
Reynosa 193
Riegle, Donald W., Jr. 169
Rio Grande 140
Rojas, Francisco 191
Roll-up issue, in rules of origin 163, 169–71, 225–27, 231, 339

Royalties, Mexican policy on 177
Rules of origin
  change-in-tariff-heading test 156–57, 164, 165, 167, 168
  factory cost test 158, 162, 170
  for automobiles 31, 161–63, 165, 169, 170, 221, 227
  for textiles and apparel 160, 276, 277
  in Canada–US FTA 31, 155–58, 160, 166, 167, 277
  in EC 163–65, 170
  in GATT 165–66
  issues for NAFTA 31, 32, 331
  maquiladoras and 97, 104
  recommendations 166–71, 338
  roll-up issue 163, 169–71, 225–27, 231, 339
  in steel 160
  substantial transformation 156, 165
  tariff preferences and 168, 169
  trinational commission on 167, 168, 331
  under Kyoto Customs Convention 156
  value-added test 157, 159, 160, 162, 165, 168, 223

Safeguards 9, 210, 233, 260, 277, 295, 330, 338
Salinas de Gortari, Carlos 3, 82, 134, 136, 137, 284, 336
Saltillo 234, 239
Same-condition drawback 97, 169, 224
Secretaría de Comercio y Fomento Industrial (SECOFI) 83, 95, 215, 281
Secretaría de Comunicaciones y Transporte 85
Secretaría de Desarrollo Urbano y de Ecología (SEDUE) 103, 136–41
Secretaría de Energía, Minas, e Industria Paraestatal (SEMIP) 190, 195, 196
Secretaría de Hacienda y Crédito Público (SHCP) 304, 314, 318, 322
Secretariat of Communications and Transport 85
Secretariat of Energy, Mining, and Parastatal Industry (SEMIP) 190, 195, 196
Secretariat of Finance and Public Credit (SHCP) 304, 314, 318, 322
Secretariat of Trade and Industrial Development (SECOFI) 83, 95, 215, 281

wages 266–68
Tijuana 91, 125, 139, 200, 252
Toluca 220, 234, 239
Tourism. *See* Travel and tourism
Toyota 161, 211, 212, 224, 226
Trade. *See also specific industry*
   Canada-Mexico 62–64, 198, 339
   environment and 331
   Mexico, composition 49, 50
   US–Canada 223, 285, 299
   US–Mexico 47, 48, 210, 213–14,
     245, 250–56, 263–65, 269,
     272–73, 279–80, 285–88
   projections 66–68, 339
Trade Act of 1974 116, 255
Trade Adjustment Assistance (TAA)
   program 114, 116, 117
Trade secrets, Mexican policy on 178,
   180
Trademarks, Mexican policy on 176
Transition periods for implementation of
   NAFTA 330
Transport, inadequate, as barrier to
   trade 290
Transportation, regulations on 84, 85
Transportation services 28
Travel and tourism 27, 28, 69, 85
Trilateral negotiations, advantages and
   disadvantages 23
Trilateralization of Canada–US FTA 35
Trinational commission on rules of
   origin 167, 168, 331
Trucking 84, 85
Trucks and buses, Mexican policy on
   manufacture 219
Tubos de Acero de México (TAMSA) 81,
   82, 244, 245, 247, 257
Turkey, as model for Mexico 8
"Two-fleet" rule 210, 211, 221, 231,
   232

Understanding on Subsidies and
   Countervailing Duties 3
Understanding Regarding Trade and
   Investment Facilitation Talks 4
Unemployment insurance, US 114–16,
   118
Unions, in Mexico 124, 125
United Auto Workers (UAW) 162, 222,
   223
United States Apparel Industry Council
   (USAIC) 276

United Steelworkers of America 256
Uruguay Round. *See also* General
   Agreement on Tariffs and Trade
   (GATT)
   agriculture in 294
   antidumping in 29
   financial services in 28, 324
   impact on NAFTA 329, 343
   intellectual property in 26
   NAFTA as complement to 42, 43
   NAFTA as model for 26
   steel in 257
   subsidies in 29
US Department of Agriculture 147, 287,
   289, 300
US Department of Transportation 85
US Environmental Protection Agency
   (EPA) 136–39, 141, 147
US–Israel Free Trade Area Agreement
   10
Used cars, ban on imports 210, 218,
   221, 227, 230, 335

Valenti, Jack 180
Value-added test, as rule of origin 157,
   159, 160, 162, 165, 168, 223
Veracruz 244
Volkswagen 169, 209, 216, 220, 224,
   228, 238
"Voluntary" restraint agreements (VRAS)
   210, 255, 256, 258–60, 291
Volvo 162

Wages
   comparative 122, 123
   impact of NAFTA on US 110, 112,
     113, 337
   in maquiladoras 121–22
   in Mexico 94, 121
   in steel 244, 254
   in textiles and apparel 266–68
   in US 122
   minimum 120
   projections 56, 57, 110
Water resources 140–41, 341. *See also*
   Environment
Weekes, John 21
Wheat 299
Wildlife conservation 135, 142
Wilson, Michael 166
Withholding taxes 88
World Bank 136, 243

Zenith 73, 112

Other Publications from the
Institute for International Economics

POLICY ANALYSES IN INTERNATIONAL ECONOMICS Series

BOOKS

Economic Sanctions Reconsidered: History and Current Policy
Gary Clyde Hufbauer, Jeffrey J. Schott, and Kimberly Ann Elliott/
  December 1990
$36.00	ISBN cloth 0-88132-136-2	288 pp.
$25.00	ISBN paper 0-88132-140-0	288 pp.

Pacific Basin Developing Countries: Prospects for the Future
Marcus Noland/*January 1991*
$29.95	ISBN cloth 0-88132-141-9	250 pp.
$19.95	ISBN paper 0-88132-081-1	250 pp.

Currency Convertibility in Eastern Europe
John Williamson, editor/*September 1991*
$39.95	ISBN cloth 0-88132-144-3	396 pp.
$28.95	ISBN paper 0-88132-128-1	396 pp.

Foreign Direct Investment in the United States
Edward M. Graham and Paul R. Krugman/*1989, rev. October 1991*
$16.95	ISBN paper 0-88132-139-7	200 pp.

International Adjustment and Financing: The Lessons of 1985–1991
C. Fred Bergsten, editor/*January 1992*
$34.95	ISBN cloth 0-88132-142-7	336 pp.
$24.95	ISBN paper 0-88132-112-5	336 pp.

American Trade Politics
I. M. Destler/*1986, rev. 1992*
$30.00	ISBN cloth 0-88132-164-8	400 pp.
$18.00	ISBN paper 0-88132-188-5	400 pp.

SPECIAL REPORTS

1 **Promoting World Recovery: A Statement on Global
   Economic Strategy**
   by Twenty-six Economists from Fourteen Countries/*December 1982*
(out of print)	ISBN paper 0-88132-013-7	45 pp.

2 **Prospects for Adjustment in Argentina, Brazil, and Mexico:
   Responding to the Debt Crisis**
   John Williamson, editor/*June 1983*
(out of print)	ISBN paper 0-88132-016-1	71 pp.

3 **Inflation and Indexation: Argentina, Brazil, and Israel**
   John Williamson, editor/*March 1985*
$12.00	ISBN paper 0-88132-037-4	191 pp.

4 **Global Economic Imbalances**
   C. Fred Bergsten, editor/*March 1986*
$25.00	ISBN cloth 0-88132-038-2	126 pp.
$10.00	ISBN paper 0-88132-042-0	126 pp.

5 **African Debt and Financing**
   Carol Lancaster and John Williamson, editors/*May 1986*
(out of print)	ISBN paper 0-88132-044-7	229 pp.

FORTHCOMING

A World Savings Shortage?
Paul R. Krugman

Who's Bashing Whom? Trade Conflict in High-Technology Industries
Laura D'Andrea Tyson

Sizing Up U.S. Export Disincentives
J. David Richardson

The Globalization of Industry and National Economic Policies
C. Fred Bergsten and Edward M. Graham

The Economics of Global Warming
William R. Cline

Trading for the Environment
John Whalley

Narrowing the U.S. Current Account Deficit: A Sectoral Assessment
Allen J. Lenz

U.S. Taxation of International Income: Blueprint for Reform
Gary Clyde Hufbauer

The Effects of Foreign-Exchange Intervention
Kathryn Dominguez and Jeffrey A. Frankel

The Future of the World Trading System
John Whalley

Adjusting to Volatile Energy Prices
Philip K. Verleger, Jr.

National Security and the World Economy
Ellen L. Frost

The United States as a Debtor Country
C. Fred Bergsten and Shafiqul Islam

International Monetary Policymaking in the United States, Germany, and Japan
C. Randall Henning